WordPerfect Encyclopedia

WordPerfect Encyclopedia

Leo J. Scanlon

BANTAM BOOKS
TORONTO • NEW YORK • LONDON • SYDNEY • AUCKLAND

WordPerfect is a trademark of WordPerfect Corporation.

IBM Personal Computer, XT, and AT are trademarks and IBM a registered trademark of International Business Machines Corporation.

Ashton-Tate and dBASE are registered trademarks of Ashton-Tate. Lotus and 1-2-3 are registered trademarks of Lotus Development Corporation.

Microsoft and Multiplan are registered trademarks of Microsoft Corporation.

MultiMate Advantage is a trademark and MultiMate a registered trademark of Multimate International, a subsidiary of Ashton-Tate.

WordStar is a trademark of MicroPro International Corp.

WORDPERFECT ENCYCLOPEDIA

A Bantam Book / October 1988

All rights reserved.
Copyright © 1988 by Leo J. Scanlon.
Cover illustration copyright © 1988 by Bantam Books
This book was produced by Publishing Synthesis, Ltd., New York, NY

No part of this book may be reproduced or transmitted
in any form or by any means, electronic or mechanical,
including photocopying, recording, or by any iformation
storrage and retrieveal system, without permission in writing from
the publisher.
For information address: Bantam Books.

ISBN 0-553-34492-7

Bantam Books are published by Bantam Books, a division of
Bantam Doubleday Dell Publishing Group, Inc. Its trademark,
consisting of the words "Bantam Books" and the portrayal of a
rooster, is Registered in U.S. Patent and Trademark Office
and in other countries. Marca Registrada, Bantam Books,
666 Fifth Avenue, New York, New York 10103

PRINTED IN THE UNITED STATES OF AMERICA

FG 0 9 8 7 6 5 4 3 2 1

Preface

This book is an alphabetized reference to WordPerfect versions 4.1, 4.2, and 5.0. It contains an entry for each feature and describes any differences a feature may have from one version to another. Knowing the differences can help a reader make a smoother transition from one version to another.

I have used two techniques to describe how a feature differs between versions of WordPerfect. Where the differences are minor, I make a short comment about them or include a separate paragraph for each version. However, where features differ widely from one version to another, I generally provide two (or sometimes three) entries. For example, the book has two separate **Print Command** entries, one for WordPerfect 4.1 and 4.2 and the other for WordPerfect 5.0.

I have also included cross-references to help you locate a feature when you don't remember the "official" term by which the WordPerfect manual refers to it. For example, the manual describes the procedure for making WordPerfect start a new page under **Page, Hard and Soft**. In this book, you can locate that procedure by looking under any of several entries, including **Hard Page Command, Page Breaks, Page, New, Page, Starting a New**, and **Starting a New Page**.

Not all entries describe features, however. Some are intended to explain occurrences a reader may not know how to cope with. For instance, if the power goes off while you're working on a Word-Perfect document (say, you absent-mindedly switch the computer off, someone dislodges the power cord, or the power fails during a thunderstorm), WordPerfect asks "Are other copies of WordPerfect currently running?" the next time you start it. This simply means that WordPerfect was not shut down properly last time, and you can bypass the message by typing **n** for no. Still, you may have trouble locating any mention of this puzzling prompt in the WordPerfect manual. You can look it up directly in this book.

The book also includes a variety of useful tips and tricks that I learned through years of working with WordPerfect. There are also many practical examples to illustrate some of the more subtle points.

Finally, the book has three appendixes, which list the features of WordPerfect 4.1, 4.2, and 5.0 (respectively) and show which keys you must press to produce them. Each appendix also summarizes WordPerfect's initial format settings (e.g., single-spaced text, one-inch margins), and tells you how to change these settings to suit your own needs.

In short, my aim in writing this book is to provide a reference that will help WordPerfect users complete their writing projects quicker and easier.

Leo J. Scanlon

Contents

A

Abbreviations, Replacing	1
Adding Rows or Columns	1
Advance Options	2
Aligning on a Character	5
Alt (Alternate) Key	6
Antonyms	6
Appending Text to a File—WordPerfect 4.1 and 4.2	7
Appending Text to a File—WordPerfect 5.0	7
Are other copies of WordPerfect currently running? Prompt	8
Arrow Keys	8
Auto Rewrite	9
Automatic Reference—WordPerfect 5.0	10
Auxiliary Files—WordPerfect 5.0	12

B

Backups	15
Backspace Key	15
Beep Sound	17
Binding Width	18
Blank Screen	19
Blank Space, Inserting	19
Block Command (Alt-F4)	19
Bold Command (F6)	22

C

Cancel Command (F1)	25
Canceling Print Jobs	26
Can't create new printer files on WP disk Message	27
Capitalizing	27
Center Command (Shift-F6)	28
Centering a Page Top to Bottom	29
Codes, Hidden—WordPerfect 4.1 and 4.2	30
Codes, Hidden—WordPerfect 5.0	37
Column Operations	47
Columns, Text	50
Compose Feature—WordPerfect 5.0	54
Concordance File	54
Conditional End of Page	55
Convert Program	56
Ctrl (Control) Key	59
Ctrl/Alt keys Option—WordPerfect 4.1 and 4.2	59
Cursor, Moving the	60

D

Dashed Line Across the Screen	61
Database Files, Using	63
Date Command (Shift-F5)—WordPerfect 4.1 and 4.2	63
Date/Outline Command (Shift-F5)—WordPerfect 5.0	66
Decimal Tabs	68
Del (Delete) Key	68
Delete [code]? (Y/N) N Prompt	69
Deleted Text, Undeleting	69
Deleting	70
Disk Directories	71
Disk full Message	73
Doc Value at Bottom of the Screen	73
Document Comments	74
Document Compare—WordPerfect 5.0	76
Document Format Option—WordPerfect 5.0	77
Document Summary—WordPerfect 4.2	78
Document Summary—WordPerfect 5.0	80
DOS Operations	82
DOS, Returning from	90
DOS Text Files	91

Dot Leaders	91
Double-Underlining	92

E

Editing Disk Documents	95
End Key	97
Endnotes	97
Enter Key	97
Equal Signs, Line of	98
ERROR: File not found Message	99
Esc (Escape) Key	99
Exit Command (F7)	100

F

Fast Save—WordPerfect 5.0	101
Filenames	102
Flush Right Command (Alt-F6)	103
Font Command (Ctrl-F8)—WordPerfect 5.0	105
Fonts, Printer—WordPerfect 4.1 and 4.2	109
Footnote Command (Ctrl-F7)—WordPerfect 4.1 and 4.2	109
Footnote Command (Ctrl-F7)—WordPerfect 5.0	111
Force Odd/Even Page—WordPerfect 5.0	114
Form Letters	116
Format Command (Shift-F8)—WordPerfect 5.0	128
Forms	128
Function Keys (F1-F10)	130

G

Go To Command (Ctrl-Home)	131
Graphics Command (Alt-F9)—WordPerfect 5.0	132

H

Hard Disk Startup File for WordPerfect	142
Hard Page Command (Ctrl-Enter)	142
Hard Space	142
Headers and Footers—WordPerfect 4.1 and 4.2	143
Headers and Footers—WordPerfect 5.0	144

Help Command (F3)	146
Home Key	147
Hyphenation	148
Hyphenation Zone	150

I

Indent Commands (F4 and Shift-F4)	153
Indexes	155
Initial Settings for WordPerfect 4.1 and 4.2	159
Initial Settings for WordPerfect 5.0	160
Ins (Insert) Key	167

J

Justification	169

K

Keeping Text Together	171
Keyboard Layout—WordPerfect 5.0	171

L

Leaving DOS	179
Leaving WordPerfect	179
Legal Size Paper	180
Letterhead Paper	181
Line Format Command (Shift-F8)—WordPerfect 4.1 and 4.2	181
Line Format Option—WordPerfect 5.0	183
Lines, Drawing	184
Lines per Inch—WordPerfect 4.1 and 4.2	188
List Files Command (F5)	189
Lists	195
Lowercase, Converting Text to	199

M

Macro Command (Alt-F10)	201
Macro Define Command (Ctrl-F10)—WordPerfect 4.1 and 4.2	201
Macro Define Command (Ctrl-F10)—WordPerfect 5.0	202

Macro Files, Operating on	204
Macro Libraries—WordPerfect 5.0	204
Macro Programming Commands—WordPerfect 5.0	204
Macro, Repeating a	235
Macros, Chaining	236
Macros, Converting from WordPerfect 4.2 to WordPerfect 5.0	238
Macros, Editing	239
Macros, Introduction to	240
Macros, Running at Startup	243
Macros that Perform Commands—WordPerfect 4.1 and 4.2	244
Macros that Perform Commands—WordPerfect 5.0	245
Margins—WordPerfect 4.1 and 4.2	248
Margins—WordPerfect 5.0	250
Mark Text Command (Alt-F5)—WordPerfect 4.1 and 4.2	251
Mark Text Command (Alt-F5)—WordPerfect 5.0	252
Master Documents—WordPerfect 5.0	254
Math/Columns Command (Alt-F7)	256
Mathematical Operations	256
Menus, Selecting Options from	265
Merge Codes Command	265
Merge E Command (Shift-F9)—WordPerfect 4.1 and 4.2	268
Merge Operations	268
Merge R Command (F9)	268
Merge/Sort Command (Ctrl-F9)	269
Minus (-) Key on Numeric Keypad	269
Move Command (Ctrl-F4)—WordPerfect 4.1 and 4.2	269
Move Command (Ctrl-F4)—WordPerfect 5.0	272
Moving Between Pages	274
Multiple Copies, Printing	275

N

New Page Number	277
New Page, Starting a	278
Numeric Keypad	278
Num Lock Key	280

O

Other Format Option—WordPerfect 5.0	281
Outlines	283

Contents

Overflow file already exists Message for WordPerfect 4.1	287
Overstrikes	287

P

Page Breaks	289
Page Format Command (Alt-F8)—WordPerfect 4.1 and 4.2	289
Page Format Option—WordPerfect 5.0	293
Page Numbering	295
Paper	296
Paragraph Numbering	297
PgUp and PgDn Keys	300
Pitch—WordPerfect 4.1 and 4.2	300
Place Markers	300
Plus (+) Key on Numeric Keypad	301
Pos Indicator	301
Power Failure	301
Primary File in Merge Operations	302
Print Command (Shift-F7)—WordPerfect 4.1 and 4.2	302
Print Command (Shift-F7)—WordPerfect 5.0	306
Print Format Command (Ctrl-F8)—WordPerfect 4.1 and 4.2	311
Print Jobs	314
Print Options—WordPerfect 4.1 and 4.2	315
Print Screen (PrtSc) Key	316
Printer Commands	316
Printer, Stopping the	317
Printing	318
Proportional Spacing	319

Q

Quit Printing	321

R

Rectangular Blocks of Text—WordPerfect 4.1 and 4.2	323
Rectangular Blocks of Text—WordPerfect 5.0	324
Redlining Text—WordPerfect 4.1 and 4.2	325
Redlining Text—WordPerfect 5.0	326
Reformatting Documents	328
Replace Command (Alt-F2)	330
Retrieve Command (Shift-F10)	338

Returning from DOS	339
Reveal Codes Command (Alt-F3)	340
Roman Numerals for Numbering Pages	341

S

Save Command (F10)	343
Screen Command (Ctrl-F3)—WordPerfect 4.1 and 4.2	344
Screen Command (Ctrl-F3)—WordPerfect 5.0	347
Scroll Lock Key	349
Search Commands (F2 and Shift-F2)	349
Secondary Merge File	352
Set-up—WordPerfect 4.1 and 4.2	353
Set-up—WordPerfect 5.0	355
Shell Command (Ctrl-F1)	358
Soft Page Breaks	359
Sorting	360
Spacing	372
Special Characters	372
Spell Command (Ctrl-F2)	374
Spell Utility Program	381
Splitting the Screen	385
Spreadsheet Files, Using	386
Starting WordPerfect	389
Status Line	390
Stop Merging	390
Stop Printing	391
Stop Replacing	392
Strikeout Text—WordPerfect 4.1 and 4.2	392
Strikeout Text—WordPerfect 5.0	393
Style Command (Alt-F8)—WordPerfect 5.0	395
Super/Subscript Command (Shift-F1)—WordPerfect 4.1 and 4.2	400
Switch Documents Command (Shift-F3)	402
Switching Printers—WordPerfect 4.1 and 4.2	402
Switching Printers—WordPerfect 5.0	403

T

Tab Align Command (Ctrl-F6)	405
Tab Key	406
Table of Authorities	407
Table of Contents—WordPerfect 4.1 and 4.2	407

Table of Contents—WordPerfect 5.0	410
Tab Ruler	414
Tabs	415
Text Files	418
Text In/Out Command (Ctrl-F5)—WordPerfect 4.1	418
Text In/Out Command (Ctrl-F5)—WordPerfect 4.2	420
Text In/Out Command (Ctrl-F5)—WordPerfect 5.0	424
Thesaurus Command (Alt-F1)	426
Top Margin	428
Typeover Mode (Ins)	430
Typing Directly to the Printer	431

U

Undeleting	433
Underlining	434
Units of Measure—WordPerfect 5.0	436

V

Variables—WordPerfect 5.0	439
View Document Option—WordPerfect 5.0	440

W

Widow and Orphan Lines	443
Windows, Document	444
Word Count	446
Word Left and Right Commands (Ctrl-← and Ctrl-→)	447
Word Search	447
WordPerfect, Leaving	447
Appendix A: WordPerfect 4.1 Features	449
Appendix B: WordPerfect 4.2 Features	459
Appendix C: WordPerfect 5.0 Features	469
Index	483

Abbreviations, Replacing

To save time, you may sometimes want to type abbreviations into your document, and expand them when you finish. For example, if you are writing a report on European sales, you may simply type UK for United Kingdom, WG (West Germany) for Federal Republic of Germany, and EEC for European Economic Community.

When you finish, do replace operations (see **Replace Command**) to expand the abbreviations. Be sure that your abbreviations are distinct (note, for instance, that you find US in USSR) and do not conflict with each other (such as using UF for United Fund and University of Florida). *Replace* has the advantage of making Word-Perfect—not *you*—expand the abbreviations.

Adding Rows or Columns

WordPerfect can perform math operations on numeric tables. For example, it can add a column of numbers to produce a *subtotal*. It can then add subtotals to produce a *total*, and add totals to produce a *grand total*. WordPerfect can also perform calculations on the rows

2 Advance Options

in a table. It can add, subtract, multiply, or divide rows of numbers based on simple formulas that you enter. For details, see **Math/Columns Command**.

Advance Options

Elsewhere in this book, I describe the *Subscript* and *Superscript* options, which let you print a character or a block of text one-half line below or above the current line. WordPerfect also provides several *Advance* options that let you move the cursor to a specified place on the page. When you print the document, these commands will move the printer's printing element to the same page location. WordPerfect 4.1 and 4.2 can only move the cursor vertically (up, down, or to a specific line), but version 5.0 can also move it horizontally (left, right, or to a specific column).

To move the cursor with version 4.1 or 4.2, you must specify the advance distances in terms of line numbers. By contrast, version 5.0's Advance provides a variety of ways to tell WordPerfect where to move the cursor. Specifically, 5.0 lets you indicate the distance in inches, centimeters, points, units of horizontal measure (pitch), or units of vertical measure (lines). In short, the Advance options give you total control over the cursor position; that is, control over where material will be printed.

When you advance the cursor, WordPerfect does *not* move it on the screen, but simply reports its new location in the *Ln* and *Pos* values on the bottom line.

The Advance options for WordPerfect 4.1 and 4.2 are contained in the Shift-F1 (Super/Subscript) menu. With version 5.0, they are contained in the Format (Shift-F8) command's *Other* submenu.

Advance Options for WordPerfect 4.1 and 4.2

> 4.1
> 4.2

The Super/Subscript menu for WordPerfect 4.1 and 4.2 has three movement options: *Adv Up*, *Adv Dn*, and *Adv Ln* (Advance to Line). Adv Up and Adv Dn move the cursor up or down a half-line (which is handy for superscripting or subscripting a string of text), while Adv Ln moves it to a specified line.

To superscript the next string of characters you type, press Shift and F1 to give a Super/Subscript command. When the following menu appears:

1 Superscript; **2** Subscript; **3** Overstrike; **4** Adv Up; **5** Adv Dn; **6** Adv Ln: **0**

type 4 for *Adv Up* (a ▲ symbol appears at the bottom left-hand corner). When you finish typing the superscripted material, press Shift-F1 to get the Super/Subscript menu and type 5 for *Adv Dn*. For example, to produce 2^{36}, enter **2**, press Shift-F1 and **4**, type **36**, then press Shift-F1 and **5**.

Similarly, **to subscript the next string of characters you type**, press Shift-F1 and type **5** for *Adv Dn* (a ▼ symbol appears at the bottom left-hand corner). Then type the subscripted material, press Shift-F1 to get the Super/Subscript menu, and type **4** for *Adv Up*. Note that this procedure is the reverse of what you do for a superscript.

To superscript existing material, move to the first superscript character, press Shift-F1, and type **4**. Then move just past the last superscripted character, press Shift-F1, and type **5**. **To subscript existing material**, do the opposite. That is, insert an *Adv Dn* ahead of it and an *Adv Up* after it.

The Adv Up and Adv Dn features are also convenient for centering a title in an even-numbered list of items. For example, in the following list, an *Adv Dn* precedes "Divisions" and an *Adv Up* follows "International":

Boxco Corp.
Etc., Ltd.
Daywear Fashions
Petrie High-Tech Associates

Divisions of Acme International

The third Advance option, *Adv Ln* (for Advance to Line), lets you insert an area of blank space on a page. This can be used to reserve room for a drawing or picture that you will paste on the final document. It can also be used to leave space for text that you will enter later.

To create the blank space, move the cursor to where it should begin and press Shift-F1 to obtain the menu, then type **6** to select *Adv Ln*. When **Adv.** appears at the bottom of the screen, enter the line number where the blank space should end. WordPerfect inserts the space and moves to the end of it. Whatever you type next will appear on the line you specified when the document is printed. As I mentioned earlier, note that *the cursor does not physically move down the screen*; only the line (Ln) number at the bottom changes.

For Adv Ln to work correctly, you must give it a valid line number—one that is on or between the top and bottom margin settings for this page. If you enter **0** or a number that is outside the page's margins, WordPerfect ignores the command and leaves the cursor where it is.

Adv Ln also lets you advance *up* the page! For example, if the cursor is on line 40 and you give an Adv Ln to line 4, whatever you type next will be printed on line 4. That is, when the printer finishes printing line 40, it moves the paper backward to line 4 and continues printing from *that* point. This can be useful for filling in preprinted forms; see the **Forms** entry for more details.

Advance Options for WordPerfect 5.0

5.0 WordPerfect 5.0 provides the same vertical printer movement options as versions 4.1 and 4.2 (although it labels them *Up*, *Down*, and *Line*), but it also has three horizontal movement options: *Left*, *Right*, and *Column*. These options are contained in an Advance submenu that appears when you give a Format (Shift-F8) command, and choose *Other* (**4**), then *Advance* (**1**). The Advance menu looks like this:

Advance: 1 Up; 2 Down; 3 Line; 4 Left; 5 Right; 6 Column: 0

As I mentioned earlier, version 5.0 lets you specify movement distances in any of five different forms: inches, centimeters, points, units of horizontal measure, or units of vertical measure.

Whenever you give a movement command, WordPerfect displays a prompt asking for the distance you want the cursor (and print head) to move. To respond, type a number and a one-character measurement unit suffix, then press Enter. The measurement unit suffixes are: *i* or " for inches, *c* for centimeters, *p* for points, *h* for units of horizontal measure (pitch), and *v* for units of vertical measure (lines).

For example, to move the cursor 4 inches down the page, press Shift-F8 to give a Format command, then type **4** for *Other*, **1** for *Advance*, and (finally!) **2** for *Down*. When WordPerfect displays **Adv. down**, enter **4"**.

Unit of horizontal measure refers to the width of a character based on the pitch (characters per inch) of the active print font. Thus, if you are using a 10-pitch (i.e., 10 characters per inch) font, entering **10h** in response to *Left* tells WordPerfect to move the cursor ten character positions (or one inch) to the left. Similarly, entering **10h** for a 12-pitch font moves the cursor 10/12 or 5/6 inches.

Unit of vertical measure refers to the height of a line within the current font. If the font's lines are .15" high, entering **10v** in response to the Up prompt moves the cursor 10 lines (or 1. 5") up the page.

It's important to understand how Line relates to Up and Down, and how Column relates to Left and Right. Note the following points:

- Up and Down move the cursor up or down by a specified number of units (inches, centimeters, etc.) *from the current line.*
- Line moves the cursor down by a specified number of units *from the top of the page.*
- Left and Right move the cursor left or right by a specified number of units *from its current position.*
- Column moves the cursor right by a specified number of units *from the left-hand edge of the page.*

For example, if you give a Down command and enter **10v** in response to the prompt, WordPerfect moves the cursor down 10 lines from its current position. By contrast, if you give a Line command and enter **10v** in response to the prompt, WordPerfect moves the cursor down 10 lines from the top.

For any of these movement operations, the final position must be a valid line or column number; one that lies within the margins for that page. If the resulting position is beyond the margins, WordPerfect moves the cursor to the appropriate margin. (Note that this differs from the version 4.1 and 4.2 Advance options, where WordPerfect simply ignores illegal movement commands and leaves the cursor at its original position.)

On the other hand, you can use this margin-limiting characteristic to reach a margin without knowing where it is: Simply enter a very large number at the prompt. WordPerfect will then try to move there, but will give up when it encounters a margin. To reach the right-hand margin, for instance, you could give a Right or Column command and enter **500** at the prompt.

Aligning on a Character

WordPerfect can line up a column of text or numbers on a character. For example, the second column of the following list is aligned on a decimal point, WordPerfect's preset alignment character:

Member	Collections
Brown, John	$1,504.36
Carlson, Ray	965.77
Decker, Patricia	1,668.43
Garnett, Vance	769.03
Evans, Sue	779.56

Here, WordPerfect shifts numbers left until you type a decimal point. It then puts anything else you type to the right.

To align a number with WordPerfect 4.1, you must press Ctrl-F6 (for Tab Align) to reach its tab stop. With WordPerfect 4.2 or 5.0, you can define a tab as "Decimal," and simply press Tab to reach it. WordPerfect aligns material entered at a decimal tab stop automatically. For more information about decimal tabs, see **Tabs**.

Alt (Alternate) Key

Like Ctrl and Shift, Alt is a *control* key. Pressing Alt alone does nothing, but holding it down and pressing another key makes WordPerfect do whatever that key combination indicates (if anything). Pressing Alt and a function key (F1 through F10) gives WordPerfect one of the commands that are printed in blue on the keyboard template. For example, pressing Alt and F7 together gives WordPerfect a Math/Columns command.

You can also define macros that activate when you press Alt and a letter key; for details, see the **Macros, Introduction to** entry.

With WordPerfect 4.1 and 4.2, you can also make Alt-letter key combinations insert geometric shapes, foreign characters, and other non-keyboard characters in a document (see **Special Characters**). However, if you assign a key combination to a character, you cannot use the same combination to run a macro; it will then only produce the character. In effect, WordPerfect will ignore the fact that this combination should replay a macro.

Antonyms

Starting with WordPerfect 4.2, the thesaurus displays antonyms (opposites) as well as synonyms when you look up a word. Lists of antonyms are marked with *ant*.

Appending Text to a File — WordPerfect 4.1 and 4.2

4.1
4.2

WordPerfect can attach a block of text to the end of any document file (even *locked* files) on your data disk. To make it do this:

1. Move the cursor to the beginning of the block.
2. Press Alt-F4 to get into Block mode.
3. Move the cursor to the end of the block.
4. Press Ctrl-F4 to give a Move command.
5. When the Move menu appears, press **3** for Append.
6. When the **Append to:** prompt appears, enter the name of the file to which you want to append the block. If WordPerfect cannot find that file, it reports **ERROR: File not found** and discontinues the Append operation.

Note that appending a block simply adds a copy of it to the end of the specified file; the original block remains in your document.

Appending Text to a File — WordPerfect 5.0

5.0

In WordPerfect 4.1 or 4.2, you can attach or *append* a block of text to the end of a document file on disk. WordPerfect 5.0 is more versatile; it can also append a column or rectangle selected in Block mode, or a sentence, paragraph, or page selected in regular editing mode. Further, WordPerfect 4.1 and 4.2 can only append to an existing file; WordPerfect 5.0 will *create* the file if it's not already on the disk.

Appending Blocks, Columns, and Rectangles

To append a block, column, or rectangle, do the following:

1. Move the cursor to the beginning of the text to be appended.
2. Press Alt-F4 to get into Block mode.
3. Move the cursor to the end of the affected text.
4. Press Ctrl-F4 to give a Move command.
5. When the Move menu appears, select Block (1), Tabular Column (2), or Rectangle (3).
6. When the next menu appears, type **4** for *Append*.

7. When the **Append to:** prompt appears, enter the name of the file to which you want to append the block.

Appending Sentences, Paragraphs, and Pages

To append a sentence, paragraph, or page, do the following:

1. Move the cursor anywhere within the text to be appended.
2. Press Ctrl-F4 to give a Move command.
3. When the Move menu appears, select Sentence (1), Paragraph (2), or Page (3).
6. When the next menu appears, type **4** for *Append*.
7. When the **Append to:** prompt appears, enter the name of the file to which you want to append the text.

Are other copies of WordPerfect currently running? **Prompt**

This prompt appears when you try to start WordPerfect 4.2 or 5.0 after a power failure. To bypass it, and start WordPerfect, type **n** for "no."

Arrow Keys

The →, ←, ↑, and ↓ keys on the numeric keypad move the cursor in the direction they point—that is, right (6), left (4), up (8), and down (2). The ← and → keys move the cursor a character at a time horizontally; the ↑ and ↓ keys move it a line at a time vertically. These keys *repeat*. They keep the cursor moving as long as you hold them down. You can also use the Ctrl key to move the cursor a word at a time. Pressing Ctrl and ← together moves it one word to the left, while pressing Ctrl and → moves it one word to the right. Like the arrow keys, these key combinations repeat; that is, the cursor keeps moving as long as you hold them down.

While you can certainly move through a document one character or one line at a time, you will often want to move greater distances. See **Cursor, Moving the** for details.

ASCII Text Files

— See **DOS Text Files**

Auto Rewrite

WordPerfect normally rearranges the screen automatically when you insert or delete material. If you find this distracting, you can turn off this so-called *auto rewrite* feature, and make WordPerfect update the screen at your command.

With the release of WordPerfect 5.0, the *Auto Rewrite* option was moved from the Screen (Ctrl-F3) key to the Setup (Shift-F1) key. Therefore, to avoid confusion, I will now describe the two Auto Rewrite procedures separately.

Auto Rewrite for WordPerfect 4.1 and 4.2

| 4.1 4.2 | To turn off auto rewriting, press Ctrl and F3 to give a Screen command. When the Screen menu appears, press **5** to choose *Auto Rewrite*. When the prompt appears, type **n** to turn automatic formatting off.

WordPerfect will then only update an altered line when you move the cursor downward, switch pages, or give another Screen command and choose *Rewrite* (0).

Auto Rewrite for WordPerfect 5.0

| 5.0 | To turn off auto rewriting, press Shift and F1 to give a Setup command. When the Setup menu appears, type **3** to obtain the Display Setup menu. Then type **3** again to select *Automatically Format and Rewrite*, and type **n** to turn automatic formatting off. Finally, press F7 (Exit) to leave the Setup menu.

WordPerfect will then only update an altered line when you move the cursor downward or switch pages.

Automatic Reference — WordPerfect 5.0

5.0

Reports, manuals, proposals, and other large documents often include references to pages, sections, chapters, figures, tables, or notes. For example, your document may include "As the Sales by Division graph on page 12 shows, . . ."

With WordPerfect 4.1 and 4.2, you must keep track of such references yourself, and change the reference number if the associated "target" (figure, page, footnote, etc.) is renumbered. However, WordPerfect 5.0 provides an *automatic reference* feature that maintains cross-references for you.

Creating an Automatic Reference

To create an automatic reference, you must insert a Reference code where a reference number belongs, then insert a Target code to mark the item to which the Reference code refers. If the reference and target are in the same document, you can mark them both in one operation. If either the reference or the target has not yet been created, or they're in different documents, you can mark them separately. When you finish marking all the references and targets in a document, you must *generate* the references to make WordPerfect insert the reference numbers.

To mark both a reference and its target:

1. Move the cursor to where the reference number belongs; e.g., perhaps just after "Sales by Division graph on page."
2. Press Alt-F5 to give a Mark Text command.
3. When the Mark Text menu appears, type **1** to select *Auto Ref*.
4. When the Automatic Reference menu appears, type **3** to *Mark Both Reference and Target*.
5. Specify the type of number you're referring to: Page (1), Paragraph/Outline (2), Footnote (3), Endnote (4), or Graphics Box (5). If you specify *Graphics Box Number*, WordPerfect shows

    `1 Figure; 2 Table; 3 Text Box; 4 User-defined Box: 0`

    Type the number of the box type you want.
6. When a prompt of the form **Press Enter to select** *item* appears (where *item* is page, paragraph, footnote, etc.), move the cursor

to the end of the number you're referring to (the target) and press Enter.
7. When WordPerfect asks for the **Target Name:**, enter an appropriate name for this item (e.g., enter **sales by division graph**).

The cursor then returns to the reference number location, and you can finish typing any text that belongs there.

To mark only a target:

1. Move the cursor to the target.
2. Press Alt-F5 to give a Mark Text command.
3. When the Mark Text menu appears, type **1** to select *Auto Ref*.
4. When the Automatic Reference menu appears, type **2** to *Mark Target*.
5. When WordPerfect asks for the **Target Name:**, enter an appropriate name for this item (e.g., enter **sales by division graph**).

To mark only a reference:

1. Move the cursor to where the reference number belongs; e.g., perhaps just after "Sales by Division graph on page."
2. Press Alt-F5 to give a Mark Text command.
3. When the Mark Text menu appears, type **1** to select *Auto Ref*.
4. When the Automatic Reference menu appears, type **2** to *Mark Reference*.
5. Specify the type of number you're referring to: Page (1), Paragraph/Outline (2), Footnote (3), Endnote (4), or Graphics Box (5). If you specify *Graphics Box Number*, WordPerfect shows

```
1 Figure; 2 Table; 3 Text Box; 4 User-defined Box: 0
```

Type the number of the box type you want.
6. When asked for the **Target Name:**, enter the name you have given (or will give) to the target this reference refers to.

WordPerfect inserts a question mark (?) at the reference location. It will replace the ? with a number when you *generate* the references.

Generating References

To generate the references in a document, put the cursor anywhere in the document and do the following:

1. Press Alt-F5 to give a Mark Text command.
2. When the Mark Text menu appears, type **6** for *Generate*.
3. When the Generate menu appears, type **5** for *Generate Tables, Indexes, Automatic References, etc.*
4. When **Existing tables, lists, and indexes will be replaced. Continue? (Y/N) Yes** appears, type **y** or press Enter. (Or, to return to the document without generating references, type **n**.)

WordPerfect displays **Generation in progress** while it inserts the reference numbers. Of course, it can only insert numbers for references whose targets are in the same document. Those it can't resolve remain marked with a ?.

Multiple References

In some cases you may want to use more than one reference to refer to an item, as in

Figure 3 on page 12 lists the major accounts in the Southeast region.

Here, you would do two Automatic Reference operations, to insert the figure number and the page number, and specify the same *Target Name* both times.

Auxiliary Files — WordPerfect 5.0

5.0   If your computer has only floppy disk drives, you must sometimes switch disks for certain WordPerfect operations. For example, you must insert the Speller disk to do a spell-check operation, or insert the Thesaurus disk to do a Thesaurus operation. With floppy disks, then, WordPerfect always knows to look on one of your disk drives (A or B) to find the auxiliary files it needs.

However, a computer that has a hard disk can hold hundreds or even thousands of disk files. The usual way to keep things organized is to store related files in sections of the disk called *directories*. For example, you could put WordPerfect's system files—the program and data files that we collectively call "WordPerfect"—in one directory and put document files in another directory. You could also create separate directories for the Speller and Thesaurus files.

WordPerfect 4.1 and 4.2 assume that all of your files (programs, data, documents, macros, and so on) are in the main *WP* directory. However, by using the Set-up menu for these versions, you can put the Speller's dictionaries (main and supplementary) and the Thesaurus file in directories of your choice.

Like its predecessors, WordPerfect 5.0 expects to find all files in the main WordPerfect directory, but has a Setup menu option that lets you specify alternate directories for auxiliary files. This option, *Location of Auxiliary Files*, lets you store auxiliary files in up to eight different directories.

To begin, press Shift and F1 to give a Setup command. When the Setup menu appears, type **7** to obtain the *Location of Auxiliary Files* menu shown in Figure A-1.

Here is an explanation of these fields:

1 *Backup Directory* is where WordPerfect is to store files created by a Backup option (see **Backups**).
2 *Hyphenation Module(s)* is the directory that contains WordPerfect's Auto Hyphenation file. The English language version of this file is called WP{WP}EN.HYL; WordPerfect Corporation also offers hyphenation files for other languages.
3 *Keyboard/Macro Files* is the directory that holds keyboard (.WPK), macro (.WPM), and macro resource (.MRS) files.
4 *Main Dictionary(s)* is the directory that contains the Speller's main dictionary file. The English language version of this file is called WP{WP}EN.LEX; WordPerfect Corporation also offers dictionary files for other languages.

Figure A-1. WordPerfect 5.0's Location of Auxiliary Files menu.

```
    Setup: Location of Auxiliary Files

         1 - Backup Directory
         2 - Hyphenation Module(s)
         3 - Keyboard/Macro Files
         4 - Main Dictionary(s)
         5 - Printer Files
         6 - Style Library Filename
         7 - Supplementary Dictionary(s)
         8 - Thesaurus

    Selection: 0
```

5 *Printer Files* is the directory that holds printer definition (.PRS) files.
6 *Style Library Filename* refers to a file used with WordPerfect 5.0's Style (Alt-F8) command. Here, you must specify the name of the file as well as its directory. (All other entries in this menu require only a directory name.) For example, if your style library is called MYSTYLE.LIB and it's in a hard disk (Drive C) directory called STYLE, enter **c:\style\mystyle.lib** here.
7 *Supplementary Dictionary(s)* names the directory in which WordPerfect should store the dictionary it uses when you tell the Speller to add a word to the dictionary. When creating a supplementary dictionary file, WordPerfect gives it the same name as the current main dictionary, but with a .SUP extension. For example, WordPerfect will name the English language supplementary dictionary WP{WP}EN.SUP.
8 *Thesaurus* is the directory that contains the Thesaurus file. The English language version of this file is called WP{WP}EN.THS; WordPerfect Corporation also offers thesaurus files for other languages.

When you finish with the menu, press F7 (Exit) to return to your document.

Specifying the Language

The files that WordPerfect uses for fields 2, 4, 7, 8 depends on the abbreviation in the *Language* field of the Other Format submenu. For example, the abbreviation *EN* makes WordPerfect select English-language files.

To change the *Language* setting for the current document, press Shift-F8 to give a Format command and type 4 to obtain the Other Format submenu. Similarly, to change the *Language* setting for all documents, press Shift-F1 to give a Setup command, type 5 for *Initial Settings*, then 4 for *Initial Codes*. When the Reveal Codes screen appears, press Shift-F8 to give a Format command and type 4 to obtain the Other Format submenu.

Backspace Key

Backspace is the key with the left arrow above Enter. On a typewriter, pressing Backspace moves the carriage or typing element to the left. When using WordPerfect, pressing Backspace not only moves to the preceding character, but deletes it as well.

Backspace is a *repeating* key. It keeps deleting characters as long as you hold it down.

Backups

Your documents represent a lot of time and effort, and you should be sure to keep at least one additional copy of the important documents. After all, floppy disks are cheap; your time isn't. You can either create backup files manually or let WordPerfect create them automatically.

Manual Backups

There are two ways to back up a document manually: (1) from within WordPerfect, give a List Files (F5) command and select *Copy;*

or (2) from the DOS prompt, enter a Copy command. For example, if the DOS prompt is A>, put the disk that contains the document you want to copy in drive A and the disk that is to receive the copy in drive B. Then enter a command of the form

copy a:docname.ext b:

if you want the copy to have the same name as the original, or

copy a:docname.ext b:newname.ext

if you want the copy to have a different name.

Automatic Backups

WordPerfect will make backup copies of your documents automatically, if you tell it to. To make WordPerfect produce backups, you must change its initial or *setup* options. The procedure differs between WordPerfect versions 4.x and version 5.0.

> 4.1
> 4.2

With WordPerfect 4.1 or 4.2, start the computer as usual, but when the B> prompt appears, enter **a:wp/s** (instead of the usual **a:wp**). When the Setup Menu appears, enter **4** for *Set Backup Options*.

> 5.0

With WordPerfect 5.0, obtain the Setup menu from within WordPerfect, by pressing Shift-F1. When the Setup menu appears, type **1** for *Backup*.

WordPerfect provides options called Timed Backup and Original Backup.

The *Timed Backup* option guards against an unexpected power failure by saving the documents you're working on at regular, specified intervals. At each interval, it stores the documents on the Doc 1 and Doc 2 screens in files called {WP}BACK.1 and {WP}BACK.2. Then, if the power ever goes off when WordPerfect is running, restart it (see **Power Failure**), retrieve the {WP}BACK file and save it under the document's original name. Note that {WP}BACK.1 and .2 are temporary files; if you exit normally, with an Exit (F7) command, WordPerfect deletes them.

The *Original Backup* option makes WordPerfect create a backup when you save a document with the Save (F10) or Exit (F7) command. Here, WordPerfect gives the backup the same name, but with the extension *.BK!*. For example, if you edit a document named ROSTER.DOC and save it, WordPerfect saves the edited version as ROSTER.DOC and the original as ROSTER.BK!.

Fortunately, if you somehow foul up a document beyond repair, you can always go back to the original. Simply retrieve the .BK! file and then save it under the original name.

Timed Backup Versus Original Backup

Both automatic backup options have advantages and disadvantages. Timed Backup lets you work without having to remember to save to disk periodically. Furthermore, it ensures that you are only in danger of losing whatever you entered since the last backup interval.

On the other hand, Timed Backup's save operations can disrupt your train of thought, in that you can't do anything when it's saving to disk. Moreover, if your backup interval is short (say, only a few minutes), Timed Backup puts a lot of wear and tear on your disk. This is especially destructive to a hard disk over a period of time: a lot of save operations can ruin it.

The Original Backup option guarantees that you always have two copies of your document on disk, one from the last time you saved and another from the save operation before that. Although Original Backup's value depends on how often you save, it has one possible advantage over Timed Backup: it creates a separate backup file for every document you save. Timed Backup only maintains two backup files ({WP}BACK.1 and {WP}BACK.2) and always uses them to store the active documents. Then again, creating a backup for each document tends to clutter your disk with backup files.

It's up to you to determine which backup technique to use. Just be sure to back up documents in *some* way, even if you do it manually.

Beep Sound

WordPerfect sounds a "beep" through the computer's built-in speaker whenever you attempt to perform an illegal command. For example, it beeps if you have selected a block of text in Block mode, then press Alt-F1 for a Thesaurus command. There's no reason you should be calling for the thesaurus in Block mode, so WordPerfect scolds you by beeping.

More Beeping

WordPerfect can also sound a beep whenever a search fails, an error message appears, or it needs hyphenation help. To make it do this, you must change WordPerfect's initial or *setup* options. The setup procedure differs between versions 4.x and 5.0.

4.1 / 4.2 — **With version 4.1 or 4.2,** start WordPerfect with **wp/s** (instead of the usual **wp**). When the Set-up menu appears, type **3** to select *Set Screen and Beep Options* (with version 4.1, type **5** for *Set Beep Options*) and answer the search, error, and hyphenation prompts.

5.0 — **With WordPerfect 5.0,** press Shift-F1 to give a Setup command. When the Setup menu appears, press **5** to obtain the *Initial Settings* menu, then press **2** to select *Beep Options*. Type **y** to turn on each option you want, then press F7 (Exit) to leave the Beep Options menu.

Binding Width

If your document is to be printed as double-sided pages, you must allow for holes or other bindings. That is, you must give pages a "gutter" at either the left (for odd-numbered or right-hand pages) or right (for even-numbered or left-hand pages).

4.1 / 4.2 — **With WordPerfect 4.1 or 4.2,** specify the width of the gutter or *binding width* as follows:

1. Press Shift-F7 to do a Print command.
2. When the Print menu appears, you have two options:
   A. To change the binding width of the next document you print, press **3** for Options.
   B. To change the binding width for all print jobs until you leave WordPerfect, press **4** for Printer Control, then **1** for Select Print Options.
3. When the Select Print Options screen appears, press **3** for Binding Width.
4. Type the binding width you want, then press Enter. Binding width is specified in tenths of an inch, so enter **5** if you want a half-inch gutter.

5.0 — With WordPerfect 5.0, specify the binding width as follows:

1. Press Shift-F7 to do a Print command.
2. When the Print menu appears, type **b** to select Binding.

3. Enter athe binding width, in inches.
4. Press F7 (Exit) to leave the menus.

BK! Files

— See **Backups**

Blank Screen

If the screen goes blank when you press Shift and a function key, you have pressed Shift and *F3*. This is WordPerfect's Switch command. WordPerfect lets you edit two documents at the same time, one on the main screen (called Doc 1 on the status line) and the other on an alternate (Doc 2) screen. If that's not what you want to do, press Shift-F3 again to get back to your original document.

Blank Space, Inserting

WordPerfect has an *Adv Ln* (Advance to Line) that lets you insert blank space in your document, to leave room for a figure or table you will paste in later. See **Advance** for details.

Block Command (Alt-F4)

WordPerfect lets you work with blocks of text, where a block can be anything from a single character to an entire document. To define text as a block, move the cursor to the beginning of it and press Alt-F4 to give a Block command. This produces a flashing **Block on** at

20 Block Command (Alt-F4)

the bottom left-hand corner of the screen, which means that WordPerfect is in Block mode. (If you pressed Alt-F4 accidentally, press F1 to leave Block mode.)

Once WordPerfect is in Block mode, it highlights everything the cursor passes over. To move the cursor in Block mode, you can either use the standard cursor-moving commands (the arrow keys, End, PgUp, PgDn, and so on) or simply type a character.

Typing a character makes WordPerfect extend the highlighting to the first occurrence of that character. For example, if you put the cursor at the beginning of the sentence "Bill, you're such a good friend.", and press Alt-F4 (for Block), then type **s**, WordPerfect will highlight "Bill, you're s". (Note that the *s* is included in the highlighting.) If you then press the space bar, WordPerfect extends the highlighting to cover "such" and the space that follows it.

Block Operations

Once you highlight a block, you can perform many different operations on it. (Some operations differ between versions 4.1 and 4.2 [collectively called 4.x] and version 5.0.) Specifically:

To perform this command:	Press
Bold	F6
Cancel (leave Block mode)	F1
Center each line in the block	Shift-F6
Comment, convert block to (5.0)	Ctrl-F5, then y
Delete	Del, then y
Flush Right lines in the block	Alt-F6, then y
Font (5.0)	Ctrl-F6
Size/Position	1
Appearance	2
Help	F3
Lowercase	Shift-F3, then 2
Mark Text	Alt-F5
Table of Contents	1
List	2
Redline (4.x)	3
Strikeout (4.x)	4
Index	5 (4.x) or 3 (5.0)
Table of Authorities	6 (4.2) or 4 (5.0)
Move (4.x)	Ctrl-F4

Block Command (Alt-F4)

Cut Block	1
Copy Block	2
Append	3
Cut/Copy Column	4
Cut/Copy Rectangle	5
Move (5.0)	Ctrl-F4
Block	1
Column	2
Rectangle	3
Print	Shift-F7, then **y**
Protect (keep together on a page)	Alt-F8, then **y** (4.x) or Shift-F8, then **y** (5.0)
Replace	Alt-F2
Reveal Codes	Alt-F3
Save	F10
Screen	Ctrl-F3
Search Backward	Shift-F2
Search Forward	F2
Sort	Ctrl-F9
Spell-check	Ctrl-F2
Style (5.0)	Alt-F8
Super/Subscript (4.x)	Shift-F1
Underline	F8
Uppercase	Shift-F3, then **1**

Other function key combinations make the computer beep.

With versions 4.1 and 4.2, some of the preceding operations leave WordPerfect in Block mode; press F1 (Cancel) to turn it off.

In WordPerfect 4.1 and 4.2, common Block mode operations include Cut (Ctrl-F4, 1), Copy (Ctrl-F4, 2), and Protect (Alt-F8). In WordPerfect 5.0, the corresponding operations are Move (Ctrl-F4, 1, 1), Copy (Ctrl-F4, 1, 2), and Protect (Shift-F8). Protecting a block makes WordPerfect keep it together on a page during reformatting. You will often want to protect tables, for example.

To protect a specific number of lines of text without selecting them in Block mode, give a Conditional End of Page command. See that entry for details.

Rehighlighting a Block

Sometimes you will want to do a second operation on the same block. To do this, press Alt-F4 to turn Block mode on, then press Ctrl-Home *twice* to rehighlight the block. Ctrl-Home is

WordPerfect's *Go To* command. Pressing it twice makes the cursor return to its previous location.

Bold Command (F6)

To make something print in **bold** type, press F6. WordPerfect emboldens the *Pos* value at the bottom right-hand corner of the screen. This means it will embolden everything you type until you press F6 again. (Emboldened text is displayed brighter than normal on the screen, but you may have to reduce the display's contrast to see the difference.) To embolden existing text, highlight it in Block mode, then press F6.

Removing Emboldening

WordPerfect precedes emboldened text with a [B] code and follows it with a [b] code (or, in version 5.0, [BOLD] and [bold]). To remove emboldening, do a Reveal Codes (Alt-F3) command, then move the cursor just ahead of either code and press Del to delete it. Finally, press Alt-F3 again to leave Reveal Codes.

Bold Letters in WordPerfect 5.0 Menus

— See **Menus, Selecting Options from**

Boxes, Drawing

— See **Lines, Drawing**

Breaking Pages

—See **Hard Page Command**

Cancel Command (F1)

The F1 key is marked Cancel on the WordPerfect template, but it actually has a variety of uses. By pressing F1, you can:

1. Cancel a WordPerfect command that you started accidentally, or one that you started on purpose, but decided against. Here, you may have to press F1 several times, depending on how far you have proceeded into the operation.
2. Recover deleted text. WordPerfect saves text from your last three deletions. When you press F1, it shows the text you deleted most recently (in highlighted form) at the current cursor position and displays this menu at the bottom of the screen:

        Undelete: 1 Restore; 2 Show Previous Deletion: 0

    To insert the highlighted material into the text, press **1**; to insert the next most recent deletion, press **2**, then **1**; to insert the earliest deletion, press **2** *twice*, then **1**. To get back to editing without undeleting anything, press the F1 key again.
3. Turn the Block mode off.
4. Cancel a Hyphenation request when Hyphenation is on.

You cannot press F1 to cancel a macro definition, however. Once **Macro Def** appears on the screen, you must press Ctrl-F10 (Macro Define) to return to editing. The second Macro Define command saves the macro on disk; to get rid of it, you must delete it.

Canceling Print Jobs

To cancel a print operation or "job":

1. Press Shift-F7 for Print, then **4** for *Printer Control*.
2. When the Printer Control menu appears, press **c** (versions 4.x) or **1** (version 5.0) for *Cancel*. WordPerfect shows

   ```
   Cancel which job? (*=All Jobs) n
   ```

   below "Selection:". Here, *n* is the number of the job that is being printed.
3. You now have three options:
   A. To cancel the current job, press Enter
   B. To cancel an upcoming job, enter its "Job Number" from the *Job List* at the bottom
   C. To cancel all jobs, type an asterisk (*), then press Enter. Since this is a drastic action, WordPerfect lets you change your mind by displaying **Cancel All Jobs? (Y/N) N**. Press **y** to cancel the jobs or Enter to proceed with printing.

In any case, WordPerfect shows **Press ENTER if Printer Does not Respond**.

A Macro to Cancel Printing

When you want to cancel a print job, you generally want to do it quickly, and don't want to have to think about which keys to press. Following is the procedure to create a macro that does the preceding steps 1 and 2 when you press Alt and C:

1. Press Ctrl and F10 to give WordPerfect a Macro Define command.
2. When **Define Macro:** appears at the bottom of the screen, press Alt and C simultaneously. WordPerfect shows a blinking **Macro Def** message at the bottom.

3. Press Shift and F7 (for Print).
4. When the Print menu appears, type **4** for Printer Control.
5. When the Printer Control menu appears, type **c** (4.1 or 4.2) or **1** (5.0) for Cancel Print Job(s).
6. Press Ctrl-F10 to end the macro definition and save the Alt-C macro on disk.

Note that when you run the Alt-C macro, all you must do is tell WordPerfect which print job (or jobs) to cancel.

Can't create new printer files on WP disk Message

This means that you have asked for the Select Printers option on the Printer Control menu, but there isn't enough space on your WordPerfect disk to save printer information. Delete any unnecessary files and try again.

Capitalizing

WordPerfect can capitalize text as you enter it or capitalize existing text.

Capitalizing New Text

To enter text in capital (uppercase) letters, you can either hold the Shift key down or press Caps Lock, then type.

Caps Lock is a handy variation of a shift lock key; it locks in capital letters but *leaves the nonletter keys in lowercase*. Be careful with Caps Lock. Pressing it once locks in capital letters, but pressing it again returns the keyboard to lowercase. The IBM PC AT keyboard has a green indicator that lights when Caps Lock is on, but the PC and XT keyboards do not. Fortunately, WordPerfect provides its own indicator: it shows the abbreviation *POS* at the bottom right-hand corner of the screen.

Of course, you can always press a letter key and see what appears on the screen. One added feature is that when Caps Lock is on, you can press Shift to enter lowercase letters. Nonletter keys always work normally.

Capitalizing Existing Text

To capitalize existing text, put WordPerfect in Block mode (by pressing Alt-F4), move the cursor to highlight the text, and press Shift-F3. When this menu appears

```
Block: 1 Upper Case 2 Lower Case: 0
```

select *Upper Case*, then press F1 to leave Block mode. This operation affects only letter characters; numbers and symbols are unchanged.

Caps Lock Key

— See **Capitalizing**

Center Command (Shift-F6)

WordPerfect can center an individual line or all lines in a block of text between the left and right margins. It can also center a heading over a column. (WordPerfect can also center text on a page vertically, and put equal space above and below it. See **Centering a Page Top to Bottom** for details.)

Centering a Line

To center a line you are about to type, press Shift-F6 (the cursor moves to the center of the screen) and enter the line. To center an existing line, put the cursor on the first character and press Shift-F6.

Centering a Block of Text

To center a block, select it in Block mode, then press Shift-F6. When the **[Center]? (Y/N) N** prompt appears, press **y** for yes.

Centering a Column Heading

To center a heading over a column of text or numbers, move the cursor to the center of the column and press Shift-F6. Then type the heading and press → or Tab to move right or press Enter to move to the next line.

Uncentering

WordPerfect precedes centered text with a hidden [C] code and follows it with a [c] code (or, in WordPerfect 5.0, [Cntr] and [c/a/flrt]). To uncenter a line, give a Reveal Codes (Alt-F3) command, then move the cursor just ahead of either code and press Del to delete it. Finally, press Alt-F3 again to leave Reveal Codes. To uncenter a block of text, you must uncenter each line in it individually.

Centering a Page Top to Bottom

To center text top to bottom on a page, first move the cursor to the very beginning of the page, ahead of all codes. (Move to the top line, press Home *three times*, then ←.) Then:

| 4.1 4.2 |
- **For WordPerfect 4.1 or 4.2,** press Alt-F8 to obtain the Page Format menu, then press **3** to select *Center Page Top to Bottom* and Enter to leave the menu.

| 5.0 |
- **For WordPerfect 5.0,** press Shift-F8 to display the Format menu, press **2** to select *Page*, **1** to select *Center page (top to bottom)*, and F7 (Exit) to return to editing.

WordPerfect doesn't actually center the page on the screen (in fact, it doesn't even change the text's line numbers to reflect the centering), but the page will be centered when you print it.

Uncentering

WordPerfect puts a hidden [Center Pg] code at the beginning of a centered page. To uncenter a page, do a Reveal Codes (Alt-F3) command, then move the cursor just ahead of the code and press Del to delete it. Finally, press Alt-F3 again to leave Reveal Codes.

Centering a Paragraph

— See *Indenting from Both Margins* under **Indent Commands**

Characters per Inch

— See **Pitch**

Codes, Hidden — WordPerfect 4.1 and 4.2

4.1
4.2

WordPerfect tells your printer how to format text by sending it special codes. The printer interprets each code as a command and does whatever that particular command signifies. For example, when you press Ctrl and Enter to switch pages, WordPerfect inserts a "new page" code in your document. When you print the document, the printer receives that code and advances the paper to the next page before it starts printing.

WordPerfect does not show these codes on the screen; it hides them. However, you can display the codes by pressing Alt-F3, to give a *Reveal Codes* command. Reveal Codes shows the current cursor position as a blinking underline. To delete a code, move the cursor to the left of it and press Del, or to the right of it and press Backspace. To leave the Reveal Codes screen, press Alt-F3 again.

Here is a list of all the hidden codes, and what they indicate. Two codes on a line indicate that WordPerfect inserts the first one ahead of your text and the second one after it. For example, when you center a line, WordPerfect puts [C] at the beginning of it and [c] at the end of it.

[ ]	Hard space
[-]	Hard hyphen (one you typed)
*	Do grand total
=	Do total
!	Formula calculation

-	Soft hyphen (one that WordPerfect inserted)
+	Do subtotal
/	Cancel hyphenation
[A][a]	Tab Align or Flush Right
[Adv ▲]	Advance up 1/2 line
[Adv ▼]	Advance down 1/2 line
[AdvLn:*n*]	Advance to line *n*
[Align Char:*char*]	Decimal alignment character
[B],[b]	Bold print
[Bin#:*b*]	Sheet feeder bin number
[Block]	Beginning of block
[BlockPro:On][BlockPro:Off]	Block protection on, off
[C][c]	Center
[Cmnd:*command*]	Embedded printer command
[CndlEOP:*n*]	Conditional end of page (*n* = number of lines)
[Col Def:*d*]	Column definition (*d* = definition codes)
[Col On][Col Off]	Beginning, end of text columns
[Date:*f*]	Date/Time insert function (*f* = format)
[DefMark:Index,*n;con*]	Index definition (*n* = numbering style; *con* = name of concordance file)
[DefMark:List,*n*]	List definition (*n* = list number)
[DefMark:ToC,*l*]	Table of contents definition (*l* = table of contents level)
[EndDef]	End of index, list, or table of contents
[EndMark:Index,*f*]	End of text marked for index (*f* = format)
[EndMark:List,*n*]	End of text marked for list (*n* = list number)
[EndMark:ToC,*l*]	End of text marked for table of contents (*l* = table of contents level)
[E-Tabs:*n,s*]	Extended tabs (begin at column *n*, every *s* spaces) in WordPerfect version 4.1.
[FontChange:*p,f*]	Specify new font or print wheel (*p,f* = pitch, font)
[FtnOpt]	Footnote/endnote options

Codes, Hidden — WordPerfect 4.1 and 4.2

[Hdr/Ftr:*t,o*;text]	Header or footer definition (*t,o* = type, occurrence)
[HPg]	Hard page break (Ctrl-Enter keys)
[HRt]	Hard return (Enter key)
[Hyph on][Hyph off]	Hyphenation on, off
[HZone Set:*l,r*]	Reset size of hyphenation zone (*l,r* = left, right)
[-Indent]	Beginning of left indent
[-Indent]	Beginning of left/right indent
[Index:*h;s*]	Index mark (*h,s* = heading, subheading)
[LnNum:On][LnNum:Off]	Line numbering turned on, off
[LPI:*n*]	Lines per inch (*n* = 6 or 8)
[-Mar Rel:*n*]	Left margin release (*n* = number of positions moved)
[Margin Set:*l,r*]	Change left and right margin settings
[Mark:List,*n*]	Beginning of text marked for list (*n* = list number)
[Mark:ToC,*l*]	Beginning of text marked for table of contents (*l* = table of contents level)
[Math Def]	Definition of math columns
[Math On][Math Off]	Beginning, end of math
[Note:End,*e*; [Note #]*text*]	Endnote (*e* = endnote number)
[Note:Foot,*f*; [Note #]*text*]	Footnote (*f* = footnote number)
[Ovrstk]	Overstrike preceding character
[Par#:Auto]	Automatic paragraph/outline number
[Par#:*n*] (*n* = level number)	Permanent paragraph number
[Par#Def]	Paragraph numbering definition
[Pg#:*n*]	New page number
[Pg#Col:*l,c,r*]	Column position for page numbers (*l,c,r* = left, center, right)
[Pg Lnth:*f,t*]	Set page length (*f,t* = no. of total lines, no. of text lines)
[Pos Pg#:*n*]	Set position for page numbers
[RedLn][r]	Redline

[Rt Just On][Rt Just Off]	Right justification on, off
[Set Ftn:#*n*]	New footnote number
[Smry/Cmnt: *text*]	Document comment
[Smry/Cmnt: *date, author, typist, comment*]	Document summary
[Spacing Set:*n*]	Spacing set
[SPg]	Soft page break (page is full, WordPerfect has started a new one)
[SRt]	Soft return (end of lines within a paragraph)
[StrkOut][s]	Strikeout (overtype with hyphens)
[SubScrpt]	Subscript
[SuprScrpt]	Superscript
[Suppress:*o*]	Suppress page format options (*o* = options suppressed)
t (blinking)	Subtotal entry
T (blinking)	Total entry
[TAB]	Move to next tab stop (Tab key)
[Tab Set:*tabs*]	Change tab settings
[ToA:*;ShortForm;*] or [ToA:*s;ShortForm;* <FullForm>]	Mark for Table of Authorities (*s* = *(section number)*)
[Top Mar:*n*]	Set top margin (*n* = number of half-lines)
[U][u]	Underlining
[Undrl Style:*s*]	Underline style (*s* = style code)
[W/O On][W/O Off]	Widow/Orphan protection turned on, off

Searching for Hidden Codes

At the beginning of this entry, I mentioned that you can delete a hidden code by moving to it in Reveal Codes and pressing Del or Backspace. Of course, that assumes you know roughly where a code is located; sometimes you may not. Instead of spending a lot of time scrolling through the text in Reveal Codes, you can use WordPerfect's *Search* commands (see separate entry) to locate the code.

There are two search commands. F2 searches forward through the document, while Search-F2 searches backward. When you press either key, WordPerfect displays a *Srch:* prompt at the bottom of the screen. Insert the hidden code you want to locate (details are upcoming), then press F2 to start searching. WordPerfect stops at the first instance of the code and puts the cursor just after it. You can then press Backspace, if you want to delete the code.

WordPerfect's *Replace* (Alt-F2) command can locate hidden codes, and replace or delete them. For example, you could use Replace to change all Indents to Tabs or to remove underlining from some or all of the text in a document. Replace operates with two strings, a search string and a replacement string (see **Search Commands** for details), and you can insert hidden codes in either or both of them.

In general, to insert a hidden code in a search or replacement string, you simply enter the command that produces that feature. For example, to search for the [Bold] code that precedes emboldened text, press F6 in your search string. The following table should help save you from having to remember which key commands produce which codes in a search string. It gives the name of each code, the keystroke(s) you must type to insert it, and the code that WordPerfect puts in the search string.

To search for...	Press	Code in string
* (Math grand total)	Alt-F7 6	*
= (Math total)	Alt-F7 5	=
! (Math formula calculation)	Alt-F7 9	!
- (Soft hyphen)	Ctrl-Hyphen	-
+ (Math subtotal)	Alt-F7 4	+
/ (Cancel hyphenation)	Shift-F8 6	/
Advance down	Shift-F1 5	[Adv ▼]
Advance to line	Shift-F1 6	[AdvLn]
Advance up	Shift-F1 4	[Adv ▲]
Alignment character, decimal	Shift-F8 7	[Align Char]
Block protect on or off	Alt-F8 7	[BlockPro]
Bold off	F6 F6	[Bold][b]
Bold on	F6	[Bold]
Cancel hyphenation (/)	Shift-F8 6	/
Center	Shift-F6	[Center]
Center page top to bottom	Alt-F8 3	[Center Pg]
Column position for page number	Alt-F8 1	[Pos Pg#]
Columns definition, text	Alt-F7 B	[Col Def]
Columns off	Alt-F7 D	[Col off]
Columns on	Alt-F7 C	[Col on]

Comment, document	Ctrl-F5	[Smry/Cmnt]
Conditional end of page	Alt-F8 9	[CndlEOP]
Date/Time function	Shift-F5	[Date]
Decimal alignment character	Shift-F8 7	[Align Char]
Document comment or summary	Ctrl-F5	[Smry/Cmnt]
^E (Merge E)	Shift-F9	^E
End of definition	Alt-F5 8	[EndDef]
Endnote	Ctrl-F7 1	[Note]
Endnote number	Ctrl-F7 4	[Note #]
Endnote number, set new	Ctrl-F7 2	[Set Note #]
Endnote options	Ctrl-F7 3	[FtnOpt]
Extended tabs (WordPerfect 4.1)		
Flush Right	Alt-F6	[Aln/FlshR]
Font change	Ctrl-F8 1	[Font Change]
Footer or header definition	Alt-F8 6	[Hdr/Ftr]
Footnote	Ctrl-F7 1	[Note]
Footnote number	Ctrl-F7 4	[Note #]
Footnote number, set new	Ctrl-F7 2	[Set Note #]
Footnote options	Ctrl-F7 3	[FtnOpt]
Formula calculation (!)	Alt-F7 9	!
Grand total (*)	Alt-F7 6	*
Hard hyphen	-	[-]
Hard page break	Ctrl-Enter	[HPg]
Hard return (Enter key)	Enter	[HRt]
Hard space	Home Space	[ ]
Header or footer definition	Alt-F8 6	[Hdr/Ftr]
Hyphenation, cancel (/)	Shift-F8 6	/
Hyphenation off	Shift-F8 8	[Hyph off]
Hyphenation on	Shift-F8 9	[Hyph on]
Hyphenation Zone, set	Shift-F8 5	[HZone Set]
Index definition	Alt-F5 7	[DefMark]
Index entry	Alt-F5 3	[Index]
Left indent	F4	[->Indent]
Left/right indent	Shift-F4	[->Indent<-]
Left margin release	Shift-Tab	[<-Mar Rel]
Line numbering on or off	Ctrl-F8 8	[LnNum]
Lines per inch	Ctrl-F8 2	[LPI]

Codes, Hidden — WordPerfect 4.1 and 4.2

List definition	Alt-F5 7	[DefMark]
List or table of contents entry	Alt-F5 1	[Mark]
Margin release	Shift-Tab	[<-Mar Rel]
Margin, top	Alt-F8 5	[Top Mar]
Margins, left and right	Shift-F8 3	[Margin Set]
Math definition	Alt-F7 1	[Math Def]
Math off	Alt-F7 3	[Math Off]
Math on	Alt-F7 2	[Math On]
Merge E (^E)	Shift-F9	^E
Merge R (^R)	F9	^R
Negative (N) operator	Alt-F7 A	N
New footnote/endnote number	Ctrl-F7 2	[Set Note #]
New page number	Alt-F8 2	[Pg#]
Outline numbering definition	Alt-F5 7	[DefMark]
Overstrike	Shift-F1 3	[Ovrstk]
Page, center top to bottom	Alt-F8 3	[Center Pg]
Page length, set	Alt-F8 4	[Pg Lnth]
Page number, new	Alt-F8 2	[Pg#]
Page number position	Alt-F8 1	[Pos Pg#]
Paragraph number	Alt-F5 2	[Par#]
Paragraph numbering definition	Alt-F5 6	[Par#Def]
Pitch change	Ctrl-F8 1	[Font Change]
Printer command	Ctrl-F8 7	[Cmnd]
^R (Merge R)	F9	^R
Redline	Alt-F5 4	[RedLn]
Right justification off	Ctrl-F8 3	[Rt Just Off]
Right justification on	Ctrl-F8 4	[Rt Just On]
Sheet feeder bin number	Ctrl-F8 6	[Bin#]
Soft hyphen	Ctrl-Hyphen	-
Soft page break	Ctrl-VK	[SPg]
Soft return	Ctrl-M	[SRt]
Spacing	Shift-F8 4	[Spacing Set]
Special character	Ctrl-V *n*	*character*
Strikeout	Alt-F5 5	[StrkOut]
Subscript	Shift-F1 2	[SubScrpt]
Subtotal (+)	Alt-F7 4	+
Subtotal entry	Alt-F7 7	t
Summary, document	Ctrl-F5	[Smry/Cmnt]

Superscript	Shift-F1 1	[SuprScrpt]
Suppress page format options	Alt-F8 8	[Suppress]
Tab	Tab	[TAB]
Tab Align	Ctrl-F6	[Aln/FlshR]
Tab settings	Shift-F8 1	[Tab Set]
Table of Authorities definition	Alt-F5 7	[DefMark]
Table of Authorities entry	Alt-F5 9	[ToA]
Table of contents definition	Alt-F5 7	[DefMark]
Table of contents or list entry	Alt-F5 1	[Mark]
Text columns definition	Alt-F7 B	[Col Def]
Text columns off	Alt-F7 D	[Col off]
Text columns on	Alt-F7 C	[Col on]
Top margin	Alt-F8 5	[Top Mar]
Total (=)	Alt-F7 5	=
Total entry	Alt-F7 8	T
Underline style	Ctrl-F8 5	[Undrl Style]
Underlining off	F8 F8	[Undrline][u]
Underlining on	F8	[Undrline]
Widow/Orphan protection off	Alt-F8 B	[W/O off]
Widow/Orphan protection on	Alt-F8 A	[W/O on]

Note that for Bold (F6) and Underline (F8), you can press the command key *twice* to insert the ending code ([b] or [u]) in a search or replacement string. (Note also that the first keystroke produces [Bold] or [Undrline], codes you will probably want to delete.) With most commands, you can only search for the beginning code.

It's also worth observing that you can't search directly for the definition of an outline, list, index, table of contents or table of authorities. WordPerfect can only search for a generic [DefMark] code. It's up to you to determine which feature the code applies to; use Reveal Codes to do that.

Codes, Hidden — WordPerfect 5.0

5.0 WordPerfect tells your printer how to format text by sending it special codes. The printer interprets each code as a command and does whatever that particular command signifies. For example, when you press Ctrl and Enter to switch pages, WordPerfect inserts a "new page" code in your document. When you print the document, the printer receives that code and advances the paper to the next page before it starts printing.

WordPerfect does not show these codes on the screen; it hides them. However, you can display the codes by pressing Alt-F3, to give a *Reveal Codes* command. Reveal Codes shows the current cursor position as a solid rectangle. To delete a code, move the cursor to the left of it and press Del, or to the right of it and press Backspace. To leave the Reveal Codes screen, press Alt-F3 again.

Here is a list of all the hidden codes, and what they indicate. Two codes on a line indicate that WordPerfect inserts the first one ahead of your text and the second one after it. For example, when you make text **bold**, WordPerfect puts [BOLD] at the beginning of it and [bold] at the end of it.

[ ]	Hard space
[-]	Hard hyphen (one you typed)
*	Do grand total
=	Do total
!	Formula calculation
-	Soft hyphen (one that WordPerfect inserted)
+	Do subtotal
/	Cancel hyphenation
[Align][C/A/Flrt]	Tab Align
[Adv Dn:*n*]	Advance down *n* units
[Adv Up:*n*]	Advance up *n* units
[Adv Lft:*n*]	Advance left *n* units
[Adv Rgt:*n*]	Advance right *n* units
[Adv To:*n*]	Advance to line or column
[BOLD],[bold]	Bold print
[Block]	Beginning of block
[BlockPro:On][BlockPro:Off]	Block protection on, off
[C/A/Flrt]	End of Center, Tab Align, or Flush Right
[Center Pg]	Center page
[CndlEOP:*n*]	Conditional end of page (*n* = number of lines)
[Cntr][C/A/Flrt]	Center
[Col Def:*d*]	Column definition (*d* = definition codes)

[Col On][Col Off]	Beginning, end of text columns
[Color:*color*]	Print color
[Comment]	Document comment
[Date:*f*]	Date/Time insert function (*f* = format)
[DBL UND][dbl und]	Double underline
[Decml Char:*dec,thou*]	Decimal characters for decimal and thousands
[DefMark:Index,*n;con*]	Index definition (*n* = numbering style; *con* = name of concordance file)
[DefMark:List,*n*]	List definition (*n* = list number)
[DefMark:ToC,*l*]	Table of contents definition (*l* = table of contents level)
[EndDef]	End of index, list, or table of contents
[EndMark:Index,*f*]	End of text marked for index (*f* = format)
[EndMark:List,*n*]	End of text marked for list (*n* = list number)
[EndMark:ToC,*l*]	End of text marked for table of contents (*l* = table of contents level)
[Endnote:*n*]	Endnote
[Endnote Placement]	Endnote placement
[EndOpt]	Endnote options
[EXT LARGE][ext large]	Extra large print
[Figure]	Figure box
[FigOpt]	Figure box options
[FINE][fine]	Fine print
[Flsh Rt][C/A/Flrt]	Flush right
[Font:*font-spec*]	Base font
[Footer A/B:*n;text*]	Footer A or B
[Footnote:*n*]	Footnote
[Force:Odd][Force:Even]	Force odd or even page
[Form:*size,type*]	Specify form size and type
[Form Typ]	Form type
[FtnOpt]	Footnote options
[Full Form]	Table of Authorities, Full Form
[Header A/B:*n;text*]	Header A or B
[HLine]	Horizontal line
[HPg]	Hard page break (Ctrl-Enter keys)
[HRt]	Hard return (Enter key)
[Hyph on][Hyph off]	Hyphenation on, off

[HZone:*l,r*]	Reset size of hyphenation zone (*l,r* = left, right)
[->Indent]	Beginning of left indent
[->Indent<-]	Beginning of left/right indent
[Index:*h;s*]	Index mark (*h,s* = heading, subheading)
[ISRt]	Invisible Soft Return
[ITALC][italc]	Italics
[Kern:On][Kern:Off]	Kerning on, off
[L/R Mar:*left,right*]	Change margin settings
[Lang:*lang*]	Language change
[LARGE][large]	Large print
[Line Hgt:*leading*]	Line height (leading)
[LnNum:On][LnNum:Off]	Line numbering turned on, off
[Ln Spacing:*n*]	Line spacing
[<-Mar Rel:*n*]	Left margin release (*n* = number of positions moved)
[Mark:List,*n*]	Beginning of text marked for list (*n* = list number)
[Mark:ToC,*l*]	Beginning of text marked for table of contents (*l* = table of contents level)
[Math Def]	Definition of math columns
[Math On][Math Off]	Beginning, end of math
[Open Style:*name*]	Turn open style on
[OUTLN][outln]	Outline print
[Ovride:*o*]	Suppress page format options (*o* = options suppressed)
[Ovrstk]	Overstrike preceding character
[Paper Sz/Typ:*size,type*]	Paper size and type
[Par#:Auto]	Automatic paragraph/outline number
[Par#:*n*]	Permanent paragraph number (*n* = level number)
[Par#Def]	Paragraph numbering definition
[Pg Num:*n*]	New page number
[Pg Num Pos:*n*]	Page number position
[Ptr Cmnd:*command*]	Embedded printer command
[REDLN][redln]	Redline
[Ref(*name*)]	Automatic reference, with target *name*

Codes, Hidden — WordPerfect 5.0

[Rt Just On][Rt Just Off]	Right justification on, off
[SHADW][shadw]	Shadow print
[SM CAP][sm cap]	Small caps
[SMALL][small]	Small print
[SPg]	Soft page break (page is full, WordPerfect has started a new one)
[SRt]	Soft return (end of lines within a paragraph)
[STKOUT][stkout]	Strikeout
[Style On:*name*]	Paired style
[Style Off:*name*]	
[Subdoc:*filename*]	Include subdocument
[Subdoc Start:*filename*]	Subdocument
[Subdoc End:filename]	
[SUBSCPT][subscpt]	Subscript
[SUPRSCPT][suprscpt]	Superscript
t (blinking)	Subtotal entry
T (blinking)	Total entry
[T/B Mar:*top,bottom*]	Top and bottom margins
[TAB]	Move to next tab stop (Tab key)
[TabOpt]	Table box options
[Tab Set:*tabs*]	Change tab settings
[Table]	Table box
[Target(*name*)]	Target of an automatic reference
[Text Box]	Text box
[TxtOpt]	Text box options
[ToA:;*ShortForm*;] or [ToA:*s*;*ShortForm*; <FullForm>]	Mark for Table of Authorities (*s* = section number)
[Undrl:Spaces,Tabs]	Underline definition
[UNDRLN][undrln]	Underlining
[Usr Box]	User box
[UsrOpt]	User box options
[VLine]	Vertical line
[VRY LARGE][vry large]	Very large print
[W/O On][W/O Off]	Widow/Orphan protection turned on, off

42 Codes, Hidden — WordPerfect 5.0

Searching for Hidden Codes

At the beginning of this entry, I mentioned that you can delete a hidden code by moving to it in Reveal Codes and pressing Del or Backspace. Of course, that assumes you know roughly where a code is located; sometimes you may not. Instead of spending a lot of time scrolling through the text in Reveal Codes, you can use WordPerfect's *Search* commands (see separate entry) to locate the code.

There are two search commands. F2 searches forward through the document, while Search-F2 searches backward. When you press either key, WordPerfect displays a *Srch:* prompt at the bottom of the screen. Insert the hidden code you want to locate (details are upcoming), then press F2 to start searching. WordPerfect stops at the first instance of the code and puts the cursor just after it. You can then press Backspace, if you want to delete the code.

WordPerfect's *Replace* (Alt-F2) command can locate hidden codes, and replace or delete them. For example, you could use Replace to change all Indents to Tabs or to remove underlining from some or all of the text in a document. Replace operates with two strings, a search string and a replacement string (see **Search Commands** for details), and you can insert hidden codes in either or both of them.

In general, to insert a hidden code in a search or replacement string, you simply enter the command that produces that feature. For example, to search for the [BOLD] code that precedes emboldened text, press F6 in your search string. The following table should help save you from having to remember which key commands produce which codes in a search string. It gives the name of each code, the keystroke(s) you must type to insert it, and the code that WordPerfect puts in the search string.

To search for ...	Press	Code in string
* (Math grand total)	Alt-F7 6	*
= (Math total)	Alt-F7 5	=
! (Math formula calculation)	Alt-F7 9	!
- (Soft hyphen)	Ctrl-Hyphen	-
+ (Math subtotal)	Alt-F7 4	+
/(Cancel hyphenation)	Shift-F8 6	/
Advance (any direction)	Shift-F8 3 1	[Adv]
Automatic reference	Alt-F5 5 3	[Ref]
Automatic reference target	Alt-F5 5 4	[Target]

Base font	Ctrl-F8 4	[Font]
Block protect on or off	Shift-F8 3 2	[BlockPro]
Bold on	F6	[BOLD]
Box number, graphics	Alt-F9 1 4	[Box Num]
Cancel hyphenation (/)	Shift-F8 1 3	/
Center	Shift-F6	[Cntr]
Center page top to bottom	Shift-F8 2 1	[Center Pg]
Character width adjustment	Shift-F8 3 7 3	[Width Adj]
Color, print	Ctrl-F8 5	[Color]
Column position for page number	Shift-F8 2 7	[Pg Numbering]
Columns definition, text	Alt-F7 B	[Col Def]
Columns off	Alt-F7 D	[Col Off]
Columns on	Alt-F7 C	[Col On]
Comment, document	Ctrl-F5	[Comment]
Conditional end of page	Shift-F8 3 3	[Cndl EOP]
Date code	Shift-F5 1	[Date]
Decimal character	Shift-F8 3 4	[Decml/Algn Char]
Document comment	Ctrl-F5	[Comment]
Double underline	Ctrl-F8 2 3	[DBL UND]
End of definition	Alt-F5 5 2	[End Def]
End of marked text	Alt-F5 2	[End Mark]
Endnote code	Ctrl-F7 2 1	[Endnote]
Endnote number	Ctrl-F7 2 2	[Note Num]
Endnote number, set new	Ctrl-F7 2 3	[New End Num]
Endnote options	Ctrl-F7 2 4	[End Opt]
Endnote placement	Ctrl F7 3	[Endnote Placement]
Extra large print	Ctrl-F8 1 7	[EXT LARGE]
Figure box	Alt-F9 1 1	[Figure]
Figure box number, new	Alt-F9 1 2	[New Fig Num]
Figure box options	Alt-F9 1 3	[Fig Opt]
Fine print	Ctrl-F8 1 3	[FINE]
Flush Right	Alt-F6	[Flsh Rt]
Footer A definition	Shift-F8 2 4 1	[Footer A]
Footer B definition	Shift-F8 2 4 2	[Footer B]
Footnote code	Ctrl-F7 1 1	[Footnote]
Footnote number	Ctrl-F7 1 2	[Note Num]
Footnote number, set new	Ctrl-F7 1 3	[New Ftn Num]
Footnote options	Ctrl-F7 1 4	[FtnOpt]
Force odd or even page number	Shift-F8 2 2	[Force]

Formula calculation (!)	Alt-F7 9	!
Grand total (*)	Alt-F7 6	*
Graphics box number	Alt-F9 1 4	[Box Num]
Hard hyphen	-	[-]
Hard page break	Ctrl-Enter	[HPg]
Hard return (Enter key)	Enter	[HRt]
Hard space	Home Space	[ ]
Header A definition	Shift-F8 2 3 1	[Header A]
Header B definition	Shift-F8 2 3 2	[Header B]
Horizontal line	Alt-F9 5 1	[HLine]
Hyphenation, cancel (/)	Shift-F8 1 3	
Hyphenation off	Shift-F8 1 1 2	[Hyph Off]
Hyphenation on	Shift-F8 1 1 1	[Hyph On]
Hyphenation Zone, set	-Shift-F8 1 2	[HZone]
Include subdocument	Alt-F5 6 1	[Subdoc]
Index definition	Alt-F5 5 1	[DefMark]
Index entry	Alt-F5 3	[Index]
Italics	Ctrl-F8 2 4	[ITALC]
Kerning change	Shift-F8 3 7 1	[Kern]
Language change	Shift-F8 3 5	[Lang]
Large print	Ctrl-F8 1 5	[LARGE]
Left indent	F4	[->Indent]
Left/right indent	Shift-F4	[<-Indent->]
Left margin release	Shift-Tab	[<-Mar Rel]
Line height	Shift-F8 1 5 1	[Ln Height]
Line numbering on or off	Shift-F8 1 5 2	[Ln Num]
Line spacing	Shift-F8 1 5 3	[Ln Spacing]
List definition	Alt-F5 5 1	[DefMark]
List or table of contents entry	Alt-F5 1	[Mark]
Margin release, left	Shift-Tab	[<-Mar Rel]
Margin, left or right	Shift-F8 1 6	[L/R Mar]
Margin, top or bottom	Shift-F8 2 5	[T/B Mar]
Mark for list or table of contents	Alt-F5 1	[Mark]
Math definition	Alt-F7 1	[Math Def]
Math off	Alt-F7 3	[Math Off]
Math on	Alt-F7 2	[Math On]
Merge codes	Shift-F9	^*letter*
Merge R (^R)	F9	^R

Negative (N) operator	Alt-F7 A	N
New page number	Shift-F8 2 6	[Pg Num]
Open style	Alt-F8 3	[Open Style]
Outline numbering definition	Alt-F5 5 1	[DefMark]
Outline print	Ctrl-F8 2 5	[OUTLN]
Overstrike	Shift-F8 3 7	[Ovrstk]
Page, center top to bottom	Shift-F8 2 1	[Center Pg]
Page number, new	Shift-F8 2 6	[Pg Num]
Page number position	Shift-F8 2 7	[Pg Numbering]
Paper size/type	Shift-F8 2 8	[Paper Sz/Typ]
Paragraph number	Shift-F5 2	[Par Num]
Paragraph numbering definition	Shift-F5 3	[Par Num Def]
Print color	Ctrl-F8 5	[Color]
Printer command	Shift-F8 3 7 2	[Ptr Cmnd]
^R (Merge R)	F9	^R
Redline	Ctrl-F8 2 8	[REDLN]
Right justification off	Shift-F8 1 4 2	[Rt Just Off]
Right justification on	Shift-F8 1 4 1	[Rt Just On]
Shadow print	Ctrl-F8 2 6	[SHADW]
Small caps	Ctrl-F8 2 7	[SM CAP]
Small print	Ctrl-F8 1 4	[SMALL]
Soft hyphen	Ctrl-Hyphen	-
Soft page break	Ctrl-VK	[SPg]
Soft return	Ctrl-M	[SRt]
Spacing, line	Shift-F8 1 5 3	[Ln Spacing]
Special character	Ctrl-V *n*	*character*
Strikeout	Ctrl-F8 2 9	[STKOUT]
Style off	Alt-F8 2	[Style Off]
Style on	Alt-F8 1	[Style On]
Subdocument end	Alt-F5 6 3	[Subdoc End]
Subdocument include	Alt-F5 5 1	[Subdoc]
Subdocument start	Alt-F5 6 2	[Subdoc Start]
Subscript	Ctrl-F8 1 2	[SUBSCPT]
Subtotal (+)	Alt-F7 4	+
Subtotal entry	Alt-F7 7	t
Superscript	Ctrl-F8 1 1	[SUPRSCPT]
Suppress page format options	Shift-F8 2 9	[Suppress]
Tab	Tab	[TAB]

Tab Align	Ctrl-F6	[Align]
Tab Align character	Shift-F8 3 4	[Decml/Algn Char]
Tab settings	Shift-F8 1 7	[Tab Set]
Table box	Alt-F9 2 1	[Table]
Table box number, set	Alt-F9 2 2	[New Tab Num]
Table box options	Alt-F9 2 3	[Tab Opt]
Table of Authorities definition	Alt-F5 5 1	[DefMark]
Table of Authorities entry	Alt-F5 4	[ToA]
Table of contents definition	Alt-F5 5 1	[DefMark]
Table of contents or list entry	Alt-F5 1	[Mark]
Text box	Alt-F9 3 1	[Text Box]
Text box number, set	Alt-F9 3 2	[New Txt Num]
Text box options	Alt-F9 3 3	[Txt Opt]
Text columns definition	Alt-F7 B	[Col Def]
Text columns off	Alt-F7 D	[Col Off]
Text columns on	Alt-F7 C	[Col On]
Top or bottom margin	Shift-F8 2 5	[T/B Mar]
Total (=)	Alt-F7 5	=
Total entry	Alt-F7 8	T
Underline style	Shift-F8 3 8	[Undrln]
Underlining on	F8	[UNDRLN]
User-defined box	Alt-F9 4 1	[Usr Box]
User-defined box number, set	Alt-F9 4 2	[New Usr Num]
User-defined box options	Alt-F9 4 3	[UsrOpt]
Vertical line	Alt-F9 5 2	[VLine]
Very large print	Ctrl-F8 1 6	[VRY LARGE]
Widow/Orphan protection off	Shift-F8 1 8 2	[W/O Off]
Widow/Orphan protection on	Shift-F8 1 8 1	[W/O On]
Word spacing justification limits	Shift-F8 3 7 4	[Just Lim]

WordPerfect contains many options that let you send styling commands to the printer. These include Bold (F6), Underline (F8), and the Font (Ctrl-F8) command's Size/Position options (Subscpt, Suprscpt, Fine, etc.) and Appearance options (Dbl Und, Italc, Outln, etc.). Each of these features produces two codes: one that turns the style on at the beginning of the text (e.g., [BOLD]) and another that turns the style off at the end (e.g., [bold]).

The preceding table lists only the keystrokes that insert the starting code in a search or replacement string. However, you can press the command keys *twice* to insert the ending code ([bold], [undrl], and so on) in a string. Here, the first key command inserts the starting code, while the second inserts the ending code. For example, pressing F6 inserts [BOLD], while pressing F6 F6 inserts [BOLD][bold]. To search for just the ending code, you must delete the starting code from the string.

It's also worth observing that you can't search directly for the definition of an outline, list, index, table of contents or table of authorities. WordPerfect can only search for a generic [DefMark] code. It's up to you to determine which feature the code applies to; use Reveal Codes to do that.

Column Operations

WordPerfect can move, copy, delete, and insert columns of text or numbers. (It can also add numeric columns to produce a total, as described under **Math/Columns Command**.)

Moving and Copying Columns

To move or copy a column, start as you would for a block: obtain Block mode (Alt-F4) and highlight everything between the top left corner and bottom right corner of the column. (Of course, doing that also makes WordPerfect highlight everything in between.) Then press Ctrl and F4 to give a Move command, and do one of the following:

4.1
4.2

•**WordPerfect 4.1 or 4.2** shows this menu:

1 Cut Block; 2 Copy Block; 3 Append; 4 Cut/Copy Column; 5 Cut/Copy Rectangle: 0

Type **4** for Cut/Copy Column, then **1** to Cut or **2** to Copy. To paste the column, do another Move and select Column from the menu.

5.0

•**WordPerfect 5.0** shows this menu:

Move: 1 Block; 2 Tabular Column; 3 Rectangle: 0

Type **2** for Tabular Column, then **1** to Move or **2** to Copy. To paste the column, do another Move and select Retrieve from the Move menu, then Tabular Column from the Retrieve menu.

Adjusting the Format

When you paste a moved or copied column, it takes on the format settings (tabs, margins, spacing, etc.) of the new location. Thus, for example, if you move single-spaced material to a double-spaced page, WordPerfect double-spaces it.

To restore the original format, perform the move or copy, then correct the format at the new location by doing Line Format operations (Shift-F8 in WordPerfect 4.1 and 4.2, Shift-F8 and **1** in WordPerfect 5.0) just ahead of and just after the pasted text. (The number of Line Formats this requires depends on how many parameters differ between the original location and the new one.) The Line Formats that precede the pasted text should restore the original format; the ones that follow it should restore the destination format.

Inserting Columns

To insert a new column into a table, proceed as follows:

1. Insert the heading for the column.
2. Use Reveal Codes to find the [Tab Set:] code that set the tabs for the table. Move the cursor just past that code and press Alt-F3 to get back to editing.
3. Obtain a copy of the current tab settings. **In WordPerfect 4.1 or 4.2**, do a Line Format command (Shift-F8) and select the Tabs option. **In WordPerfect 5.0**, give a Format command (Shift-F8), type **1** to select Line and **8** to select Tab Set.
4. Change the tabs to reflect an additional column. That is, set a tab for the new column and move the remaining tabs right to provide space for the insertion. (To move a tab right, delete it, then set it at its new location.) Finally, return to editing.
5. Put the cursor on the first data line, then move it to where the new column should start.
6. Enter the first data item in the new column, then press Tab to shift the remaining columns to the right.
7. Enter the rest of the data items in the new column by repeating steps 5 and 6.

Column Insert Example

As an example, suppose you have prepared a list of your company's major customers, and it looks like this:

Column Operations   49

Account	Buyer	Sales Rep.
Wilburg Sons	Paul Wilkinson	R. Roberts
Jenco	Carrie Black	C. Chamber
Symtech	Wayne Beck	P. Grogan
Chicago Gear	Morris Daley	J. Wilkes
Hart Foods	Sandy Karras	P. Wallach
Pacifico	Bill Anderson	D. Kim
Storr Bros.	Lee Walters	B. Lloyd

As usual, you used tabs at the beginning of each column to enter the data. Here, they are at columns 25 and 42.

After finishing the list, you decide to insert a column for the buyer's telephone number between "Buyer" and "Sales Rep." Since each number is 12 characters long, and you want three spaces between it and the next column, the new column must be 15 characters wide. To insert it, proceed as follows:

1. Put the cursor on the heading line and press Alt-F3 for Reveal Codes.
2. Move the cursor just beyond the [Tab Set:] code, then press Alt-F3 to leave Reveal Codes.
3. Use the Line Format (WordPerfect 4.1 or 4.2) or Format (5.0) command to set a new tab at column 57. This is where the "Sales Rep." column will move after the insertion.

Now you can enter the heading and data for the telephone number column. The final list will look similar to this:

Account	Buyer	Phone #	Sales Rep.
Wilburg Sons	Paul Wilkinson	212-555-3589	R. Roberts
Jenco	Carrie Black	904-388-6743	C. Chamber
Symtech	Wayne Beck	404-783-8832	P. Grogan
Chicago Gear	Morris Daley	312-395-1904	J. Wilkes
Hart Foods	Sandy Karras	406-184-5683	P. Wallach
Pacifico	Bill Anderson	503-438-9532	D. Kim
Storr Bros.	Lee Walters	213-679-4260	B. Lloyd

Deleting Columns

To delete a column, move the cursor to the beginning of it and proceed as follows:

1. Press Alt-F4 to put WordPerfect in Block mode.
2. Move the cursor to the last character of the column. WordPerfect highlights everything in between.
3. Press Ctrl-F4 to give a Move command.
4. When the menu appears, type **4** for *Cut/Copy Column* (WordPerfect 4.1 or 4.2) or **2** for *Tabular Column* (WordPerfect 5.0). WordPerfect highlights the column.
5. When the next menu appears, type **3** for *Delete*. (Version 4.1 has no Delete option; select *Cut* instead.) WordPerfect closes the gap by moving the remaining columns to the left.

Columns, Text

Newspaper and magazine articles, newsletters, dramatic scripts, and some legal documents are printed with several columns on a page. WordPerfect 4.1 and 4.2 let you arrange text in either of two column styles: Newspaper-Style and Parallel with Block Protect. WordPerfect 5.0 offers an additional Parallel style that provides no block protection.

Column Styles

Newspaper-Style Columns are designed for text that continues from the bottom of one column to the top of the next, in winding fashion. You may want to use this style for a newsletter.

Parallel Columns are designed for scripts, side-by-side translations, inventory lists, and other documents where information is arranged left-to-right across the page. For example, an inventory list may have four columns—for the product name, part number, quantity in stock, and comments.

"Parallel Columns With Block Protect," the style offered by all three versions of WordPerfect, keeps each group of columns on the same page. (If text in any column crosses the page boundary, the entire group is moved to the next page.) WordPerfect 5.0's "Parallel Columns" variation is similar, but it does not protect groups from being split between pages. This is handy for material where a column may be longer than a page, and thus cannot be block-protected.

WordPerfect 4.2 and 5.0 can provide up to 24 columns, whereas version 4.1 limits you to five columns. You can tell WordPerfect to make each column the same width or use column margin settings you specify. Moreover, WordPerfect normally displays text columns side-by-side on the screen, but you can make it display each column on a separate page.

Defining the Columns

To make WordPerfect produce text columns, move the cursor to where they should begin and press Alt and F7 for Math/Columns. When the menu appears, type **4** for *Column Def*. WordPerfect displays a Text Column Definition form. Figure C-1 shows the form for WordPerfect 5.0. The forms for versions 4.1 and 4.2 look somewhat different, but do the same job.

Note that WordPerfect makes some assumptions about what you want. Specifically, it assumes you want two Newspaper-Style Columns, each three inches wide with a half-inch gap between

Figure C-1. WordPerfect 5.0's Text Column Definition form.

```
         Text Column Definition

         1 - Type                        Newspaper
         2 - Number of Columns           2
         3 - Distance Between Columns
         4 - Margins

         Column    Left     Right    Column   Left    Right
           1:       1"        4"       13:
           2:       4.5"      7.5"     14:
           3:                          15:
           4:                          16:
           5:                          17:
           6:                          18:
           7:                          19:
           8:                          20:
           9:                          21:
          10:                          22:
          11:                          23:
          12:                          24:
```

them. If you want something else, change the Definition form as follows:

1. To specify the column style, press **1** to reach the *Type* field. When this menu appears:

   ```
   1 Newspaper; 2 Parallel; 3 Parallel with Block Protect: 0
   ```

   make your selection.
2. To specify the number of columns on a page, type **2** to reach *Number of Columns* and enter a number from 2 to 24. WordPerfect assumes every column is to have the same width, so it calculates the left and right margin values and records them in the Margins table at the bottom.
3. If you want evenly-spaced columns, type **3** to reach *Distance Between Columns* (the value **0.5"** appears) and enter the size of the gap, in inches.
4. At this point, WordPerfect has supplied the margin values that divide each page into the specified number of columns with the same size gap between each one. To change this arrangement, type **4** to reach the *Left* field for Column 1, and enter margin values for each column you want to change.
5. When you finish, press F7 (Exit) to return to the Math/Columns menu.

Turning Columns On

Once the Math/Columns menu reappears, you can turn on the Text Columns mode immediately by typing **3** to select *Column On/Off*. Otherwise, to turn it on past that point, press F7 to leave the Math/Columns menu, and move to where you want columns to start. Then press Alt-F7 and type **3** for *Column On/Off*.

When WordPerfect enters a Text Columns mode, it shows the column number as a *Col* value on the status line. From then on, it arranges everything you enter in column format.

Entering Newspaper-Style Columns

To enter text as Newspaper-Style Columns, simply keep typing. WordPerfect advances to the next column when the current one is full, and starts a new page when the last column is full. When you finish entering column material, press Alt-F7 to obtain the menu and type **3** to turn columns off.

Columns, Text 53

Entering Parallel Columns

To enter text as Parallel Columns (with or without Block Protect), type the material for the current column, then press Ctrl-Enter to reach the beginning of the next column. Pressing Ctrl-Enter from the last column moves the cursor two lines below the longest column, then back to the beginning of the first column. (Note that Ctrl-Enter here does *not* start a new page, as it does in regular text.)

To start a new page for Parallel Columns, press Alt-F7 to obtain the menu and type 3 to turn columns off, then press Ctrl-Enter to insert the page break. WordPerfect is in regular text mode on the new page. To enter more Parallel Columns, press Alt-F7 again and type 3 to turn columns back on. (Note that you did not have to do another *Column Def* because the preceding column definition is still in effect.)

Editing Columns

You can use the standard cursor-moving keys (←, →, Home-←, PgDn, etc.) to move within a column. To make editing changes in a different column, move to it using one of the following key sequences:

Pressing	Moves the cursor to ...
Ctrl-Home ←	Preceding column
Ctrl-Home, →	Next column
Ctrl-Home, Home, ←	First column
Ctrl-Home, Home, →	Last column

The key combinations that delete material (e.g., Ctrl-Backspace to delete the current word) work as they do in regular full-screen text, except Ctrl-PgDn (delete the rest of the current page) deletes only to the bottom of the current column. Pressing Ctrl-PgDn within a Newspaper-Style Column (and answering the prompt with y) makes WordPerfect rearrange the remaining columns to fill the gap.

Displaying Individual Columns

Sometimes you may want to work on one column without viewing the others. WordPerfect 4.2 and 5.0 let you display columns as if they're on separate pages. As with a multi-column display, you can use the regular movement commands to move between columns.

With WordPerfect 4.2, press Alt-F7 for Math/Columns and type **5** to select *Column Display*. When the **Display columns side by side? (Y/N) Y** prompt appears, type **n** for No.

With WordPerfect 5.0, press Shift-F1 for Setup and type **3** to select *Display*. When the Display menu appears, type **8** to reach the *Side-by-side Columns Display* field and type **n** for No. Finally, press F7 (Exit) to return to your document.

Compose Feature — WordPerfect 5.0

5.0 WordPerfect 5.0 provides a Compose feature that lets you print two characters at the same location. You can print two letters to form a digraph or print a letter and an accent mark to form a diacritic. Press Ctrl-2 to activate Compose, then type the two characters you want, in either order. For example, to produce the English "pounds" sign, type **-** and **L**.

Compose also lets you insert a geometric shape, foreign language character, or other non-keyboard character in a document, by selecting it from 12 built-in character sets or a user-defined character set. To insert one of these characters, press Ctrl-2 for Compose, then type a command of the form **set,char** and press Enter. For example, if you turn Compose on and enter **1,23**, WordPerfect inserts the German double-s character. For details, see *WordPerfect Characters* in the Appendix of the WordPerfect manual.

Concordance File

With WordPerfect 4.1, you must build an index by marking each entry individually. However, quite often you will want the index to contain *every* occurrence of a specific word or phrase. With version 4.2 or 5.0, you can make WordPerfect mark all occurrences of specific words or phrases by putting them in a *concordance file*. A concordance file is simply a WordPerfect document that contains entries for an index, one per line. WordPerfect asks for the name of the concordance file when you define the index's numbering style.

Concordance Entries as Headings or Subheadings

WordPerfect always assumes that an entry in a concordance file is to be a heading in the index. However, just as you can specify words or phrases as headings or subheadings when you mark them manually, you can mark concordance entries as headings or subheadings as you create the file. The procedure differs slightly for words and phrases.

To mark a word as a heading, put the cursor anywhere in it and press Alt-F5 to give a Mark Text command. When the menu appears, type **5** (WordPerfect 4.2) or **3** (WordPerfect 5.0) for *Index.* When **Index Heading:** appears, press Enter. When **Index Subheading:** appears, press Enter again.

To mark a word as a subheading, do the same thing, but when **Index Heading:** appears, enter the heading. When **Index Subheading:** appears, press Enter.

To mark a phrase as a heading or subheading, follow the procedures just given, but select the phrase in Block mode before pressing Alt-F5.

Conditional End of Page

Sometimes you may want to keep a paragraph or table together on a page. Or you may want to keep a section title on the same page as the first few lines of the paragraph that follows it.

To keep lines of text together, give WordPerfect a Conditional End of Page command. This tells it "If the current page has fewer lines remaining than the number I specify, start a new page." To begin, move the cursor to the line above the first line you want to protect. What you do next depends on which version of WordPerfect you have, as follows:

[4.1 4.2]
1. **With WordPerfect 4.1 or 4.2,** press Alt and F8 to obtain the Page Format menu (see **Page Format Command**). Type **9** to select *Conditional End of Page,* then type the number of lines you want to protect and press Enter.

[5.0]
2. **With WordPerfect 5.0,** press Shift and F8 to obtain the Format menu (see **Format Command**). Type **4** to select *Other* and **3** to select *Conditional End of Page,* then type the number of lines you want to protect and press Enter. Finally, press F7 (Exit) to return to your document.

You can also keep a block of text together on a page with a Block Protect command. (See **Block Command** for details.) Conditional End of Page is convenient for protecting a specific number of lines, while Block Protect is handy when you don't want to count lines, or when the line count may change due to additions or deletions in the text.

Continuous Paper

— See **Paper**

Convert Program

In practice, you may want to combine a document with a financial report generated by a spreadsheet or a list obtained from a database. If every computer program produced results in the same form, you could simply copy material between them. For example, you could use WordPerfect's Retrieve command to copy a *Lotus 1-2-3* spreadsheet directly into a report you are writing. Alas, things aren't that easy.

Spreadsheet programs generally produce results in a different form than word processing programs. Likewise, database programs produce results in a different form than spreadsheets or word processors. Thus, in general, most programs are incompatible.

Fortunately, WordPerfect includes a program that can convert the results of various kinds of programs into WordPerfect documents. Conversely, it can also convert WordPerfect documents into a form that can be used by another program. This entry describes the conversion procedure. It also includes examples of using the results of spreadsheets and databases with WordPerfect.

WordPerfect contains a special program called *CONVERT* that can convert material from one format to another. To use it, start your computer as usual and obtain the B> prompt, then proceed as follows:

```
1 WordPerfect to another format
2 Revisable-Form-Text (IBM DCA Format) to WordPerfect
3 Navy DIF Standard to WordPerfect
4 WordStar 3.3 to WordPerfect
5 MultiMate 3.22 to WordPerfect
6 Seven-bit transfer format to WordPerfect
7 Mail Merge to WordPerfect Secondary Merge
8 WordPerfect Secondary Merge to Spreadsheet DIF
9 Spreadsheet DIF to WordPerfect Secondary Merge

Enter number of Conversion desired
```

Figure C-2. WordPerfect 4.2's Convert menu.

1. Insert the Learning disk into drive A and insert the disk that has the file to be converted into drive B.
2. Enter **a:convert**. This produces a copyright notice, then the prompt **Name of Input File?**
3. Enter the name of the file you want to convert. For a computer with floppy disks, the name should be of the form **b:**_filename_. With a hard disk, enter just the name if the file is in the WordPerfect subdirectory (e.g., enter report.doc). If it is in a different subdirectory, precede the file name with a \, the subdirectory name, and another \ (e.g., \mm\report.doc specifies the REPORT.DOC file in a MultiMate subdirectory).
4. When the prompt **Name of Output File?** appears, enter the name you want the converted file to have (it must be different from the original name). This makes the Convert menu appear. Figure C-2 shows the Convert menu that WordPerfect 4.2 produces.
5. Enter the number of the conversion procedure you want.

Option 1 (WordPerfect) lets you convert a WordPerfect document to any of six formats. They are:

- *Revisable-Form-Text* and *Final-Form Text* are DCA (Document Content Architecture) formats used by large IBM "mainframe" computers.
- *Navy DIF* (for Data Interchange Format) is a U.S. Navy spreadsheet format. (Someone once said, "If you're in the Navy, you already

know enough about Navy DIF. If you aren't in the Navy, you already know enough about Navy DIF.")

- *WordStar* is the format used by MicroPro International Corporation's word processor.
- *MultiMate* is the format used by Multimate International's MultiMate and MultiMate Advantage word processors.
- *Seven-bit transfer format* is used by modems (devices that transfer data over telephone lines).

Option 8 (WordPerfect Secondary Merge) is similar, but it works with secondary merge files rather than regular WordPerfect documents. Specifically, it converts a secondary merge file to the DIF format that many spreadsheet programs (including Lotus 1-2-3) use to represent numerical data. In the converted file, records become rows, and fields become entries or *cells*.

The remaining options convert various kinds of program files to WordPerfect, as follows:

- Options 2 through 5 convert DCA, Navy DIF, WordStar, and MultiMate files to WordPerfect format.
- Option 6 restores a previously-converted WordPerfect file from seven-bit transfer format (see option 1) to its original form.
- Option 7 (Mail Merge) converts files to secondary merge format. It can operate on WordStar Mail Merge files or on files produced by Ashton-Tate's popular dBASE II and dBASE III database management programs. For details on using dBASE II and III files with WordPerfect, see Database Files, Using.
- Option 9 (Spreadsheet DIF) does the opposite of option 8. That is, it converts a spreadsheet DIF file to secondary merge format. In the converted file, rows become records and cells become fields. For details, see **Spreadsheet Files, Using**.

Copy Operations

— See **Move Command**

Ctrl (Control) Key

Pressing *Ctrl*, the key above the left-hand Shift key, together with a function key (F1 through F10) gives WordPerfect one of the commands that appear in red on the template. For example, to start a Spell operation, hold Ctrl down and press F2.

Ctrl also performs a variety of other functions, as follows:

- Pressing Ctrl and ← together moves the cursor to the preceding word, while pressing Ctrl and → moves it to the next word. These key combinations repeat; that is, the cursor keeps moving as long as you hold them down.
- Pressing Ctrl and Backspace deletes the current word.
- Pressing Ctrl and End deletes from the cursor position to the end of the line, while pressing Ctrl and PgDn deletes from the cursor position to the end of the page.
- Pressing Ctrl and Enter makes WordPerfect start a new page, by inserting a so-called *hard page break.*

Further, pressing Ctrl and Home at the same time gives WordPerfect a *Go To* command. When **Go to** appears at the bottom of the screen, enter the number of the page or the character you want to reach, or press ↑ or ↓ to reach the beginning or end of the current page. Pressing Ctrl-Home *twice* moves the cursor to where you were when you gave a preceding cursor-moving or Search command.

Finally, with WordPerfect 4.1 and 4.2, you can use Ctrl to insert geometric shapes, foreign characters, and other non-keyboard characters into a document. See **Special Characters** for details.

Ctrl/Alt keys Option — WordPerfect 4.1 and 4.2

| 4.1 4.2 | This option on the Screen (Ctrl-F3) command menu lets you make WordPerfect insert a special, non-keyboard character (such as a geometric shape or a Greek letter) when you press Ctrl or Alt and a letter key. See **Special Characters** for details.

Cursor, Moving the

While you can certainly use the arrow keys to move through a document one character or one line at a time, you will often want to move greater distances. WordPerfect's other cursor-moving commands are:

Pressing...	Moves the cursor to the...
Home ↑	Top of the screen.
Home ↓	Bottom of the screen.
End	End of the current line.
Home Home ←	Beginning of the current line, but following any codes.
Home Home Home ←	Beginning of the current line, preceding any codes.
Home Home ↑	Beginning of the document.
Home Home ↓	End of the document.
PgUp	Beginning of the preceding page.
PgDn	Beginning of the next page or end of this page, if it's the last one.
Ctrl-Home	Page whose number you enter.
Ctrl-Home ↑	Beginning of the page.
Ctrl-Home ↓	End of the page.
Ctrl-Home Ctrl-Home	Location in the document where you last gave a cursor-moving or Search command.
Ctrl-←	Preceding word.
Ctrl-→	Next word

Cut and Copy Operations

— See **Move Command**

Dashed Line Across the Screen

When you have filled a page with text, WordPerfect starts a new page automatically and draws a line of dashes across the screen. In WordPerfect terminology, this is called a *soft page break*. The word "soft" here distinguishes a page break that WordPerfect has produced to one that you have produced (a so-called *hard* page break) by pressing the Ctrl and Enter keys simultaneously. WordPerfect versions 4.2 and later show hard page breaks as a line of equal signs across the screen.

Database Files, Using

Database management programs let you create, search, sort, combine, and perform arithmetic operations on lists of text and numbers. For example, you could enter purchase orders into a database, then have it produce a list of customers who bought more than, say, 100 units in the last year. Or you could make the database produce a file of customers in a given state, sorted by city.

Producing Form Letters from Database Files

You can easily produce form letters with WordPerfect. To do this, you must merge a generalized copy of the letter (primary file) with a data file (secondary merge file) containing the items you want to insert—name, address, account status, etc. I will now describe how to use a data file produced by *dBASE II* or *dBASE III*, the popular database management programs from Ashton-Tate.

Suppose you have a dBASE file called CUSTMRS that holds current information about your company's customers. Each entry or *record* in the file has the following format:

company, street, city, state, zipcode, indtype, buyer, salutation, telephone, salesyr, region

At the beginning of a new year, you want to write a letter offering special terms to each customer who bought at least $100,000 worth of goods last year. So you must select these customers' records from the dBASE file.

To begin, start dBASE, then enter the following commands to select the qualifying customers (assuming your data files are on drive B):

USE B:CUSTMRS
COPY TO B:BIGSLS.DB FOR SALESYR>=100000 DELIMITED WITH, QUIT

The commands and qualifiers here have the following meanings:

- *USE B:CUSTMRS* specifies which database file dBASE is to use.
- *COPY* copies from the database in USE to another file.
- *TO B:BIGSLS.DB* assigns the name of the new file (DB stands for database).
- *FOR SALESYR>=100000* selects records with yearly sales greater than or equal to 100000 (>= means "greater than or equal to").
- *DELIMITED WITH ,* separates fields with commas.
- *QUIT* makes the computer leave dBASE.

The entries in the BIGSLS.DB file will look like the following:

Bay Tea Co.,105 Federal Ave.,Boston,MA,01284,Food,Mr. Thomas Wheaton,Tom,617-555-1776,123000,NE
XYZ Computers,34 Lake Rd.,Big Palm,FL,32650,Computer,Ms. Carrie Raye,Carrie,904-987-2854,140000,SE

This represents two records, one for Bay Tea Co. and another for XYZ Computers.

Now you must convert the BIGSLS.DB file to WordPerfect's secondary merge file format. Do this as follows:

1. Put your WordPerfect Learning disk in drive A, replacing the dBASE disk, and enter **a:convert**.
2. When the *Name of Input File?* prompt appears, enter **bigsls.db**.
3. When the *Name of Output File?* prompt appears, enter **bigsls.sf** (for secondary file).
4. When the Convert menu appears, type 7 to select *Mail Merge to WordPerfect Secondary Merge*.
5. CONVERT now needs some information about the makeup of your database file. When it asks for the *Field delimiter*, type a comma and press Enter. When it asks for the *Record delimiter*, enter {13}{10}. When it asks for the *Characters to be stripped from file*, press Enter.

Finally, you can prepare the primary merge file—the letter you want to send to the BIGSLS customer list. This letter is shown in Figure D-1. (Note that the ^Fn^ numbers assume you know the order of the fields in the database file. If you aren't sure of this order, enter DISPLAY STRUCTURE while in dBASE to obtain it.) When you finish the letter, do a Merge command to print the copies.

Date Command (Shift-F5) — WordPerfect 4.1 and 4.2

4.1
4.2

WordPerfect can insert the current date or time, or both, at the cursor position. To make it do this, press Shift-F5 to give a *Date* command. WordPerfect displays:

        Date: 1 Insert Text; 2 Format; 3 Insert Function: 0

Insert Text and Insert Function Options

If you select option 1 or 3 from the Date menu, WordPerfect will insert the date in the common month-day-year format (e.g., *May 29, 1988*). These two options are quite different, however.

November 6, 1988

^F7^
^F1^
^F2^
^F3^, ^F4^ ^F5^

Dear ^F8^:

   We are pleased to inform you that your company has qualified for our 1988 Special Discount Program. As a valued customer, you are entitled to the following privileges:

   1) 45-day terms on all purchases.

   2) An extra 2% discount in advance, as well as our usual 2% discount for payments made within 15 days.

   3) Free returns (you pay shipping costs only) on all goods unsold after 90 days.

We appreciate your patronage and plan to do all we can to continue this important relationship.

                            Sincerely,

                            Ray Cornell
                            National Sales Manager

^T^N^P^P

Figure D-1 Form letter to be sent to customer list selected by dBASE II or III.

Specifically, *Insert Text* (option 1) produces regular text; once you insert the date, it's in your document permanently. By contrast, *Insert Function* (option 3) inserts a hidden [Date:] code that WordPerfect replaces with the current whenever you edit the document or print it.

For example, if you do an Insert Function on June 4, 1988, that date appears in your document. However, if you print the document, say, one week later, the date will appear as June *11*, 1988. Insert Function is handy for use in form letters and in documents that you work on over a period of time.

However, Insert Function's variable-date feature can also be a drawback. If you need to print the document for filing purposes later, it will have *that* day's date, not the original date. To eliminate this problem, you can keep the Insert Function date while you're working on a document, then delete it and replace it with Insert Text on the day you want saved for posterity.

Format Option

The Date menu's Format option (2) lets you specify the format for the date and time. When you select it, WordPerfect displays the *Date Format* screen shown in Figure D-2.

Here, the *Character* column lists the available codes you can use to specify the form in which the date and/or time are to appear when you give an Insert Text or Insert Function command. The *Meaning* column describes what each code produces. Below these columns are some examples of possible format combinations.

The *Date Format* prompt at the bottom shows the current format. The combination "3 1, 4" indicates that only the date should be shown, and it should be arranged as month spelled out (character 3), a space, the day of the month (1), a comma and space, and all four digits of the year (4). To accept this format, press Enter. To specify a different format, type its codes and any symbols that separate them, then press Enter.

For example, suppose you are preparing a document in which you want WordPerfect to produce a date and time of the form

Wednesday, 27 January 1988 — 10:33 am

To get this, enter **6, 1 3 4 — 8:9 0** for the Date Format prompt.

```
Date Format

Character  Meaning
    1      Day of the month
    2      Month (number)
    3      Month (word)
    4      Year (all four digits)
    5      Year (last two digits)
    6      Day of the month (word)
    7      Hour (24-hour clock)
    8      Hour (12-hour clock)
    9      Minutes
    0      am / pm
    %      Include leading zero for numbers less than 10
           (must directly precede number)

Examples:  3 1, 4              = December 25, 1984
           %2/%1/5 (6)          = 01/01/85 (Tuesday)
           8:90                 = 10:55am

Date Format: 3 1,4
```

Figure D-2 Date Format screen.

Date/Outline Command (Shift-F5) — WordPerfect 5.0

5.0 When you press Shift-F5 to give a Date/Outline command, WordPerfect 5.0 displays

1 Date Text; 2 Date Code; 3 Date Format; 4 Outline; 5 Para Num; 6 Define: 0

Here, the first three options deal with the date, while the last three deal with outline and paragraph numbering.

Date Text and Date Code Options

If you select option 1 or 2 from the Date/Outline menu, WordPerfect inserts the date in the common month-day-year format (e.g., *May 29, 1988*). These two options are quite different, however.

Specifically, *Date Text* (option 1) produces regular text; once you insert the date, it's in your document permanently. By contrast, *Date Code* (option 2) inserts a hidden [Date:] code that WordPerfect replaces with the current date whenever you edit the document or print it.

For example, if you select Date Code on June 4, 1988, that date appears in your document. However, if you print the document, say, one week later, the date will appear as June *11*, 1988. Date Code is handy for use in form letters and in documents that you work on over a period of time.

However, Date Code's variable-date feature can also be a drawback. If you need to print the document for filing purposes later, it will have *that* day's date, not the original date. To eliminate this problem, you could keep the Insert Function date while you're working on a document, then delete it and replace it with Date Text on the day you want saved for posterity.

Date Format Option

The Date/Outline menu's *Date Format* option (3) lets you specify the format for the date and time. When you select it, WordPerfect displays the Date Format screen shown in Figure D-2 (see preceding **Date Command** entry).

Here, the *Character* column lists the codes you can use to specify the form in which the date and/or time are to appear when you give a Date Text or Date Code command. The *Meaning* column describes what each code produces. Below these columns are some examples of possible format combinations.

The **Date Format** prompt at the bottom shows the current format. The combination "3 1, 4" indicates that only the date should be shown, and it should be arranged as month spelled out (character 3), a space, the day of the month (1), a comma and space, and all four digits of the year (4). To accept this format, press Enter. To specify a different format, type its codes and any symbols that separate them, then press Enter.

For example, suppose you are preparing a document in which you want WordPerfect to produce a date and time of the form

Wednesday, 27 January 1988 — 10:33 am

To get this, enter **6, 1 3 4 — 8:9 0** for the Date Format prompt.

Outline, Para Num, and Define Options

These options are covered in the **Outlines** and **Paragraph Numbering** entries.

dBASE II and dBASE III Files

— See **Convert Program** and **Database Files, Using**

DCA (Document Content Architecture) Files

— See **Convert Program**

Decimal Tabs

WordPerfect can align numbers around a decimal point or any other character you specify. If you have WordPerfect version 4.2 or later, see **Tabs**; if you have 4.1, see **Tab Align Command**.

Del (Delete) Key

Pressing the Del key (bottom right-hand corner of the keyboard) makes WordPerfect delete the character or hidden code at the cursor position. If you have selected a block of text in Block mode, pressing Del and typing y deletes the block. If you accidentally press Del (say, you meant to press Ins), you can restore the deleted text by pressing F1 to give a *Cancel* command, then selecting *Restore* from the menu.

Delete [code]? (Y/N) N **Prompt**

When you embolden, center, underline, or style text in some other manner, WordPerfect marks the styling change with a hidden code (see **Codes, Hidden** for details). Because these codes are invisible during normal editing, WordPerfect warns when you try to delete one by pressing Del or Backspace. It gives you a chance to preserve the code by displaying a prompt of the form *Delete [code]? (Y/N) N* at the bottom of the screen. To delete the code, type **y**; to preserve it, type **n** or press Enter.

Of course, the choice is yours. If you really intended to delete that code (e.g., you want to remove underlining or uncenter a line), do so.

Sometimes, however, you will receive a *Delete [code]?* prompt unexpectedly. For example, WordPerfect might show *Delete [Bold]?* when there's seemingly nothing emboldened. This occurs when you have deleted bold text, but not the hidden codes that enclosed it. The codes are still in the document, they just aren't operating on any text. In this case, of course, you would type **y** to delete the code. If you're ever in doubt about what a code is operating on, press Alt and F3 to give WordPerfect a Reveal Codes command. When the code appears, delete it if you want to.

Deleted Text, Undeleting

When you delete text, WordPerfect does not immediately discard it, but instead, temporarily saves it in the computer's memory. In fact, WordPerfect keeps text from the last *three* deletions in memory!

To recycle deleted text, simply move the cursor to where you want to insert it and press the F1 (*Cancel*) key. This makes WordPerfect display the text, in inverse video, at the cursor position and show the following option list at the bottom of the screen:

```
Undelete: 1 Restore; 2 Show Previous Deletion: 0
```

Now you have three choices: to restore the highlighted text, type **1**; to show the text you deleted before this deletion, type **2**; to return to editing (if you pressed F1 by mistake), press Enter.

As an illustration of restoring deleted text, let's suppose you absent-mindedly transposed Raymond Morris' name in a computerized telephone list—entering *Raymond, Morris* instead of *Morris, Raymond*—so you want to switch these words. To do this, move the cursor to the "R" in "Raymond," then press Ctrl and Backspace. "Raymond, " disappears. Now move the cursor to the space after *Morris* and type a comma and a space. The cursor is now where *Raymond* belongs, so press F1, then **1**, to retrieve "Raymond, " from memory and insert it. (Note that the word is still in memory, so you could use it again later if you wanted to.) Finally, press Backspace twice to delete the extra space and the comma.

Deleting

WordPerfect lets you erase or delete text or hidden codes. To delete tabs, see **Tabs**; to delete disk files, see **List Files Command**.

Deleting Text

WordPerfect provides key combinations to delete a character, word, sentence, paragraph, or page. They are:

- To delete the current character or the preceding one, press Del or Backspace. Both Del and Backspace *repeat*; they delete characters as long as you hold them down.
- To delete the current word, put the cursor anywhere in it and press Ctrl-Backspace.
- To delete left of the cursor to the beginning of the word, press Home, then Backspace. If the cursor is at the beginning of a word, pressing Home and Backspace deletes the previous word.
- To delete from the cursor to the beginning of the next word, press Home, then Del.
- To delete from the cursor to the end of the current line, press Ctrl and End.
- To delete a sentence, paragraph, or page, press Ctrl-F4 to obtain the *Move* menu, type **1** (Sentence) **2** (Paragraph), or **3** (Page), then type **3** for *Delete*.

To delete consecutive words, sentences, or whatever, put the cursor on the first character to be deleted and press Alt-F4 to put Word-

Perfect in Block mode. When the flashing *Block on* message appears at the bottom of the screen, move the cursor to the last character to be deleted (WordPerfect highlights text as you move) and press Del. When the *Delete Block?* prompt appears, type **y**, then press Enter.

If you delete something accidentally, you can restore it using the Cancel (F1) command; see **Deleted Text, Undeleting**.

Deleting Hidden Codes

Sometimes you may discover that an entire paragraph or page is emboldened when you only intended to make a single word bold. Or you may accidentally center something when you only wanted to insert the date. Here, you apparently forgot to turn off a feature (e.g., emboldening) or pressed the wrong command keys (e.g., Shift-F6 for Center instead of Shift-F5 for Date). To correct the problem, you must locate and delete the errant code.

If you realize your error immediately, simply press Alt-F3 to give a Reveal Codes command. Then move the cursor just past the code and press Backspace, or just ahead of it and press Del. If you don't know where the code is located, search backward or forward for it (see **Search Commands**), then do a Reveal Codes and delete it.

DIF (Data Interchange Format) Spreadsheets

— See **Convert Program**

Disk Directories

A computer's hard disk can hold thousands of files. To keep related files together, most people divide the hard disk into functional areas called *directories*. If you think of the hard disk as a house, you may think of each directory as a room in that house.

The main directory (the "house" itself) is called the *root directory*. This is the directory the computer is "in" when you turn it on. The root directory is named \ or, more properly, C:\. That is, it's the \ directory on the computer's C drive. (Floppy disk drives are named A and B; hard disk drives have names with the letters C and higher.)

If you have set up WordPerfect according to the manual, it is in a directory called \wp. Thus, to put the computer into that directory, you must give it the command **cd \wp** (where *cd* stands for "change directory").

Creating Subdirectories for Documents

WordPerfect always assumes that you want to store documents in its main directory, C:\WP. However, if you work with a lot of different kinds of documents (perhaps reports, business letters, and personal letters), you may want to keep them in separate directories. The most reasonable approach is to create a *subdirectory* (a closet in WordPerfect's room) for each type of document. To create a subdirectory from within WordPerfect:

1. Press F5 to give a List Files command.
2. When **Dir C:\wp*.*** appears at the bottom of the screen, press Enter.
3. When the List Files menu appears, type **7** to select *Change Directory*. WordPerfect shows

```
New Directory = C:\WP
```

4. Enter the full name of the new subdirectory (e.g., *c:\wp\reports*).
5. When you are asked **Create c:\wp\reports? (Y/N) N**, or whatever name you used, type **y** for Yes.

WordPerfect creates the new subdirectory and puts its name in the list with <DIR> beside it. This entry simply acknowledges that the subdirectory exists. To make WordPerfect store documents in it, you must do another *Change Directory* operation.

Making WordPerfect Use a Subdirectory

To switch to a document subdirectory, give a List Files command and select *Change Directory* from the menu. When

```
New Directory = C:\WP
```

appears, enter the name of the subdirectory you want (e.g., c:\wp\reports). WordPerfect assumes you want to work on a document in that subdirectory, and shows

```
Dir C:\wp\reports\*.*
```

Here, the *.* indicates "all files" in the REPORTS subdirectory (see *Operating on Groups of Files* under **DOS Operations**). Press Enter to obtain a list of those files. Then highlight the one you want and Retrieve it or, to create a new document, select Exit by pressing 0.

Deleting Subdirectories

If you don't need any of the files in a subdirectory (say, they're from a project you have finished), delete each one, then delete the subdirectory itself. To delete a subdirectory, highlight its name in the List Files list and select Delete from the menu. When WordPerfect asks if you're sure, type y for Yes.

Disk Files (Documents), Operating on

— See **List Files Command** and **DOS Operations**

Disk full Message

This message indicates that the data disk on which you have attempted to save a document is full. When that happens, you can either try saving on another formatted data disk or make room on the current disk by removing documents you no longer need. For details on how to remove documents from a disk, see **List Files Command**.

Doc Value at Bottom of the Screen

WordPerfect lets you work with two different documents at the same time, and shows which one you're currently in by displaying its *Doc* number at the bottom right-hand corner of the screen. The document on the main screen (the one you start in) is numbered 1. If you do a Switch command, by pressing Alt and F3, WordPerfect clears the screen and shows *Doc 2* at the bottom.

This second, alternate screen is identical to the first one, and you can use it to create a new document or retrieve an existing one. In fact, it's almost like having two separate computers. Perhaps it's *better* in that you can easily transfer (move or copy) information between the two screens. For more details, see **Switch Documents Command**.

Document Comments

WordPerfect versions 4.2 and later let you insert nonprinting comments in your documents. This is convenient for including questions, suggestions, or reminders within a document in progress. For example, if you're reviewing someone else's work, you might want to insert a note to the author, such as "Are you sure of these prices?" or "This is a good point. Please expand on it."

Creating Comments

To insert a comment, move to where it belongs and press Ctrl-F5 to give a Text In/Out command. When the menu appears, type **b** for *Create Comment* (WordPerfect 4.2) or type **5** for *Comment*, then **1** for *Create* (WordPerfect 5.0). WordPerfect clears the screen and shows a box with the cursor at the beginning of it, waiting for you to enter text.

Comments can be up to 1024 characters long, and may include bold and underlined text. You can also press Ins to put WordPerfect in the Typeover mode, in which characters you type replace those on the screen. You cannot center comment text, however, nor make it flush right. Further, comment text cannot include tabs or indents, nor can you undelete material.

When you finish entering the comment, press F7 (Exit) to return to your document. WordPerfect inserts the comment at the place where you gave the Text In/Out command.

Editing Comments

To edit a comment, move past it (WordPerfect always assumes you want to edit the preceding comment) and press Ctrl-F5 to give a Text In/Out command. When the menu appears, type **c** for *Edit Comment* (WordPerfect 4.2) or type **5** for *Comment*, then **2** for *Edit* (WordPerfect 5.0). WordPerfect moves the cursor to the beginning of the comment. Make your changes, then press F7 (Exit) to return to your document.

Hiding Comments

Once you create a comment, WordPerfect will display it unless you say otherwise. If you find the comments distracting, you can hide them, as follows:

| 4.2 |

- **With WordPerfect 4.2**, press Ctrl-F5 to give a Text In/Out command and type **d** to select *Display Summary and Comments*. WordPerfect asks **Display Summary? (Y/N) N**. This refers to a nonprinting summary you can display at the beginning of a document; see **Document Summary**. Type **y** to display it or **n** to keep it hidden. When the **Display Comments? (Y/N) Y** prompt appears, type **n** for no.

| 5.0 |

- **With WordPerfect 5.0**, press Shift-F1 to give a Setup command and type **3** for *Display*. When the Display menu appears, type **3** to reach the *Display Document Comments* field and type **n** to hide comments.

WordPerfect then redisplays your document, but hides the comments. You can reinstate them at any time by repeating the same procedure, but typing **y** to *Display Comments*.

Comment Codes

WordPerfect 4.2 marks document comments with a hidden code of the form [Smry/Comment: *text*], where *text* is the first 100 characters of the comment. (Thus, you can view the comment text by giving a Reveal Codes command.) By contrast, WordPerfect 5.0 marks document comments with a hidden [Comment] code, which doesn't show the text.

Converting Between Comments and Text

WordPerfect 5.0 lets you convert a comment to regular text, or vice versa. To change a comment to text, move past it, press Ctrl-F5 for Text In/Out, and type **5** for *Comment*, then **3** for*Convert to Text*. To change text to a comment, select it in Block mode, press Ctrl-F5 for Text In/Out, and type **y** in response to the prompt.

Document Compare—WordPerfect 5.0

5.0 WordPerfect 5.0 lets you compare the document on the screen with one on disk, to find out whether the two are identical. After comparing the two documents, it redlines any on-screen text that is not on the disk, and inserts (in strikeout form) any disk text that is not in the screen document. Moreover, if a block of text has been moved, WordPerfect inserts (in strikeout) "The Following Text was Moved" in front of the text and "The Preceding Text was Moved" after it.

To compare a document on the screen with one on disk, do the following:

1. Press Alt-F5 to give a Mark Text command.
2. Type **6** to select *Generate*.
3. Type **2** to select *Compare screen and disk documents for redline and strikeout*.
4. Press Enter to accept the displayed filename or enter a filename of your own.

Removing Redline Markings and Strikeout Text

When you finish comparing the documents, you can restore the on-screen document to its original form by removing the redline marks and strikeout text. To do this:

1. Press Alt-F5 to give a Mark Text command.
2. Type **6** to select *Generate*.
3. Type **1** to select *Remove redline markings and strikeout text from document*, and type **y** in response to the prompt.

Document Format Option — WordPerfect 5.0

WordPerfect's Format (Shift-F8) menu provides four options, of which *Document* controls the format settings that are active for the current document. When you type 3 from the Format menu, WordPerfect displays the Document Format menu shown in Figure D-3.

The Document Format menu lets you make the following changes within a document:

- *Display Pitch* (option 1) controls the width of characters displayed on the screen.
- *Initial/Codes* lets you display and change the active format settings for the current document. When you select this option, WordPerfect displays a Reveal Codes screen that will show you settings as you give commands. See **Initial/Codes** for more details.
- *Redline Method* is the technique WordPerfect uses to mark text that is proposed for inclusion in the document. See **Redlining Text**.
- *Summary* lets you create a nonprinting summary for a document. The document summary shows the date the document was created and has fields where you can enter the names of the author and typist, and comments of your choice. See **Document Summary**.

Figure D-3 WordPerfect 5.0's Document Format menu.

```
Format: Document

1 - Display Pitch - Automatic        Yes
                    Width            0.1"
2 - Initial Codes
3 - Initial Font                     Printer Dependent
4 - Redline Method
5 - Summary                          10 CPI

Selection: 0
```

Document Names

— See **Filenames**

Document Summary — WordPerfect 4.2

WordPerfect 4.2 lets you create a nonprinting summary for any document. The document summary screen lists the name of the document file and the date it was created, and has fields where you can enter the names of the author and typist, and comments of your choice (e.g., the reason a letter was written or a list of tasks that still need to be done).

Creating and Editing a Document Summary

You can create a document summary or edit an existing one from anywhere in a document. The procedure is:

1. Press Ctrl and F5 to give WordPerfect a *Text In/Out* command.
2. When the Document Conversion, Summary and Comments menu appears, type **A** to select *Create/Edit Summary*.
3. When the Document Summary screen (Figure D-4) appears, enter the names of the author and typist (up to 40 characters each), then your comments (up to 880 characters).

Figure D-4 WordPerfect 4.2's Document Summary menu.

```
Document: Summary

         Filename:                    C:\WP\REPORT.DOC

         Date of Creation:            September 14, 1988

    1 - Author:
    2 - Typist:
    3 - Comments
```

3. When the Document Summary screen (Figure D-4) appears, enter the names of the author and typist (up to 40 characters each), then your comments (up to 880 characters).

4. When you finish entering comments, press F7 (Exit) to exit the Comments box, then press Enter to return to your document.

Comments may include bold and underlined text. You can also press Ins, to put WordPerfect in the Typeover mode, in which characters you type replace those on the screen. You cannot center comment text, however, nor make it flush right. Further, comment text cannot include tabs or indents, nor can you undelete material.

Hiding a Document Summary

Once you create a document summary, WordPerfect will display it at the beginning of your document, unless you say otherwise. To hide the summary, press Ctrl-F5 to give a Text In/Out command and type **D** for *Display Summary and Comments*. When WordPerfect asks *Display Summary? (Y/N)*, type **n** for no. The next prompt, *Display Comments? (Y/N)*, refers to nonprinting comments you can insert within documents; see **Document Comments**. Type **y** to display them or **n** to keep them hidden.

When you finish responding to the prompts, WordPerfect redisplays your document, but hides the summary box. You can reinstate it at any time by repeating the procedure I just gave, but typing **y** in response to *Display Summary?*.

Viewing a Document Summary

Sometimes you may want to examine a summary without displaying it in your document. To do this, move the cursor to the beginning of the document (by pressing Home twice, then ↑) and press Alt-F3 to give a *Reveal Codes* command. Reveal Codes shows the first 100 characters of the summary.

You can also view the summary for any document on your disk, by choosing *Look* from the List Files (F5) menu. You might even want to Look at the document you're working on (provided it's on disk), to see the summary without physically moving to the first page.

Document Summary — WordPerfect 5.0

5.0
WordPerfect 5.0 lets you create a nonprinting summary for any document. The document summary screen lists the name of the document file and the date it was created. It also has blank fields where you can enter a descriptive name for the file, the subject or account the material in this file pertains to, the names of the author and typist, and comments of your choice (e.g., the reason a letter was written or a list of tasks that still need to be done).

Creating and Editing a Document Summary

You can create a document summary or edit an existing one from anywhere in a document. The procedure is:

1. Press Shift and F8 to give WordPerfect a Format command.
2. When the Format menu appears, type **3** to select *Document*, then **4** to select *Summary*.
3. When the Document Summary screen (Figure D-5) appears, type the number of the entry you want to work on. You may enter up to 40 characters in the first four entries and up to 780 characters in the *Comments* box. (WordPerfect inserts the first 400 characters of the document in the Comments box automatically.)

Figure D-5 WordPerfect 5.0's Document Summary screen.

```
Document: Summary

    System Filename    C:\WP\REPORT.DOC

    Date of Creation   September 14, 1988

 1 - Descriptive Filename
 2 - Subject/Account
 3 - Author
 4 - Typist
 5 - Comments

Selection: 0
```

4. When you finish with an entry, press Enter to return to *Selection*. If you are done working on the document summary, press F7 (Exit) to save the changes and return to your document.

Comments may include bold and underlined text. You can also press Ins, to put WordPerfect in the Typeover mode, in which characters you type replace those on the screen. You cannot center comment text, however, nor make it flush right. Further, comment text cannot include tabs or indents, nor can you undelete material.

Displaying a Document Summary

Once you create a document summary, you can obtain it at any time by following the procedure I just gave; that is, by selecting *Summary* from the Format (Shift-F8) command's Document submenu. You can also view the summary for any document on your disk, by giving a List Files (F5) command and choosing *Look*.

However, both of these procedures require you to press keys to get the summary. WordPerfect can also display the summary automatically whenever you Save (F10) or (Exit) the document. To make it do this:

1. Press Shift and F1 to give a Setup command.
2. When the Setup menu appears, type **5** to select *Initial Settings*.
3. When the Initial Settings menu appears, type **3** to select *Document Summary*.
4. Type **1** for *Create on Save/Exit*, then **y** for Yes.
5. Press F7 (Exit) to return to your document.

From then on, WordPerfect will display the document summary whenever you Save or Exit.

Letting WordPerfect Fill In the Subject/Account Field

WordPerfect 5.0 always looks for a particular sequence of characters in the first 400 characters of every document. If it finds that sequence (called the *subject search text*), it automatically puts a copy of the rest of the paragraph in the document summary's *Subject/Account* field. This is convenient in that it saves you from having to remember the subject of a document while you are creating the summary.

WordPerfect is preset to search for the string *RE:* (the classic abbreviation in memos), but you can make it search for another string of your choice by doing the following:

1. Press Shift and F1 to give a Setup command.
2. When the Setup menu appears, type 5 to select *Initial Settings*.
3. When the Initial Settings menu appears, type 3 to select *Document Summary*.
4. Type 2 to reach the *Subject Search Text* field, then enter the character(s) you want WordPerfect to search for.
5. Press F7 (Exit) to return to your document.

Thereafter, WordPerfect will search for the string you specified in every document you work on.

Documents, Reformatting

— See **Reformatting Documents**

DOS Operations

You may occasionally want to do some general "housekeeping" work on disks that contain WordPerfect documents. For example, you may want to copy an entire disk or a single document, or give a document a new name that is easier to remember. You can do some of these operations from within WordPerfect, using the List Files command (F5), but it is often quicker and easier to do them from the computer's Disk Operating System, or *DOS*. This entry describes common DOS operations; for others or more details, refer to the DOS manual that came with your computer.

Starting DOS

To start DOS, insert the DOS disk in the left-hand drive (A) and switch the power on. Press Enter when the computer asks for the date and time. The *A>* on the screen tells you that the computer is waiting for a DOS command. If you want to do something that involves one disk (e.g., delete a file or format a disk), put the disk in the right-hand drive (B). If you want to do something that involves two disks (e.g., copy a disk), replace the DOS disk with the source disk and put the second, destination disk in drive B.

Filenames

Every disk file has a name of up to eight characters. Optionally, it can have an "extension"—a period followed by one to three characters that describes what kind of information the file contains. For example, you may give letters the extension *.LET*, reports the extension *.RPT*, and so on.

When using DOS to operate on a file, you must enter both its name and its extension. For example, to operate on a disk file named *SALES.RPT*, you would enter **SALES.RPT**. Furthermore, if the file you want is not on the active drive, you must tell DOS where to locate it by preceding the filename with the drive name and a colon. Floppy disk drives are named *A* and *B*, while hard disk drives are named *C* or some higher letter. Hence, you would enter **B:SALES.RPT** if A is the active drive and *SALES.RPT* is in B.

Finally, if you are working from a hard disk and the file is not in the active directory, you must enter a directory description, called a path, in front of the filename. Hence, if *SALES.RPT* is in the REPORTS directory of drive C, you would enter **C:\REPORTS\SALES.RPT**. The combination of drive name, path, filename, and extension is referred to as a file specification or "filespec."

Operating on Groups of Files

DOS lets you operate on entire groups of similarly-named files. You can, for example, copy or display a directory of a group of files with a single command. To do this, you use *wild card* characters that act as shorthand for "any character" or "any group of characters." You can compare them with the Joker in popular card games, a free number in Bingo, or a blank tile in Scrabble.

The character *?* means "any single character." You can put *?* anywhere in a filename—even several times. For example, the command **dir rptq28?.rpt** displays a list (directory) of report files for all second-quarter sales reports for the 1980s. Similarly, the command **dir rptq?8?.rpt** displays a list of *all* quarterly sales reports for the 1980s.

The * (asterisk) is an even more all-encompassing wild card. It tells DOS that any character can occupy that position and all remaining positions in the filename or extension. For example, the

84   DOS Operations

command **dir rptq*.rpt** displays all *RPTQ* report files, regardless of their quarter or year. Similarly, the command **dir rptq*.*** displays all files whose names begin with *RPTQ*, regardless of their extension.

Common DOS Commands

Table D-1 summarizes the DOS commands you will probably use most often. Here, items shown in brackets are optional.

Table D-1 Common DOS commands.

Command	Action	Comments
CD \path	Makes the named directory active.	
CHKDSK [d:]	Displays a disk and memory status report.	
COPY old-filespec [new-filespec]	Copies files.	
DIR [filespec]	Displays name, size, date, and time of file(s) on disk.	If you omit the filespec, DIR summarizes the current floppy disk or hard disk directory.
DISKCOPY source-drive target-drive	Copies an entire disk.	Target disk need not be formatted.
ERASE filespec	Deletes files.	
FORMAT a: or FORMAT b:	Prepares a disk to accept DOS files.	Deletes any files currently on the disk
MD \path	Creates the named directory.	
RD \path	Deletes the named directory.	The directory to be deleted must be empty.
RENAME old-filespec new-filespec	Changes a file's name.	

CD (Change Directory) Command

This command puts the computer "in" the specified hard disk directory. The general form of the CD command is

CD \path

where *path* gives the location of the directory in respect to the higher-level directories above it.

Once you change to a directory, DOS assumes that every command you give applies to that directory. For example, if you give the command **ERASE REPORT.DOC**, DOS expects to find the REPORT.DOC file in the current directory.

The simplest CD command is **CD **, which puts the computer in the main or *root* directory, the directory that the computer starts in when you turn it on. Similarly, **CD \WP** puts the computer in the WordPerfect directory, whereas **CD \WP\DOCS** puts it in a DOCS (documents) subdirectory within the WP directory.

If the directory you specified does not exist, DOS ignores your CD command and displays "Invalid directory."

CHKDSK (Check Disk) Command

CHKDSK tells how many files a disk contains and how many bytes (characters) are unused. It also reports on memory use. CHKDSK reports on the active disk unless you follow it with a drive name.

A typical report from CHKDSK looks like this:

```
362496 bytes total disk space
350000 bytes in 12 user files
 12496 bytes available on disk

655360 bytes total memory
386672 bytes free
```

The top lines tell the disk's status. This particular disk is nearly full, since only 12,496 bytes of its 362,496-byte capacity are still available.

If you try to copy a file to a disk that doesn't have room for it, DOS ignores your Copy command and displays an **Insufficient disk space** message. As a rule of thumb, when a data disk has less than 20,000 bytes available, you should change disks. Disks are inexpensive, and you do not want to lose some work because a disk is full.

COPY Command

As you might expect, COPY copies files. If you copy files onto another disk, you can give them the same names as the originals. If you copy them onto the floppy disk or into the hard disk directory where they are now, you must rename them. Either way, COPY does not affect the original files.

COPY obviously requires two filespecs—a source and a destination—where the source's filespec comes first. You may omit the destination's name if it is the same as the source's. The following command copies SALES.RPT from drive A to drive B:

```
COPY SALES.RPT B:
```

You might also want to copy all document files to a new disk, to make a backup. If you named the files with a .DOC extension, copy them with

```
COPY *.DOC B:
```

Finally, you might want to copy a document to use as a starting point for preparing a new document. For example, the following command makes a copy of 1988's sales report as a starting point for preparing 1989's:

```
COPY SALES88.RPT SALES89.RPT
```

DIR (Directory) Command

DIR displays the following information about files on a disk: filename and extension, size in characters, and the date and time it was most recently saved. A typical entry looks like this:

```
REPORT88 DOC 1920 5-29-88 9:45p
```

This tells you that the file REPORT88 has the extension DOC and is 1920 characters long. Further, 5-29-88 (May 29, 1988) is the date on which you last saved REPORT88.DOC and 9:45 p.m. is the time at which you saved it. Of course, these are correct only if you entered the time and date when DOS asked for them.

You can follow DIR with a filespec, to limit the display to files in a particular group. Typical examples are:

```
DIR                (Display all files on the active drive.)
DIR B:             (Display all files on drive B.)
```

DIR B:*.DOC (Display all DOC files on drive B.)
DIR B:NEW*.DOC (Same, but display only DOC files whose filenames start with NEW.)

If your disk has many files, the directory entries may move or "scroll" by so quickly that you can't read them. To stop the scrolling temporarily, press Ctrl and Num Lock simultaneously; to stop the scrolling altogether, press Ctrl and Break.

DISKCOPY Command

DISKCOPY copies an entire disk. The general form is:

DISKCOPY source-drive target-drive

Note that the source drive comes first. The target drive need not be formatted, since DOS will format it automatically before copying to it.

ERASE Command

ERASE deletes files. It can delete a single file or a group of files. Typical examples are:

ERASE REPORT86.DOC (Delete only REPORT86.DOC.)
ERASE REPORT.* (Delete every REPORT file.)
ERASE B:NEW*.DOC (Delete DOC files that begin with NEW.)

Be careful if you use ? and * to erase a group of files, because a single misplaced character may result in the deletion of files you want to keep. To avoid disaster, run DIR with the filespec you plan to use with ERASE. This will provide a list of all files that ERASE will delete.

If you tell DOS to delete all the files on a disk (by entering, say, **ERASE A:*.***), it gives you a chance to change your mind by displaying an **Are you sure (Y/N)?** prompt. To proceed with the deletion, type **n** and press Enter; to retain the files, type **y** and Enter.

FORMAT Command

FORMAT prepares a disk to accept DOS files, including WordPerfect files. You can compare formatting a disk with drawing lines on a baseball or football field, or marking the origins and axes on a piece of graph paper. That is, formatting prepares the disk for use but doesn't actually do anything with it.

The drive name after FORMAT specifies the disk to be formatted, as in

FORMAT B:

This is the form you would normally use to prepare a new WordPerfect document disk. **Warning:** If your computer has a hard disk drive (C, D, or whatever), do *not* enter **FORMAT C:**. DOS will wipe your hard disk clean and you will lose everything!

MD (Make Directory) Command

This command creates a new directory on a hard disk. The general form of the MD command is

MD \path

where *path* gives the location of the new directory in respect to the higher-level directories above it. For example, the command **MD \LETTERS** creates a directory called LETTERS that is one level below the root directory.

The similar command **MD \WP\LETTERS** also creates a LETTERS directory, but the term WP\ makes LETTERS a subdirectory *within* the WP directory. Such a subdirectory is handy for storing files produced by the program contained in the directory above it. In this case, LETTERS could be used to hold letters that you create with WordPerfect.

The MD command simply creates a directory. To make the computer use that directory, you must give a CD (Change Directory) command. For example, the command **CD \WP\LETTERS** puts the computer in the LETTERS subdirectory that is contained in the WP directory.

RD (Remove Directory) Command

This command deletes the specified directory from a hard disk. The general form of the RD command is

RD \path

where *path* gives the location of the directory in respect to the higher-level directories above it. For example, the command **RD \LETTERS** deletes a directory called LETTERS that is one level below the root directory. The similar command **RD \WP\LETTERS** erases a LETTERS subdirectory that is contained in the WP directory.

DOS will only remove a directory that is empty. (Attempting to remove a directory that still contains files makes DOS ignore your RD command and display an **Invalid path, not directory, or directory not empty** message.) To remove all the files from a directory, give a command of the form

ERASE *path**.*

where *.* stands for "all files and any extension." For example, the command **ERASE \WP\LETTERS*.*** empties the LETTERS subdirectory that is contained in the WP directory.

RENAME Command

RENAME changes a file's name. This command obviously requires two filespecs; the old one comes first. For example, the command

RENAME B:SALESRPT.BK! OLDSALES

changes the name of SALESRPT.BK! on drive B to OLDSALES. WordPerfect has a Backup feature that copies document files to a temporary file whose extension is *BK!* (see **Backups**). Hence, this particular command converts a backup file into a regular document file.

RENAME can also preserve files while you are deleting an entire group. For example, suppose you have documents named SALES86, SALES87, SALES88, and SALES89. If you want to delete all except SALES89, you can do so with the sequence

RENAME SALES89 TEMP
ERASE SALES8*
RENAME TEMP SALES89

Here, the TEMP file serves as a temporary "hideout" for SALES89, keeping it from being ERASEd.

List Files Equivalents of DOS Commands

WordPerfect's List Files command (obtained by pressing F5) produces a list of files that's similar to the list produced by the DOS *DIR* (Directory) command. List Files also reports the status of the specified disk or hard disk directory at the top of the screen, and thereby serves as a WordPerfect version of the DOS *CHKDSK* (Check Disk) command.

Further, List Files provides a menu that lets you perform some DOS-like commands on the disk files in its list. Specifically, the menu has *Delete, Rename, Change Directory,* and *Copy* options that do the same jobs as the DOS *ERASE, RENAME, CD,* and *COPY* commands.

What's more, List Files's Delete command provides a safety feature that you don't get with DOS's ERASE. Before erasing a file, Delete displays a **Delete** *file?* prompt that makes you confirm that you really want to proceed with the deletion. ERASE only asks for a confirmation when you give it an ERASE *.* type command, which tells it to delete every file on a disk or hard disk directory.

DOS, Returning from

The Shell command (Ctrl-F1) lets you leave WordPerfect temporarily and do something from DOS—perhaps, run another program or format a data disk. When you finish, you must enter the word **exit** to return to WordPerfect. Note that you must manually type the word **exit**, *not* press the Exit key (F7).

DOS Text Files

Information is generally transferred between computers as pure text; that is, as characters and spaces with no underlining, bold print, or other control characters. The WordPerfect manual refers to this format as *DOS text*; within the computer field, it's usually called *ASCII*, short for "American Standard Code for Information Interchange." DOS text is, in essence, the generic computer format. Nearly every program can both read text information and produce text results.

DOS text is often used to communicate with programs that cannot produce any of the formats on which WordPerfect's CONVERT program can operate. For example, you would work with it to use documents produced by a non-CONVERTible word processor. WordPerfect has a Text In/Out command that transfers DOS text files into or out of WordPerfect.

Dot Leaders

A dot leader is a string of periods between two pieces of text. Dot leaders are often used in a table of contents, to separate an entry from its page number, as in

```
BASIC HAND TOOLS  . . . . . 23
   How to Drive a Nail  . . . . . 24
   First Aid for Thumbs . . . . . 25
```

In fact, WordPerfect will use dot leaders within a table of contents, if you tell it to; see **Table of Contents**. It can also insert dot leaders in a list, index, or table of authorities.

However, all of those features put a page number at the end of each dot leader. Sometimes you may want dot leaders in some other kind of list, such as a price list or an inventory of your valuable possessions or insured items. WordPerfect 4.2 and 5.0 let you set up tab stops that are marked for dot leaders. When you press Tab to reach one of these stops, WordPerfect inserts a dot leader between where you were and the tab stop. For details about leader-producing tab stops, see **Tabs**.

Double-Sided Pages, Printing

— See **Binding Width**

Double-Spacing

— See **Spacing**

Double-Underlining

Besides underlining material, WordPerfect can also put a double underline beneath it. With WordPerfect 4.1 and 4.2, you select double-underlining from the Print Format menu; with WordPerfect 5.0, you select it from the Font menu.

Double-Underlining with WordPerfect 4.1 and 4.2

4.1 4.2 To produce double-underlining with WordPerfect 4.1 or 4.2, you must switch the "underlining style" from Single to Double. To do this, press Ctrl and F8 to obtain the Print Format menu. When it appears, select either *Non-continuous Double* (6) or *Continuous Double* (8), then press Enter. (The non-continuous style does not underline tabs; continuous does.) After that, whenever you underline something, WordPerfect will show a single underline on the screen, but print with a double underline.

WordPerfect keeps using the active underline style until you tell it to use another. Thus, to get back to single-underlining, repeat the selection process and choose one of the Single styles.

When you switch underlining styles, WordPerfect puts a hidden [Undrl Style:*n*] code in your document, where *n* is the style number (5, 6, 7, or 8).

Double-Underlining with WordPerfect 5.0

5.0

To double-underline text you are about to type:

1. Press Ctrl and F8 to give a Font command.
2. When the Font menu appears, type **2** to select *Appearance*.
3. Type **3** to select *Dbl Und*.
4. Type the text you want double-underlined. When you finish, press → to move past the Double Underline Off ([dbl und]) code.

You can also double-underline existing text, by selecting it in Block mode, then performing steps 1 through 3 above.

Drawing Boxes and Lines

— See **Lines, Drawing**

Editing Disk Documents

Once you have documents on a disk, you will probably spend more time editing them than creating new ones. To retrieve a document from disk, press Shift and F10 to give WordPerfect a *Retrieve* command. When the screen shows

```
Document to be Retrieved:
```

enter the file's name and extension (e.g., report.doc), then press Enter. WordPerfect displays the document on the screen as if you had entered it.

Saving an Edited Document

When you finish making changes, you will want to save the document on disk. There are two ways to do this. If you want to continue editing the document, press F10 to give a Save command; if you want to work on another document or leave WordPerfect entirely, press F7 to give an Exit command. Pressing F7 brings on the prompt

Editing Two Documents

```
           Save Document? (Y/N) Y
```

Press Enter to accept WordPerfect's default, Y (for Yes). When the screen shows

```
        Document to be Saved: B:\filename
```
press Enter again.

WordPerfect then asks if you're sure you want to replace the document on disk with the one on the screen. It displays

```
           Replace B:\filename? (Y/N) N
```

Type y to tell it Yes. The screen shows

```
              Saving B:\filename
```

When

```
              Exit WP? (Y/N) N
```

appears, press Enter to stay in WordPerfect. Now WordPerfect clears the screen, and you may retrieve a new document from disk. If you don't remember its name, you can get a list of the available documents by pressing F5 to give a List Files command. See List Files Command for details.

Editing Two Documents

—See **Switch Documents Command**

Emboldened Text

—See **Bold Command**

End Key

Pressing the End key (1 on the numeric keypad) moves the cursor to the end of the current line. Pressing Ctrl and End simulataneously deletes everything from the cursor position to the end of the line.

Endnotes

Endnotes are footnotes that WordPerfect prints at the end of a document or, with WordPerfect 5.0, wherever else you tell it to put them. See **Footnote Command** for more about endnotes.

Enter Key

Enter is the gray key with the bent left arrow that's between the regular keyboard and the numeric keypad. It's the equivalent of Return on a typewriter. On a typewriter, you press Return at the end of each line; when using WordPerfect, press Enter only at the end of a paragraph or when you want to skip a line.

Pressing Enter in a Menu

You can also use Enter to select the default option (the option that WordPerfect assumes you want) from a menu or the default choice from a Yes or No (Y/N) prompt. For most menus, the default is 0 (zero), as in this one produced by the Merge Sort (Ctrl-F9) command:

```
1 Merge; 2 Sort; 3 Sorting Sequence: 0
```

Here, the 0 indicates "no choice," and pressing Enter makes the menu disappear, as if you had never given the command.

Similarly, with a prompt such as **Save Document? (Y/N) Y**, pressing Enter makes WordPerfect choose the default (Y, for Yes, here). WordPerfect's defaults are designed to provide the choice you probably want, and keep you out of trouble. For example, Save Document's default is Y, because if it were N (No) you may inadvertently leave WordPerfect without first saving your work.

Ctrl and Enter Starts a New Page

Pressing Ctrl and Enter together makes WordPerfect start a new page. It tells you it has done this by drawing a line of equal signs across the screen and displaying *Ln 1* at the bottom right-hand corner. It also inserts a hidden [HPg] code where you pressed Ctrl-Enter. If you pressed Ctrl-Enter by mistake (say, you intended Ctrl-Home), press Alt-F3 to see the hidden codes and delete [HPg].

Envelopes, Printing

— See *Printing Envelopes* under **Form Letters**

Equal Signs, Line of

A line of equal signs across the screen indicates that you have pressed Ctrl and Enter together, thereby telling WordPerfect to start a new page. WordPerfect inserts a hidden [HPg] code where you pressed Ctrl-Enter. If you pressed Ctrl-Enter by mistake (say, you intended Ctrl-Home), press Alt-F3 to see the hidden codes and delete [HPg].

Erasing Material

— See **Deleting**

ERROR: *File not found* Message

This message appears when you attempt to retrieve or print a document that WordPerfect cannot find. You probably misspelled the file's name, had the wrong disk in the data drive, or gave the wrong extension to the file name. Remember, every file has a name, but it may also have an extension. For example, the file REPORT.Q2 has the name REPORT and the extension Q2. The extension is always optional, but if a file has one, you must supply it to WordPerfect when you refer to that file.

Esc (Escape) Key

Pressing Esc lets you repeat the next command a specified number of times. WordPerfect assumes you want to repeat the command eight times, and shows **n = 8** (or **Repeat Value = 8**, for WordPerfect 5.0) at the bottom left-hand corner of the screen. To repeat it eight times, simply give the command; to repeat it some other number of times, type the repetition count, then give the command. Here is what you can use Esc to do:

To...	Press...
Move the cursor *n* lines up	Esc **n** ↑
Move the cursor *n* lines down	Esc **n** ↓
Move the cursor *n* spaces to the left	Esc **n** ←
Move the cursor *n* spaces to the right	Esc **n** →
Move the cursor *n* tab stops to the right	Esc **n** Tab
Move the cursor *n* words to the left	Esc **n** Ctrl- ←
Move the cursor *n* words to the right	Esc **n** Ctrl- →
Move the cursor *n* pages backward	Esc **n** PgUp
Move the cursor *n* pages forward	Esc **n** PgDn
Perform a macro *n* times	Esc **n** (Replay macro)
Delete *n* characters	Esc **n** Del
Delete *n* words	Esc **n** Ctrl-Backspace
Delete *n* lines, starting at the cursor	Esc **n** Ctrl-End

Insert *n* copies of a character   Esc **n** *character*

You might use the insert-characters operation to draw a dashed line across the screen. For example, if the cursor is at the left-hand margin and your margins are 10 and 74 (the default values), press Esc, then type **65** and **-** (hyphen).

If you often use a repetition count other than 8, you can easily make Esc produce that count each time. Simply press Esc, type your repetition count, then press Enter. Esc will then use the new count value until you leave WordPerfect.

Exit Command (F7)

You should always press F7 (Exit) to leave WordPerfect, rather than just turning the computer off. Pressing F7 makes WordPerfect display the prompt **Save Document? (Y/N) Y** at the bottom left corner of the screen. If you already saved the current version of the document on disk, WordPerfect 4.2 and 5.0 also show *(Text was not modified)* at the bottom right corner. (**Note:** Take the word "Text" here literally. If you only changed hidden formatting codes, and didn't disturb the text, WordPerfect will still report that *Text was not modified*. If you don't save here, you'll lose the formatting changes.)

You can then press Enter or type **y** to save the document on disk or type **n** to exit without saving. If you tell WordPerfect to save the document, it asks **Replace** *filename* **(Y/N)? N**. Type **y** to update the disk file or **n** to exit without replacing. Finally, type **y** in response to **Exit WP (Y/N) N**. When the DOS prompt (usually B> or C>) appears, switch the power off if you are done.

The F7 key is also used to complete some operations, such as setting tabs or creating a header or footer. Here, WordPerfect's on-screen messages refer to F7 as *EXIT*, as in, "Press EXIT when done."

F

F1 – F10 Keys

— See **Function Keys**

Fast Save — WordPerfect 5.0

WordPerfect 5.0 speeds up the process of saving documents on disk by storing them in unformatted form, using a feature called *Fast Save*.

However, Fast Saved documents cannot be printed directly from disk. (Trying to print one brings on the message **ERROR: Document was Fast Saved — Must be retrieved to print**.) To print a disk document with Fast Save active, you must either retrieve it and print it from the screen, or format it by pressing Home *twice*, then ↓, before you save it.

WordPerfect comes preset with Fast Save on. To turn it off, and save documents in printable, formatted form:

1. Press Shift and F1 to give a Setup command.
2. Type **4** to select Fast Save.

3. Type **n** to turn Fast Save off.
4. Press F7 (Exit) to get back to editing.

Feeders, Paper

— See **Sheet Feeders**

Filenames

Each file (program, WordPerfect document, or whatever) on a disk must have a unique name. With WordPerfect, you must give each document a name when you first store it on disk with an Exit (F7), Save (F10), or Text In/Out (Ctrl-F5) command. Similarly, you must enter this name whenever you want to retrieve a disk document into WordPerfect (see **Retrieve Command** or **Text In/Out Command**) or operate on it using DOS (see **DOS Operations**).

Disk files have names of the general form *filename.ext*, where *filename* is up to eight characters long, and *ext* is an optional "extension"; a period (.), followed by up to three characters. Filenames and extensions may consist of letters (A-Z), numbers (0-9), or any of the following symbols:

$ & # @ ! % ' - ( ) { } _ ' ^

Extensions are useful for reminding you what kind of information a file contains. For example, if you write a report on your company's sales for 1988, you may want to call it *SALES88.RPT*. Similarly, if there is a cover letter for the report, you could call it *SALES88.LET*.

Furthermore, you must put the drive name (A:, B:, or C:) in front of the filename if the file is not on the active drive. Hence, you would enter **B:SALES.RPT** if A is the active drive and *SALES.RPT* is in B.

Finally, if you are working from a hard disk (usually drive C) and the file is not in the active directory, you must put the path in front of the filename. Hence, you would enter **C:\REPORTS\SALES.RPT** if SALES.RPT is in the REPORTS directory. The combination of drive name, path, filename, and extension is referred to as a file specification or "filespec."

Reserved Extensions

In general, you can give a document file any extension you want. However, WordPerfect, DOS, and BASIC employ certain extensions for their program and data files, and you should avoid using them for your documents. "Reserved" extensions include the following:

BAS	EXE	TST
BAT	FIL	TV1
BV1	MAC	TV2
BV2	SPC	WP
CHK	SUP	
COM	SYS	

File Operations

— See **DOS Operations** and **List Files Command**

Flush Right Command (Alt-F6)

WordPerfect normally aligns text along the left-hand margin, but you can make it align along the right-hand margin by pressing Alt and F6 to give a Flush Right command. Flush right text is particularly handy for headers or footers on odd-numbered (right-hand) pages. WordPerfect 4.1 and 4.2 precedes right-aligned text with an [A] code and follows it with an [a] code; WordPerfect 5.0 encloses it with the codes [Flsh Rt] and [c/a/flrt].

Right-Aligning a Block of Text

You can also right-align each line in a block of text. To do this, select the text in Block mode and press Alt-F6. When the prompt

[Aln/FlshR]? (Y/N) N appears, type **y** for yes. WordPerfect then puts Flush Right codes ahead of each line and after it.

Flush Right with Dot Leaders for WordPerfect 4.2

4.2

When you define a list, index, table of contents, table of authorities, or outline, you can tell WordPerfect to insert a line of dots, or *dot leaders*, between the text at the left and the page number at the right. Although WordPerfect does not provide a "with Dot Leaders" option for the Flush Right command, you can trick it into doing essentially the same thing. (Provided you have WordPerfect 4.2; this doesn't work with version 4.1.) You might want to use dot leaders in lists that you create; say, in a telephone list or a list of your insured valuables.

The "trick" I refer to involves setting up a Right-justify with Dot Leaders-style tab (see **Tabs**) at the right-hand margin, then putting WordPerfect into a pseudo *Flush Right with Dot Leaders* mode. Here, whenever you press Tab, WordPerfect draws a dot leader to the right-hand margin, and right-aligns text until you press Enter. When you finish entering your leadered list, press the right-arrow key to reactivate the document's previous tab settings.

Obtaining the Flush Right with Dot Leaders mode requires typing a series of keystrokes that's long enough to warrant defining as a macro. Following are the keystrokes you need to set up a macro called DOTLEAD. (If you're unfamiliar with macros, see the various **Macros** entries in this book.) Once you have created DOTLEAD, you can put WordPerfect into the Flush Right with Dot Leaders mode at any place in your document by pressing Alt-F10 (to give a *Macro* command) and entering **dotlead** in response to the prompt. To create DOTLEAD, press the following keys (don't enter the comments at the right, however):

Ctrl-F10	Begin the macro definition
DOTLEAD Enter	Name the macro DOTLEAD
Shift-F8 1 F7	Insert a copy of the current tab settings
←	Move just ahead of the [Tab Set:] code
Shift-F8 1 →	Get the Tabs menu again and move right one column position
Ctrl-End F7	Clear all remaining tab stops and exit
Alt-F6 Shift-F8 1	Give a Flush Right command to move just past the right margin, then prepare to set a tab
←r. F7	Move to the right margin, set a right-justified tab stop with dot leaders, and exit

←Backspace y	Delete the [A] (Flush Right) code
→	Move past the [Tab Set:] code that produces dot leaders
Ctrl-F10	End the macro definition

DOTLEAD performs the following steps:

1. Insert a copy of the current tab settings, so they can be reinstated at the end of the flush-right material.
2. Move ahead of these settings and clear all tabs that follow the cursor position.
3. Set a right-justified (R) tab stop with dot leaders at the right margin.
4. Return the cursor to its starting position.

Since WordPerfect provides no way to locate the right margin from within the Tabs menu, steps 3 and 4 required some fancy keystroking. After clearing the tabs, I returned to the document and did a Flush Right. This moves the cursor just past the right margin. Then I called up the Tabs menu (WordPerfect places the cursor where it was in the text), moved to the right margin, set my *R-period* tab, and exited. The cursor remained at the right margin, so I then moved ahead of the new [Tab Set:] and deleted Flush Right's hidden code.

Of course, if you know where the right margin is located, you can simplify DOTLEAD quite a bit. After clearing the remaining tabs on the line, enter the right margin's column number (WordPerfect moves there and displays an *L*), type **r** and a period, then exit. The cursor will be just past the [Tab Set:] code, exactly where you want it.

Font Command (Ctrl-F8) — WordPerfect 5.0

5.0 WordPerfect 5.0's Font command lets you specify your base font (the one with which text is printed) and change the size, style, or color of printed text. When you press Ctrl and F8, WordPerfect displays the following menu:

```
1 Size/Position; 2 Appearance; 3 Normal; 4 Base Font; 5 Print Color: 0
```

Size/Position

Pressing 1 for Size/Position brings on a menu of five print sizes and two positions, as follows:

1 Subscpt; 2 Suprscpt; 3 Fine; 4 Small; 5 Large; 6 Vry Large; 7 Ext Large: 0

Choosing any of these options makes WordPerfect insert a hidden starting code ahead of the cursor and an ending code after it. Thus, when you type something, it will have the attribute you selected. For example, if you select *Subscpt* (Subscript), WordPerfect assumes that whatever you type next is to be printed below the line. (It precedes the cursor with a [SUBSCPT] code and follows it with a [subscpt] code.) When you finish typing the affected text, press the → key to get past the hidden ending code.

You can also apply a size/position attribute to existing text, by selecting it in Block mode, then choosing the appropriate attribute.

Appearance

Pressing 2 for Appearance brings on a menu of nine print styles, as follows:

1 Bold; 2 Undrln; 3 Dbl Und; 4 Italc; 5 Outln; 6 Shadw; 7 Sm Cap; 8 Redln; 9 Stkout: 0

Note that the first two styles, Bold and Underline, are also available as separate key commands: F6 and F8, respectively. The next five styles—Double Underline, Italics, Outline, Shadow, and Small Caps—can add an attractive, professional appearance to documents, provided your printer can produce them.

The Redline feature prints a mark (usually a vertical line) beside the text, indicating that it is a proposed addition to the document. Finally, the Strikeout feature overwrites text with hyphens, indicating a proposed deletion; this is a common practice when lawyers or legislators change a legal document.

You can also apply an appearance attribute to existing text, by selecting it in Block mode, then choosing the appropriate attribute.

Normal

When you type 3 to select Normal, WordPerfect turns off all active attributes (Bold, Underline, etc.), and makes the printer produce standard, unstyled text. This option is handy for situations in which you have applied an attribute (or several attributes) to more text than you intended. Simply put the cursor on the first character you want to unstyle and select Normal.

Base Font

When you install WordPerfect, you tell it which fonts you need for your particular printer(s). This option lets you select the *base font*; the one WordPerfect is to use to print regular text. To select the base font, move the highlighting to it, then type **1** for *Select*.

Selecting a base font makes WordPerfect insert a hidden code of the general form [Font:*font-spec*] in your document, where MIfont-spec gives the font's type, size in points, and pitch (characters per inch). A typical example is [Font:Courier 10pt 10 Pitch].

Figure F-1 Print Color submenu

```
Print Color

                        Primary Color Mixture

                        Red    Blue   Green

        1 - Black        0%     0%     0%
        2 - White       100%   100%   100%
        3 - Red          67%    0%     0%
        4 - Green         0%   67%     0%
        5 - Blue          0%    0%    67%
        6 - Yellow       67%   67%     0%
        7 - Purple       67%    0%    67%
        8 - Cyan          0%   67%    67%
        9 - Orange       67%   25%     0%
        A - Gray         50%   50%    50%
        N - Brown        67%   33%     0%
        O - Other

        Current Color    0%     0%     0%

   Selection: 0
```

Print Color

This option lets you select a color for the printer to use (provided, of course, you have a color printer). Typing **5** for *Print Color* brings on the menu shown in Figure F-1. Note that WordPerfect shows how each color is derived from the primary colors red, green, and blue. The percentages here indicate the intensity of each primary color, where *0%* indicates the complete absence of a color and *100%* indicates a color at its maximum intensity. To specify a print color, simply type its number or letter (WordPerfect makes it the "Current Color"), then press F7 (Exit) to return to editing.

Print Color's *Other* selection lets you define a color as some combination of the primary colors red, green, and blue. Here, typing **o** moves the cursor to the Other *Red* column. To specify the percentage of red in your new color, type it (without the percent sign), then press Enter. Do the same thing for the *Green* and *Blue* values, or press Enter to retain 0% and move to the next column. Finally, when the cursor returns to *Selection*, press F7 to leave the menu.

Selecting a print color makes WordPerfect insert a hidden code of the form [Color:*color*] in your document. Or, if you change *Other*, it inserts a code of the form [Color:*%red,%green,%blue*], where the % values are the ones you entered for each color.

Fonts, Printer — WordPerfect 4.1 and 4.2

4.1
4.2

Some dot-matrix printers are designed to produce several different print styles or *fonts*, and you can make WordPerfect use any one of them. To switch fonts, press Ctrl and F8 to give a Print Format command. When the Print Format menu appears, type **1** for Pitch and enter the pitch (characters per inch) value. Then type the font number (a number from 1 to 8) and press Enter to leave the menu. WordPerfect puts a [Font Change] code at the place where you switched fonts.

A daisy wheel printer will stop when it encounters a Font Change code. When this happens, change the print wheel, then press Shift-F7 and 4 to give a *Printer Control* command. When the Printer Control menu appears, type **g** (for go) to resume printing, then Enter to get back to editing.

Footers

— See **Headers and Footers**

Footnote Command (Ctrl-F7) — WordPerfect 4.1 and 4.2

4.1
4.2

WordPerfect lets you add footnotes to any page. Once you have created a footnote, WordPerfect automatically numbers it and "attaches" that number to the text that refers to it. If changes move the reference to a different page, WordPerfect moves the footnote along with it. Similarly, if you delete a footnote reference, WordPerfect deletes its footnote as well.

Endnotes are the same as footnotes, except WordPerfect puts them at the end of the document. You can have both footnotes and endnotes in the same document.

Footnotes do not appear on the screen during regular editing (nor do endnotes), but WordPerfect prints them at the bottom of the page where their references appear. It also prints a line above the footnotes, to set them off from regular text.

Creating Notes

To create a footnote or endnote, move the cursor to where you want the note number inserted, then press Ctrl and F7 to give a Footnote command. When this menu appears:

```
1 Create; 2 Edit; 3 New #; 4 Options; 5 Create Endnote; 6 Edit Endnote: 0
```

type **1** to create a footnote or **5** to create an endnote. WordPerfect shows a blank screen that looks like the one you use to create a header or footer. It has a number at the top—the reference number WordPerfect has assigned to this note—and **Press EXIT when done** at the bottom. Enter the text for your note, then press the F7 (Exit) key to return to the regular text. Now WordPerfect has put the reference number at the place where you pressed Ctrl-F7.

For example, suppose you are writing a term paper on "Alaskan Explorers" that includes the sentence

Their journey took them through the Shelikov Strait.

and you want "Shelikov Strait" to refer to the footnote

> A strait 30 miles wide between the Alaskan Peninsula and the Kodiak and Afognak Islands.

To put this footnote at the bottom of the page, type the reference sentence in the text, then press Ctrl-F7 and type **1** for *Create*. When the blank screen appears, enter the footnote text and press F7. When you print the term paper, the reference sentence will appear in the text in this form:

> Their journey took them through the Shelikov Strait.[1]

and the footnote will appear at the bottom of the page in this form:

---

[1] A strait 30 miles wide between the Alaskan Peninsula and the Kodiak and Afognak Islands.

(Of course, the superscript "1" here assumes that this is the first footnote in the term paper. If other footnotes precede it, the reference number will be higher.)

Editing Notes

You can edit a note from anywhere in your document. To begin, press Ctrl-F7 to obtain the Footnote menu, then type **2** for a footnote or **6** for an endnote. WordPerfect displays **Ftn #?** or **Endn #?**, and a number. If this is the number of the note you want to edit, press Enter; otherwise, type the correct number, then press Enter. When WordPerfect displays the note, make your changes, then press F7 to get back to editing.

Deleting Notes

To delete a note, put the cursor on its reference number in the text and press Del. When WordPerfect asks **Delete [Note]? (Y/N) N**, type **y**. Deleting the number also deletes the note it refers to. As with regular text, you can undelete a note by pressing F1 (Cancel) and then typing **1** for *Restore*.

Footnote Command (Ctrl-F7) — WordPerfect 5.0

5.0 WordPerfect lets you add footnotes to any page. Once you have created a footnote, WordPerfect automatically numbers it and "attaches" that number to the text that refers to it. If changes move the reference to a different page, WordPerfect moves the footnote along with it. Similarly, if you delete a footnote reference, WordPerfect deletes its footnote as well.

Endnotes are the same as footnotes, except WordPerfect puts them at the end of the document or wherever else you specify. You can have both footnotes and endnotes in the same document.

Footnotes do not appear on the screen during regular editing (nor do endnotes), but WordPerfect prints them at the bottom of the page where their references appear. It also prints a line above the footnotes, to set them off from regular text.

Creating Notes

To create a footnote or endnote, move the cursor to where you want the note number inserted, then press Ctrl and F7 to give a Footnote command. When this menu appears:

```
1 Footnote; 2 Endnote; 3 Endnote Placement: 0
```

type **1** to create a footnote or **2** to create an endnote. Then, when the following submenu appears:

```
1 Create; 2 Edit; 3 New Number; 4 Options: 0
```

type **1** to select *Create*.

WordPerfect shows a blank screen that has a number at the top—the reference number WordPerfect has assigned to this note—and **Press EXIT when done** at the bottom. Enter the note, then press the F7 (Exit) key to return to the regular text. Now WordPerfect has put the reference number at the place where you pressed Ctrl-F7.

For example, suppose you are writing a term paper on "Alaskan Explorers" that includes the sentence

Their journey took them through the Shelikov Strait.

and you want "Shelikov Strait" to refer to the footnote

A strait 30 miles wide between the Alaskan Peninsula and the Kodiak and Afognak Islands.

To put this footnote at the bottom of the page, type the reference sentence in the text, then press Ctrl-F7, type **1** for *Footnote*, and **1** for *Create*. When the blank screen appears, enter the footnote text and press F7. When you print the term paper, the reference sentence will appear in the text in this form:

Their journey took them through the Shelikov Strait.[1]

and the footnote will appear at the bottom of the page in this form:

[1]A strait 30 miles wide between the Alaskan Peninsula and the Kodiak and Afognak Islands.

(Of course, the superscript "1" here assumes that this is the first footnote in the term paper. If other footnotes precede it, the reference number will be higher.)

Editing Notes

You can edit a note from anywhere in your document. To begin, press Ctrl-F7 to obtain the Footnote/Endnote menu, type **1** for a footnote or **2** for an endnote, then type **2** for *Edit*. WordPerfect displays **Footnote number?** or **Endnote number?**, and a number. If this is the number of the note you want to edit, press Enter; otherwise, type the correct number, then press Enter. When the note appears, make your changes, then press F7 to get back to editing.

Deleting Notes

To delete a note, put the cursor on its reference number in the text and press Del. When WordPerfect asks if you really want to delete this note, type **y**. Deleting the number also deletes the note it refers to (and renumbers the rest of the notes in the document). As with regular text, you can undelete a note by pressing F1 (Cancel) and typing **1** for *Restore*.

Renumbering Notes

WordPerfect always assumes you want footnotes and endnotes numbered sequentially, starting with *1*. However, if your document consists of several disk files, or you want to restart the numbering with each new chapter in a book, you will want to assign a number of your choice to a note. To do this, press Ctrl-F7 to obtain the Footnote/Endnote menu, type **1** for *Footnote* or **2** for *Endnote*, then type **3** to select *New Number*. When WordPerfect displays **Footnote number?** or **Endnote number?**, type the number you want the next note to have, then press Enter.

Generating Endnotes

WordPerfect always assumes that you want endnotes printed at the end of your document. However, if you're writing a book that consists of several chapters, you may want the corresponding set of endnotes to be printed at the end of each chapter.

To tell WordPerfect where to print endnotes, move the cursor there and press Ctrl-F7 to give a Footnote command, then type **3** to select *Endnote Placement*. When WordPerfect asks

```
Restart endnote numbering? (Y/N) Yes
```

type **y** to restart the numbering for subsequent endnotes or type **n** to continue the current endnote numbering sequence.

Either way, a hidden [Endnote Placement] code is inserted in your document. This marks the place where WordPerfect should print the endnotes that have been created between that code and the preceding one—or to the beginning of the document, if there is no preceding code. Along with the [Endnote Placement] code, WordPerfect displays a box that contains:

```
Endnote Placement
It is not known how much space endnotes will occupy
here.
Generate to determine.
```

This indicates that WordPerfect has recorded your endnotes, but has not yet combined them, and therefore doesn't know how much space to reserve for them. To reserve the space, you must *generate* the endnote list, as follows:

1. Press Alt and F5 to give a *Mark Text* command.
2. When the Mark Text menu appears, type 6 for *Generate*.
3. When the Generate submenu appears, type **5** for *Generate tables, indexes, automatic references, etc*. WordPerfect gives you the chance to change your mind. It displays

> **E**xisting tables, lists, and indexes will be replaced.
> Continue (Y/N)? Yes

4. Type y to continue. WordPerfect shows **Generation in progress**, then displays **Endnote Placement** in the box.

The box now occupies the number of lines your endnotes require. You can see just how many lines that is by moving the cursor up or down past the box; the *Ln* value on the status line will decrease or increase by the box's height.

Note Options

WordPerfect makes some assumptions about how you want footnotes and endnotes printed. This includes the spacing within and between notes, the number of lines to keep together, and the numbering style. If these assumptions aren't what you want, you can change them by selecting *Options* from the Footnote or Endnote submenu.

Figure F-2 shows the Footnote Options submenu. Note that WordPerfect assumes (in option 1) you want to single-space the footnotes and leave 0.16 inches—or one line, on a page that has six lines per inch—between them. It also assumes (in option 2) you want to keep 0.5 inches—or three lines—together when a note needs to be split between two pages.

In particular, you may want to change option 5, Footnote Numbering Method, to make WordPerfect assign *Letters* rather than *Numbers* to your footnotes. You can also make it use up to five different *Characters*. After it has used all the characters you specified, it prints two repetitions of them, then three repetitions, and so on.

Figure F-3 shows the similar, but shorter, Endnote Options submenu.

Force Odd/Even Page — WordPerfect 5.0

5.0 The Force Odd/Even Page option on the Format (Shift-F8) command's *Page* menu forces the current page to have an odd or even number. This is especially handy for ensuring that the first page of each chapter of a book or report is odd-numbered.

```
Footnote Options

    1 - Spacing Within Footnotes              1
                Between Footnotes             0.16"

    2 - Amount of Note to Keep Together       0.5"

    3 - Style for Number in Text              [SUPRSCPT][Note Num][su

    4 - Style for Number in Note              [SUPRSCPT][Note

    5 - Footnote Numbering Method             Numbers

    6 - Start Footnote Numbers Each Page      No

    7 - Line Separating Text and Footnotes    2-inch Line

    8 - Print Continued Message               No

    9 - Footnotes at Bottom of Page           Yes
```

Figure F-2. Footnote Options submenu.

```
Endnote Options

    1 - Spacing Within Endnotes               1
                Between Endnotes              0.16"

    2 - Amount of Endnote to Keep Together    0.5"

    3 - Style for Number in Text              [SUPRSCPT][Note Num][su

    4 - Style for Number in Note              [Note Num]

    5 - Endnote Numbering Method              Numbers
```

Figure F-3. Endnote Options submenu.

To specify odd or even numbering, move the cursor to the top of the page you want to renumber and do the following:

1. Press Shift and F8 to give a Format command.
2. When the Format menu appears, type **2** to select *Page*.
3. When the Page Format menu appears, type **2** to select *Force Odd/Even Page*.
4. Type **1** to make this page odd-numbered or **2** to make it even-numbered.
5. Press F7 (Exit) to return to editing.

Note that this option only takes effect if necessary. For example, if you specify an odd number for page 3 (which is already odd), WordPerfect ignores the Force command. However, specifying an odd number on an even-numbered page (or vice-versa) makes WordPerfect increase the page number. For example, forcing page 4 to an odd numbered page makes WordPerfect renumber it as 5.

Foreign Characters

— See **Special Characters**

Formatting Disks

— See **DOS Operations**

Form Letters

There are two ways to generate form letters with WordPerfect. If you're sending the letter to a mailing list, you can combine or *merge* the disk file that contains the letter with another file that contains the names and addresses. Otherwise, if you aren't working from a mailing list, or you want to send the form letter to one or more individuals, you can prepare the letter as a macro. Here, you can use WordPerfect's *pause* (Ctrl-PgUp) command to mark places where the macro should allow you to enter personalized data, such as a name or number.

Creating Form Letters from Mailing Lists

Sometimes you must send the same letter (such as a request for payment, notice of credit terms, order acknowledgment, or report on account status) to an entire list of recipients. Direct mail solicitors often use personalized letters that have the recipient's name and address in various places. The following is typical of the kind of letters that fill our mailboxes and wastebaskets:

```
Dear Mr. Brown:

Would you like the name James C. Brown to be associated
with success? Yes, Mr. Brown, you can be a dynamic,
successful person if you attend our seminar.
```

With WordPerfect, creating this kind of personalized form letter takes three steps:

1. Prepare a generalized version of the letter in which you name places or fields that will vary (e.g., the recipient's name, address, account number, outstanding balance, etc.)
2. Prepare a data file containing the items WordPerfect must insert into the multiple copies.
3. Use a *Merge* command to combine the form with the data and print the letters.

The WordPerfect manual refers to the generalized letter as the *primary file* and to the data file as a *secondary merge file*.

I will first discuss the simple situation in which WordPerfect replaces fields in the primary file with items from the secondary merge file on a one-for-one basis. I will then describe WordPerfect's features for creating more elaborate form letters. These include customizing letters from the keyboard and the use of macros to automate merge operations.

As an example of a simple form letter, let us produce an invitation to a company's anniversary party. All that's needed here is to insert an individual address, a salutation, and a single reference to the recipient's affiliation. I will now describe the procedures for creating a secondary merge file, entering the primary file, merging the files, and printing the copies.

Contents of a Secondary Merge File

A secondary merge file is a data document containing the entries to be merged into the generalized primary document to produce the copies. Within a secondary merge file, each entry (e.g., an individual's name and address) is called a *record*. Records are separated by "Merge E" codes, which you produce by pressing Shift-F9 (WordPerfect 4.1 and 4.2) or pressing Shift-F9 and typing **e** (WordPerfect 5.0). WordPerfect shows ^E on the screen and moves the cursor to the next line.

Each record is comprised of *fields*. Fields are separated by "Merge R" codes, which you produce by pressing F9. WordPerfect shows ^R and moves the cursor to the next line. Fields are numbered from top to bottom; thus, *1* is the field that starts on the first line.

Fields in secondary merge files can contain as many lines as you want. For example, to create an address list of business associates, you may want to reserve three lines for the "company name" field. That way, you can construct records that require only a company name (one line), a company name and division name (two lines), or a company, division, and department name (three lines). To start a new line within a field, press Enter.

You can put any number of fields in a record, but any given field must always contain the same type of information or nothing at all. For example, suppose you are creating a secondary merge file that contains the names and addresses of both your friends and business associates. If field 2 is set aside for a company name, you would enter the name and ^R for business associates, but enter only ^R for friends.

Figure F-4 shows the secondary merge file for the invitation. Each entry consists of five fields: name, company, street, city, and first name. Prepare this file just as you would any document, then save it under the name *guests.sf*, where *sf* stands for secondary file. Use the Exit (F7) command to perform the save, so that you end up with a blank screen on which to create the primary file.

Creating a Primary File

Now you may enter the generalized letter as shown in Figure F-5. Note that the return address, the closing, and the writer's name and title are at the center of the page. Before entering them, you should

```
Mr. Phillip T. Grange^R
Newton Plastics Corporation^R
1865 Industrial Way^R
Newton, FL 32786^R
Phil^R
^E
Mrs. Viola Wilson^R
Wilson and Associates, Inc.^R
4399 Beach St.^R
Ocala, FL 32787^R
Vi^R
^E
```

Figure F-4 Secondary merge file for a simple form letter.

set a tab at the center, position 42. With WordPerfect 4.1 or 4.2, use the Line Format (Shift-F8) command to set the tab; with WordPerfect 5.0; use the *Line* option of the Format (Shift-F8) command.

The symbols ^F1^ through ^F5^ tell WordPerfect which data field to insert when merging letters. They are numbered according to the order in which fields occur in the secondary merge file; ^F1^ specifies the name field, ^F2^ specifies the company field, and so on. To produce them, do the following:

1. Press Alt-F9 (WordPerfect 4.1 or 4.2) or Shift-F9 (WordPerfect 5.0) to give a *Merge Codes* command. WordPerfect shows the following list:

   ^C; ^D; ^F; ^G; ^N; ^O; ^P; ^Q; ^S; ^T; ^U; ^V:

2. Type **f** to select ^F. WordPerfect shows "Field Number?" at the bottom.
3. Type the number of the field you want to insert (e.g., type **1** for the name field or **2** for the company field), then press Enter. WordPerfect inserts a symbol of the form ^F*n*^, where *n* is the field number.

When you finish entering the letter, save it under the name *invite.pf* (where *pf* stands for primary file). As with the secondary file, use Exit (F7) to perform the save, so you end up with a blank screen.

Merging Form Letters

To produce the personalized invitations (that is, to *merge* the primary and secondary files), proceed as follows:

```
                                    Gutenberg Printing, Inc.
                                    1243 Flamingo Lane
                                    Newton, FL 32786
                                    September 24, 1988

^F1^
^F2^
^F3^
^F4^

Dear ^F5^:

This year is Gutenberg Printing's fifth anniversary in business.
To mark the occasion, we are hosting a cocktail party on
Wednesday, October 5, from 4:30 to 7:00 PM at the Newton Inn.  As
one of our most valued customers and friends at ^F2^, we would be
honored by your presence.  I hope to see you there!

                    Best wishes,


                    James A. Anderson
                    President
```

Figure F-5. Simple form letter before merging.

1. Press Ctrl-F9 to give a *Merge/Sort* command.
2. When the following menu appears:

    1 Merge; **2** Sort; **3** Sorting Sequences: **0**

    type **1** to select Merge.

3. Enter **invite.pf** for "Primary file:" and **guests.sf** for "Secondary file:".

WordPerfect shows *Merging* while it does the merge. When it finishes, the completed invitations appear, one per page, and the cursor is at the end of the last page.

Figure F-6 shows the completed letter to Phillip Grange. Note that WordPerfect has replaced all the ^Fn^ symbols with specific fields from the secondary file.

Printing Form Letters

Since WordPerfect has produced the form letters as a regular document, press Shift-F7 to do a Print command and type **1** to select *Full Text* (called *Full Document* in WordPerfect 5.0). Of course, you can also save the letters on disk (as, say, *invite.ltr*), and print them later.

Merging to the Printer

Sometimes you may want WordPerfect to send completed form letters to the printer instead of the screen. To make it do this, put a ^T code at the end of your primary file, by giving a Merge Codes command (Alt-F9 in WordPerfect 4.1 and 4.2, Shift-F9 in WordPerfect 5.0) and typing **t**.

The ^T tells WordPerfect to send merged text up to that point. You should know, however, that merging to the printer is not only very slow, but ties up your computer; you can't do other work until merging has finished.

To print multiple copies of the form letters, do a Print command before you do the merge. **With WordPerfect 4.1 or 4.2,** choose Printer Control (4); when the Printer Control menu appears, choose Select Print Options (1), then change Number of Copies to what you want. **With WordPerfect 5.0,** choose Number of Copies and change it to what you want.

```
                              Gutenberg Printing, Inc.
                              1243 Flamingo Lane
                              Newton, FL 32786
                              September 24, 1988

Mr. Phillip T. Grange
Newton Plastics Corporation
1865 Industrial Way
Newton, FL 32786

Dear Phil:

This year is Gutenberg Printing's fifth anniversary in business.
To mark the occasion, we are hosting a cocktail party on
Wednesday, October 5, from 4:30 to 7:00 PM at the Newton Inn.  As
one of our most valued customers and friends at Newton Plastics
Corporation, we would be honored by your presence.  I hope to see
you there!

                              Best wishes,



                              James A. Anderson
                              President
```

Figure F-6 Form letter after merging.

Canceling a Merge Operation

Suppose that while WordPerfect is doing a merge operation you spot a mistake in the form letter, or you suddenly realize you're merging with the wrong secondary file. When that happens, you will want to stop merging immediately. To cancel a merge operation, press the F1 (Cancel) key. The *Merging* message disappears and WordPerfect returns to regular editing mode.

Printing Envelopes

You can also make WordPerfect address envelopes. Here, the primary file contains only your return address (unless you have preprinted envelopes) and ^Fn^ symbols for the recipient's name, company, street address, and city. Figure F-7 shows a typical primary file for use on standard 4-1/8-inch by 9-1/2-inch business-size envelopes.

I have started the recipient's fields at line 12 and column 45, so they print 2 inches from the top and 4-1/2 inches from the left edge. (You may want different values.) Furthermore, printing envelopes also requires you to use your printer in "hand-fed" mode, so that it pauses between envelopes.

Customizing Form Letters from the Keyboard

WordPerfect lets you add information to a form letter from the keyboard. You can use this feature to insert specific dates, times, places, subjects, event names, sponsors, numbers, or messages to a generalized letter.

WordPerfect provides this capability through the merge code ^C. The ^C code makes it stop and wait for you to enter text (type the text, then press F9). WordPerfect can also display a prompt on the

Figure F-7. Primary file for printing envelopes

```
Susan Briggs
Universal Bridge Co.
12366 West 10th Street
Bridge City, PA  16589
```

status line when it needs keyboard information. To make it do this, precede ^C with the sequence ^O*message*^O.

For example, say you want to notify all sales representatives of their last quarter's total and current quarter's goal for a particular item. Figure F-8 shows the standard letter. Note that we use ^F1^, ^F2^, and ^F3^ for the representative's name, street address, and city, and ^O*prompt*^O^C for last quarter's sales and this quarter's goals. Note also the ^T^N^P^P at the end, to send the copies directly to the printer.

When you merge this memorandum, WordPerfect obtains the first name and address from the secondary file and displays the memorandum. It puts the cursor at the end of the first sentence (where you entered ^OSales^O^C) and shows the prompt *Sales* at the bottom of the screen. Type the sales amount for the first representative, then press F9. Type the goal amount and press F9 again when the prompt *Goal* appears. WordPerfect will now print the first memorandum, then display the second one. It repeats this procedure for each record in the secondary file.

Using Macros With Merge Operations

You can also use macros to automate merge operations. One way is to set up a macro that starts the merge and supplies the name of the primary file and perhaps the secondary file.

Figure F-8. Sales memorandum using keyboard insertions.

```
From: Richard Gordon, National Sales Manager
To:  ^F1^
     ^F2^
     ^F3^

Subject: Sales for third quarter 1988.

   According to our records, your sales for the third quarter of
1988 were ^OSales^O^C.  Your goal for the current quarter is
^OGoal^O^C.  If either of these do not concur with your records,
please notify me.  These numbers will be used to calculate
commissions and determine progress toward overall sales goals.
Please acknowledge receipt of this notification and report any
discrepancies before the end of the current quarter.
^T^N^P^P
```

For example, suppose you have a form letter in a primary file called *FORM* (there is no secondary file, you insert specifics from the keyboard). To save yourself the bother of doing a Merge command each time, you could assign a merge-starting macro to the Alt-F key combination. To define the *ALTF* macro, you would do the following:

1. Press Ctrl-F9 to do a Merge/Sort.
2. Type **1** to select Merge.
3. When "Primary file:" appears, enter **form**.
4. When "Secondary file:" appears, press Enter (because there is no secondary file). WordPerfect begins merging.
5. Press Shift-F9 (WordPerfect 4.1 or 4.2) or press Shift-F9 and type **e** (WordPerfect 5.0) to end the merge and save the macro.

You can also make WordPerfect start a macro when it finishes merging. This is handy for beginning a second merge operation or for sending the merged text to the printer. To make WordPerfect proceed from merging to a macro, enter a command of the form ^G*macro name*^G at the end of your primary file.

Using Multiple Primary Files

The merge code sequence ^P*filename*^P makes WordPerfect retrieve a file from the disk and use it as a new primary file. This is especially useful for building form letters from files that contain various kinds of "boilerplate" text. It also has the advantage that by changing only one file, you automatically change all the merge files that use it.

The similar sequence ^P^C^P lets the user enter the name of the file to be retrieved during the merge operation. The WordPerfect manual gives an example that uses these commands to "assemble" a contract.

Form Letter Prepared as a Macro

Suppose you want to notify a customer that your company is canceling credit due to unpaid bills. Figure F-9 shows the general form of a letter you could use. (Key commands in this letter are designed for WordPerfect 4.1 and 4.2; they would be slightly different for WordPerfect 5.0.) The line **Shift-F5 3** below the return address shows the keystrokes you must enter to make WordPerfect insert the current date. The underlined material in brackets indicates places where WordPerfect should allow you to insert personalized items.

To define this letter as a macro, do the following:

1. Start a new document. When the blank first page appears, delete the automatic tabs and set a new tab at the center (column 42).
2. Press Ctrl-F10 to start defining a macro.
3. When WordPerfect shows the prompt *Define Macro:*, enter **nocredit**.
4. Enter the return address shown in Figure F-9. On the line below it, press Tab to reach the center, then press Shift-F5 for *Date*. When the Date menu appears, type **3** for *Insert Function* and press Enter twice to reach the line where the customer's address belongs.
5. Press Ctrl-PgUp to insert a pause command for the customer's name. When the computer beeps, press Enter twice to continue, then press Enter once more to reach the company name line.
6. Enter pause commands for the company's name, street address, and city, then move the cursor to the salutation line.
7. Enter the start of the salutation (**Dear**) and insert a pause command for the name.
8. [Complete the letter, inserting two more pause commands in the first sentence—one after "close of business on " and the other at the end of the sentence.
9. Press Ctrl-F10 to save the macro on disk.
10. Clear the screen by doing an Exit operation.

Let's use the *nocredit* macro to produce a credit cancellation letter to Harold "Bug" Rogers of Pest-B-Gone, Inc. As of October 11, 1988, Pest-B-Gone has accumulated $1287.67 in unpaid invoices. With the screen now blank, proceed as follows:

1. Press Alt-F10 to start a macro.
2. When WordPerfect shows the *Macro:* prompt at the bottom of the screen, enter **nocredit**. WordPerfect produces the return address and date, then beeps the computer.
3. Respond to the beep by entering **Mr. Harold "Bug" Rogers**.
4. Respond to the next three beeps by entering these lines:

```
Pest-B-Gone, Inc.
2786 Mayflower St.
San Diego, CA 92121
```

Figure F-8. Sales memorandum using keyboard insertions.

```
                          211 Washington Street
                          San Diego, CA 92121
                          Shift-F5 3

[Customer's name and address]

Dear [Name]:

As of the close of business on [Date], your company has
outstanding invoices over 30 days old totaling [Amount].  We must
request immediate payment of these invoices or we will be forced
to add a 1 1/2% monthly service charge.

Until we receive payment, we cannot extend credit to your company
or process further orders.  Please remit this payment to my
attention as soon as possible.

                          Sincerely yours,



                          Marie F. Gerard
                          Assistant Credit Manager
```

Figure F-9. Generalized letter showing insertion points

5. When the computer beeps after "Dear " in the salutation, enter Mr. Rogers.
6. When it beeps after "close of business on ", enter October 11, 1988.
7. When it beeps after "totaling ", enter $1286.67.

When WordPerfect finishes, print the letter.

Format Command (Shift-F8) — WordPerfect 5.0

5.0 WordPerfect comes preset to arrange documents using a format that's acceptable to most people. For example, it sets up each document for single-spaced, justified text and tab stops every half-inch. If these settings are not what you want, you can change them using the Format (Shift-F8) command.

As Figure F-10 shows, when you press Shift and F8, WordPerfect displays a menu that has four options: *Line* (1), *Page* (2), *Document* (3), and *Other* (4). Choosing one of these options brings on a submenu that shows the current setting for each of the listed parameters. Each option is covered as a separate entry elsewhere in this book.

Forms

You can use WordPerfect to help fill out invoices and other preprinted forms, by defining a *macro* that does the basic work of accepting the operator's keystrokes and moving the cursor between fields. (If you're unfamiliar with macros, see the various **Macros** entries in this book.) This macro should take the operator from one field to the next, in the proper sequence. Thus, the macro must have movement commands that tell WordPerfect where each field is located (which line it's on, which tab position it's at) and which field is to be processed next.

Contents of a Form-Processing Macro

In general, a macro that processes forms must do some or all of the following tasks:

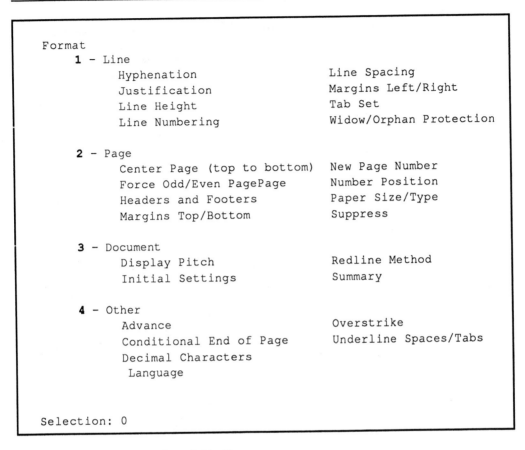

Figure F-10 WordPerfect 5.0's Format menu.

- Change tab settings when the fields on a line are in a different location from those on the previous line; see **Tabs** for information on changing the tab settings.
- Accept the number or text that the operator enters in a field. When defining a macro, press Ctrl-PgUp wherever you want WordPerfect to pause for a keyboard insertion.
- Move the cursor to the next line to be processed. If that's the line below the current one, your macro should include the keystroke sequence

    ↓ Home ← Tab

to move down, then to the beginning of the line and, finally, to the first tab stop.

Otherwise, if the next line to be processed is somewhere else on the form, you need the services of WordPerfect's *Adv Ln* (Advance to Line) option. Adv Ln moves the cursor to whatever line you specify, regardless of whether it's above or below the current line. See the **Advance** entry for details.

- Perform any required math operations, such as adding columns of numbers or calculating sales tax, shipping charges, or commissions. These topics are covered under **Mathematical Operations**.

Function Keys (F1 - F10)

The dark keys at the far left-hand side of the keyboard are *function keys* labeled F1 through F10. With WordPerfect, you use these keys to give the computer special commands such as print, indent, or save a document on disk. The function keys are multipurpose command keys in that they do different things depending on whether you press them alone or at the same time as Alt, Shift, or Ctrl. For example, pressing F6 gives WordPerfect a command, while pressing Shift and F6 together gives it a *Center* command.

The keyboard template that comes with WordPerfect summarizes these combinations. It shows Ctrl commands in red, Shift commands in green, Alt commands in blue, and single-key commands in black.

Go To Command (Ctrl-Home)

You can use the Ctrl and Home key combination to move the cursor within your document. When the **Go to** prompt appears, you may

- Type a character to move the cursor to it.
- Type a page number to move the cursor there.
- Press ↑ or ↓ to move the cursor to the top or bottom of the current page.

When WordPerfect is in Block mode, pressing Ctrl-Home, then Alt-F4, moves the cursor to the beginning of the block and removes the highlighting, but keeps **Block on**.

If you have just completed a Block operation (say, you emboldened it), you can rehighlight the block for another operation by pressing Alt-F4 (Block), then pressing Ctrl-Home *twice*.

Backtracking With the Go To Command

If you press Ctrl-Home *twice* after any of the following commands, WordPerfect moves the cursor to its original position:

Esc
Go To (Ctrl-Home)
Home, Home, and an arrow key
PgUp or PgDn
Replace (Alt-F2)
Search Forward (F2) or Backward (Shift-F2)

Go to DOS

—See **Shell Command**

Graphics Command (Alt-F9) — WordPerfect 5.0

5.0 In some documents you may want to include text from a disk file or graphic images (pictures or drawings) that were created using a commercial drawing program. WordPerfect 5.0's Graphics feature lets you do that. That is, it lets you set up boxes that have the size and position you want. Once a box is in place, WordPerfect will surround it with regular text, giving your document the professional look one finds in newspapers and books. The Graphics feature also lets you draw horizontal or vertical lines on a page; see **Lines, Drawing** for details.

Creating a Graphics Box

To create a graphics box, do the following:

1. Press Alt and F9 to give a Graphics command. WordPerfect displays the following menu:

    ```
    1 Figure; 2 Table; 3 Text Box; 4 User-defined Box; 5 Line: 0
    ```

2. Select the *type* of box you want (details are upcoming).
3. [When the box's menu appears, type **1** to select *Create*.
4. Specify the size and position of the box, and which file you want to retrieve into it, by filling out a *Definition* form.

5. Press F7 (Exit) to return to your document.

Once you have created a graphics box, WordPerfect draws an outline of it (along with its type and number) as you move down the page it's on. Furthermore, WordPerfect arranges the text on that page so that it "wraps" around the box.

Box Types

WordPerfect's Graphics menu lets you create four types of boxes, called *Figure, Table, Text,* and *User-defined.* These names refer to the definition form that WordPerfect assigns to the box, not to its contents.

Figure boxes are intended to hold graphic images and charts. Similarly, Table boxes are intended for tables of numbers and other tabular data, while Text boxes are intended for short articles (or "sidebars") that relate to the main text. User-defined boxes are useful for holding information that doesn't fit in any of the other categories.

Defining Boxes

When you choose *Create* from a box menu, WordPerfect displays the Definition form for that type. Figure G-1 shows the Definition form for a Figure box. The forms for the other three boxes have the same entries.

Taking the entries one by one:

- *Filename* is a blank field in which you can enter the name of a disk file (graphics or text) that is to be retrieved into the box. WordPerfect marks text filenames with *(Text)* and graphic images with *(Graphic).* You can also leave the field blank, and enter text into the box manually.

- *Caption* provides a place to enter a caption for the box. When you choose this field, WordPerfect inserts the box number; you type the text that accompanies that number.

- *Type* determines whether the box stays with the text that surrounds it (Paragraph type), stays at a specified position on the page (Page type), or is treated as part of the text on a line (Character type).

- *Vertical Position* specifies the box's vertical orientation.

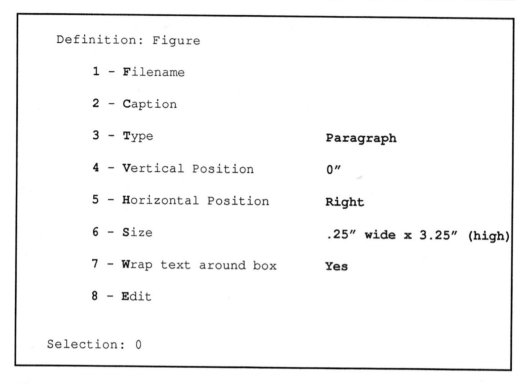

Figure G-1 Figure box definition form.

For a *Paragraph* type box, the Vertical Position is the distance of the cursor from the beginning of the current paragraph. For example, if you create a box on the first line of a paragraph, WordPerfect will set Vertical Position to 0". On a standard page that has six lines per inch, each line occupies about 0.16 inches.

A *Page* type box can occupy the full page, be aligned with the top (first line of text on the page) or bottom (above any footers or footnotes) of the page, be centered top-to-bottom on the page, or start some set position from the top edge of the page.

A *Character* type box can be positioned so that the rest of the text on the line is even with the top, middle, or bottom of the box.

•*Horizontal Position* specifies where the box is placed across the page.

A *Paragraph* type box can be aligned with the left or right margin, centered between the margins, or occupy the space between them.

With a *Character* type box, Horizontal Position is unused because WordPerfect always puts the box after the character to its left.
- *Size* gives the width and height of the box. There are three Size options: Set Width, Set Height, and Set Both Width and Height. If the box contains text, you can only Set Width (to let WordPerfect calculate the height based on the line count) or Set Both Width and Height.
- *Wrap Text Around Box* should usually be Yes. If you set it to No, WordPerfect will extend the text from margin to margin, and disregard the box.
- *Edit* lets you edit the text in a box (or enter text in an empty box) or rotate, scale, and move the image in a box.

Editing Options for Graphic Images

When you choose *Edit* for a box definition that contains a graphic image, WordPerfect draws the box and image on the screen and shows this menu at the bottom:

```
1 Move; 2 Scale; 3 Rotate; 4 Switch: 0        (%10)
```

and this line at the top:

```
Arrow keys = Move; PgUp/Dn = Scale; +/- = Rotate; Ins = % change
```

Here is what the menu options do:

- *Move* lets you move the image horizontally and vertically in the box, by entering values in response to its *Horizontal =* and *Vertical =* prompts. Positive values move the figure up or to the right; negative values move it down or to the left.
  You can also press the arrow keys to move the image by the percentage shown in the lower right-hand corner.
- *Scale* lets you enter a scale factor that expands or contracts the image in the horizontal (*Scale X:*) or vertical (*Scale Y:*) direction. For example, *Scale X: 50* decreases the width of the image by 50 percent.
  You can also press PgUp or PgDn to expand or contract the entire image by the percentage shown in the lower right-hand corner.
- Choosing *Rotate* displays the prompt **Enter # of degrees (0-360):**, which lets you rotate the image by a specified number of degrees from its original position (*not* its current position). The second

prompt, **Mirror image (Y/N)?**, lets you indicate whether to rotate clockwise (**y**) or counter-clockwise (**n**).

You can also press + or - on the numeric keypad to rotate the image clockwise or counter-clockwise by the percentage shown in the lower right-hand corner. Here, 1% = 36 degrees, 5% = 18 degrees, 10% = 36 degrees, and 25% = 90 degrees.

- If the image is a bitmap image (rather than a line drawing), *Switch* displays the opposite (or complementary) color of each dot. For example, black on white becomes white on black.

The notation *Ins = % change* at the top of the screen signifies that pressing the Ins key advances the number at the bottom right corner through the sequence 1%, 5%, 10%, and 25%.

Viewing Boxes

When you create a box in a document, WordPerfect displays its outline, but not its contents or caption. To see how the box will look when you print the page, you must look at the page using WordPerfect's *View* feature.

View is an option in the Print menu, so begin by pressing Shift and F7 to give a Print command (see that entry). When the menu appears, type **6** to select *View Document*. WordPerfect clears the screen and draws a miniaturized version of the page. At the bottom, it displays the following menu:

```
1 100%; 2 200%; 3 Full Page; 4 Facing Pages: 3
```

Currently the screen shows how the page looks under the *Full Page* option (note that 3 is selected). To see how the page will look in its true, printed size, select *100%*; to see it double the true size, select *200%*. (Neither view can display the entire page, but you can use the arrow keys to move from one part to another.) On any page but the first one, you can also select *Facing Pages*, to obtain a "full page" size view of that page and the one that faces it. That is, you can view pages 2 and 3, 4 and 5, and so on. When you finish looking at your handiwork, press F7 (Exit) to return to your document.

Editing Boxes

You can edit a box from anywhere in a document. Simply press Alt-F9 to give a Graphics command, select the type of box to be edited, type **2** to choose *Edit* from the menu, and enter the number of the box. When the Definition form appears, change the options you want and press F7 (Exit) to return to your document.

Renumbering Boxes

WordPerfect numbers boxes consecutively, starting with 1. However, if your document is divided among several disk files, you may want to correct the numbering in files that follow the first one. To change box numbering, move the cursor ahead of the first box that is to be renumbered and press Alt-F9 to give a Graphics command. When the Graphics menu appears, select the type of box you want to renumber, type **3** to select *New Number*, then enter a number. From there on, WordPerfect renumbers boxes of the type you selected.

Box Options

WordPerfect makes assumptions about the borders, spacing, caption style, and other characteristics of boxes you create. If these assumptions don't suit you, you can change them by modifying the box type's *Options* list.

To change the options for a certain type of box, move the cursor ahead of the first box to be changed and press Alt-F9 to give a Graphics command. When the Graphics menu appears, select the box type, then press **4** for *Options*. When the Options list appears, make the changes you want, then press F7 (Exit) to return to your document.

Figure G-2 shows the Options list for *Figure* boxes. The lists for other box types look the same, but some of the initial settings differ. (For example, Table and Text boxes have no borders on the left or right, but have Thick—rather than Single—borders on the top and bottom. User-Defined boxes have no borders at all, initially.)

Here's what the entries in the Options list do:

1. *Border Style* specifies the kind of line WordPerfect is to use in drawing the four edges of the box. As you proceed through the edge options, WordPerfect displays the border style choices with this menu:

   1 None; **2** Single; **3** Double; **4** Dashed; **5** Dotted; **6** Thick; **7** Extra Thick: **0**

138 Graphics Command (Alt-F9) — WordPerfect 5.0

```
Options:   Figure

     1 - Border Style
            Left                            Single
            Right                           Single
            Top                             Single
            Bottom                          Single
     2 - Outside Border Space
            Left                            0.16"
            Right                           0.16"
            Top                             0.16"
            Bottom                          0.16"
     3 - Inside Border Space
            Left                            0"
            Right                           0"
            Top                             0"
            Bottom                          0"
     4 - First Level Numbering Method       Numbers
     5 - Second Level Numbering Method      Off
     6 - Caption Number Style               [BOLD]Figure 1[bold]
     7 - Position of Caption                Below box, Outside borders
     8 - Minimum Offset from Paragraph      0"
     9 - Gray Shading (% of black)          0%

Selection: 0
```

Figure G-2. Figure box Options list.

1. *Border Style* specifies the kind of line WordPerfect is to use in drawing the four edges of the box. As you proceed through the edge options, WordPerfect displays the border style choices with this menu:

   1 None; 2 Single; 3 Double; 4 Dashed; 5 Dotted; 6 Thick; 7 Extra Thick: 0

2. *Outside Border Space* is the amount of space between each edge and the text outside of the box. The default value, 0.16", is about one-sixth of an inch, or one line vertically.
3. *Inside Border Space* is the amount of space between each edge and the text or figure inside the box. The value 0" is acceptable for a graphic image; you may want to change it to, say, 0.16" for a box that contains text.

5. *Second Level Numbering Method* refers to the second number in a two-level numbering system. WordPerfect produces the same menu as for option 4.
6. *Caption Number Style* tells how WordPerfect will display the caption number. It assumes you want the word "Figure" and the number in bold print. Here, the number 1 stands for the first level of the box number. If your boxes have a two-level numbering system, insert a 2 where the second-level number belongs. A typical string for two-level figure numbering is [BOLD]Figure 1-2[bold].
7. Choosing *Position of Caption* brings on two menus in succession. The first is:

    Caption Position: 1 Below Box; 2 Above Box: 1

    the second is:

    Caption: 1 Outside of Border; 2 Inside of Border: 1

8. *Minimum Offset from Paragraph* tells WordPerfect how far from the top of the paragraph a box can move to avoid being put on the next page. The value 0" indicates that boxes may be aligned with the top of the paragraph, if necessary.
9. *Gray Shading* lets you shade a box with a specified percentage of black, from 0% for no shading to 100% for solid black.

Gutter

— See **Binding Width**

Half-Spacing

— See **Advance Options**

Hand-Fed Paper

— See **Paper**

Hanging Paragraphs

— See **Indent Commands**

Hard Disk Startup File for WordPerfect

When you turn on a computer that has a hard disk, it always starts in the primary or *root* directory. To switch it to the WordPerfect subdirectory, you must first type **cd\wp** (or **cd\wp50**, in WordPerfect 5.0). Then, to start WordPerfect, you must type **wp** and press Enter. This requires only a few simple commands, but remembering commands is bothersome. To make your job easier, let's create a short program or *file* that changes directories and starts WordPerfect when you type **wp** and Enter.

To create the startup file, proceed as follows:

1. Type **cd** and press Enter to put the computer in the root directory (in case it isn't there already).
2. Type **copy con: wp.bat** and Enter.
3. Type **cd \wp** and Enter.
4. Type **wp %1** and press the *F6* function key, then Enter.

Hard Page Command (Ctrl-Enter)

If you press Ctrl and Enter, WordPerfect will automatically start a new page. To inform you that it has done this, it shows a line of equal signs across the screen (or a dashed line, in WordPerfect 4.1) and displays *Ln 1* at the bottom right-hand corner. It also inserts a hidden [HPg] code where you pressed Ctrl-Enter. If you pressed Ctrl-Enter by mistake (say, you intended Ctrl-Home), press Alt-F3 to see the hidden codes and delete [HPg].

Hard Space

Sometimes you may want to keep two or more words, or terms in an equation, together on a line. To do this, you must separate them with a so-called *hard* space. To produce a hard space, press Home and then the space bar. WordPerfect marks each hard space with a hidden [ ] code.

Headers and Footers — WordPerfect 4.1 and 4.2

4.1
4.2

WordPerfect can print text at the top of every page (a *header*) or at the bottom of every page (a *footer*). When you create a header or footer, you must tell WordPerfect which pages to put it on (every page, odd- or even-numbered pages) and where to print it on those pages. You can specify up to two headers and two footers. For example, you can have a section title at the top of right-hand (odd-numbered) pages, the report title at the top of left-hand (even-numbered) pages, and the page number at the bottom of every page.

Creating a Header or Footer

To create a header or footer, move the cursor to the top of the first page where you want one, then press Alt-F8 to obtain the Page Format menu. When it appears, type **6** to select *Headers or Footers* to obtain the Header/Footer Specification menu (see Figure H-1).

Now proceed as follows:

1. Select the *Type* you want, Header A or B or Footer A or B. (*A* is the first header or footer, while *B* is the second.)
2. Select the *Occurrence*. This can be Discontinue (to omit a previously-defined header or footer), Every Page, Odd Pages, Even Pages, or Edit (to change an existing header or footer). WordPerfect clears the screen and shows **Press EXIT when done** at the bottom.

Figure H-1. Header/Footer Specification menu.

```
Header/Footer Specification

      Type                 Occurrence
      1 - Header A    0 - Discontinue
      2 - Header B    1 - Every Page
      3 - Footer A    2 - Odd Pages
      4 - Footer B    3 - Even Pages
                      4 - Edit

  Selection:    0  Selection:   0
```

3. Enter the text for the header or footer just as you would enter regular text. You can center, underline, or embolden it using standard methods.

   To make WordPerfect print the page number in a header or footer, press Ctrl and B where you want it to appear. The screen shows ^B there.
4. Press F7, the *Exit* key, to return to the Page Format menu, then Enter to return to your document.

Editing and Canceling Headers and Footers

WordPerfect also provides options that let you edit a header or footer, or cancel one, to stop it from printing. In either case, you can reach the text for a header or footer—that is, reach its *definition*—from anywhere in your document, by starting as you did when you created it. WordPerfect will locate the definition and move the cursor to the beginning of its text.

To edit a header or footer, obtain the Header/Footer Specification menu and specify the Type, then choose *Edit* from the Occurrence options. When the header or footer appears, make your changes just as you would with regular text, then press F7 to save the changes.

To cancel an active header or footer, select *Discontinue* from the Header/Footer Specifications menu's Occurrence list. WordPerfect retains discontinued headers and footers, it just doesn't print them. Thus, you can reactivate one by obtaining it and selecting *Every Page*, *Odd Pages*, or *Even Pages*.

Searching Through Headers and Footers

WordPerfect normally searches only regular text, but with version 4.2, you can make it include headers, footers, footnotes, and endnotes as well. To do this, press Home before entering your Search or Replace command.

Headers and Footers — WordPerfect 5.0

5.0 WordPerfect can print text at the top of every page (a *header*) or at the bottom of every page (a *footer*). When you create a header or footer, you must tell WordPerfect which pages to put it on (every page, odd- or even-numbered pages) and where to print it on those pages. You can specify up to two headers and two footers. For example, you can have a section title at the top of right-hand (odd-numbered) pages, the report title at the top of left-hand (even-numbered) pages, and the page number at the bottom of every page.

Creating a Header or Footer

To create a header or footer, do the following:

1. Move the cursor to the top of the first page where you want the header or footer.
2. Press Shift-F8 to give a Format command.
3. When the Format menu appears, type **2** to select *Page*.
4. When the Page Format menu appears, type **3** for *Headers* or **4** for *Footers*. WordPerfect displays a menu with two choices, **1** for Header or Footer A and **2** for Header or Footer B.
5. Specify the header or footer you want to create, A or B, where A is the first header or footer and B is the second.
6. When this menu appears:

    ```
    1 Discontinue; 2 Every page; 3 Odd pages; 4 Even pages; 5 Edit: 0
    ```

    type **2, 3,** or **4** to indicate the pages on which the new header or footer is to be printed. WordPerfect clears the screen and shows *Press EXIT when done* at the bottom.
7. Enter the text for the header or footer just as you would enter regular text. You can use formatting features such as Center, Underline, Flush Right, and Bold, just as in regular text.
    To make WordPerfect print the page number in a header or footer, press Ctrl and B where you want it to appear. The screen shows ^B there.
8. Press F7 (*Exit*) to return to the Page Format menu. In the *Headers* or *Footers* fields, WordPerfect shows a two-letter code and an occurrence description for each active header or footer. For example, **HA Every Page** indicates that your Header A text will be printed on every page of the document.
9. Press F7 again to return to your document.

Editing and Canceling Headers and Footers

WordPerfect also provides options that let you edit a header or footer, or cancel one, to stop it from printing. In either case, you can reach the text for a header or footer—that is, reach its *definition*—from anywhere in your document, by starting as you did when you created it. WordPerfect will search for the definition and move the cursor to the beginning of its text.

To edit a header or footer, obtain the Page Format menu and select *Headers* or *Footers*, then *A* or *B*. When the Header/Footer menu appears, type 5 for *Edit*. When the header or footer appears, make your changes just as you would with regular text, then press F7 to save the changes.

To cancel an active header or footer, select *Discontinue* from the Header/Footer menu. WordPerfect retains discontinued headers and footers, it just doesn't print them. Thus, you can reactivate one by obtaining it and selecting *Every Page*, *Odd Pages*, or *Even Pages*.

Searching Through Headers and Footers

WordPerfect normally searches only regular text, but you can make it include headers, footers, footnotes, and endnotes as well. To do this, press Home before entering your Search or Replace command.

Help Command (F3)

The Help command lets you obtain a description of any WordPerfect feature without referring to the manual. Pressing the F3 key brings on a screen that lets you do any of three things. You can:

1. Press a letter key to obtain a list of features that start with that letter.
2. Press a function key (or Alt, Shift, or Ctrl and a function key) to obtain a description of what that command does.
3. Press F3 again to obtain a picture of the keyboard template.

You can keep pressing keys until you have read about every feature you want. To leave Help and return to editing, press Enter or the space bar.

Hidden Codes

— See **Codes, Hidden**

Highlighting

— See **Block Command**

Home Key

Home, the 7 key on the numeric keypad, is primarily used to move the cursor. The key sequences are:

These keys:	Move the cursor to the ...
Home ↑	Top of the screen
Home ↓	Bottom of the screen
Home Home ←	Beginning of the line, but following any codes
Home Home ↑	Beginning of the document
Home Home ↓	End of the document
Home Home Home ←	Beginning of the line, preceding any codes

Pressing Ctrl and Home together gives WordPerfect a Go To command. When Go to appears at the bottom of the screen, you can move to a character by typing it, move to a page by entering its number, or move to the top or bottom of the current page by pressing ↑ or ↓.

Home also has some other miscellaneous uses, as follows:

These keys:	Do the following:
Home Backspace	Deletes left of the cursor to the beginning of the word
Home Del	Deletes right of the cursor to the end of the word

148   Hyphenation

Home Spacebar	Inserts a "hard space" between words, to keep them on the same line
Home F2	Searches forward through headers, footers, footnotes, and endnotes as well as regular text
Home Shift-F2	Same as Home F2, but searches backward
Home Alt-F2	Replaces in headers, footers, footnotes, and endnotes as well as in regular text

Hyphenation

When you enter text in a document, WordPerfect normally fills each line with as many words as it can hold, and starts a new line when a word crosses the right-hand margin. Although this saves you from having to tell WordPerfect how to divide lines, it can make a page of unjustified text look extremely ragged or put a lot of blank space between words of justified text.

Fortunately, WordPerfect has a Hyphenation feature that can enhance the appearance of your text by hyphenating words. This feature provides an *Aided* option (called *Manual* in WordPerfect 5.0) that lets you specify where hyphens belong, and an *Auto* option that makes WordPerfect insert hyphens automatically, based on a set of prescribed rules.

Turning Hyphenation On and Off

To use the Hyphenation feature, start by moving the cursor to where you want hyphenation turned on. This is usually the beginning of the document, in which case you can press Home *twice*, then ↑, to get there. What you do next depends on which version of WordPerfect you have.

4.1
4.2

With WordPerfect 4.1 or 4.2, turn on Hyphenation as follows:

1. Press Shift-F8 to give a Line Format command.
2. When the Line Format menu appears, type 5 to obtain the following Hyphenation menu:

[HZone Set] 7,0   Off Aided **1** On; **2** Off; **3** Set H-Zone; **4** Aided; **5** Auto: 0

3. Type **1** to turn Hyphenation *On*.
4. WordPerfect assumes you want Aided hyphenation (the words *On Aided* precede the menu's option list); if so, press Enter to get back to editing. If you want Auto hyphenation instead, type **5**, then press Enter.

5.0

With WordPerfect 5.0, turn on Hyphenation as follows:

1. Press Shift-F8 to give a Format command.
2. When the Format menu appears, type **1** to select *Line*.
3. When the Line Format Menu appears, press **1** to select *Hyphenation*.
4. When this Hyphenation menu appears:

    1 Off; 2 Manual; 3 Auto: 0

    type **2** for *Manual* or **3** for *Auto*. WordPerfect records your choice in the Line Format menu.
5. Press F7 (Exit) to return to your document.

To turn hyphenation off, obtain the Hyphenation menu again and select *Off*, then press Enter (WordPerfect 4.1 or 4.2) or F7 (WordPerfect 5.0) to return to your document. When you turn hyphenation on or off, WordPerfect inserts a hidden [Hyph on] or [Hyph off] code in your document.

Aided (Manual) and Auto Hyphenation

With Hyphenation on, WordPerfect watches the words you type toward the end of each line. If a word starts before or at its so-called *Hyphenation Zone* (see separate entry) and extends past it, WordPerfect asks for a hyphenation decision or inserts the hyphen itself, depending on whether you selected *Aided* (*Manual* in WordPerfect 5.0) or *Auto* hyphenation.

With *Aided/Manual* hyphenation on, WordPerfect asks for hyphenation help by beeping the computer and showing **Position hyphen; Press ESC** and the word to be hyphenated at the bottom of the screen. You then have three options:

1. Press Esc to insert a hyphen where WordPerfect has suggested.
2. Move the cursor left or right to where you want the hyphen, then press Esc.

3. Press F1 (Cancel) to leave the word unhyphenated and move it to the next line.

With *Auto* hyphenation on, WordPerfect uses a set of hyphenation rules to determine where to insert a needed hyphen. If the rules don't apply there, WordPerfect switches to *Aided* for that particular word.

Soft Hyphens

The hyphens that WordPerfect inserts in your document look like regular hyphens on the screen, but they are only temporary or *soft* hyphens. If you insert or delete text on a line that ends with a soft hyphen, WordPerfect will, if necessary, remove the hyphen.

Soft hyphens also look different than regular hyphens on the Reveal Codes (Alt-F3) screen. In Reveal Codes for WordPerfect 4.1 or 4.2, soft hyphens are emboldened, regular hyphens are not. For WordPerfect 5.0, regular hyphens appear as [-], whereas soft hyphens appear as - (no brackets).

Hyphenation Zone

WordPerfect uses an invisible strip of character positions called the Hyphenation Zone (or *H-Zone*) to determine whether words should be hyphenated. As Figure H-2 shows, the Hyphenation Zone extends from a Left H-Zone that precedes the right-hand margin to a Right H-Zone that follows the right-hand margin.

If a word starts ahead of or at the Left H-Zone and extends past the Right H-Zone, WordPerfect asks you to hyphenate it. If a word starts after the Left H-Zone and extends past the right-hand margin, WordPerfect moves it to the next line.

4.1
4.2

With WordPerfect 4.1 and 4.2, the Left H-Zone is preset to 7 (i.e., seven character positions left of the right-hand margin) and the Right H-Zone is preset to 0 (it is at the right-hand margin). **With**

5.0

WordPerfect 5.0, the Left H-Zone is preset to .7" and the Right H-Zone is preset to .25" (i.e., just right of the right-hand margin). These are reasonable settings insofar as they provide a fairly wide H-Zone. The Left H-Zone value, 7 or .7", helps ensure that words having more than seven letters will not be moved to the next line, which would make the text more ragged.

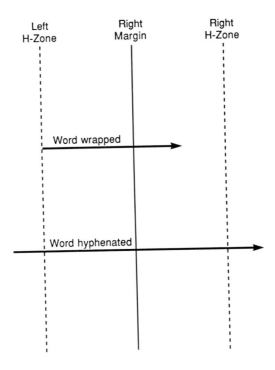

Figure H-2. H-Zone

With WordPerfect 4.1 or 4.2, you can change the H-Zone margins by selecting *Set H-Zone* (option 3) from the Hyphenation menu. With WordPerfect 5.0, you can change them by selecting *Hyphenation Zone* (option 2) from the Line Format menu. Just realize that a narrow H-Zone requires more hyphenation while a wide one requires less hyphenation.

Indent Commands (F4 and Shift-F4)

WordPerfect can indent a paragraph from the left-hand margin or from both side margins, left and right. In both cases, it uses tab stops to determine where the indentation starts.

Indenting From the Left Margin

When people type a list of items, they often indent them and set them off with numbers, letters, dashes, or "bullets." For example, suppose you want to indent three numbered sentences in a letter, as in

```
In response to your recent request, we need the
following information to complete a credit application:

1) Name and address of your bank, along with your
   account number.
2) Three credit references.
3) A signed corporate resolution indicating
   responsibility for payment.
```

To indent material, set a tab where you want the indented left-hand margin. Then, whenever you want to indent something, press

F4 (->Indent)—rather than Tab—to start indenting. WordPerfect will indent everything you type until you press Enter. In other words, it will indent a paragraph worth of text.

You can also indent an existing paragraph, by putting the cursor on the first character and pressing F4. Of course, if you have a tab at the beginning of a paragraph, press F4 at the left-hand margin rather than at the first character. Either way, WordPerfect will indent only the current paragraph.

Indenting From Both Margins

You can also indent material from both the left- and right-hand margins, to set it off from regular text. To do this, press Shift-F4 (rather than just F4) before you type the material. As you type, WordPerfect arranges lines so that they are the same distance from both the left- and right-hand margin.

On the left, WordPerfect indents text to the first tab stop; on the right, it indents text the same *distance* from the right-hand margin. Note that it does *not* use a tab stop to indent the right edge of the paragraph.

For example, suppose your left and right margins are at columns 10 and 74 and your first tab stop is at column 15. Pressing Shift-F4 from the left-hand margin makes WordPerfect indent to column 15 on the left and to column 69 (74 - 5) on the right. For example, you may want to produce a letter that includes the following:

```
     Your contract is generally acceptable, but I would
like an advance for this project. Thus, please add the
following clause (or something similar) and send me a
revised contract:

     17. ADVANCE. The Publisher agrees to pay to the
     Author an advance against royalties of $1,000,
     payable as follows:

          $500 within 30 days of receipt of signed
          contract; $500 on acceptance by the
          Publisher of the complete manuscript.
```

Here, the "17. ADVANCE." paragraph is indented one tab stop from both margins, so you would press Shift-F4 once before typing it. The next paragraph is indented two tab stops from the margins, so you would press Shift-F4 *twice* before typing it.

Hanging Paragraphs

WordPerfect also lets you create a "hanging" paragraph, in which the first line starts at the left-hand margin but all other lines are indented. An example is:

```
This is an example of a hanging paragraph. The first
    line starts at the left-hand margin, but the last
    two lines start at the first tab stop.
```

To produce a hanging paragraph, press F4 or Shift-F4 to indent, then press Shift-Tab (the *Margin Release* command) and enter the paragraph as usual. **Note:** Shift-Tab moves the cursor one tab stop to the left, so for the margin release to work, you must have a tab set ahead of the one to which you indented.

Removing Indentation

Sometimes you may accidentally press F4 when you mean to press the Tab key (after all, they're next to each other), and end up with an indented paragraph. WordPerfect precedes indented paragraphs with a [->Indent] or [->Indent<-] code; you must delete this code to remove the indentation. To do this, move the cursor to the beginning of the paragraph and press Backspace. WordPerfect 4.1 asks you to verify that you want to delete the Indent code, later versions do not.

Indexes

You can make WordPerfect generate an index for your document, based on words or phrases you specify. Creating an index involves three procedures. You must *build* it by marking the entries you want in it, *define* the numbering style, then *generate* the index.

Headings and Subheadings

In addition to regular index entries or *headings*, WordPerfect also lets you define *subheadings*; that is, entries that fall under a general heading. For example, the index for a financial report may include

Sales
   and commission record 271
   to accounts receivables 167
   to cash 180
   to fixed assets 185
   to inventories 190

Here, "Sales" is a heading and the indented lines are subheadings.

Building an Index

With WordPerfect version 4.1, you must build an index by marking the select words or phrases in it individually. With versions 4.2 and higher, you can give WordPerfect a list of the entries you want as a *concordance file*. I will now describe how to mark words and phrases for inclusion in an index. For details on how to create a concordance file, see **Concordance File.**

To mark a word for an index, simply move the cursor to it. **To mark a phrase**, move the cursor to the beginning of it and put WordPerfect in Block mode. Then highlight the phrase by pressing either the right-arrow key to select characters or Ctrl and right-arrow to select words. Either way, proceed as follows:

1. Press Alt-F5 to give a Mark Text command.
2. When the menu appears, type **5** (in WordPerfect 4.2) or **3** (WordPerfect 5.0) to select Index. WordPerfect shows *Index Heading:* and the word or phrase you selected.
3. Now you can do either of two things:

   • To make the entry a heading, press Enter. When the prompt **Subheading:** appears at the bottom of the screen, enter a subheading (if you want one), then press Enter.

   • To make the entry a subheading, type a heading, then press Enter. When **Subheading:** and your entry appear at the bottom of the screen, press Enter again.

Repeat these steps for each word or phrase you want included in the index. When you finish, move the cursor to the end of your document (press Home twice, then down-arrow) and start a new page (Ctrl-Enter). Then set tabs for the index and enter a heading. Now you must tell WordPerfect which numbering style to use.

Defining the Numbering Style

WordPerfect can generate an index in any of five numbering styles. They are:

1. No page numbers
2. Page numbers follow entries
3. Page numbers follow entries, but are enclosed in parentheses. For example, if the "Truman" entry is on page 43, this option would produce

    Truman (43)

4. Flush right page numbers; that is, numbers aligned along the right-hand margin.
5. Flush right page numbers with leaders (i.e., with periods between the entry and the page number).

To select the style, begin by pressing Alt-F5. Then

- **For WordPerfect 4.1**, type **6** for Define. When the Mark Text Definition menu appears, type **8** for Index.
- **For WordPerfect 4.2**, type **6** for Other Options. When the Other Mark Text Options menu appears, type **5** for Define Index.
- **For WordPerfect 5.0**, type **5** for Define. When the Mark Text: Define menu appears, type **3** for Define Index.

When WordPerfect asks for a concordance filename, type it (if applicable), then press Enter. When the *Index Definition* menu (Figure I-1) appears, type the number of the style you want.

Figure I-1 Index Definition menu.

```
Index Definition

    1- No Page Numbers
    2 -Page Numbers Follow Entries
    3 -(Page Numbers) Follow Entries
    4- Flush Right Page Numbers
    5- Flush Right Page Numbers with Leaders
```

158   Indexes

Generating an Index

To make WordPerfect generate the index, obtain the Mark Text menu (Alt-F5), then:

- **For WordPerfect 4.1**, select Generate.
- **For WordPerfect 4.2**, select Other Options, then Generate Tables and Index.
- **For WordPerfect 5.0**, select Generate, then Generate Tables, Indexes, Automatic References, etc.

When the screen shows

```
Existing tables, lists, and indexes will be replaced.
Continue? (Y/N): Y
```

type y. WordPerfect begins creating the index, and displays

```
                Generation in progress.
```

at the bottom of the screen. When it finishes, the index appears.

WordPerfect puts headings at the first tab stop on the line (at the left-hand margin, if a tab is set there) and indents subheadings to the next tab stop. It also lists both headings and subheadings alphabetically, thus saving you the trouble of rearranging them. Each index entry will have the same form as in the document (e.g., bold text will be bold in the index). You may want to edit the index to remove these print formats.

Removing Entries from an Index

Sometimes you may decide that you don't want a certain entry in your index. Removing an entry is easiest if it's in a concordance file; simply delete the entry from the file and generate the index again. If you marked occurrences of the entry in the document manually, however, you must search for them and unmark them.

When you mark text for the index, WordPerfect puts an invisible [Index] code immediately ahead of it (for a word) or after it (for a phrase). Hence, to remove an entry from an index, you must locate the [Index] code and delete it. To do this, move the cursor ahead of the first occurrence and give a Replace (Alt-F2) command. To put the [Index] code in your search string, press Alt-F5 and type **3** to select Index.

For example, to remove all references to "Acme Corporation" from an index, move the cursor to the beginning of your document and do the following:

1. Press Shift and F2 to give a Search command.
2. When the **w/Confirm?** prompt appears, press Enter to accept the default, N (No).
3. For **->Srch:**, type **Acme Corporation** and press Alt-F5.
4. When the menu appears, type **3** to select Index (WordPerfect inserts [Index] on the Srch line), then press F2.
5. For **Replace with:**, type **Acme Corporation** and press F2 again.

Now that the entry has been unmarked throughout your document, you can generate the new index.

Initial Settings for WordPerfect 4.1 and 4.2

| 4.1 |
| 4.2 |

WordPerfect provides key commands that let you change format settings in the current document. For example, pressing Shift-F8 produces a *Line Format* menu that lets you change the tabs, side margins, and line spacing. You can also specify settings for all new documents by changing WordPerfect's *Set-up* menu.

Initial Settings in the Set-up Menu

To obtain the Set-up menu, start WordPerfect by entering **wp/s**, instead of the usual **wp**. When the Set-up menu appears, type **2** for *Set Initial Settings*. This brings on the Initial Settings menu shown in Figure I-2. (Note that this is WordPerfect 4.2's menu. WordPerfect 4.1's menu is similar, except it doesn't list features introduced with 4.2, such as the Table of Authorities and Document Summary.)

WordPerfect 4.1 and 4.2 come with features preset to the values summarized in Table I-1. With the Initial Settings menu on the screen, obtain the feature you want to change by pressing the keys listed in the right-hand column.

```
Change Initial Settings

Press any of the keys listed below to change initial
settings

Key                    Initial Settings
Line Format            Tabs, Margins, Spacing, Hyphenation,
                       Align Character
Page Format            Page # Pos, Page Length, Top Margin,
                       Page # Col Pos, W/O
Print Format           Print, Font, Lines/Inch, Right Just,
Underlining,
                       SF Bin #
Print                  Printer, Copies, Binding Width
Date                   Date Format
Insert/Typeover        Insert/Typeover Mode
Mark Text              Paragraph Number Definition, Table of
                       Authorities Definition
Footnote               Footnote/Endnote Options
Escape                 Set N
Screen                 Set Auto-rewrite
Text In/Out            Set Insert Document Summary on
                       Save/Exit

Selection:

Press Enter to return to the Set-up Menu
```

Figure I-2. WordPerfect 4.2's Initial Settings menu.

Initial Settings for WordPerfect 5.0

5.0 WordPerfect provides key commands that let you change format settings in the current document. For example, pressing Shift-F8 and typing 1 produces a *Line Format* menu that lets you change the tabs, side margins, and line spacing. You can also specify settings for all new documents by changing WordPerfect's *Setup* menu.

Table I-1. Initial settings for WordPerfect 4.1 and 4.2.

Feature	Initially set to	To obtain, press
Align Character	. (period)	Shift-F8, 6
Auto Rewrite	On (reformat screen automatically)	Ctrl-F3
Binding Width	0 (Enter 1/10-inch values)	Shift-F7, 3
Date Format	Month Day, Year (e.g., May 29, 1988)	Shift-F5
Endnote numbering mode	0 (Numbers)	Ctrl-F7, 6
**Enter Document Summary on Save/Exit	No	Ctrl-F5
*E-Tabs	Every 10 spaces	Shift-F8-2
Font	1	Ctrl-F8, 1, Enter
Footnote numbering mode	0 (Numbers)	Ctrl-F7, 5
Footnotes at bottom of page	Yes	Ctrl-F7, 8
Hyphenation	Off	Shift-F8, 5
Insert/Typeover	Insert mode	Ins
Line Numbering	Off	Ctrl-F8, B
Line separating text and footnotes	1 (2-inch line)	Ctrl-F7, 7
Line Spacing	Single	Shift-F8, 4
Lines in notes to keep together	3	Ctrl-F7, 3

Note: Features marked with * are available only in WordPerfect 4.1; those marked with ** are available only in WordPerfect 4.2.

Table I-1 *(continued)*

Feature	Initially set to	To obtain, press
Lines per inch	6	Ctrl-F8, 2
Margin, Top	12 half-lines (one inch)	Alt-F8, 5
Margins, Side	Left = 10, Right = 74 (one-inch margins)	Shift-F8, 3
Note numbering mode	Numbers	Ctrl-F7, 4
Number of Copies	1	Shift-F7, 2
Outline Numbering Style	Outline	Alt-F5, 1
Page Length	66 lines total, 54 text lines (8-1/2 by 11-inch paper)	Alt-F8, 4
Page Number Column Positions	Left = 10, Center = 42, Right = 74	Alt-F8, 7
Page Number Position	No page numbers	Alt-F8, 1
Paragraph/Outline Numbering Style	Outline	Alt-F5, 1
Pitch	10 characters per inch	Ctrl-F8, 1
Printer Number	1	Shift-F7, 1
Repeat value for Esc	8	Esc
Right Justification	On (Even right-hand margin)	Ctrl-F8, 3 or 4
Sheet Feeder Bin Number	1	Ctrl-F8, 9
Spacing, line	Single	Shift-F8, 4

Note: Features marked with * are available only in WordPerfect 4.1; those marked with ** are available only in WordPerfect 4.2.

Table I-1 *(continued)*

Feature	Initially set to	To obtain, press
Spacing between notes	1	Ctrl-F7, 2
Spacing within notes	1	Ctrl-F7, 1
**Table of Authorities	Dot leaders, no underlining, blank line between authorities	Alt-F5, 2
Tabs	Every 5 spaces	Shift-F8, 1
Top Margin	12 half-lines (one inch)	Alt-F8, 5
Underline Style	Non-continuous single	Ctrl-F8, 5-8
Widow/Orphan Protect	No	Alt-F8, A

Note: Features marked with * are available only in WordPerfect 4.1; those marked with ** are available only in WordPerfect 4.2.

To obtain the Setup menu, press Shift-F1 from within WordPerfect. WordPerfect 5.0 comes with features preset to the values summarized in Table I-2. With the Setup menu on the screen, obtain the feature you want to change by pressing the keys listed in the right-hand column.

Initial Settings in the Set-up Menu

Note that most of the key sequences in the table begin with 5, which selects *Initial Settings*. Figure I-3 shows the Initial Settings menu. Its options are:

- *Beep Options* (1) is preset to make the computer beep when WordPerfect needs a hyphenation decision. You can also make it beep when an error message is displayed and/or a Search operation fails.

```
Setup: Initial Settings

     1 - Beep Options

     2 - Date Format                    3 1, 4

     3 - Document Summary

     4 - Initial Codes

     5 - Repeat Value                   8

     6 - Table of Authorities


Selection: 0
```

Figure I-3. WordPerfect 5.0's Initial Settings menu.

Table I-2. Initial settings for WordPerfect 5.0

Feature	Initially set to	Setup Menu keys
Automatically Format and Rewrite	Yes	3, 1
Auxiliary Files, Location of	Main WordPerfect directory	7
Backup		
Original Document	No	1, 2
Timed Document	No	1, 1
Beep Options		
Beep on Error	No	5, 1, 1
Beep on Hyphenation	Yes	5, 1, 2
Beep on Search Failure	No	5, 1, 3
Center Page top-to-bottom	No	5, 4, Shift-F8, 2, 1
Cursor Speed	30 chars/second	2
Date Format	Month Day, Year (e.g., May 29, 1988)	5, 2

Table I-2 *(continued)*

Feature	Initially set to	Setup Menu keys
Decimal/Align Character	. (period)	5, 4, Shift-F8, 4, 3
Display Document Comments	Yes	3, 3
Display Pitch	Auto	5, 4, Shift-F8, 3, 1
Document Comments, Display	Yes	3, 3
Document Summary		
Create on Save/Exit	No	5, 3, 1
Subject Search String	RE:	5, 3, 2
Esc key, Repeat Value for	8	5, 5
Fast Save (unformatted)	Yes	4
Filename on Status Line	Yes	3, 4
Hard Return Display Char.	Space	3, 6
Hyphenation	No (off)	5, 4, Shift-F8, 1, 1
Hyphenation Zone	L=0.7", R=0.25"	5, 4, Shift-F8, 1, 2
Justification	Yes (even right margin)	5, 4, Shift-F8, 1, 3
Kerning	No (off)	5, 4, Shift-F8, 4, 6, 1
Keyboard Layout	Standard	6
Language	EN (English)	5, 4, Shift-F8, 4, 4
Left and Right Margins	L=1", R=1"	5, 4, Shift-F8, 1, 7
Line Height	Auto	5, 4, Shift-F8, 1, 4
Line Numbering	No	5, 4, Shift-F8, 1, 5
Line Spacing	1 (single-space)	5, 4, Shift-F8, 1, 6
Location of Auxiliary Files	Main WordPerfect directory	7
Margins, Left and Right	L=1", R=1"	5, 4, Shift-F8, 1, 7
Margins, Top and Bottom	T=1", B=1"	5, 4, Shift-F8, 2, 5
Menu Letter Display	Bold	3, 7
New Page Number	1	5, 4, Shift-F8, 2, 6
Original Document Backup	No	1, 2

Table I-2 *(continued)*

Feature	Initially set to	Setup Menu keys
Page Number, New	1	5, 4, Shift-F8, 2, 6
Page Number Position	No page numbers	5, 4, Shift-F8, 2, 7
Paper		5, 4, Shift-F8, 4, 6
Size	8.5" x 11"	
Type	Standard	
Print Color	Black	5, 4, Ctrl-F8, 5
Redline Method	Printer Depend.	5, 4, Shift-F8, 3, 3
Repeat Value for Esc key	8	5, 5
Side-by-side Columns Display	Yes	3, 8
Spacing, Line	1 (single-space)	5, 4, Shift-F8, 1, 6
Tab Set	Every 0.5"	5, 4, Shift-F8, 1, 8
Table of Authorities		
Dot Leaders	Yes	5, 6, 1
Underlining Allowed	No	5, 6, 2
Blank Line between Authorities	Yes	5, 6, 3
Thousands Separator	, (comma)	5, 4, Shift-F8, 4, 3
Timed Document Backup	No	1, 1
Top and Bottom Margins	T=1", B=1"	5, 4, Shift-F8, 2, 5
Underline Spaces, Tabs	S=Yes, T=No	5, 4, Shift-F8, 4, 7
Units of Measure		
Numbers for Margins, Tabs, etc.	" (inches)	8, 1
Status Line Display	u (lines/columns)	8, 2
Widow/Orphan Protection	No	5, 4, Shift-F8, 1, 9
Width Adjustment		5, 4, Shift-F8, 4, 6, 3
Word Spacing	Optimal	
Letter Spacing	Optimal	
Word Spacing Justification		5, 4, Shift-F8, 4, 6, 4
Compressed to	60%	
Expanded to	400%	

- *Date Format* (2) is preset to insert the date in the general form Month Day, Year (e.g., May 29, 1988), but you can make it use a different date format and/or insert the current time.
- *Document Summary* (3) can be set to prompt you for a Document Summary whenever you Save (F10) or Exit (F7) a document.
- *Initial Codes* (4) makes the Reveal Codes screen appear. You can then give the command that controls whichever settings you want to change. For example, WordPerfect normally single-spaces new documents. To make it double-space them, press Shift-F8 for Format, then type 1 for Line, **6** for Line Spacing, and **2** for double-spacing.
- *Repeat Value* (5) controls the repetition count that is used when you press the Esc key.
- *Table of Authorities* (6) controls the display format for these tables.

If you make changes to the Initial Settings menu, press F7 (Exit) to save them and return to your document.

Ins (Insert) Key

When you type new characters into existing text, WordPerfect *inserts* them by shifting the original characters to the right. However, if you press the Ins key (bottom left-hand corner of the numeric keypad), WordPerfect enters a *Typeover* mode in which it replaces existing characters with ones you type. WordPerfect stays in typeover mode until you press Ins again. For more details, see **Typeover Mode**.

Invisible Codes

— See **Codes, Hidden**

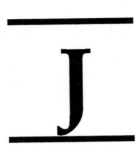

Justification

WordPerfect comes set up to print text *right-justified*; that is, with an even right-hand margin. It produces the even margin by inserting spaces between words. To switch to a non-justified or "ragged" right-hand margin, move the cursor to the beginning of your document (by pressing Home twice, then the ↑ key) and do one of the following:

4.1 4.2	•**For WordPerfect 4.1 and 4.2,** press Ctrl-F8 to give a Print Format command. When the Print Format menu appears, type 3 to *Turn off right justification,* then press Enter to return to your document.
5.0	•**For WordPerfect 5.0,** press Shift-F8 to give a Format command and type 1 for Line. When the Line Format menu appears, type 3 to reach the *Justification* field and type **n** to turn justification off. Finally, press F7 (Exit) to return to your document.

Changing Justification Permanently

The preceding procedure only affects justification in the current document. To give all of your new documents ragged right-hand margins, you must obtain WordPerfect's Set-up menu.

Justification

To obtain the Set-up menu for WordPerfect 4.1 or 4.2, start WordPerfect by entering **wp/s**, instead of **wp**. When the Set-up menu appears, type **2** for *Set Initial Settings*. When the menu appears, press Ctrl-F8 for Print Format and type **3** to *Turn off* Right Justification.

To obtain the Set-up menu for WordPerfect 5.0, press Shift-F1 from within WordPerfect. When the Set-up menu appears, type **5** for *Initial Settings*, then **4** for *Initial Codes*. When the Reveal Codes screen appears, type Shift-F8 for Format, **1** for Line, **3** for Justification, and type **n** to turn justification off.

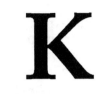

Keeping Text Together

Sometimes you may want to keep a block of text (such as a table) or a group of consecutive lines together on the same page. To make WordPerfect keep a block together, you must *protect* it; see **Block Command**. To make it keep lines together, you must give it a Conditional End of Page command (see that entry).

You may also want to keep two words, such as someone's name, on the same line. To do this, you must type a so-called *hard* space between them, by pressing Home and then the space bar.

Keyboard Layout — WordPerfect 5.0

| 5.0 | Within WordPerfect, pressing a function key (F1 through F10)—either by itself or with Ctrl, Shift, or Alt held down—makes WordPerfect perform a specific command. Similarly, pressing a key on the numeric keypad at the right of the keyboard moves the cursor through the document on the screen.

With WordPerfect 4.1 and 4.2, these keys can only perform their predefined tasks. If you want to activate additional tasks from the keyboard, you must define these tasks as mini-programs called *macros*.

By contrast, WordPerfect 5.0 lets you treat the original keyboard layout as simply a starting point, and make any key or key combination do whatever you want. To reassign a key or combination, you define its operation in a *keyboard definition file*. A keyboard definition file contains a set of key assignments that WordPerfect uses when you activate that file. Once activated, the key definitions in the file override any predefined definitions.

Predefined Keyboard Definition Files

WordPerfect 5.0's *Learning* disk—that is, the version I have now, while I'm writing this book—includes three keyboard definition files that you can either use directly or change to meet your own needs. Two of these files, ALTRNAT.WPK and ENHANCED.WPK, reassign command keys; the third, MACROS.WPK, contains a variety of useful macros.

The ALTRNAT (Alternate) file reassigns three keys: It moves the *Help* function to the F1 key, the *Cancel* function to the Esc (Escape) key, and the *Repeat Value* function to the F3 key.

The ENHANCED file only works on computers that have an "enhanced" keyboard—one that includes the additional F11 and F12 function keys—such as IBM's Personal System/2 (PS/2) series. Table K-1 summarizes the key definitions contained in ENHANCED.

The MACROS file reassigns only one command key combination (Alt-F9 lists files instead of giving a Graphics command); its other key definitions are macros that you replay by pressing Alt or Ctrl and a letter key. Table K-2 summarizes the key definitions contained in MACROS.

Many users may find the *Generate Standard Documents* (Ctrl-D) operation more useful than some of the others. This key definition generates personalized "boilerplate" text for a memorandum, letter, or itinerary. Pressing Ctrl-D makes an **Enter Author's Name:** prompt appear on the bottom line. When you have entered a name, WordPerfect displays

```
1 Memo; 2 Letter; 3 Itinerary: 0
```

Choose the kind of document you want to create.

Table K-1. Key definitions in the ENHANCED.WPK file.

Description	Key(s)

Operations that use the F11 and F12 function keys

Italics	Shift-F11
Retrieve Block	Shift-F12
Large (print)	Ctrl-F11
Very Large (print)	Alt-F11
Move block	Ctrl-F12
Copy block	Alt-F12

Cursor-moving operations

Home Home Home Left (Move cursor tobeginning of line, ahead of codes)	Home
Home	5 on numeric keypad
Go To	Ctrl-5 (on keypad)
Move Up by Sentence	Ctrl-↑
Move Down by Sentence	Ctrl-↓
Move Up by Paragraph	Alt-↑
Move Down by Paragraph	Alt-↓
Move Left One Column	Alt-←
Move Right One Column	Alt-→
Move Up by Sentence	Ctrl-e ↑
Move Down by Sentence	Ctrl-e ↓

For a memo, WordPerfect centers **MEMORANDUM** at the top, and shows **Date:** and the current date, **From:** and the author's name, and a blank **To:** field, where you can enter the addressee's name.

WordPerfect starts a letter at the end, by inserting "Sincerely," and the name you entered, then prompts for the author's title. It next prompts for the addressee's name, and it inserts both at the beginning (to serve as the start of an address) and after "Dear", to form the salutation.

For an itinerary, WordPerfect sets up seven labels (*Name:*, *Dates of Trip:*, *Destination:*, *Purpose:*, *Cost Estimate:*, *Schedule*, and *Names and Addresses*) and fills in *Name:*.

Most other MACROS definitions are self-explanatory, but a few deserve additional comments, as follows:

Table K-2. Key definitions in the MACROS.WPK file.

Description	Keys
Get to Main Editing Screen	Alt-E
Transpose two preceding characters	Alt-T
Delete a line (this line)	Alt-D
Insert a line (above this one)	Alt-I
Move Down by Sentence (to next sentence)	Alt-S
Move Down by Paragraph (to next paragraph)	Alt-P
Print the address to an envelope	Alt-A
Insert Bookmark	Alt-M
Find the Bookmark (and delete it)	Alt-F
Send GO to printer	Alt-G
Capitalize first letter of current word	Alt-C
Restore the previous block	Alt-B
Edit the Next or Previous Note	Alt-N
List Files from Graphics key	Alt-F9
Generate Standard Documents	Ctrl-D
Make (printer) Font Changes	Ctrl-F
Glossary Macro - Expand Abbreviations	Ctrl-G
Move Up by Sentence (to preceding sentence)	Ctrl-S
Move Up by Paragraph (to preceding paragraph)	Ctrl-P

- *Get to Main Editing Screen* (Alt-E) completes the current operation and makes your document reappear. You can use it to leave the List Files screen or any of the editing screens (Header, Footer, Footnote, etc.) without having to remember which key is needed to exit.

- *Print the address to an envelope* (Alt-A) prints an address you select in Block mode.

- *Insert Bookmark* (Alt-M) inserts the symbol <MARK> and an Enter at the cursor position. This is handy for marking the place where you stopped working on a document. *Find the Bookmark* (Alt-F) searches forward, then backward, for the Bookmark symbol, and deletes it.

- *Restore the previous block* (Alt-B) rehighlights a block that you highlighted, then turns Block mode off.

- *List Files from Graphics Key* makes the Alt-F9 key combination give WordPerfect a List Files command rather than a Graphics command.

- *Glossary Macro - Expand Abbreviations* (Ctrl-G) replaces the abbreviation that precedes the cursor into the words that abbreviation represents. In the definition I had while writing this book, Ctrl-G expands *wp* into *WordPerfect, wpc* into *WordPerfect Corporation, asap* into *as soon as possible,* and *sy* into *Sincerely yours,* followed by four blank lines.

Note that the last three functions (those for Alt-B, Alt-F9, and Ctrl-G) aren't very useful in themselves. They are included simply to demonstrate some of the things you can do with key definitions.

Using Keyboard Files

To make WordPerfect use the key assignments in keyboard files, press Shift and F1 to give a Setup command and type **6** for *Keyboard Layout*. WordPerfect displays a list of the available keyboard definition files (i.e., files that have the extension .WPK) and shows this menu at the bottom of the screen:

```
1 Select; 2 Delete; 3 Rename; 4 Create; 5 Edit; 6 Original; N Name Search: 1
```

Press the ↑ or ↓ key until the file you want is highlighted, then type **1** to choose *Select*. When you select a file, WordPerfect returns you to the Setup menu and shows the filename in the *Keyboard Layout* field. Press F7 (Exit) if you are done using the Setup menu.

Since the Keyboard Layout screen displays a list of files, you can probably guess what most of its other menu options do. As in WordPerfect's List Files (F5) command, *Delete* and *Rename* let you delete or rename the highlighted file, while *Name Search* moves the highlighting as you type a filename. *Original* turns off the Keyboard Layout feature, and clears the *Keyboard Layout* field to indicate that no keyboard file is active. As their labels imply, the *Create* and *Edit* options let you create a new keyboard file or edit the highlighted file.

Creating Keyboard Files

To create a keyboard file, choose *Create* from the menu. When WordPerfect asks for the **Keyboard Filename:**, enter a name of up to eight characters. (Don't enter an extension, however. Since this is a keyboard file, WordPerfect gives it a .WPK extension automatically.)

WordPerfect then displays an Edit Keyboard screen that shows the name of the keyboard file you're creating; column headings for *Key*, *Description*, and *Macro*; and the following menu:

Key: 1 Edit; 2 Delete; 3 Move; 4 Create; **Macro:** 5 Save; 6 Retrieve: 1

Creating Key Definitions

To create a key definition, type **4** to select *Create* from the Edit Keyboard menu. When the **Key:** prompt appears, press the keys with which you want to activate this definition. This can be any key combination, but in most cases you will probably want to use a combination that doesn't do anything presently. For example, you can use Ctrl and a letter key, because WordPerfect 5.0 does not use those keys otherwise. You could use Alt and another key, provided you haven't created a macro with that combination.

When you respond to the **Key:** prompt, WordPerfect displays an Edit Key screen that has a *Name* field with your key combination (e.g., if you pressed Alt and D, the *Name* field shows Alt-D), plus a blank *Description* entry and an *Action* entry with a large box below it.

The *Description* field lets you enter a short description of what this key combination does. To fill it in, type **1**, type your descriptive text, and press Enter to get back to *Selection*.

The *Action* box is where you record the operations that WordPerfect is to perform when you press the specified keys. Type **2** to reach the box, then press the sequence of keys that defines this operation. Within the box, WordPerfect shows your key commands as codes enclosed in braces. For example, it shows {Bold} if you press F6, {Underline} if you press F8, and so on. If you make a mistake, you can delete a code by moving to it and pressing Del. When you finish entering the key sequence, press F7 to get back to *Selection*. If you're done defining this key combination, press F7 to return to the Edit Keyboard screen.

The Edit Keyboard screen lists the *Key* combination you just defined, any *Description* you entered for it, and a *Macro* number. WordPerfect numbers the first macro definition 1, the next definition 2, and so on.

Operating on Key Definitions

Note that you can modify a definition (if, say, you remembered something you accidentally left out), delete it entirely, or assign it to a different key combination, by selecting *Edit* (1), *Delete* (2), or

Move (3) from the menu. You can also select *Save* (5) to create a macro (.WPM) file that contains the highlighted definition, or select *Retrieve* (6) to enter an existing macro file into the keyboard file.

Keypad, Numeric

— See **Numeric Keypad**

Leaving DOS

WordPerfect's Shell command (Ctrl-F1) lets you go to DOS, do whatever operations you want, and then return to WordPerfect. While the DOS prompt (A, B, or whatever) is on the screen, the message

```
Enter 'EXIT' to return to WordPerfect
```

appears just above it. Note that this message is *not* telling you to press the Exit (F7) key, as some messages do within WordPerfect. Instead, it is telling you to actually *type* the word **EXIT** (the forms **exit** and **Exit** will also do), then press the Enter key.

Leaving WordPerfect

You should always use the Exit command to leave WordPerfect, rather than just turning the computer off. That is, press F7 to select *Exit*, save the current document (unless you have already done so or want to discard it), then type **y** in response to the "Exit WP?"

prompt. When the DOS prompt (B> or C>) appears, simply switch the power off if you are done.

Left Indent

—See **Indent Commands**

Legal Size Paper

WordPerfect is preset to print on standard 8-1/2 by 11-inch paper, but you can easily make it print on 8-1/2 by 14-inch legal size paper, by doing the following:

4.1
4.2
- **With WordPerfect 4.1 or 4.2**, press Alt and F8 to give a Page Format command. When the Page Format menu appears, type **4** for *Page Length*. The menu that appears lets you tell WordPerfect how long your paper is (in sixths of an inch) and how many single-spaced lines to put on it. To print on legal size paper, type **2** to select *Legal Size Paper*, which has Form Length = 84 lines and Single Spaced Text Lines = 72.

5.0
- **With WordPerfect 5.0**, press Shift and F8 to give a Format command. This brings on the first of four consecutive menus. Type **2** to select *Page* from the Format menu, **8** to select *Paper Size* from the Page Format menu, **3** to select *Legal* from the Paper Size menu, and then **1** (Standard) or **2** (Bond) to select the type from the Paper Type menu.

In both cases, press F7 (Exit) to return to your document.

Letterhead Paper

Before WordPerfect prints a page, it makes the printer advance the paper one-inch to produce a margin at the top. However, if you are printing on letterhead paper, you must allow more space at the top—perhaps 1-1/2 inches. **With WordPerfect 4.1 and 4.2**, you must specify the width of the top margin by entering it in the Page Format menu (see **Top Margin**).

By contrast, **WordPerfect 5.0's** Page Format menu has a Paper Size option that lets you select from lists of common form sizes (standard, legal, envelope, etc.) and types (standard, bond, etc.). To specify letterhead paper, press Shift and F8 to give a Format command. Then select *Page* from the Format menu, *Paper Size* from the Page Format menu, *Standard* from the Paper Size menu, and *Letterhead* from the Paper Type menu. Finally, press F7 (Exit) to get back to your document.

Line Format Command (Shift-F8) — WordPerfect 4.1 and 4.2

4.1
4.2

To change the line format, press Shift-F8 to do a Line Format command. WordPerfect displays the following Line Format menu:

    1 2 Tabs; 3 Margins; 4 Spacing; 5 Hyphenation; 6 Align Char: 0

The changes you can make are:

1. *Different tabs* (option 1 or 2). WordPerfect has preset tabs at every fifth column. To add a tab, type its column number and press Enter; to delete one, move the cursor to it and press Del; to delete all tabs, move the cursor to the beginning of the line (by pressing Home twice, then ←), then press Ctrl and End. There are different kinds of tabs; for details, see **Tabs**.
2. *Different margins* (option 3). WordPerfect's default margins are at columns 10 and 74. To get shorter or longer lines, type new values and press Enter after each one.
3. *Different spacing* (option 4). The default value of 1 makes WordPerfect print single-spaced. To get double- or triple-spacing, change it to 2 or 3. To get space-and-a-half, change it to 1.5.
4. Turn the Hyphenation feature on or off, or change the H-Zone (option 5). See **Hyphenation** for details.
5. *Different decimal align character* (option 6). WordPerfect normally aligns decimal numbers around a decimal point (.), but you can make it align around a comma or any other character you want.

Changing Line Format Settings Permanently

Giving a Line Format command from within WordPerfect only affects the settings in that particular document. To make WordPerfect apply customized line format settings to all of your new documents, you must obtain the Set-up menu (by starting WordPerfect with **wp/s** instead of just **wp**) and select *Set Initial Settings*. When the Change Initial Settings menu appears, press Shift-F8 and make your changes. When you finish, press Enter to leave the menu, then type 0 (zero) to leave Set-up and enter WordPerfect.

Figure L-1. WordPerfect 5.0's Line Format menu.

```
Format: Line

        1 - Hyphenation                        Off

        2 - Hyphenation Zone - Left            10%
                             Right             4%

        3 - Justification                      Yes

        4 - Line Height                        Auto

        5 - Line Numbering                     No

        6 - Line Spacing                       1

        7 - Margins - Left                     1"
                     Right                     1"

        8 - Tab Set                            0", every 0.5"

        9 - Widow/Orphan Protection            No

Selection: 0
```

Line Format Option — WordPerfect 5.0

5.0

WordPerfect's Format (Shift-F8) menu provides four options, of which *Line* controls how text is arranged on each line and how lines are arranged on a page. When you type 1 from the Format menu, WordPerfect displays the Line Format menu shown in Figure L-1.

The Line Format menu lets you make the following format changes within a document:

1. *Hyphenation* is initially off, which makes WordPerfect keep words together, and move any that cross the right-hand margin to the next line. However, you can enhance the appearance of text by hyphenating it. See **Hyphenation** for details.
2. *Hyphenation Zone* is an imaginary vertical strip that determines whether a word needs hyphenating; see the **Hyphenation Zone** entry.
3. *Justification*. WordPerfect is preset to right-justify text; that is, insert spaces between words to produce an even right-hand margin. By turning Justification off (setting it to *No*), you can produce a ragged right margin.
4. *Line Height*. WordPerfect normally prints six lines per inch on a page, and makes each line one-sixth of an inch high. However, you can compress or expand the space a line occupies by changing this parameter. (The WordPerfect manual sometimes refers to line height as "leading," the formal term that's used by typesetters.)
5. *Line Numbering* lets you print line numbers at the left-hand margin, a common requirement for legal documents.
6. *Line Spacing* is preset to *1*, to produce single-spacing. To switch to double-spacing, make it 2; to switch to space-and-a-half, make it *1.5*; and so on.
7. *Margins*. WordPerfect is preset to provide one-inch margins on the left and right. To make these margins wider or narrower, increase or decrease the *Left* and *Right* values. (The top and bottom margin settings are controlled by the Format command's *Page* option.)
8. *Tab Set*. WordPerfect has preset tabs every half inch. To add a tab, type its position in inches and press Enter; to delete one, move the cursor to it and press Del; to delete all tabs, move the cursor to the beginning of the line (by pressing Home twice, then ←), then press Ctrl and End. For details on the different kinds of tabs, see **Tabs**.

9 *Widow/Orphan Protection*. Normally, WordPerfect simply fills each page to capacity. Unlike a good typist, it may leave the first line of a paragraph alone at the bottom of a page (a *widow*) or the last line at the top of a new page (an *orphan*). This option lets you break it of this sloppy habit.

Changing Line Format Settings Permanently

Changing Line Format values from within WordPerfect only affects the settings in that particular document. To make WordPerfect apply customized line format settings to every new document, press Shift and F1 to give a Setup command. When the Setup menu appears, type 5 for *Initial Settings*, then 4 for *Initial Codes*. When the Reveal Codes screen appears, type Shift-F8 for Format and 1 for Line, then make your changes. When you finish, press F7 (Exit) to leave the menu and return to WordPerfect.

Line Numbering

— See **Print Format Command** (WordPerfect 4.2) or **Line Format Option** (WordPerfect 5.0).

Lines, Drawing

WordPerfect's Screen (Ctrl-F3) command has a *Line Draw* feature that lets you draw lines and boxes using a single line, double line, asterisk, or other character of your choice. Once you turn Line Draw on, WordPerfect draws a line as you move the cursor. This feature is handy for creating bar charts and decorative borders.

Line Draw's drawings are acceptable if you have a daisy wheel printer or a dot matrix printer that can't produce graphics. However, since the lines are drawn with characters, they tend to look rather unprofessional. Fortunately, if you have WordPerfect 5.0 and your printer can produce graphics, there's another way to draw lines.

WordPerfect 5.0's Graphics (Alt-F9) command provides a *Line* option that can draw a solid horizontal or vertical line of any width, length, and darkness you specify. This is convenient for drawing lines to separate items on a page. WordPerfect does not show graphics lines on the editing screen. You must use the Print (Shift-F7) command's *View Document* feature to see them.

Drawing With the Cursor

To draw a line or box, move the cursor to where you want it to begin, then press Ctrl and F3 to give a Screen command. When the Screen menu appears, type **2** to obtain the following *Line Draw* menu:

```
1| ; 2|| ; 3 *; 4 Change; 5 Erase; 6 Move: 1
```

The first three options (single line, double line, and asterisk) are commonly-used drawing characters. Typing **4** for *Change* lets you substitute one of eight other characters—or any character of your choice (say, $, #, or @)—for the asterisk.

Of course, your printer must be able to produce the character you select. If you're not sure it can, use the character to draw a simple figure, then print it.

Note that WordPerfect assumes you want to use the single line (option 1). If you want the double line, asterisk, or some other character, type **2**, **3** or **4**. After doing that, simply move the cursor using the arrow keys; WordPerfect will draw the line. If you change direction, it will insert a corner. When you finish drawing, press F7 to get back to editing.

You can also erase a drawing or any part of it. To do this, move the cursor to where you want to start erasing, then obtain the Line Draw menu and select *Erase*. WordPerfect will then erase every character the cursor passes. To leave the Erase mode, make another choice from the menu or press F1.

Finally, Line Draw's *Move* option lets you move the cursor through the drawing without affecting any of its characters. This is handy for adding lines to a drawing or positioning the cursor for an **Erase**.

Drawing Graphics Lines with WordPerfect 5.0

5.0 To draw a graphics line in a WordPerfect 5.0 document, move the cursor to the line or column where you want the line. Then press Alt and F9 to give a Graphics command and type **5** for *Line*. When the following menu appears at the bottom of the screen:

```
1 Horizontal Line; 2 Vertical Line: 0
```

186 Lines, Drawing

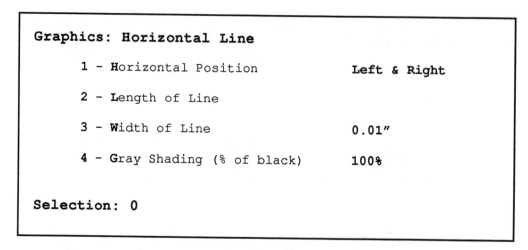

Figure L-2. The Graphics command's Horizontal Line menu.

select the kind of line you want to draw.

Choosing *Horizontal Line* from the Line submenu brings on the menu shown in Figure L-2. Here, WordPerfect assumes you want a thin (0.01-inch), solid-black line that extends from the left margin to the right margin. If that's what you're after, press F7 (Exit) to return to your document. Otherwise, make the necessary changes, then press F7 to get back to editing.

If you type **1** for *Horizontal Position*, WordPerfect displays

```
Horizontal Pos: 1 Left; 2 Right; 3 Center; 4 Both Left & Right; 5 Set Position: 0
```

The *Left* and *Right* options draw a line from the left- or right-hand margin to the cursor position, and show its length in the *Length of Line* field. (Change that value to make the line longer or shorter.) *Center* tells WordPerfect to draw a line that's centered between the margins, but sets its length to 0" (change it to what you want).

Set Position draws a line from the right-hand margin to a point you specify. Initially, it displays a prompt of the form **Offset from left of page:** *d"*, where *d"* is the distance from the left edge of the paper to the cursor. For example, if the cursor is at the left margin, the Offset will be 1". Press Enter to accept that value, or type a different value, then press Enter.

Choosing *Vertical Line* from the Line submenu brings on the menu shown in Figure L-3. Here, WordPerfect assumes you want a thin (0.01-inch), solid-black line slightly to the left of the left-hand margin, extending from the top margin to the bottom margin. If this is

```
Graphics: Vertical Line

    1 - Horizontal Position           Left Margin

    2 - Vertical Position             Full Page

    3 - Length of Line

    4 - Width of Line                 0.01"

    5 - Gray Shading (% of black)     100%


Selection: 0
```

Figure L-3. The Graphics command's Vertical Line menu.

what you're after, press F7 (Exit) to return to your document. Otherwise, make the necessary changes, then press F7 to get back to editing.

If you type **1** for *Horizontal Position*, WordPerfect displays

```
Horizontal Position: 1 Left; 2 Right; 3 Between Columns; 4 Set Position: 0
```

The *Left* and *Right* options place the line slightly left of the left-hand margin or slightly right of the right-hand margin. *Between Columns* places it between a specified text column (see **Columns, Text**) and the column to its right. *Set Position* places it at the cursor's column position, and displays the distance of that position from the left edge, in inches.

If you type **2** for *Vertical Position*, WordPerfect displays

```
Vertical Position: 1 Full Page; 2 Top; 3 Center; 4 Bottom; 5 Set Position: 0
```

The *Full Page* option extends the line from the top margin to the bottom margin. *Top* and *Bottom* draw a line from the top or bottom margin to the cursor position, and fill in the *Length of Line*. *Center* tells WordPerfect to draw a line that's centered between the top and bottom margins. Its length is set to **9"** initially, the distance between the margins; change the length to what you want. Finally, choosing *Set Position* draws a line from the cursor to the bottom margin, and displays the distance from the top edge to the cursor, in inches. *Set Position* also fills in *Length of Line*.

Viewing Graphics Lines

WordPerfect does not display graphics lines on the editing screen. To see how the line will look when you print the page, you must display the page using WordPerfect's *View Document* feature.

To begin, press Shift and F7 to give a Print command. When the menu appears, type 6 to select *View Document*. WordPerfect clears the screen and draws a miniaturized version of the page. At the bottom, it displays the following menu:

```
1 100%; 2 200%; 3 Full Page; 4 Facing Pages: 3
```

The screen shows how the page looks under the *Full Page* option (note that 3 is selected). To see how the page will look in its true, printed size, select *100%*; to see it double-size, select *200%*. Neither option can display the entire page, but you can use the arrow keys to move from one part to another.

On any page but the first one, you can select *Facing Pages* to obtain a "full page" size view of that page and the one that faces it. That is, you can view pages 2 and 3, 4 and 5, and so on. When you finish admiring your handiwork, press F7 (Exit) to return to your document.

Lines Per Inch — WordPerfect 4.1 and 4.2

4.1
4.2

Note: While WordPerfect 4.1 and 4.2 regulate the number of lines on a page with the *Lines Per Inch* parameter described here, WordPerfect 5.0 regulates lines with a *Line Height* parameter. See **Line Format Option — WordPerfect 5.0** for details.

WordPerfect is preset to print 6 lines per inch, but you can change it to 8. You can do this to print with a small type size—say, 16.5 characters per inch.

To change the lines per inch setting, press Ctrl and F8 to give a Print Format command. When the Print Format menu appears, type 2 to select *Lines per Inch*, type your new value, then press Enter. Press Enter again if you are finished using the Print Format menu.

When you change the Lines per Inch setting, WordPerfect inserts a hidden [LPI:*n*] code in your document, where *n* is whatever value you entered.

Of course, changing the Lines per Inch setting from within WordPerfect simply changes it in that document. To change the setting for all of your new documents, see the procedure given under **Page Format Command**.

Lines Per Page

—See **Page Format Command (WordPerfect 4.1 and 4.2)**

List Files Command (F5)

The List Files command allows you to operate on the files on a data disk. That is, it lets you copy files, rename them, retrieve them into WordPerfect, and so on.

When you press the F5 key, WordPerfect assumes you want a list or *directory* of the files on the current data disk, and puts **Dir B:*.*** at the bottom of the screen. (On a hard disk, this is usually **Dir C:\WP*.*.**) Here, the * (asterisk) is a *wildcard* character that acts as shorthand for "any group of characters." Thus, *.* means "any file name and any extension"; in other words, *every* file.

Specifying the Files to be Listed

Sometimes (and especially with a hard disk) you don't want to list every file; you want just the ones you intend to work with. If you want just one file, type its name (and extension, if it has one) and press Enter. To list a group of similarly-named files, you can include the asterisk in the filename. Some examples are:

- Entering ***.let** lists all files that have the extension *let*.
- Entering **sales*.doc** lists files whose names begin with *sales* and have the extension *doc*.

190   List Files Command (F5)

- Entering **sales*.*** lists files whose names begin with *sales*, regardless of their extension.

You can also include a question mark (?) in a filename, to represent "any single character." You can compare it with the Joker in popular card games, a free number in Bingo, or a blank tile in Scrabble. You can put ? anywhere in a filename—even several times. For example, entering **Dir rptq28?.doc** produces a list of report documents for all second-quarter sales reports for the 1980s. Similarly, **Dir rptq?8?.doc** lists all quarterly sales reports for the 1980s.

The List Files Screen

When you enter the file specifier for the Dir prompt (or press Enter to accept WordPerfect's default, *.*), WordPerfect produces an alphabetized list of the files you asked for and shows a menu below it. WordPerfect 5.0's List Files menu looks like this:

```
1 Retrieve; 2 Delete; 3 Rename; 4 Print; 5 Text In; 6 Look; 7 Other Directory; 8 Copy;
9 Word Search; N Name Search: 6
```

Note: WordPerfect 4.1's menu has no *Name Search* option and lists 0 as the default selection, which means you can type 0 or press Enter to leave List Files. WordPerfect 4.2's menu has a 0 *Exit* option in place of *Name Search*.

The lighted bar (initially at the top left corner of the list) is used to select the file(s) you want to operate on. To select a file, move the bar to its name by pressing the arrow keys.

Note that the menu's default option is 6. This means that if you simply press Enter, WordPerfect will do a Look operation (details are upcoming) on whichever file is highlighted.

Operating on Multiple Files

With WordPerfect 4.2 or 5.0, you can Delete, Print, or Copy a group of files with one operation. Simply highlight each file you want and type an asterisk (*). WordPerfect puts * to the right of the third entry, the file size, and advances to the next file name. You can also mark *every* file on the List Files screen; press Alt-F5 (Mark Text) or press Home, then type *.

When you finish selecting files, choose *Delete* (2), *Print* (4), or *Copy* (8). When the following kind of message appears:

```
Copy Marked Files? (Y/N) N
```

type **y** to operate on the marked files or press Enter to operate only on the file that's highlighted.

Retrieve

Retrieve leaves List Files and copies the highlighted file onto the screen. Using Retrieve does the same thing as pressing Shift-F10 from within WordPerfect, except you highlight the filename rather than enter it manually. (Of course, you can only Retrieve files that contain WordPerfect documents; to retrieve a text file, use the *Text In* option.)

A word of caution: WordPerfect does *not* clear the editing screen before it retrieves a document. Thus, if you Retrieve onto a screen that already contains text, WordPerfect will *insert the retrieved document into your text* at the cursor position. WordPerfect 4.1 and 4.2 make this insertion without warning. Fortunately, WordPerfect 5.0 is more polite. If the screen is not blank, it asks you to confirm that you really want to insert the new text into what's already there.

Of course, you may want to insert text on purpose if, say, the disk document contains "boilerplate" text you want to reproduce in a contract or form letter. However, if you absent-mindedly Retrieve a document without first clearing the screen, you must either Exit the document without saving it (by pressing F7, then typing **n** and **y**) or delete the retrieved text manually.

Delete

Delete displays a precautionary **Delete** *filename*? **(Y/N) N prompt, and erases the highlighted file if you answer y.** But be careful. Once you delete a file, it's gone forever.

Rename

Rename lets you change the name of the highlighted file, by responding to a New Name: prompt. You can also use Rename to move a file to a different disk or hard disk directory. For example, to remove a file called REPORT.DOC from its current disk and save it on the disk in drive A, enter **a:report.doc** for **New Name:**. Here, Rename does the same thing as a Copy followed by a Delete.

Print

Print prints a copy of the highlighted file. With WordPerfect 4.2 and 5.0, you can also print several different files, by marking them in the list. See *Operating on Multiple Files* toward the beginning of this entry.

Note: WordPerfect 5.0 is preset to save documents on disk in unformatted form, using a Fast Save feature. To print a Fast-Saved document, you must Retrieve it onto the screen and print it using a Print (Shift-F7) command.

Text In

Text In copies the highlighted text file onto the screen and arranges it within the margins. Unfortunately, this option only works well for files that contain line-oriented material such as lists.

If a line extends past the right-hand margin, Text In moves the excess material to the next line and puts a hidden [SRt] (Soft Return) code at the end of the shortened line. It also puts a [HRt] (Hard Return) code at the original end-of-line position.

In regular text, WordPerfect inserts an [SRt] code when it moves excess material to a new line, and inserts an [HRt] code when *you* press Enter at the end of a paragraph. Thus, in effect, Text In splits a text file paragraph into several paragraphs. As Figure L-4 shows, Text In's paragraph-reformatting technique may produce WordPerfect text that's nowhere near what you want.

Fortunately, there's another way to load a text file into WordPerfect: Press Ctrl and F5 to give a Text In/Out command, then (with WordPerfect 4.2) type **3** for *Retrieve (CR/LF in H-Zone becomes [SRt])* or (with WordPerfect 5.0) type **1** for *DOS Text* and **3** for *Retrieve (CR/LF to [SRt] in HZone)*. When **Document to be Retrieved:** appears at the bottom of the screen, type the text file's name, then press Enter.

```
The following is a paragraph within a text file:

    Text files are files on disk that contain only characters;
that is, letters or symbols. They contain no special control
codes (not even tabs), and therefore cannot represent bold,
underlined, subscripted, or superscripted material.

This is how the same paragraph is arranged when you load it into
WordPerfect using the List Files Text In option:

    Text files are files on disk that contain only characters;
that is, letters
or symbols. They contain no special control codes (not even
tabs), and therefore
cannot represent bold, underlined, subscripted, or superscripted
material.
```

Figure L-4. The effect of the List Files command's *Text In* option on a paragraph within a text file.

Unlike List Files' *Text In* option (and Text In/Out's equivalent, option 2), the option 3 *Retrieve* simply rearranges a text file paragraph to fit within WordPerfect's margins. It remains one paragraph, not several.

Look

Look lets you examine the highlighted document without retrieving it. You can, for example, check a chart, table, or quotation while preparing a description of it. You can also look at an earlier part of a report, to avoid repetitions and (worse) contradictions. Thus, Look gives you quick access to a document without going to all the bother of loading it onto the screen.

With WordPerfect 4.1 or 4.2, you can only move forward in the displayed document. That is, you can press ↓ to move down the screen, + (Screen Down) on the numeric keypad to reach the bottom of the screen, or PgDn to reach the next page. However, with WordPerfect 5.0, you can use the regular cursor-moving keys to move backward or forward, and use the Search commands (F2 and Shift-F2) to find a specific word or phrase.

In WordPerfect 4.2 and 5.0, *6* is the default; it's the option that gets selected if you press Enter. WordPerfect 4.1's default option is *0*, so pressing Enter makes your document reappear.

Other Directory

List Files always assumes you want to operate on the files on the current disk or hard disk directory. This option lets you work with some other disk or directory.

When you type **7** to select *Other Directory* (labeled *Change Directory* in the WordPerfect 4.1 and 4.2 menus), WordPerfect shows **New Directory =** at the bottom of the screen. You can then enter the disk or directory name just as you would for the initial *Dir* message. As with Dir, you can also include ? and * wildcard characters. For example, to list the files on drive A that have the extension .LET, enter **a:*.let**.

Copy

This option copies the highlighted file to a specified disk or hard disk directory. Note that since this is a copy operation, and not a move, the original version of the file is unaffected.

With WordPerfect 4.2 and 5.0, you can copy multiple files. See *Operating on Multiple Files* toward the beginning of this entry.

Word Search

This option makes WordPerfect produce a smaller list, one that names all the files in the current list that contain a specified word or word pattern. Selecting *Word Search* makes WordPerfect display a **Word Pattern:** prompt at the bottom of the screen. You can then enter a specific word, to list the files that contain that word, or enter a word pattern, to list the files that contain any word that matches that pattern.

A word pattern can include a question mark (?) to represent a single letter or an asterisk (*) to represent an unspecified number of consecutive letters. For example, entering **197?** makes WordPerfect search for all occurrences of dates in the 1970s. (Of course, it doesn't know that this is a date; it will also find all occurrences of the number 197.) Similarly, entering **Corp*** makes WordPerfect search for all variations of *Corp*, regardless of whether they are abbreviations (Corp.) or full words (Corporation or Corporations).

The word pattern is case-sensitive. If you include a capital letter, WordPerfect will only find occurrences in which that particular letter is capitalized. For example, entering **International** makes it locate *International* or *INTERNATIONAL*, but not *international*. On the other hand, entering a lowercase word such as *international* makes it locate all occurrences.

You can also search for several words. If you separate them with a semicolon (;) or space, WordPerfect will list all files that contain both words. For example, entering **Smith;Jones** or **Smith Jones** produces a list of the files that contain *Smith* and *Jones*. (The order of the words is unimportant here. Entering **Jones;Smith** would produce the same list.)

You can also separate words in a pattern with a comma, to make WordPerfect list the files that contain either word. For example, entering **Smith,Jones** makes WordPerfect list the files that contain *Smith* or *Jones*, or both names.

Finally, you can combine semicolons, commas, and spaces in a word pattern. For example, entering **Smith;Jones Wilson** lists the files that contain either *Smith* or *Jones* and also *Wilson*.

Name Search

This option lets you move quickly to any filename in the list. When you type **n**, WordPerfect displays **Name Search:** at the bottom of the screen. Type the name you want. As you press keys, WordPerfect anticipates what you're after, and moves the highlighting to the next name that starts with those characters.

WordPerfect 4.1 and 4.2 also provide the Name Search feature, but don't list it in their menus. Like version 5.0, they home in on a filename as you type it.

Leaving List Files

To leave List Files and return to editing, type **0** or press Enter in WordPerfect 4.1, type **0** in WordPerfect 4.2, or press F7 (Exit) in WordPerfect 5.0.

Lists

WordPerfect can produce up to five different lists, based on words or phrases you specify. This is handy to summarize page numbers for figures, illustrations, and tables in a document.

To create a list, you must *build* it by marking entries, *define* the numbering style, then *generate* the list.

Building a List

To build a list, you must tell WordPerfect what to include. To begin, move the cursor to the beginning of the word or phrase you want and obtain Block mode. Then highlight the text by either pressing the → key to select characters or pressing Ctrl and → to select words. With that done, proceed as follows:

1. Press Alt-F5 to give a Mark Text command.
2. When the menu appears, type **2** to select List.
3. When *List #:* appears, enter a number between 1 and 5 to specify the list you want the entry included in.

Repeat these steps for each word or phrase you want to include in the list. When you finish, move the cursor to where the list should appear and enter a heading, if you want one. Now you must tell WordPerfect which numbering style to use.

Defining the Numbering Style

WordPerfect can generate a list in any of five numbering styles. They are:

1. No page numbers
2. Page numbers follow entries
3. Page numbers follow entries, but are enclosed in parentheses. For example, if the "Truman" entry is on page 43, this option would produce

```
                    Truman (43)
```

4. Flush right page numbers; that is, numbers aligned along the right-hand margin.
5. Flush right page numbers with leaders; that is, with periods between the entry and the page number.

To select the style, begin by pressing Alt-F5. Then

- **For WordPerfect 4.1**, type **6** for *Define*.
- **For WordPerfect 4.2**, type **6** for *Other Options*, then **3** for *Define List*.
- **For WordPerfect 5.0**, type **5** for *Define*, then **2** for *Define List*.

When requested, type the number of the list you want to generate. When the *List Definition* menu (Figure L-5) appears, type the number of the style you want.
Generating a List
To make WordPerfect generate the list, obtain the Mark Text menu (Alt-F5), then:

Figure L-5. List Definition menu.

```
List n Definition

    1 - No Page Numbers
    2 - Page Numbers Follow Entries
    3 - (Page Numbers) Follow Entries
    4 - Flush Right Page Numbers
    5 - Flush Right Page Numbers with Leaders
```

Generating a List

To make WordPerfect generate the list, obtain the Mark Text menu (Alt-F5), then:

- **For WordPerfect 4.1**, select *Generate*.
- **For WordPerfect 4.2**, select *Other Options*, then *Generate Tables and Index*.
- **For WordPerfect 5.0**, select *Generate*, then *Generate Tables, Indexes, Automatic References, etc.*

When the screen shows

```
Existing tables, lists, and indexes will be replaced.
Continue? (Y/N): Y
```

type **y**. WordPerfect begins creating the list, and displays **Generation in progress** at the bottom of the screen. When it finishes, the list appears.

WordPerfect puts each list entry at the left-hand margin. It also arranges them in ascending order, by page number, but (unfortunately) does not sort them alphabetically. For any given page number, WordPerfect simply lists the entries in the order you typed them. (To sort a list, see **Sorting**.) Each list entry has the same form as in the document (e.g., bold material in the text is bold in the list). You may want to edit the list to remove these print formats.

Removing Entries from a List

Sometimes you may decide that you don't want a certain entry in your list. Removing an entry involves searching for each occurrence of it in the document and unmarking it.

When you mark text for a list, WordPerfect puts a hidden [Mark:List,n] code ahead of it and an [EndMark:List,n] code after it. Hence, to remove an entry from a list, you must locate the [Mark] code and delete it. (When you do, WordPerfect deletes the [EndMark] code automatically.) To do this, move the cursor ahead of the first occurrence and give a Replace (Alt-F2) command. To put the [Mark] code in your search string, press Alt-F5 for Math/Columns and type **1** to select *List/ToC*.

For example, to remove all references to "Acme Corporation" from a list, move the cursor to the beginning of your document and do the following:

1. Press Shift and F2 to give a Search command.
2. When the **w/Confirm?** prompt appears, press Enter to accept the default, N (No).
3. For **Srch:**, type **Acme Corporation** and press Alt-F5.
4. When the menu appears, type **1** to select List/ToC (WordPerfect inserts [Mark] on the Srch line), then press F2.
5. For **Replace with:**, type **Acme Corporation** and press F2 again.

Now that the entry has been unmarked throughout your document, you can generate the new list.

Loading Documents from Disk

— See **Retrieve Command** or *Retrieve (0)* under **List Files Command**

Locking Documents

— See **Text In/Out Command**

Looking at a Document

— See *Look (6/)* under **List Files Command**

Lotus 1-2-3 Spreadsheets

— See **Convert Program**

Lowercase, Converting Text to

To convert existing text to lowercase, put WordPerfect in Block mode (by pressing Alt-F4), move the cursor to highlight the text, and press Shift-F3. When this menu appears

```
Block: 1 Upper Case 2 Lower Case: 0
```

select *Lower Case*, then press F1 to leave Block mode. This operation affects only letter characters; numbers and symbols are unchanged.

M

Macro Command (Alt-F10)

Pressing Alt and F10 lets you run a macro that was created using the Macro Define (Ctrl-F10) command. When the **Macro:** prompt appears, enter the macro's name. If you misspell it, WordPerfect displays **ERROR: File not found**, then puts you back in editing.

Macro Define Command (Ctrl-F10) — WordPerfect 4.1 and 4.2

4.1
4.2

Pressing Ctrl and F10 makes WordPerfect display a **Define macro:** prompt on the status line and wait for you to enter the name of a macro. When you do, WordPerfect checks your data disk or hard disk directory for that macro. If it finds no macro with that name, it assumes you want to create it. Otherwise, if there's already a macro with that name, WordPerfect assumes you want to replace it.

Defining New Macros

When you define a new macro, the type of name you enter determines whether the macro will be *permanent* (one that WordPerfect saves on disk) or *temporary* (one that only exists during the current work session).

To create a permanent macro, enter two to eight characters, or hold Alt down and type a letter from A to Z. To create a temporary macro, press Enter or type a single letter, then press Enter. Either way, proceed as follows:

1. When the blinking **Macro Def** prompt appears, type the keystrokes you want WordPerfect to play back. Besides text, this can include tab or margin commands, print formats (e.g., Center, Bold, Underline, Subscript), or anything else you can use in a regular document.
2. Wherever you want WordPerfect to pause for a keyboard insertion, press Ctrl and PgUp. When the computer beeps, press Enter *twice* to continue defining the macro.
3. When you finish, press Ctrl and F10 again. WordPerfect saves the macro on your data disk (provided it's of the permanent variety) and then returns to editing.
4. Clear the screen by doing an F7 (Exit) operation.

To replay a named macro (temporary or permanent), press Alt-F10 to give a Macro command, and enter the macro's name at the **Macro:** prompt. To replay an Alt-key macro, press Alt and the letter key together.

Replacing Macros

If your data disk or hard disk directory already has a macro with the name you entered at the Define Macro prompt, WordPerfect shows

```
Replace macroname.MAC? (Y/N) N
```

Type **y** to redefine the macro, or type **n** or press Enter to make Define Macro: reappear.

Macro Define Command (Ctrl-F10) — WordPerfect 5.0

5.0 Pressing Ctrl and F10 makes WordPerfect display a **Define macro:** prompt on the status line and wait for you to enter the name of a macro. When you do, WordPerfect checks your data disk or hard disk directory for that macro. If it finds no macro with that name, it assumes you want to create it. Otherwise, if there's already a macro with that name, WordPerfect assumes you want to replace it.

Defining New Macros

When you define a new macro, the type of name you enter determines whether the macro will be *permanent* (one that WordPerfect saves on disk) or *temporary* (one that only exists during the current work session).

To create a permanent macro, enter one to eight characters, or hold Alt down and type a letter from A to Z. To create a temporary macro, press Enter. Either way, proceed as follows:

1. When the screen shows **Description:**, you may enter a comment (up to 60 characters) that tells what the macro does. To omit the comment, press Enter.
2. When the blinking Macro Def prompt appears at the bottom of the screen, type the keystrokes you want WordPerfect to play back. Besides text, this can include tab or margin commands, print formats (e.g., Center, Bold, Underline, Subscript), or anything else you can use in a regular document.
3. Wherever you want WordPerfect to pause for a keyboard insertion, press Ctrl and PgUp. When the following menu appears:

    1 Pause; **2** Display; **3** Assign; **4** Comment: 0

    type 1 for *Pause*, then press Enter to continue defining the macro.
4. When you finish, press Ctrl and F10 again. WordPerfect saves the macro on your data disk (provided it's of the permanent variety) and then returns to editing.
5. Clear the screen by doing an Exit (F7) operation.

To replay a named macro, press Alt-F10 (to give a Macro command) and enter its name at the **Macro:** prompt. To replay an Alt-key macro, press Alt and the letter key together.

Replacing and Editing Macros

If your data disk or hard disk directory already has a macro with the name you entered at the Define Macro prompt, WordPerfect shows

```
macroname.WPM is Already Defined. 1 Replace; 2 Edit: 0
```

Type **1** to redefine the macro or **2** to edit it. See **Macros, Editing** for details about editing macros.

Macro Files, Operating on

Sometimes you may want to operate on macro files. For example, if a macro name is inappropriate or hard to remember, you will want to rename it. Similarly, you may want to delete a macro you no longer need.

As with regular document files, you can rename, delete, or copy macro files using a List Files command (F5). To list only macro files, enter ***.mac** (for WordPerfect 4.1 or 4.2) or ***.wpm** (for WordPerfect 5.0) when the *Dir* prompt appears. Named macros have file names of the form *macroname*.MAC or *macroname*.WPM; Alt-key macros have file names of the form ALT*L*.MAC or ALT*L*.WPM, where *L* is the letter.

Macro Libraries — WordPerfect 5.0

5.0 WordPerfect 5.0 has a Keyboard Layout feature that lets you create disk files that contain one or more key definitions. Each key definition holds command sequences that tell WordPerfect which operation(s) to perform when you press the associated key or key combination.

You can use a key definition file to change how WordPerfect's command keys operate. (For example, rather than activate the Help feature, you could make F3 move the cursor to the beginning of the line.) However, you can also put a group of macros in a key definition file, to produce a *macro library* that you can activate for a given application. For details, see **Keyboard Layout**.

Macro Programming Commands — WordPerfect 5.0

5.0 WordPerfect 4.1 and 4.2 execute a macro like an actor reading from a script. That is, they replay a macro's keystrokes one after the other, in the exact order you typed them into the macro definition.

While that's handy, in that it saves you from typing the same commands every time, the macros in these earlier versions are pretty dumb. For one thing, they do their work (that is, replay their keystrokes) whenever you activate or *invoke* them, regardless of what WordPerfect is doing at the time. For example, if you designed a macro to operate from regular editing mode (e.g., print the current page), it may do something entirely different if you invoke it from, say, the Footnote or Sort screen.

In short, a WordPerfect 4.1 or 4.2 macro does nothing to ensure that you're using it correctly. It simply replays the keystrokes, regardless of whether they make sense in that context.

WordPerfect 5.0 has a built-in Macro Editor that can help in situations like this, by restricting a macro to specific operating states. You can control how and when a macro operates by including the Macro Editor's *programming commands* in your macros.

These programming commands can also help with jobs that you can't do easily, if at all, using WordPerfect's regular features. For example, you can display prompts, and perform any of several tasks, depending on what the user types in response. You can also generate menus, just as WordPerfect does, and design the macro to react differently to each option the user selects.

But that's enough generalizing; it's now time to take a look at the actual programming commands. The Appendix of the WordPerfect 5.0 manual describes them in alphabetical order. That's fine for reference purposes, but to help you learn how the commands relate to each other, I have divided them into functional groups.

Types of Programming Commands

Macro Editor programming commands have the general form {*command*}*operand(s)*~, where the *operand* specifies data that the command uses. Some programming commands have no operand, others have one, two, or an entire list of them. The operand or operand list is always followed with a tilde (~) character, which tells WordPerfect where this command ends.

Table M-1 summarizes the programming commands and divides them into seven functional groups, as follows:

- User interface commands display messages and prompts, and obtain the user's response from the keyboard.

- *Execution control commands* can alter the sequence in which WordPerfect processes or "executes" the keystrokes in a macro definition.

Table M-1. Macro Editor programming commands.

User Interface Commands

{ASSIGN}*variable~value~*
Set the specified *variable* (0 through 9) to *value*.

{BELL}
Sound a beep through the computer's speaker.

{CHAR}*variable~message~*
Display a *message* on the bottom line and assign the next keyboard character to the specified *variable*.
   See also TEXT, which obtains a string of characters from the user.

{DISPLAY OFF}
Hide any status messages and menus this macro produces. WordPerfect still displays any error messages, however. *Note:* When you create a macro, WordPerfect inserts a DISPLAY OFF command at the beginning of it automatically.

{DISPLAY ON}
Display any messages and menus this macro produces.

{LOOK}*variable~*
If the user has typed a character, assign it to the specified *variable*; otherwise, continue executing the macro. LOOK is similar to CHAR, except it doesn't wait for a key from the user.

{ORIGINAL KEY}
Return the user's most recent keystroke. This can be a single key or a combination, such as Ctrl-Enter.

{PAUSE}
Pause to let the user enter text from the keyboard.

{PROMPT}*message~*
Display a *message* on the bottom line.

{TEXT}*variable~message~*
Display a *message* on the bottom line, and assign whatever the user enters next (up to 120 characters) to the specified *variable*.
   See also CHAR and LOOK, which obtain a single character from the user.

Table M-1 *(continued)*

{WAIT}*interval*~
Pause for the specified *interval* (in tenths of a second), then resume executing the macro.

Execution Control Commands

{BREAK}
Skip to the end of the current IF structure or, if {BREAK} is not in an IF structure, to the end of the macro.

{CALL}*label*~
Call (run) the subroutine that starts at *label*.

{CANCEL OFF}
If the user presses the F1 (Cancel) key, disregard it.

{CANCEL ON}
Cancel the current operation if the user presses the F1 key.

{CASE}*value~case1~label1~case2~label2~...caseN~labelN~~*
Compare the specified *value* with each *case* value. If there is a match, transfer to the corresponding *label*. If no match is found, continue at the line that follows CASE.
  Note that the last label in the list must be followed by two tildes (~~) rather than one.

{CASE CALL}*value~case1~label1~case2~label2~...caseN~labelN~~*
Like CASE, except if a match is found, CASE CALL calls the subroutine that has the corresponding *label*.

{GO}*label*~
Transfer to the line that has the specified label.

{LABEL}*label*~
Define a label to serve as the "target" for a GO, CALL, CASE, or CASE CALL command. A label can be as long as you want and can include any character, even a space.

{QUIT}
Stop executing all macros immediately.

Table M-1 *(continued)*

{RESTART}
Stop executing all macros when the current subroutine or macro finishes.

{RETURN}
Return from the current subroutine or leave the current macro.

{SPEED}*interval*~
Slow down the macro by waiting for the specified *interval* (in hundredths of a second) between each keystroke in the definition.

Exception Commands

{ON CANCEL}*command*~
Execute the specified *command* if the user presses F1 (Cancel) or a subroutine or nested macro signals "cancel" upon return. The legal commands here are BREAK, CALL, GO, RESTART, RETURN, RETURN ERROR, RETURN NOT FOUND, and QUIT.

Since the label in a GO or CALL command must be followed by a tilde (~), these forms of ON CANCEL must have two tildes at the end. Thus, the generalized formats are:
{ON CANCEL}GO*label*~~
{ON CANCEL}CALL*label*~~

{ON ERROR}*command*~
Execute the specified *command* if a macro or subroutine signals an error upon return or an error occurs during a regular WordPerfect operation or a DOS operation. See {ON CANCEL} for the list of legal commands and a note about tildes for the GO and CALL forms.

{ON NOT FOUND}*command*~
Execute the specified *command* if a Search, Word Search, or Name Search operation fails. See {ON CANCEL} for the list of legal commands and a note about tildes for the GO and CALL forms.

{RETURN CANCEL}
Return from the current subroutine or macro and indicate "cancel" to the higher level. RETURN CANCEL must be preceded by an ON CANCEL command, to tell WordPerfect what to do if it receives a cancel signal.

Table M-1 *(continued)*

{RETURN ERROR}
Return from the current subroutine or macro and indicate "error" to the higher level. RETURN ERROR must be preceded by an ON ERROR command, to tell WordPerfect what to do if it receives an error signal.

{RETURN NOT FOUND}
Return from the current subroutine or macro and indicate "not found" to the higher level. RETURN NOT FOUND must be preceded by an ON NOT FOUND command, to tell WordPerfect what to do if it receives a not found signal.

STATE Command

{STATE}
Return a number that indicates WordPerfect's current operating state. The number is the sum of all active conditions, as follows:

1,2,3	Current document number. Set to 3 when the Sort screen is being displayed; set to 1 or 2 (for *Doc 1* or *Doc 2*) otherwise.
4	An editing screen is being displayed.
8	A Header, Footer, Footnote, or Endnote editing screen is being displayed.
16	The macro definition (Macro Def) screen is being displayed.
32	A macro is being executed. Since you can only read STATE from within a macro, this condition is always true.
64	A Merge operation is taking place.
128	Block mode is on.
256	Typeover mode is on.
512	The Reveal Codes screen is being displayed.
1024	A Yes/No question is being displayed.

IF Structures

{IF}*value~*
..
..
{END IF}
If *value* is nonzero, execute the lines between {IF} and {END IF}; otherwise, if it is zero, skip to the line that follows {END IF}.

Table M-1 *(continued)*

{IF}*value*~
..
..
{ELSE}
..
..
{END IF}
If *value* is nonzero, execute the lines between {IF} and {ELSE}; otherwise, if it is zero, execute the lines between {ELSE} and {END IF}.

{IF EXISTS}*variable*~
..
..
{END IF}
If the *variable* exists, execute the lines between {IF EXISTS} and {END IF}; otherwise, skip to the line that follows {END IF}.

{IF EXISTS}*variable*~
..
..
{ELSE}
..
..
{END IF}
If the *variable* exists, execute the lines between {IF EXISTS} and {ELSE}; otherwise, execute the lines between {ELSE} and {END IF}.

Macro-Chaining Commands

{CHAIN}*macro*~
Execute the specified *macro* when the current macro finishes.

{NEST}*macro*~
Execute the specified *macro*, then resume the current macro.

Single-Step Commands

{STEP ON}
Execute the macro one keystroke at a time. Proceed to the next keystroke when the user presses a key.

Table M-1 (continued)

{STEP OFF}
Turn off single-stepping.

• If the user presses Cancel, an error occurs, or a search operation doesn't find what it's looking for, WordPerfect activates a "cancel," "error," or "not found" signal. The *exception commands* tell WordPerfect what to do if it receives one of these signals. There are also commands that let you turn on these "exception" signals to indicate some occurrence within your macro.

• The *STATE command* returns a number that indicates what the user was doing (editing text, defining a macro, etc.) when he or she invoked the macro.

• The *IF structure* is used to execute commands conditionally, based on whether an operand has a nonzero ("true") or zero ("false") value. If the operand is nonzero, WordPerfect processes the lines between the structure's IF and END IF terms. Otherwise, if the operand is zero, WordPerfect skips to the line that follows END IF. You can also include an ELSE term in the structure, to execute one set of lines if the operand is nonzero and another set of lines if it's zero.

There is also an IF EXISTS structure that bases its execution decision on whether a variable is in use, or "exists."

• *Macro-chaining commands* let you invoke one macro from within another.

• *Single-step commands* let you execute a macro one keystroke at a time, to locate errors in it.

The Macro Editor also lets you include *comments* in a macro description, to tell what the macro is doing. Comments have the general form {;}*text*~. Since comments aren't commands (they don't *do* anything), WordPerfect ignores them when it executes a macro.

Inserting Programming Commands

To insert a comment or a PAUSE, DISPLAY ON or OFF, or ASSIGN command in a macro you're defining, press Ctrl-PgUp and select from the menu. However, the other commands can only be inserted in existing macros. thus, you must create the macro, then *edit* it.

To edit a macro definition, press Ctrl-F10 to give a Macro Define command. When the **Define macro:** prompt appears, enter the macro's name or press its Alt-*letter* key combination. Since this macro already exists, WordPerfect notifies you that

macroname.WPM is Already Defined. 1 Replace; 2 Edit: 0

Type 2 for *Edit*. When the Macro: Edit screen appears, type 2 to reach the *Action* box.

Move the cursor to where you want a programming command inserted, then press Ctrl and PgUp simultaneously. Pressing Ctrl-PgUp (for *Macro Commands*) makes WordPerfect produce an alphabetized list of the available commands and highlight the first one. To insert that command, press Enter; to insert some other command, move the highlighting to it, then press Enter.

Note that although most programming commands require an operand (e.g., the CALL command requires a label), WordPerfect inserts only the command term. You must enter the operand and the tilde (~) that ends it.

Inserting Cursor-Moving and Text-Editing Commands

You can also insert WordPerfect's *cursor-moving* and *text-editing* commands in a macro definition. Let me explain. If you press, say, Tab or Enter while you're creating a macro, WordPerfect records the key as a command, and moves the cursor to the next tab stop or line when you execute the macro. However, if you press Tab or Enter while you're editing a macro definition, WordPerfect assumes you're simply formatting the definition, so it moves the cursor but doesn't generate a code.

WordPerfect also assumes that you're editing a definition if you press any other key that moves the cursor (such as End, an arrow key, or PgUp) or operates on the text (such as Del or Backspace). Similarly, it assumes that you want to cancel changes to the definition if you press F1, or leave the definition if you press F7.

There are two ways to insert these cursor-moving and text-editing functions as executable commands:

- To insert just one of these functions, press Ctrl-V, then the key you want. For example, to insert a Tab command, press Ctrl-V, then Tab.

- To insert several of these functions in succession, press Ctrl-F10 to give a Macro Define command. When **Press Macro Define to enable editing** appears, press the keys you want. When you finish, press Ctrl-F10 again to return to editing. For example, to insert the

Macro Programming Commands — WordPerfect 5.0

sequence that sends WordPerfect to the beginning of a document, press Ctrl-F10, Home, Home, up-arrow, and Ctrl-F10.

As with the programming commands, the Macro Editor displays your key commands as codes enclosed in braces. That is, it shows {Tab} where you pressed Tab, {Up} where you pressed the up-arrow key, {Cancel} where you pressed F1, and so on.

Inserting Variables

WordPerfect 5.0 provides ten *variables* (numbered 0 through 9) that you can use to hold an integer (a number with no decimal point, such as 3, 244, or -14), a calculation, or a block of text temporarily. Once you give a variable a value, it keeps that value until you change it or leave WordPerfect, in which case all ten variables disappear.

The **Variables — WordPerfect 5.0** entry in this book describes how to use the *Macro Commands* (Ctrl-PgUp) feature to define a variable from within a document. As you may recall, once a variable has been defined, you can insert its value anywhere by typing its Alt-*number* combination (Alt-0, Alt-1, or whatever).

You can also include these operations in a macro that you're creating. However, inserting them into an existing macro requires some different procedures. In the next section, I describe the Macro Editor programming commands that you can use to assign a value to a variable. For now, I'll concentrate on how to insert the name of a variable in a macro definition, to make WordPerfect obtain that variable's value when it executes the macro.

As with the cursor-moving and text-editing functions, if you simply press Alt-*number* (say, Alt-3 for variable 3) in a macro definition you're editing, the Macro Editor inserts the variable's current value. To register an Alt-*number* combination as an executable command, you must precede it with either Ctrl-V (to insert one variable name) or Ctrl-F10 (to insert several key commands). The Macro Editor will then show your variable as {VAR 0}, {VAR 1}, or whatever is appropriate.

I will now describe the Macro Editor's programming commands, starting with the user interface commands, the first of seven functional groups I listed earlier.

User Interface Commands

The Macro Editor provides a variety of commands you can use to make a macro interact or "interface" with the user. Among them are commands that read the user's keyboard responses into one of WordPerfect's ten general-purpose variables. The command I'll describe first, ASSIGN, doesn't necessarily use keyboard characters, but since it involves variables, it's better suited to this group than any other.

ASSIGN activates a variable by giving it a specified value. For example, {ASSIGN}1~3~ sets variable 1 to 3. You can also use the contents of an existing variable (even the same one) in the *value* term, as in these examples:

{ASSIGN}1~{VAR 2}~	{;}Set Var 1 = Var 2 ~
{ASSIGN}1~{VAR 2}-{VAR 3}~	{;}Set Var 1 = Var 2 - Var 3~
{ASSIGN}3~-{VAR 3}~	{;}Change the sign of Var 3~
{ASSIGN}3~2*{VAR 3}~	{;}Double the value of Var 3~

By the way, note how the comments here can help you understand what's happening. A comment such as "Set Var 1 = Var 2" is certainly more meaningful than {ASSIGN}1~{VAR 2}~.

You can also discard or unassign a variable from within a macro, by ASSIGNing an empty value to it. For example, {ASSIGN}1~~ puts variable 1 back on the "does not exist" list. The Macro Editor has an IF EXISTS feature (described under *IF Structures*) that bases an execution decision on whether a variable exists.

The CHAR and TEXT commands display a prompt on the status line and record the user's typed response in a variable. However, CHAR accepts only a single character (say, a **y** or **n** response to a question, or the number of a menu option), while TEXT accepts a string of up to 120 characters, with an Enter at the end. For example, the following displays a question and records the user's one-character answer in variable 1:

```
{CHAR}1~Do you want to continue (Y/N)? Yes~
```

Since the CHAR and TEXT messages are usually *prompts*, WordPerfect takes them off the screen as soon as the user has responded.

The LOOK command also reads a keyboard character into a variable, but unlike CHAR, neither displays a prompt nor waits for the keystroke. LOOK simply accepts a key if it's available. Otherwise, if the user hasn't pressed a key, LOOK does nothing but send WordPerfect to the next line.

LOOK can be useful in loops where you're waiting for a typed response, but need to do other things in the meantime. For example, you may be maintaining a timer that limits the time a user has to respond to a prompt or select from a menu. Here, you would decrease the timer while you wait.

Further, if your macro uses a keystroke immediately, you needn't record it in a variable. You can use the ORIGINAL KEY command to obtain it. ORIGINAL KEY always contains the last keystroke the user typed.

One of the simplest interfacing command is PAUSE, which makes WordPerfect wait until the user has entered something, but doesn't display a message. Further, while CHAR and TEXT record the user's response in a variable, PAUSE puts it directly on the screen, as regular text. Thus, CHAR and TEXT are handy when you must save what the user types for later use, but PAUSE is more appropriate if you simply want to insert the response into a document.

You could use PAUSE to let the user enter, say, a name, address, or price in a "personalized" form letter or computerized invoice-maker. For example, the following inserts "Name:" and PAUSEs while the user enters a name, then skips a line and PAUSEs again for a "Street:" entry:

Name: {PAUSE}{Enter}{Enter}
Street: {PAUSE}{Enter}{Enter}

PROMPT does the opposite of PAUSE. That is, it displays a message at the bottom of the screen, but doesn't require the user to enter anything. Recall that because CHAR and TEXT messages are usually prompts, WordPerfect takes them off the screen as soon as the user responds. By contrast, since WordPerfect has no way of knowing when you no longer want a PROMPT message, it displays this message until you turn it off.

To make WordPerfect display a message briefly, give a DISPLAY OFF, a PROMPT, and then a WAIT. DISPLAY OFF hides the status messages, prompts, and menus that a macro would normally display as it executes. While DISPLAY OFF doesn't hide PROMPT messages, it removes them as soon as the macro reaches the next line—unless that line is a WAIT command.

WAIT is not an executable command, so DISPLAY OFF doesn't affect it. In fact, WAIT is the opposite of an executable command; it makes the macro *stop* executing for a specified interval. Its general form is {WAIT}*interval*~, where *interval* is a delay period in tenths of a second. The following sequence uses DISPLAY OFF, PROMPT, and WAIT to display a message for two seconds (i.e., 20 tenths of a second):

{DISPLAY OFF}
{PROMPT}That option doesn't exist. Please try again.~
{WAIT}20~

When you create a macro, WordPerfect inserts a DISPLAY OFF command at the beginning of it automatically. However, you may really want to see a macro's messages and menus if, say, you're trying to locate an error in it. To make WordPerfect show everything, simply delete the {DISPLAY OFF}. Or, if you just want to see the messages and menus in just part of a macro, precede that part with DISPLAY ON and follow it with DISPLAY OFF.

WordPerfect lets you get fairly creative with the CHAR, PROMPT, and TEXT messages. Besides text, you can include *control characters* that style the text (e.g., underline it or make it blink) or move the cursor; see Table M-2. To insert a control character in a message string, press Ctrl-V, then press the character's Ctrl-key combination.

Note that the Macro Editor provides control characters to turn on and off three commonly-used attributes: reverse video (black letters on a white background, instead of vice versa), underlining, and bold. To work with other display attributes, you can use Ctrl-N and Ctrl-O, which turn on or off the attribute whose code follows it. Table M-3 lists the attribute codes.

For example, to produce blinking characters in a message, press Ctrl-N and Ctrl-P to turn blinking on, type the characters, then press Ctrl-O and Ctrl-P to turn blinking off. The Macro Editor displays this sequence as

```
{^N}{^P}text{^O}{^P}
```

By the way, don't bother trying to relate the on-screen codes to the attributes they represent—{Home} for Italics, {Tab} for Shadow Print, etc. These display codes are simply byproducts of their respective Ctrl-key combinations. They're the same as for the control characters in Table M-2, where they make more sense.

The Ctrl-V character helps you create WordPerfect 5.0-style menus, where the user can select an option by typing either its number or a letter in its name. WordPerfect is preset to display option-selecting letters as bold, but you can easily make it use underlining, italics, or any other attribute you want. To change the letter-display attribute, you must enter its code in a *Menu Letter Display* parameter that's contained in the Setup (Shift-F1) command's Display Setup submenu. Once you select the attribute, pressing Ctrl-V turns it on.

Table M-2 Control characters for use in CHAR, PROMPT, and TEXT message strings.

Press Ctrl-V, then	Displayed as	Action
Ctrl-H	{Home}	Move cursor to the top left-hand corner of the screen
Ctrl-J	{Enter}	Start a new line
Ctrl-K	{Del to EOL}	Delete the rest of the line
Ctrl-L	{Del to EOP}	Clear the screen and move cursor to the top left-hand corner
Ctrl-M	{^M}	Move cursor to the beginning of the line
Ctrl-N	{^N}	Turn on display attribute. Follow {^N} with one of the attribute codes listed in Table M-3.
Ctrl-O	{^O}	Turn off display attribute. Follow {^O} with one of the attribute codes listed in Table M-3.
Ctrl-P	{^P}	Move cursor to the specified screen location. Follow {^P} with a column and line code, as listed in Table M-4.
Ctrl-Q	{^Q}	Turn off all display attributes
Ctrl-R	{^R}	Turn on reverse video
Ctrl-S	{^S}	Turn off reverse video
Ctrl-T	{^T}	Turn on underlining
Ctrl-U	{^U}	Turn off underlining

Table M-2. (continued)

Press Ctrl-V, then	Displayed as	Action
Ctrl-V	{^V}	Turn on the attribute for displaying option-selecting letters in a menu
Ctrl-W	{Up}	Move to preceding line
Ctrl-X	{Right}	Move to next character
Ctrl-Y	{Left}	Move to preceding character
Ctrl-Z	{Down}	Move to next line
Ctrl-]	{^]}	Turn on bold
Ctrl-\	{^\}	Turn off bold

The Macro Editor has no control character that turns off only the option letter attribute, but you can use Ctrl-Q, which turns off *every* active display attribute at the same time. For example, suppose you want the user to choose from the following menu:

    1 Letter; 2 Memo: 0

where 1, 2, and 0 are bold, while L and M have the current selection letter attribute. The following CHAR command displays this menu and reads the user's selection character into variable 1:

{CHAR}1~{^]}1 {^V}L{^Q}etter; {^]}2 {^V}M{^Q}emo: {^]}0{^\}~

CHAR, PROMPT, and TEXT normally display their messages on the bottom (status) line, but by including a Ctrl-H, Ctrl-L, or Ctrl-P control character, you can make WordPerfect display the rest of the message on the main screen.

Ctrl-H and Ctrl-L move the cursor to the top left-hand corner of the screen, but Ctrl-P moves it to a column and line that you specify. You can't enter the column and line numbers directly; however, you

Table M-3. Display attribute codes for use with a {^N} (turn on) or {^O} (turn off) control character.

Press Ctrl-V, then	Displayed as	Attribute
Ctrl-A	{^A}	Very Large
Ctrl-B	{^B}	Large
Ctrl-C	{^C}	Small
Ctrl-D	{^D}	Fine Print
Ctrl-E	{^E}	Superscript
Ctrl-F	{^F}	Subscript
Ctrl-G	{^G}	Outline
Ctrl-H	{Home}	Italics
Ctrl-I	{Tab}	Shadow
Ctrl-J	{Enter}	Redline
Ctrl-K	{Del to EOL}	Double Underline
Ctrl-L	{Del to EOP}	Bold
Ctrl-M	{^M}	Strikeout
Ctrl-N	{^N}	Underline
Ctrl-O	{^O}	Small Caps
Ctrl-P	{^P}	Blink
Ctrl-Q	{^Q}	Reverse Video

must insert *codes* for them, as listed in Table M-4. Line values can range from 1 to 24, while column values can range from 1 to your right-hand margin.

For example, to move the cursor to column 10 and line 20, type Ctrl-P, Ctrl-J, and Ctrl-T, which WordPerfect displays as {^P}{Enter}{^T}.

Note that to specify a position value greater than 29, you must type Alt and a number. Further, *you must use the keys on the numeric keypad to type the number*; don't try to use the number keys at the top of the regular keyboard.

Execution-Control Commands

When WordPerfect executes a macro, it normally processes lines in the order they occur in the macro definition. The commands I describe here make it transfer to a line elsewhere in a macro or leave the macro entirely.

Table M-4. Codes that specify the column and line positions for the {^P} character in a message string.

Notes:
(1) Column positions can range from 1 to the right-hand margin setting, but line positions can only range from 1 to 24.
(2) Press Ctrl-V before pressing a Ctrl-key combination.
(3) To type an Alt-number combination, use the numbers on the numeric keypad, *not* those on the main keyboard.

Position	Press	Display	Position	Press	Display
1	Ctrl-A	{^A}	41	Alt-41	)
2	Ctrl-B	{^B}	42	Alt-42	*
3	Ctrl-C	{^C}	43	Alt-43	+
4	Ctrl-D	{^D}	44	Alt-44	, (comma)
5	Ctrl-E	{^E}	45	Alt-45	- (hyphen)
6	Ctrl-F	{^F}	46	Alt-46	. (period)
7	Ctrl-G	{^G}	47	Alt-47	/
8	Ctrl-H	{Home}	48	Alt-48	0
9	Ctrl-I	{Tab}	49	Alt-49	1
10	Ctrl-J	{Enter}	50	Alt-50	2
11	Ctrl-K	{Del to EOL}	51	Alt-51	3
12	Ctrl-L	{Del to EOP}	52	Alt-52	4
13	Ctrl-M	{^M}	53	Alt-53	5
14	Ctrl-N	{^N}	54	Alt-54	6
15	Ctrl-O	{^O}	55	Alt-55	7
16	Ctrl-P	{^P}	56	Alt-56	8
17	Ctrl-Q	{^Q}	57	Alt-57	9
18	Ctrl-R	{^R}	58	Alt-58	:
19	Ctrl-S	{^S}	59	Alt-59	;
20	Ctrl-T	{^T}	60	Alt-60	<
21	Ctrl-U	{^U}	61	Alt-61	=
22	Ctrl-V	(^V)	62	Alt-62	>
23	Ctrl-W	{Up}	63	Alt-63	?
24	Ctrl-X	{Right}	64	Alt-64	@
25	Ctrl-Y	{Left}	65	Alt-65	A
26	Ctrl-Z	{Down}	66	Alt-66	B
27	Ctrl-[	{Esc}	67	Alt-67	C
28	Ctrl-\	{^\}	68	Alt-68	D
29	Ctrl-]	{^]}	69	Alt-69	E
30	Alt-30	▲	70	Alt-70	F
31	Alt-31	▼	71	Alt-71	G
32	Alt-32	(space)	72	Alt-72	H

Table M-4. *(continued)*

Position	Press	Display	Position	Press	Display
33	Alt-33	!	73	Alt-73	I
34	Alt-34	"	74	Alt-74	J
35	Alt-35	#	75	Alt-75	K
36	Alt-36	$	76	Alt-76	L
37	Alt-37	%	77	Alt-77	M
38	Alt-38	&	78	Alt-78	N
39	Alt-39	'	79	Alt-79	O
40	Alt-40	(	80	Alt-80	P

The BREAK command terminates the current IF structure or macro. In an IF structure, BREAK makes WordPerfect skip to the line that follows {END IF}. In a nested macro, it makes WordPerfect resume executing the macro that invoked this one.

QUIT is similar to BREAK, except it terminates *every* active macro, not just the current one. RESTART also terminates the active macros, but not until the current subroutine or macro has finished executing.

The GO command makes WordPerfect transfer to a label (that is, to a line containing a LABEL command), as in

{GO}there~

..
..

{LABEL}there~

This particular LABEL line follows GO, but it can actually be anywhere in the macro definition.

CALL is similar to GO, except it transfers to a label that marks the beginning of a *subroutine*. A subroutine is a mini-program that WordPerfect executes, then returns to where the "call" occurred.

Before transferring to a subroutine, CALL takes note of which line follows it and saves this location in memory. Later, when the subroutine finishes executing, a RETURN command retrieves the line location that CALL saved and hands it to WordPerfect, which resumes executing there.

In short, every subroutine must start with a LABEL and end with a RETURN. (RETURN is usually the last command in a subroutine, but it need not be. It must only be the command that WordPerfect *executes* last.) Thus, a subroutine call-and-return sequence should look something like this:

```
{CALL}sub~        {;}Call a subroutine,
 ..               {;} then return here
 ..
{LABEL}sub~       {;}Beginning of subroutine
 ..
 ..
{RETURN}          {;}End of subroutine, return to caller
```

CASE and CASE CALL are similar to GO and CALL, respectively, but they provide a list of labels (rather than just one label), where each is preceded with a value. WordPerfect compares each list value with a specified test value, and transfers to the corresponding label if it finds a match. Otherwise, if no value in the list matches the test value, WordPerfect continues at the next line.

For example, the following sequence displays a yes/no question and acts on the user's response:

```
{LABEL}Ask user~
{CHAR}1~Do you want to continue? (Y/N) Yes~
{CASE}{VAR1}~n~Stop~N~Stop~y~More~Y~More~{Enter}~More~~
{GO}Ask user~     {;}Invalid response, ask again~
 ..
 ..
{LABEL}Stop~      {;}The user said not to continue~
 ..
 ..
{LABEL}More~      {;}The user said to continue~
```

Here, a CHAR command displays the question and reads the user's one-character response into variable 1. A CASE command then sends WordPerfect to *Stop* if the user typed **n** or **N** (it's good programming practice to accept either an uppercase or lowercase response), or to *More* if he or she typed **y** or **Y**, or pressed Enter. (As you may recall, inserting the {Enter} code involves pressing Ctrl-V, then Enter.) Any other key makes WordPerfect "drop through" to the next line, where a GO command sends it back up to *Ask user*, to display the question again.

Normally, the user can abort a macro by pressing the F1 (Cancel) key. However, if your macro is doing some critical job that must not be interrupted, you can give a CANCEL OFF command to make WordPerfect ignore F1.

For example, you may want to disable Cancel if a macro has cut text (or "moved" it, in WordPerfect 5.0 terminology) from a document but hasn't yet pasted it. You wouldn't want to allow a Cancel there because you'd run the risk of the user losing the cut material by doing another Move operation. Once the critical operation has finished, you can give a CANCEL ON command to rearm F1.

Finally, the SPEED command slows down the execution of a macro by making it pause for a specified interval (in hundredths of a second) between keystrokes. You might want to use SPEED to display letters in a title slower than usual—maybe in time to music playing through the speaker! SPEED is also handy for slowing down a macro so you can see what it's doing each step of the way, to try to locate a problem in it. The Macro Editor also provides some other commands that are useful for tracking down errors, and I'll discuss them under *Single-Step Commands*.

To turn off SPEED's delay, and execute keystrokes at normal speed, enter {SPEED}~

Exception Commands

If the user presses the F1 (Cancel) key, an error occurs, or a search operation doesn't find what it's looking for, a macro won't complete its intended operation. When these kinds of things happen, WordPerfect activates one of three "exception" signals: *cancel*, *error*, or *not found*.

For example, it turns on the *error* signal if you try to retrieve a nonexistent document or DOS text file, or attempt to turn on math columns before you have defined them. Similarly, it activates the *not found* signal if a Search or Replace operation is unsuccessful, or you try to edit a nonexistent footnote or endnote.

WordPerfect ignores the exception signals unless you tell it how to deal with them. To do this, you must precede the operation that may generate an exception with an ON CANCEL, ON ERROR, or ON NOT FOUND command. Each "ON" specifies a command that WordPerfect should execute if it receives the corresponding exception signal. Your command choices here are BREAK, CALL, GO, RESTART, RETURN, RETURN ERROR, RETURN NOT FOUND, and QUIT. (I'll describe RETURN ERROR and RETURN NOT FOUND shortly.)

For example, Figure M-1 shows a sequence that searches for a [Cntr] (Center) code in a document. At the beginning, an ON NOT

FOUND command instructs WordPerfect to GO to a *SearchUp* line if it receives a "not found" exception signal thereafter. This is followed by a search-forward operation.

A successful search makes WordPerfect RETURN from the macro; an unsuccessful search transfers to SearchUp, where another ON NOT FOUND tells WordPerfect to GO to *Failed* if it again receives a "not found." The next search works backward through the document, and RETURNs if it finds a [Cntr] code. If this search is unsuccessful, WordPerfect transfers to *Failed*, where it displays ERROR: Can't find a Center code and then RETURNs.

While WordPerfect only activates the exception signals in situations where it's designed to do so, the Macro Editor provides commands that let you turn them on whenever you want. These are RETURN-with-exception commands called RETURN CANCEL, RETURN ERROR, and RETURN NOT FOUND. They do the same thing as RETURN (return from a subroutine or leave a macro), but also turn on an exception signal.

For example, if your macro displays a custom menu, you may want to do a RETURN CANCEL if the user chooses an "Exit" option. Similarly, you may want to do a RETURN ERROR if the user types an invalid option number. Here, you could use ON CANCEL or ON ERROR to tell WordPerfect how to respond.

```
{DISPLAY OFF}
{ON NOT FOUND}{GO}SearchUp~~
{Home}{Search}{Center}{Search}    {;}Search forward for [Cntr]~
{RETURN}                          {;} and leave if you find it~

{LABEL}SearchUp~
{ON NOT FOUND}{GO}Failed~~
{Home}{Search Left}{Search}       {;}Otherwise, search backward~
  {RETURN}
{LABEL}Failed~                    {;}If this fails, tell the user,~
{PROMPT}ERROR: Can't find a Center code~
{WAIT}20~
{RETURN}                          {;} then leave~
```

Figure M-1. A search sequence that uses ON NOT FOUND.

STATE Command

The STATE command returns a number that summarizes the conditions under which WordPerfect is currently operating. STATE obtains this number from a special register that WordPerfect maintains internally. You can think of this register as a bank of 11 on/off switches, where the setting of each switch indicates whether a particular condition is active. For instance, one of these switches is "on" when WordPerfect is operating in Block mode and "off" otherwise.

Of course, these aren't actually switches; they're simply cells, or "bits," in the computer's memory. A bit is a storage unit in memory, that can hold a value of 1 or 0. It contains 1 if its related condition is active ("on") or 0 if the condition is not active ("off").

Thus, the STATE command reports WordPerfect's current operating state by returning a number that reflects the on/off (1/0) status of all 11 bits. Although each bit can contain only 1 or 0, STATE produces a regular decimal number. This calls for some explanation.

Figure M-2 shows the arrangement of the bits in WordPerfect's internal operating state register and lists the operating condition for each one. Note that the bit positions are numbered right-to-left (0 to 10) and that there is a decimal value above each bit number.

Here, the decimal value indicates the numeric "weight" of its bit position. Each bit position has a value of 2^x (that is, 2 raised to the power x), where x is the bit's position number. Thus, bit 0 has a value of 2^0, or 1; bit 1 has a value of 2^1, or 2; and so on—up to the leftmost bit position, 10, which has a value of 2^{10}, or 1024.

The number that STATE returns is, then, the sum of the values for each bit whose condition is active. For example, suppose you're editing text on the Doc 1 screen with both Block and Typeover off, and you run a macro that gives a STATE command. In that particular operating state, only register bits 0, 2, and 5 are set to 1; the rest are 0. Hence, STATE adds 1 + 4 + 32, and return the total, 37.

If you put just {STATE} in a macro, WordPerfect replaces it with the sum of the active conditions. However, you normally won't want the sum; instead, you will want to *interpret* that number to determine which operating conditions are active. To do this, you must combine {STATE} with the value(s) of the conditions you're testing for, using a "logical AND" operation. In case you aren't familiar with logical operations (few non-programmers are), I'll offer a brief and hopefully painless explanation.

The term "logical" here refers to the fact that this operation obeys the rules of formal logic rather than those of mathematics. A logical AND operation obeys the rule that states, "If A is true and B is true,

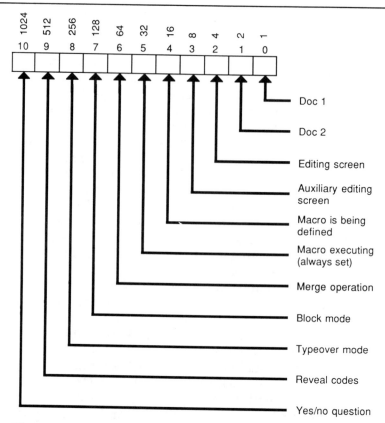

Figure M-2. The STATE command's bit assignments.

then C is true." Logical AND applies that rule to corresponding bits in two operands—STATE's sum and the test value, in this case.

Specifically, for each bit position where both operands are true (1), AND sets the bit in the result value to 1. For any other combination, AND sets the result bit to 0. In short, then, any bit ANDed with 0 becomes 0, while any bit ANDed with 1 retains its original value. In table form, this is:

Bit in Operand #1	Bit in Operand #2	Bit in Result
0	0	0
0	1	0
1	0	0
1	1	1

To perform a logical AND within the Macro Editor, put an & character between the operands. Here, you would use the form {STATE}&*n*, where *n* is the value of the condition you're testing for—from the STATE entry in Table M-1—or the sum of several condition values, if you're testing for more than one condition. For example, to test for Block mode, enter **{STATE}&128**—because as Figure M-2 shows, Block's bit position (8) has a value of 128. This operation produces 128 if Block mode is on, or 0 if it's off.

Pay special attention to bits 2 and 3, which deal with editing screens. WordPerfect sets bit 2 to 1 when the user is working in an editing screen—*any* editing screen. If that happens to be a Header, Footer, Footnote, or Endnote editing screen, WordPerfect also sets bit 3 to 1. Thus, the operation {STATE}&12 can produce three different result values. It produces:

- *0* if a menu, prompt, or question is being displayed. A question will also set bit 10 to 1.
- *4* if an editing screen is being displayed.
- *12* if a Header, Footer, Footnote, or Endnote editing screen is being displayed.

Here, a menu can be either the regular one-line, bottom-of-screen kind or a full-screen menu, such as the one the Print command produces. WordPerfect also treats the Help, Keyboard Layout, List Files, Sort, Spell, Style, Thesaurus, and View Document screens as menus.

IF Structures

An IF structure does one of two things, depending on whether its operand is zero or some other (nonzero) value. The basic form is:

{IF}*value*~
..
..
{END IF}

where WordPerfect executes the lines between {IF} and {END IF} if *value* is nonzero, and skips to the line that follows {END IF} if *value* is zero.

IF structures are often used to make a "decision" based on WordPerfect's operating state. For example, if Block mode is on, the following IF structure turns it off:

{IF}STATE&128
  {Block}
{END IF}

The IF structure's *value* can also be a relational test that compares two terms to determine whether the first term is equal to (=), not equal to (!=), greater than (>), or less than (<) the second term. Here, WordPerfect executes the IF lines if the relationship is "true" and skips them if it's "false." For example, the following sequence displays an error message and transfers to a line labeled *Restart* if variable 2 holds a negative number:

{IF}{VAR 2}<0~
  {PROMPT}You can't enter a negative number here.~
  {GO}Restart~
{END IF}

You can also include an {ELSE} term in an IF structure, to make WordPerfect execute one set of lines if the operand is nonzero and a different set of lines if the operand is zero.

IF structures are often used to put WordPerfect in the mode in which a macro is designed to operate. For example, the IF structure shown in Figure M-3 puts WordPerfect in the main editing screen by systematically checking for each possible operating mode and turning off any that are active.

You can even use an {ELSE} term by itself, to do an "IF NOT" type operation. For example, this sequence turns Block mode on if it isn't on already:

{IF}STATE&128   {;}Is Block on?
{ELSE}
  {Block}   {;}No, Turn it on.
{END IF}

The Macro Editor also provides an IF EXISTS structure that bases its execution decision on whether one of WordPerfect's ten variables (0 through 9) has a value, or "exists." To activate a variable in a macro definition, you can either ASSIGN a value to it or read keyboard characters into it with a CHAR, LOOK, or TEXT command. As I mentioned earlier, you can also free up a variable (put

```
{LABEL}Top~
{IF}{STATE}&4~                          {;}In some editing screen~
  {IF}{STATE}&8~                        {;}If in auxiliary editing screen,~
    {Exit}                              {;} leave it ~
  {ELSE}{IF}{STATE}&64~                 {;}If a Merge is taking place,~
    {^Q}                                {;} terminate it~
  {ELSE}{IF}{STATE}&128~                {;}If Block mode is on,~
    {Block}                             {;} turn it off~
  {ELSE}{IF}{STATE}&256~                {;}If Typeover is on,~
    {Typeover}                          {;} turn it off~
  {ELSE}{IF}{STATE}&512~                {;}If in Reveal Codes, ~
    {Reveal Codes}                      {;} leave it~
  {ELSE}                                {;}If in main screen with reular~
    {RETURN}                            {;} editing mode, end the macro~
  {END IF}{END IF}{END IF}{END IF}{END IF}
{ELSE}
  {IF}{STATE}&1024~                     {;}If a yes/no question is active,
    y                                   {;} answer yes
  {ELSE}                                {;}If a menu is being displayed,
    {Cancel}                            {;} leave it
  {END IF}
{END IF}
{GO}Top
```

Figure M-3. A sequence that puts WordPerfect in regular editing mode.

it back on the "does not exist" list) by ASSIGNing an empty value to it, as in {ASSIGN}1~~.

IF EXISTS can be handy for determining whether the user has responded to a prompt or selected from a menu. The following sequence waits for a keystroke, then reads it into variable 0:

```
{ASSIGN}0~~                 {;}Clear variable 0 ~
{LABEL}Wait~
{LOOK}0~                    {;}Has the user pressed a key?~
{IF EXISTS}0~
{ELSE}
  {GO}Wait~                 {;}No, go back and check again~
{END IF}
  ..                        {;}Yes, continue here~
  ..
```

To begin, an ASSIGN clears variable 0, in case it already has a value. The LABEL line marks the beginning of a Wait loop. With each pass through the loop, a LOOK command tries to read a keyboard character into variable 0. Since variable 0 won't exist until LOOK has actually read a character, the IF EXISTS that follows fails continually. That makes WordPerfect drop through to the ELSE term, where a GO sends WordPerfect back to the Wait label.

When the user finally presses a key, LOOK records it in variable 0. The IF EXISTS test then succeeds and, since there's nothing between {IF EXISTS} and {ELSE}, WordPerfect continues at the line that follows {END IF}. You may want to use that line to select a course of action based on which key the user pressed. A CASE or CASE CALL command with {VAR 0} as its test value would be a reasonable choice.

Macro-Chaining Commands

The Macro Editor has two commands that let you invoke a macro from inside the current one, or "chain" one macro to the other. NEST invokes the specified macro immediately, while CHAIN invokes it when the current macro finishes.

In either case, if the macro has a regular name, type it; if it's assigned to an Alt-*letter* combination, type **alt** and the letter. For example, {NEST}mymac~ invokes a macro called MYMAC, while {NEST}altf~ invokes the macro assigned to Alt-F.

Single-Step Commands

Sometimes a new macro doesn't do exactly what you intended, and you must locate and correct the error. If the problem is obvious (say, you turned on Bold when you meant to Underline), you can simply edit the macro and make your change. However, if the problem is more subtle, you may have a difficult time locating it. It gets even more difficult if the macro executes so fast that you can't keep track of what it's doing.

Of course, you can slow down a macro by including a SPEED command, which I described under *Execution Control Commands*. However, if you want total control over how fast a macro executes, you can use a STEP ON command to make WordPerfect "single-step" through it. Here, WordPerfect executes the macro one keystroke at a time, and proceeds to the next keystroke when you press a key. Each time, WordPerfect indicates which keystroke it will execute next at the bottom left-hand corner of the screen.

How WordPerfect represents the next keystroke depends on what that keystroke does. If it produces a character, invokes an Alt-key macro, or inserts a variable, WordPerfect shows the character, ALT *letter* (ALT A, ALT B, etc.), or VAR *number* (VAR 1, VAR 2, etc.). However, if the next keystroke is a WordPerfect command or a Macro Editor programming command, its screen message is somewhat harder to interpret.

You might expect WordPerfect key commands to be depicted by codes such as {Block} and {Bold}, as they are on the Macro Edit screen. But instead (unfortunately), WordPerfect represents them with a message of the form **KEY CMD** *n*, where *n* is a predefined number for a command. Table M-5 lists these command numbers and shows the codes that appear on the Macro Edit screen and the key(s) you press to produce them.

In a CHAR, TEXT, or PROMPT message string, some codes can represent either a command or a display attribute, depending on how they're being used. In these instances, I list both functions in the *Key(s)* column.

Table M-5. *KEY CMD* numbers displayed with STEP ON.

No.	Code on Screen	Key(s)
1	{^A}	Ctrl-A (*Very Large* attribute) in message string
2	{^B}	Ctrl-B (*Large* attribute) in message string
3	{^C}	Ctrl-C (*Small* attribute) in message string
4	{^D}	Ctrl-D (*Fine Print* attribute) in message string
5	(^E)	Ctrl-E (*Superscript* attribute) in message string
6	{^F}	Ctrl-F (*Subscript* attribute) in message string
7	{^G}	Ctrl-G (*Outline* attribute) in message string
8	{Home}	Home; Ctrl-H (*Move to Top Left Corner* command or *Italics* attribute) in message string
9	{Tab}	Tab; Ctrl-I (*Shadow* attribute) in message string
10	{Enter}	Enter; Ctrl-J (*New Line* command or *Redline* attribute) in message string
11	{Del to EOL}	Ctrl-End; Ctrl-K (*Delete to End of Line* command or *Double Underline* attribute) in message string
12	{Del to EOP}	Ctrl-PgDn; Ctrl-L (*Clear Screen, Move to Top Left Corner* command or *Bold* attribute) in message string

13	{^M}	Ctrl-M (*Move to Start of Line* command or *Strikeout* attribute) in message string
14	{^N}	Ctrl-N (*Turn On Display Attribute* command or *Underline* attribute) in message string
15	{^O}	Ctrl-O (*Turn Off Display Attribute* command or *Small Caps* attribute) in message string
16	{^P}	Ctrl-P (*Move to Specified Column and Line* command or *Blink* attribute) in message string
17	{^Q}	Ctrl-Q (*Turn Off All Display Attributes* command or *Reverse Video* attribute) in message string
18	{^R}	Ctrl-R (*Turn On Reverse Video*) in message string
19	{^S}	Ctrl-S (*Turn Off Reverse Video*) in message string
20	{^T}	Ctrl-T (*Turn On Underline*) in message string
21	{^U}	Ctrl-U (*Turn Off Underline*) in message string
22	{^V}	Ctrl-V (*Turn On Option Letter Display Attribute*) in message string
23	{Up}	Up-arrow; Ctrl-W (*Move to Preceding Line*) in message string
24	{Right}	Right-arrow; Ctrl-X (*Move to Next Character*) in message string
25	{Left}	Left-arrow; Ctrl-Y (*Move to Preceding Character*) in message string
26	{Down}	Down-arrow; Ctrl-Z (*Move to Next Line*) in message string
27	{Esc}	Esc
28	{^\}	Ctrl-\ (*Turn Off Bold*) in message string
29	{^]}	Ctrl-] (*Turn On Bold*) in message string
32	{Cancel}	F1
33	{Search}	F2
34	{Help}	F3
35	{Indent}	F4
36	{List Files}	F5
37	{Bold}	F6
38	{Exit}	F7
39	{Underline}	F8
40	{Merge R}	F9
41	{Save}	F10
44	{Setup}	Shift-F1
45	{Search Left}	Shift-F2
46	{Switch}	Shift-F3
47	{L/R Indent}	Shift-F4

Macro Programming Commands — WordPerfect 5.0

48	{Date/Outline}	Shift-F5
49	{Center}	Shift-F6
50	{Print}	Shift-F7
51	{Format}	Shift-F8
52	{Merge Codes}	Shift-F9
53	{Retrieve}	Shift-F10
56	{Thesaurus}	Alt-F1
57	{Replace}	Alt-F2
58	{Reveal Codes}	Alt-F3
59	{Block}	Alt-F4
60	{Mark Text}	Alt-F5
61	{Flush Right}	Alt-F6
62	{Math/Columns}	Alt-F7
63	{Style}	Alt-F8
64	{Graphics}	Alt-F9
65	{Macro}	Alt-F10
68	{Shell}	Ctrl-F1
69	{Spell}	Ctrl-F2
70	{Screen}	Ctrl-F3
71	{Move}	Ctrl-F4
72	{Text In/Out}	Ctrl-F5
73	{Tab Align}	Ctrl-F6
74	{Footnote}	Ctrl-F7
75	{Font}	Ctrl-F8
76	{Merge/Sort}	Ctrl-F9
77	{Macro Define}	Ctrl-F10
80	{Backspace}	Backspace
81	{Del}	Del
82	{Del Word}	Ctrl-Backspace
83	{Word Right}	Ctrl-Right arrow (Move to next word)
84	{Word Left}	Ctrl-Left arrow (Move to preceding word)
85	{End}	End
88	{Goto}	Ctrl-Home
89	{Page Up}	PgUp

No.		
90	{Page Down}	PgDn
91	{Screen Down}	+ on Numeric Keypad
92	{Screen Up}	-(minus) on Numeric Keypad
93	{Typeover}	Ins
94	{Left Mar Rel}	Shift-Tab
95	{HPg}	Ctrl-Enter (New page)
96	{SHy}	Ctrl-Hyphen (Soft hyphen)
97	{-}	Alt-Hyphen

Codes 1 through 29 can also serve as column or line position specifiers for the {^P} control character, in which case {^A} selects position 1, {^B} selects position 2, and so on. Keep this additional function in mind when you're interpreting KEY CMD codes.

Table M-6. *MACRO CMD* numbers displayed with STEP ON.

No.	Command	No.	Command
1	{ASSIGN}	28	{ON ERROR}
2	{BELL}	29	{ON NOT FOUND}
3	{BREAK}	30	{PAUSE}
4	{CALL}	31	{PROMPT}
5	{CANCEL OFF}	32	{QUIT}
6	{CANCEL ON}	33	{RESTART}
7	{CASE}	34	{RETURN}
8	{CASE CALL}	35	{RETURN CANCEL}
9	{CHAIN}	36	{RETURN ERROR}
10	{CHAR}	37	{RETURN NOT FOUND}
12	{DISPLAY OFF}	38	{SPEED}
13	{DISPLAY ON}	39	{STEP ON}
14	{ELSE}	40	{TEXT}
16	{END IF}	41	{STATE}
20	{GO}	42	{WAIT}
21	{IF}	44	{Macro Commands}
22	{LABEL}	45	{STEP OFF}
23	{LOOK}	46	{ORIGINAL KEY}
24	(NEST)	47	{IF EXISTS}
27	{ON CANCEL}		

Macro Editor programming commands are also represented as numbers, in a message of the form MACRO CMD *n* (see Table M-6). Note that {;}, the comment code, is missing from this table. That's because WordPerfect ignores comments during single-stepping just as it ignores them during regular execution. It skips past them, and shows neither a command number nor the comment's text.

As you may have guessed, the STEP OFF command makes WordPerfect stop single-stepping and return to executing the macro at normal speed.

If you think you know which key sequences are causing a problem, you may want to single-step through *them*, and execute everything else at normal speed. If that doesn't help, you can always run the entire macro in single-step mode.

Macro, Repeating a

Sometimes you want to insert the same material several times in succession. This is particularly common when you must prepare a list of names and addresses, product descriptions, or anything else in which the entries are similar. To create such lists from the keyboard, the operator would have to perform the entry procedure repeatedly until he or she has completed the list.

One way to eliminate some of this repetition is to define the general structure of an entry as a macro, then run that macro whenever you want to insert the entry. For example, if the list consists of names and addresses, the macro could produce the labels *Name:*, *Street Address:*, *City:*, *State:*, and *Zip Code:*, and pause after each one to let the operator fill in the information.

If you know how many times you want to repeat a procedure (e.g., how many names and addresses you want to enter), you can tell WordPerfect to repeat the macro. To begin, press the Esc (Escape) key. WordPerfect shows n = 8 (or **Repeat Value = 8**, in WordPerfect 5.0) at the bottom of the screen; it assumes you want to repeat the next operation (run a macro, in this case) eight times. If that's what you want, start the macro as usual. Otherwise, type the repetition count you want, then start the macro.

For example, to repeat a macro called *names* ten times, press Esc and type **10**, then press Alt-F10. When the **Macro:** prompt appears, enter **names**.

Macros, Chaining

WordPerfect lets you call or *start* one macro from inside another. The manual refers to this technique as "chaining" macros. Chaining is handy in that it lets you combine a number of small (and hopefully error-free) macros to build bigger macros. This is like having an assortment of spices that you can choose from to make different recipes.

To chain an existing macro to a new one, define the new macro as usual, but when you get to the place where WordPerfect is to run the existing macro, enter a start command for it. WordPerfect will not actually start the second macro at this point; it will start the second macro when you run the new one.

Example — Format-Changing Macro

Under **Macros That Perform Commands**, I describe macros that change the tabs, margins, and line spacing (Alt-T, Alt-M, and Alt-L, respectively). Using chaining, you could define a fourth macro that changes all three parameters. The definition of this macro (call it Alt-F, for Format) would be simply

Alt-T Alt-M Alt-L

Macros like this one are convenient if you regularly use different formats for various projects. (For example, you may use one format for letters, another for reports, and a third for memoranda). WordPerfect starts every new document with its built-in or "default" format settings. However, by creating format-changing macros such as Alt-F, you can switch formats by simply pressing the appropriate keys. This lets you get right to work without spending time giving format commands.

```
Ctrl-F10                    Begin macro definition
Alt-R                       Assign the macro to the Alt-R keys
Home Home Down-arrow        Move to the end of the document
Alt-F10                     Run a macro
REV Enter                   Macro to be run is REV
Ctrl-F10                    End macro definition

Create the REV macro with the following keystrokes:

Ctrl-F10                    Begin macro definition
REV Enter                   Name the macro REV
Ctrl-Home Up-arrow          Move to top of current page
Shift-F7 2                  Print this page
Shift-F2                    Search backward
Space F2                    Search for a space. NOTE: Macro terminates
                            when it searches backward from the first
                            page.
Alt-F10                     Run a macro
REV Enter                   Macro to be run is REV itself
Ctrl-F10                    End macro definition
```

Figure M-4. Keystrokes to create two macros for printing out in the correct page order on nonreversing laser printers.

Repeating Chains

If a macro includes a Search command, you can make WordPerfect repeat it until the search fails. To do this, simply chain the macro to itself, by starting a macro within in its own definition.

For example, Figure M-4 shows the keystrokes needed to create two macros for WordPerfect 4.1 or 4.2: Alt-R and the macro Alt-R calls, REV. Together, they print the current document in reverse order, starting at the last page and working backward. This is handy if you have a laser printer that stacks pages in the opposite order from what you want.

Here, Alt-R simply moves to the end of the document, then calls REV to do the actual printing. REV moves to the beginning of the page, prints it, then searches backward for a space. The space will, of course, be somewhere on the preceding page, so that's where WordPerfect moves. REV then calls itself to repeat the operation. However, when REV searches for a space from the top of the first page, the search will fail and REV will stop operating. When that happens, WordPerfect returns to the Alt-R macro, which puts you back in your document.

Much as I would like to take credit for these ingenious macros, I can't. They were developed by Daniel L. Lieberman, and appeared in the Power User column of the September 29, 1987 issue of *PC Magazine*.

Macros, Converting from WordPerfect 4.2 to WordPerfect 5.0

5.0

The WordPerfect 5.0 *Conversion* disk has a MACROCNV program that can convert a WordPerfect 4.2 macro to WordPerfect 5.0 format. It gives the converted macro the same filename but makes its extension WPM rather than MAC. You may have to do additional work, however.

If a command is unchanged from version 4.2 (e.g., pressing F6 produces Bold in both versions), MACROCNV converts it directly. However, if a command is different in 5.0 (e.g., Alt-F8 produces the Page Format command in 4.2, but Page Format is a submenu of the Format command in 5.0), MACROCNV inserts the comment *BAD!*, and leaves it up to you to replace the comment with the appropriate 5.0 key sequence. The procedure you need is described in **Macros, Editing**.

To use MACROCNV with a computer that has floppy disks, start as usual and obtain the B> prompt. Insert the Conversion disk into Drive A and the disk that has the macro to be converted into Drive B. Then enter a command of the form a:macrocnv *macroname*, where *macroname* is the name of the macro file, minus its .MAC extension. When it finishes, MACROCNV shows

> Done. Conversion statistics for b:*macroname*.mac
> Number of characters processed: *n*

and an additional message. If it converted the macro entirely, it shows "This macro should work without any major modifications." Otherwise, if the macro needs editing, it shows "This macro will not work properly without major modifications to *n* function(s) which require extensive hand fix-up."

Converting a macro with a hard disk is similar, except if the macro is in a different directory (as it usually is), you must precede its name with a "path." For example, to convert a WordPerfect 4.2 macro called ALTF (i.e., pressing Alt-F invokes it) in the *WP* directory, enter **macrocnv c:\wp\altf**. MACROCNV puts the converted file (ALTF.WPM, here) in the *WP* directory, so you will have to copy it to *WP50*, your WordPerfect 5.0 directory.

If your disk already has a WordPerfect 5.0 macro with the same name as the one you're converting, MACROCNV shows

```
Warning! File macroname.wpm already exists.
Ok to overwrite it? (Y/N) No
```

To replace the existing macro, type **y**; to try again, press Enter or type n.

Macros, Editing

WordPerfect 4.1 and 4.2 allow you to create macros, but do not provide a way to change or *edit* them directly. To edit these macros, you must obtain the separate *WordPerfect Library* package, which contains a Macro Editor program.

Fortunately, WordPerfect 5.0 has a macro-editing feature built in. To edit a macro, press Ctrl and F10 to give a Macro Define command

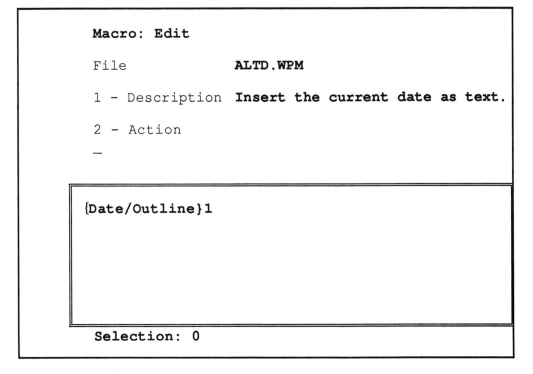

Figure M-5. Sample Macro Edit screen

and enter the macro's name. Recognizing that the macro already exists, WordPerfect displays

```
macroname.WPM is Already Defined. 1 Replace; 2 Edit: 0
```

In response, type 2 to *Edit* the macro. This brings on a screen that looks similar to Figure M-5.

This particular screen shows the entries for a simple macro that inserts the text for the current date when you press Alt and D. Here, ALTD.WPM is the name of the macro file on disk, while *Description* is an optional comment that tells what the macro does (or anything else you want to include) and *Action* refers to the box that displays the commands in the macro.

To edit the Description or the macro definition in the Action box, type &1& or &2& to reach it. Within the definition, you can use Home, End, Del and the other standard functions to edit or move the cursor. *You can also record any of these functions as a command the macro should replay, by pressing Ctrl-V before you type it.* The Typeover feature doesn't work in the Action box, however. To replace text, you must insert the new material and delete the old.

When you finish editing, press F7 (Exit) to save your changes and return to *Selection*, or press F1 (Cancel) to exit without saving the changes. If you are done working with the Edit screen, press F7 once more to return to your document.

Note that *Action* displays commands similar to the way Reveal Codes displays them in regular text, except it encloses command codes with { and } instead of [and]. Action's command codes are also generally easier to understand than Reveal Codes', because they're spelled out rather than abbreviated. For example, {Date/Outline} in the sample macro indicates that Shift-F5 was pressed when the macro was defined. Similarly, the Edit screen displays Shift-F8 as {Format}, F7 as {Exit}, F6 as {Bold}, and F8 as {Underline}.

Macros, Introduction to

Most work involves a certain amount of repetition. For example, unless you print correspondence on letterhead paper, you must enter your return address and date at the top each time. Further, if you regularly prepare documents such as price quotations, legal contracts, and response letters, you must usually enter some of the same

Macros, Introduction to 241

paragraphs (or similar paragraphs) in each one. Sometimes you may have to repeat certain WordPerfect commands, too. For instance, if you often include single-spaced lists or tables in a double-spaced document, you must change the spacing (and perhaps the margins and tabs) before and after the table.

With WordPerfect, you can save yourself from typing the same sequence of keystrokes every time by defining the sequence as a "macro." *A macro is simply a sequence of keystrokes (text or commands) that WordPerfect plays back when you tell it to.* That is, a macro makes WordPerfect perform like an actor reading from a script.

Besides saving typing time, macros also provide some other side benefits. For example, when using a macro to reproduce a block of text, you needn't worry about misspellings or typing mistakes. If you entered error-free text into the macro, WordPerfect will always replay it without errors. Moreover, because a computer is replaying the text, it will appear faster than anyone could type it. Finally, using macros to replay key commands saves you from having to remember them. Considering the many key combinations that WordPerfect furnishes for commands, you probably appreciate the benefit of *that*.

In addition to text and WordPerfect commands, macros may include *pause* commands that let you insert material from the keyboard. The pause command is convenient for including "personalized" items such as names or addresses.

Typical macro users include:

- Attorneys who want to produce stock or *boilerplate* paragraphs that refer to a specific person or company.

- Businesspeople who want to use a form letter to reply to someone who has requested the address of a local dealer or the price of a specific item.

- Engineers who want to prepare status reports that include variable items (e.g., dates, manpower estimates, and costs) within set tables or blocks of text.

- Anyone who wants to produce periodic meeting notices or bulletins that differ only in time, place, or purpose.

WordPerfect 5.0 also provides a macro-like feature that lets you assign a number, a simple calculation, or a block of text to an Alt-*number* key combination (Alt-0 through Alt-9); see **Variables** for details.

242 Macros, Introduction to

Permanent and Temporary Macros

WordPerfect lets you define two different kinds of macros. *Permanent macros* are those you define for use in any document; they are stored on disk, and remain there until you erase them. *Temporary macros* are those you define for use within the current work session; they are stored in memory, and disappear when you leave WordPerfect or turn the computer off.

In the course of defining a macro, WordPerfect must give it a name. The name determines what you must type to make WordPerfect replay the macro, and the *form* of the name tells WordPerfect whether to make the macro permanent or temporary.

Naming Permanent Macros

To define a macro as permanent, you must either give it a name (two to eight letters in WordPerfect 4.1 or 4.2, one to eight letters in WordPerfect 5.0) or assign an Alt-*letter* key combination to it. Giving a macro a regular name lets you replay it by typing that name, while assigning a key combination lets you replay it by pressing those keys. There are advantages and drawbacks to each naming technique, as follows:

- Using a name makes the macro easy to remember, but you must give a Macro (Alt-F10) command to start it, which means another keystroke.
- Using an Alt-key combination makes the macro easy to start (press Alt and the other key), but more difficult to remember.

For example, suppose you want to define a macro that makes WordPerfect switch to single-spacing. (This macro would contain the keys you must press to obtain single-spacing. In WordPerfect 4.1 or 4.2, the sequence is Shift-F8, 4, 1, and Enter.) You could either name the macro, say, *single* or assign it to a key combination such as Alt-S, where S stands for "single."

In general, if you plan to use a macro often, assign a key combination to it; otherwise, give it a regular name.

Naming Temporary Macros

To define a temporary macro, press Enter when WordPerfect asks for its name. (WordPerfect 4.1 and 4.2 also treat macros with one-letter names as temporary macros.)

Using Macros

To use a macro, you must create or *define* it, then tell WordPerfect where to replay it. For the details on defining macros, see **Macro Define Command**. When you reach the place in a document where you want to replay a macro, do one of two things:

- If you gave the macro a regular name, press Alt and F10. When WordPerfect shows Macro:, type the macro's name and press Enter.
- If you assigned the macro to an Alt-key combination, hold Alt down and press the letter key.

Macros Can Generate Commonly-Used Phrases

If you use a phrase often (say, your company name or "party of the first part"), you should define a macro for it. If there aren't too many such phrases, you can define them as Alt-key macros; otherwise give them names. For example, you might have WordPerfect type Acme International Corporation when you press Alt-A. Similarly, it's reasonable to assign "party of the first part" to Alt-P—or perhaps to Alt-F, if you have assigned "party of the second part" to Alt-S. In fact, I used an Alt-W macro to produce "WordPerfect " throughout this book.

Of course, macros are'nt limited to producing phrases. You could design one to type an entire letter. The **Form Letters** entry contains an example of a macro that does that.

Macros, Running at Startup

As you may know, WordPerfect will load a document file when you start if you give it a command of the form **wp** *filename*. You can also make it run a macro at startup. To do this, enter a command of the form **wp/m-***macroname*. For example, if you created a macro that sets up a specific format, and you want that format for the document you are about to create, you could start a new document with those alternate settings by entering wp/m-altf.

Macros That Perform Commands — WordPerfect 4.1 and 4.2

4.1
4.2

If you use some commands often, you should consider defining them as macros. Not only do macros perform commands faster than you could from the keyboard, but they also let you do commands without breaking your train of thought.

To get some ideas about what macros you might develop, consider the following list. Here, each macro is assigned an appropriate Alt-key combination, but you could just as easily give them regular names. I have also listed the contents of each macro, the key sequence that defines it.

Alt-T — Insert a copy of the tab settings, and move ahead of it.
Sequence: Shift-F8 1 F7 Left-arrow
Operation: Do a Line Format command to set up new tabs (Shift-F8 1), exit (F7) to put a copy of the current settings in the document, and move ahead of these settings (Left-arrow).
Comment: This macro is handy for situations where you want to change the tabs temporarily, but preserve the original settings so you can reinstate them. For example, you may want to insert a table, indented paragraph, or list that uses different tabs than your main text.
    Alt-T always leaves the cursor just ahead of the hidden code that has the original settings. Once you finish setting up new tabs and entering the material that uses them, press → to reinstate the previous tab settings.

Alt-M — Change the margins.
Sequence: Shift-F8 3 (Specify margins)
Operation: Do a Line Format command to set the margins.

Alt-L — Change the line spacing.
Sequence: Shift-F8 4 (Specify spacing)
Operation: Do a Line Format command to set the line spacing.

Alt-D — Insert the date as text.
Sequence: Shift-F5 1
Operation: Do a Date command (Shift-F5) and choose the Insert Text option (1).

Alt-A — Insert your address, the date, and "Dear."

Sequence: (Enter your address) Alt-D Enter Enter
Dear (space)
Operation: Type your address, insert the date using the preceding Alt-D macro, and type Dear, followed by a space.
Comment: Calling one macro from within another (as Alt-D is called here) is referred to as "chaining." See **Macros, Chaining** for more on this topic.

Alt-S — Save document, but stay in WordPerfect.
Sequence: F10 Enter y
Operation: Save the document (F10) under the same name (Enter) and replace it on disk (**y**).
Comment: Only works for existing documents, not new ones.

Alt-E — Save document and clear the screen.
Sequence: F7 Enter Enter **y n**
Operation: Exit from the document (F7), but save it (Enter) under the same name (Enter) and replace it on disk (**y**). Then clear the screen or the window (**n**).
Comment: Only works for existing documents, not new ones.

Alt-C — Stop the print operation and cancel all print jobs.
Sequence: Shift-F7 4 c * y
Operation: Do a Print command (Shift-F7) and choose the Printer Control option (4). When the Printer Control menu appears, choose Cancel Print Jobs (c) and specify all jobs (* y).

Alt-G — Send a "Go" command to the printer to print the next single-sheet page.
Sequence: Shift-F7 4 g Enter
Operation: Do a Print command (Shift-F7) and choose the Printer Control option (4). When the Printer Control menu appears, choose "Go" (g) and return to editing (Enter).

Macros That Perform Commands — WordPerfect 5.0

5.0 If you use certain commands often, you should consider defining them as macros. Not only do macros perform commands faster than you could from the keyboard, but they also let you do commands without breaking your train of thought.

To get some ideas about what macros you might develop, consider the following list. Here, each macro is assigned an appropriate Alt-key combination, but you could just as easily give them regular names. I have also listed the contents of each macro, the key sequence that defines it.

Alt-T — Insert a copy of the tab settings, and move ahead of it.
Sequence: Shift-F8 1 8 F7 F7 Left-arrow Left-arrow
Operation: Use the Format command's *Line* option (Shift-F8 1) to set up new tabs (8), exit (F7) to put a copy of the current settings in the document, then exit (F7) back to editing. Move to the Tab Set code (Left-arrow), then ahead of it (Left-arrow).
Comment: This macro is handy for situations where you want to change the tabs temporarily, but preserve the original settings so you can reinstate them. For example, you may want to insert a table, indented paragraph, or list that uses different tabs than your main text.
    Alt-T always leaves the cursor just ahead of the hidden code that has the original settings. Once you finish setting up new tabs and entering the material that uses them, press → to reinstate the previous tab settings.

Alt-M — Change the margins.
Sequence: Shift-F8 1 7 (Specify margins)
Operation: Use the Format command's *Line* option (Shift-F8 1) to set the margins (7).

Alt-L — Change the line spacing.
Sequence: Shift-F8 1 6 (Specify spacing)
Operation: Use the Format command's *Line* option (Shift-F8 1) to set the line spacing (6).

Alt-D — Insert the date as text.
Sequence: Shift-F5 1
Operation: Do a Date command (Shift-F5) and choose the Date Text option (1).

Alt-A — Insert your address, the date, and "Dear ".
Sequence: (Enter your address) Alt-D Enter Enter Dear (space)
Operation: Type your address, insert the date using the preceding Alt-D macro, and type Dear, followed by a space.

Comment: Calling one macro from within another (as Alt-D is called here) is referred to as "chaining." See **Macros, Chaining** for more on this topic.

Alt-S — Save document, but stay in WordPerfect.
Sequence: F10 Enter y
Operation: Save the document (F10) under the same name (Enter) and replace it on disk (y).
Comment: Only works for existing documents, not new ones.

Alt-E — Save document and clear the screen.
Sequence: F7 Enter Enter **y n**
Operation: Exit from the document (F7), but save it (Enter) under the same name (Enter) and replace it on disk (y). Then clear the screen or the window (**n**).
Comment: Only works for existing documents, not new ones.

Alt-C — Stop the print operation and cancel all print jobs.
Sequence: Shift-F7 4 1 * y
Operation: Do a Print command (Shift-F7) and choose the Control Printer option (4). When the Control Printer menu appears, choose Cancel Job(s) (1) and specify all jobs (* y).

Alt-G — Send a "Go" command to the printer to print the next single-sheet page.
Sequence: Shift-F7 4 4 Enter
Operation: Do a Print command (Shift-F7) and choose the Control Printer option (4). When the Control Printer menu appears, choose "Go" (4) and return to editing (Enter).

Mail Merge

— See **Merge/Sort Command**

Margin Release (Shift-Tab)

— See **Indent Commands**

Margins — WordPerfect 4.1 and 4.2

4.1
4.2

WordPerfect is preset to print on regular 8-1/2 by 11-inch paper, and (assuming your paper is aligned correctly) provides one-inch margins at the top, bottom, left, and right. If these default settings don't suit your needs, you can change them from within a document. (You can also change them for all new documents, so that WordPerfect always starts with the margins you want. See **Set-up Menu** for details.)

Top and Bottom Margins

To change the top or bottom margin, press Alt and F8 to obtain WordPerfect's Page Format menu. The *top margin* is controlled by menu option 5. If you press 5, WordPerfect displays the following prompt at the bottom of the screen:

```
Set half-lines (12/inch) from 12 to
```

Note that the top margin is measured in half-lines. WordPerfect's default lines per inch setting is 6, so the default half-line setting, 12, produces a six-line (one-inch) top margin. To get a half-inch top margin, enter 6; to get a two-inch top margin, enter 24; and so on. If you are finished using the menu, press Enter to return to your document.

The *bottom margin* is controlled by option 4 (Page Length) on the menu. If you press 4, WordPerfect displays the Page Length menu shown in Figure M-6. To make the bottom margin, wider or narrower, type **3** for *Other*. When the cursor moves to the "Form Length in Lines" field, press Enter to reach the "Number of Single Spaced Text Lines" field.

The number in this field determines how many single-spaced lines WordPerfect will put on each page. Since it prints six lines per inch, the default value (54) indicates that it is preset to print nine inches of text (54 divided by 6) vertically. And because the top

```
┌─────────────────────────────────────────────────────────────┐
│                                                             │
│     Page Length                                             │
│                                                             │
│     1 - Letter Size Paper: Form Length = 66 lines (11 inches)│
│         Single Spaced Text Lines = 54 (This includes lines  │
│         used for Headers/Footers and/or page numbers.)      │
│                                                             │
│     2 - Legal Size Paper: Form Length = 84 lines (14 inches)│
│         Single Spaced Text Lines = 72 (This includes lines  │
│         used for Headers/Footers and/or page numbers.)      │
│                                                             │
│     3 - Other (Maximum page length = 108 lines.)            │
│                                                             │
│     Current Settings                                        │
│                                                             │
│     Form Length in Lines (6 per inch): 66                   │
│                                                             │
│     Number of Single Spaced Text Lines: 54                  │
│                                                             │
└─────────────────────────────────────────────────────────────┘
```

Figure M-6. Page Length Menu

margin is set to one inch, that means that the text will end ten inches from the top. In other words, each 11-inch page will have a one-inch margin at the bottom.

To obtain a wider bottom margin, enter a smaller number in the Text Lines field; to obtain a narrower bottom margin, enter a larger number. (Just remember that on 11-inch paper, the value cannot exceed 60, which eliminates the bottom margin entirely.) Note that the Text Lines value is actually a measurement in sixths of an inch. To get a two-inch bottom margin, enter **48**; to get a half-inch bottom margin, enter **57**; and so on.

Left and Right Margins

To change the left or right margin, press Shift and F8 to obtain WordPerfect's Line Format menu, then type **3** to select *Margins*. WordPerfect displays the following prompt at the bottom of the screen:

```
[Margin Set] 10 74 to Left =
```

WordPerfect is telling you that the left and right margins are currently at column positions 10 and 74 (the default settings), respectively, and is asking you for a new value for the left margin. To change the left margin, enter a new value; to leave it set to 10 (or whatever value the prompt shows), enter 10. Note that you can't simply press Enter here; if you do, WordPerfect assumes you don't want to change either margin setting, and removes the prompt.

Once you have entered a left margin value, WordPerfect extends the prompt with *Right* =. Enter a new right margin setting or press Enter to keep the current value.

Codes for Margin Changes

When you change the top margin setting, WordPerfect inserts a hidden [Top Mar:*t*] code in your document, where *t* is the setting you specified. As I mentioned earlier, you can't change the bottom margin setting directly, but you affect it by changing the number of single-spaced text lines. Hence, WordPerfect marks a change to the bottom margin with a hidden [Pg Lnth:*f,t*] code, where *f* is the number of total lines and *t* is the number of text lines. Finally, WordPerfect marks a change to the side margins with a hidden [Mar Set:*l,r*] code.

Margins — WordPerfect 5.0

5.0 WordPerfect comes set up to print on regular 8-1/2 by 11-inch paper, and (assuming your paper is aligned correctly) provides one-inch margins at the top, bottom, left, and right. If these default settings don't suit your needs, you can change them from within a document. (You can also change them for all new documents, so that WordPerfect always starts with the margins you want. See **Set-up Menu** for details.)

Top and Bottom Margins

To change the top or bottom margin, press Shift and F8 to obtain WordPerfect's Format menu. Then type **2** to choose *Page* and **5** to choose *Margins*. Type a new value for the *Top* setting (you needn't type the " symbol), if necessary, then press Enter to reach the *Bot-*

tom field. Type a new value there, then press Enter to reach *Selection*. If you are finished using the menus, press Enter to return to your document.

Left and Right Margins

To change the left or right margin, press Shift and F8 to obtain WordPerfect's Format menu. Then type 1 to choose *Line* and 7 to choose *Margins*. Type a new value for the *Left* setting (you needn't type the " symbol), if necessary, then press Enter to reach the *Right* field. Type a new value there, then press Enter to reach *Selection*. If you are finished using the menus, press Enter to return to your document.

Codes for Margin Changes

When you change the top or bottom margin setting, WordPerfect inserts a hidden [T/B Mar:*top,bottom*] code in your document, where *top* and *bottom* are the new settings. Similarly, it marks a change to the side margins with a hidden [L/R Mar:*left,right*] code.

Mark Text Command (Alt-F5) — WordPerfect 4.1 and 4.2

4.1
4.2

The Mark Text (Alt-F5) command lets you work with some of WordPerfect's special features. They include outline and paragraph numbering, redlining, table of authorities (with WordPerfect version 4.2), index, and table of contents. What Alt-F5 does depends on whether you press it from within regular editing mode or block mode.

Mark Text in Editing Mode

When you press Alt and F5 from editing mode, WordPerfect shows this menu at the bottom of the screen:

```
1 Outline; 2 Para #; 3 Redline; 4 Short Form; 5 Index; 6 Other Options: 0
```

Briefly, these options do the following:

1. *Outline* puts WordPerfect in outline mode, in which it inserts a paragraph number (and a hidden [Par#] code) whenever you press Enter to start a new paragraph or Ctrl-Enter to start a new page.
2. *Para #* inserts a paragraph number and a hidden [Par#] code.
3. *Redline* marks the current line for redlining, and puts hidden [RedLn] and [r] codes at the cursor position. When you print the document, a vertical line precedes this line of text. (Redlining text indicates that it has been newly added.)
4. *Short Form* marks the text for inclusion in a table of authorities.
5. *Index* marks the current word for inclusion in the index.
6. *Other Options* brings on a menu of other options pertaining to redlining, index, table of authorities, and so on.

For more information on one of these topics, refer to its particular entry.

Mark Text in Block Mode

When you press Alt and F5 from Block mode, WordPerfect shows this menu at the bottom of the screen:

```
Mark for: 1 ToC; 2 List; 3 Redline; 4 Strikeout; 5 Index; 6 ToA: 0
```

By selecting these options, you can mark the highlighted text for the table of contents, a list, redlining (text has been added to the document), strikeout (text is being considered for deletion), the index, or the table of authorities. For more information on one of these topics, refer to its particular entry.

Mark Text Command (Alt-F5) — WordPerfect 5.0

5.0 The Mark Text (Alt-F5) command lets you work with some of WordPerfect's special features. They include auto reference, subdocuments, index, table of contents, table of authorities, and list.

What Alt-F5 does depends on whether you press it from regular editing mode or Block mode.

Mark Text in Editing Mode

When you press Alt and F5 from editing mode, WordPerfect shows this menu at the bottom of the screen:

`1 Auto Ref; 2 Subdoc; 3 Index; 4 ToA Short Form; 5 Define; 6 Generate: 0`

Briefly, these options do the following:

1. *Auto Ref* lets you mark a reference and/or target for WordPerfect's Automatic Reference feature.
2. *Subdoc* marks the place in a master document where WordPerfect is to insert a subdocument.
3. *Index* marks the current word for inclusion in the index.
4. *ToA Short Form* marks the text for inclusion in a table of authorities.
5. *Define* is used to define a table of contents, list, index, or table of authorities. You can also use it to edit a table of authorities (full form).
6. *Generate* produces tables, indexes, automatic references, and endnote placements. Its menu also lets you remove redline markings and strikeout text from a document, compare the document on the screen with one on disk, and expand or compress a master document (by inserting or removing subdocuments).

For more information on any of these topics, refer to its particular entry.

Mark Text in Block Mode

When you press Alt and F5 from block mode, WordPerfect shows this menu at the bottom of the screen:

`Mark for: 1 ToC; 2 List; 3 Index; 4 ToA: 0`

By selecting these options, you can mark the highlighted text for the table of contents, a list, the index, or the table of authorities. For more information on one of these topics, refer to its particular entry.

Master Documents — WordPerfect 5.0

5.0 If your document is large, or several people are involved in preparing it, it's reasonable to divide it into several disk files, then combine the files when you're ready to produce the finished work. WordPerfect 5.0 lets you divide a document by preparing one *master document* and several *subdocuments*.

In general, the master document is a "skeleton" that contains only front and back material (perhaps the table of contents and the index) and codes that insert the subdocuments. Each subdocument would, then, contain an individual chapter or section of the document.

Inserting Subdocuments into a Master Document

When you prepare a master document, you must include codes that tell WordPerfect which disk files are subdocuments and where to insert them. When you reach the place in a master document where a subdocument belongs, do the following:

1. Press Alt and F5 to give a Mark Text command.
2. When the Mark Text menu appears, type **2** to select *Subdoc*.
3. When requested, enter the name of the subdocument file you want to insert.

WordPerfect inserts a subdocument code at the cursor position and displays it on the screen as a Subdoc: *Filename* box.

Note that a subdocument is simply an ordinary WordPerfect file that you *use* as a subdocument by giving its name within a Subdoc command. Thus, you can even use a master document as a subdocument, by inserting it in some *other* master document!

Expanding Master Documents

To actually insert the text of the subdocuments, you must *expand* the master document, as follows:

1. With the cursor anywhere in the master document, press Alt and F5 to give a Mark Text command.
2. When the Mark Text menu appears, type **6** to select *Generate*.
3. When the Generate menu appears, type **3** to select *Expand Master Document*.

WordPerfect copies the subdocument from disk and replaces the *Subdoc:Filename* box with a *Subdoc Start:Filename* box, the text of the subdocument, and a *Subdoc End:Filename* box. At this point, the subdocument text is part of the master document, just as if you had entered it manually. Thus, you can edit the subdocument material just as you would edit text in any other document.

When you Exit (F7) or Save (F10) a master document that has been expanded, WordPerfect asks

```
Document is expanded, condense it? (Y/N) Yes
```

To save the expanded form of the document, type **n** for No. (WordPerfect then asks for a file name, in case you want to keep the expanded form separate from the unexpanded original.) To discard the inserted subdocuments, and save the master document in its unexpanded form, type **y** or press Enter.

Condensing Master Documents

Sometimes you will want to make changes to the subdocuments in a master document that you have expanded. For instance, you may want to incorporate suggestions made by reviewers. With Word-Perfect, you can easily *condense* an expanded master document, to remove the subdocument text and put it back in its original form. To do this:

1. With the cursor anywhere in the expanded master document, press Alt and F5 to give a Mark Text command.
2. When the Mark Text menu appears, type 6 to select *Generate*.
3. When the Generate menu appears, type 4 to select *Condense Master Document*.

If you saved the expanded master document, WordPerfect asks

```
Save Subdocs? (Y/N) Yes
```

Press **n** to remove the subdocuments without saving them; press **y** to save the subdocuments to their respective files before removing them from the master document.

If you tell WordPerfect to save the subdocuments, it displays

```
Replace Subdoc1? 1 Yes; 2 No; 3 Replace All Remaining: 0
```

where *Subdoc1* is the filename of the first subdocument. Choosing *Yes* makes WordPerfect display the **Replace** prompt for each remaining subdocument; choosing *No* brings on a prompt of the form

```
Document to be saved: Subdoc
```

to let you change your mind, and save the subdocument; choosing *Replace All Remaining* lets you bypass the individual **Replace** prompts and save all the subdocuments, including the current one.

Math/Columns Command (Alt-F7)

When you press Alt and F7, WordPerfect shows the following menu at the bottom of the screen:

```
1 Math On; 2 Math Def; 3 Column On/Off; 4 Column Def: 0
```

(WordPerfect 4.2 also has an option 5, *Column Display*.) The Math options provide mathematical capabilities; see **Mathematical Operations**. The Column options relate to WordPerfect's ability to arrange text in columns; see **Columns, Text**.

Mathematical Operations

WordPerfect can perform mathematical operations on numeric tables. For example, it can add a column of numbers to produce a *subtotal*. It can then add subtotals to produce a *total*, and add totals to produce a *grand total*. WordPerfect can also perform calculations on the rows in a table. It can add, subtract, multiply, or divide rows of numbers based on simple formulas that you enter.

WordPerfect can provide up to 24 math columns. Columns are located at tab stops. That is, column A is at the first tab stop, column B is at the second tab stop, and so on. The text at the left-hand margin can only be used to label the rows; it is not counted as a column.

Instead of entering numbers in columns, you can enter calculation formulas or text. Or you can make WordPerfect produce totals and grand totals in separate columns. How WordPerfect treats a column depends on whether you define its "type" as Numeric, Calculation, Text, or Total.

Adding Columns

WordPerfect is initially set up to add columns, so that's the easiest kind of operation to do. To add columns, you must set up tabs for them, turn the Math feature on, enter the numbers, perform the addition, then turn Math off. The procedure is:

1. For each column, set a tab where you want the decimal point to appear.
2. Press Alt and F7 to give a Math/Columns command. WordPerfect shows this menu:

```
1 Math On; 2 Math Def; 3 Column On/Off; 4 Column Def: 0
```

To just add columns vertically, skip steps 3 and 4.

3. Type **2** for *Math Def*. WordPerfect displays a Math Definition screen (see Figure M-7).

For each of the 24 possible columns (A through X), the Math Definition screen lists the type of column and tells how it intends to display answers. Unless you change these parameters, WordPerfect will make all columns Numeric, display answers with two digits to the right of the decimal point, and enclose negative numbers in parentheses (rather than precede them with a minus sign).

4. If the current Math Definition settings are what you want, press F7 to return to the Math Definition menu. If not, make your changes and then press F7.
5. Type **1** to turn Math On. The word "Math" appears at the bottom of the screen. This indicates that WordPerfect is prepared to keep track of the numbers you enter, and to add them when you tell it to.
6. Enter a label for the row (if any), then press Tab to reach the first column.
7. Enter the first number in the first column (WordPerfect aligns it around the decimal point), then press Tab to reach the next column or Enter to reach the next line.
8. Repeat steps 6 and 7 for each row in the table.

258 Mathematical Operations

```
Math Definition        Use arrow keys to position cursor

Columns                A B C D E F G H I J K L M N O P Q R S T U V W X

Type                   2 2 2 2 2 2 2 2 2 2 2 2 2 2 2 2 2 2 2 2 2 2 2 2

Negative Numbers       ( ( ( ( ( ( ( ( ( ( ( ( ( ( ( ( ( ( ( ( ( ( ( (

# of digits to         2 2 2 2 2 2 2 2 2 2 2 2 2 2 2 2 2 2 2 2 2 2 2 2
the right (0-4)

Calculation    1
Formulas       2
               3
               4

Type of Column:
       0 = Calculation          1 = Text     2 = Numeric     3 = Total

Negative Numbers
       ( = Parenthesis (50.00)         - = Minus Sign  -50.00

Press EXIT when done
```

Figure M-7. Math Definition screen.

9. Move the cursor to where each column subtotal belongs and type +. (The + marks the place where WordPerfect should insert a subtotal.) Press Enter after the last +.

10. Press Alt and F7 to obtain the following menu (WordPerfect 4.2 also has an option 5, *Column Display*):

    1 Math Off; 2 Calculate; 3 Column On/Off; 4 Column Def: 0

and type **2** for Calculate. WordPerfect precedes each + symbol with the subtotal for the column.

11. Press Alt-F7 to get the menu back, then type **1** to select Math Off. The word "Math" disappears.

Now you can print the document. WordPerfect will print the numbers, but not the + symbols.

As a simple example of a column addition, consider the following list, which summarizes how much each member of a club has collected for charity:

Member	Collections
Brown, John	$1,504.36
Carlson, Ray	965.77
Decker, Patricia	1,668.43
Garnett, Vance	796.03
Evans, Sue	779.56
Gerard, Roy	1,056.90
Morton, Mary	800.00
Stevens, George	863.96

To produce a subtotal for the list, you would set a tab below the "t" in "Collections," then turn Math on and enter the names and amounts. When you reach the line where the subtotal is to appear, type **Total**, press Tab, type **+**, and press Enter. To produce the subtotal, obtain the menu (Alt-F7) and type **2** for Calculate. WordPerfect inserts the subtotal (8,435.01 in this case) ahead of +. Finally, get the menu back and turn Math Off.

Producing Totals and Grand Totals

In some tables, a column may include several subtotals. With the Math feature, you can make WordPerfect add a column's subtotals to produce a *total*. To obtain a total, enter = (rather than +) where you want it to appear. WordPerfect will insert the total when you select Calculate from the menu.

Figure M-8 shows an expense report for a business trip, with subtotals for each employee and a total for the group. (Comparing Mr. Wilson's expenses with those of the others, he's either a top executive or now an *ex*-employee.)

Similarly, you can make WordPerfect add totals to produce a *grand total*. Do this by entering * where the grand total belongs.

Operating on Rows

Sometimes you want to perform math operations *across* the rows of your table instead of (or as well as) *down* its columns. For example,

```
       Expenses for Trip to 1988 National Sales Meeting
       Gene Murcheson
          Food                 52.45
          Lodging             155.03
          Transportation      326.09
          Misc.                 6.55
       Subtotal               540.12+

       Harry Anderson
          Food                 47.80
          Lodging             155.03
          Transportation      279.88
          Misc.                 5.82
       Subtotal               488.53+

       Earl Wilson
          Food                 87.65
          Lodging             204.40
          Transportation      279.88
          Misc.                35.82
       Subtotal               607.75+

       Estelle Campbell
          Food                 40.67
          Lodging             155.03
          Transportation      279.88
          Misc.                 3.60
       Subtotal               479.18+

       TOTAL                2,115.58=
```

Figure M-8. Adding subtotals to produce a total.

if the columns in your table represent monthly sales figures for each product your company sells, you may want to add the rows to produce sales for the year. You may also want to produce an additional column showing net profits (sales minus costs). WordPerfect will perform these and other calculations if you simply set up a *Calculation column* and enter a formula that tells it what kind of calculation to make.

A calculation formula tells WordPerfect which column (or columns) to include in the calculation and how to combine them. For example, if column C is a Calculation column and you enter the formula A+B into it, WordPerfect will add the numbers in column A to those in column B and display the sum in column C.

Plus (+) is just one symbol you can use in calculation formulas. WordPerfect also lets you use - (subtract), * (multiply), and / (divide). Some typical formulas are:

Formula	Tells WordPerfect to ...
A+B-C	Add columns A and B, then subtract column C from the result.
B*.06	Multiply column B by 0.06 (to calculate sales tax, perhaps).
B/C	Find the ratio of column B to column C.
B/C*100	Find the ratio of B to C, and display it as a percentage.

You can also use parentheses in a calculation formula, to keep WordPerfect from getting confused. For example, *(A+B)/3* yields one-third the sum of columns A and B. If you omit the parentheses, WordPerfect would add column A to one-third the value in column B.

There are also four special formulas you can use in Calculation columns:

+	Add numbers in the Numeric columns
+/	Average numbers in the Numeric columns
=	Add numbers in the Total columns
=/	Average numbers in the Total columns

Note that these are complete formulas; you cannot combine them with column names or numeric values.

To define a Calculation column, obtain the Math Definition screen (shown previously in Figure M-7), then do the following:

1. Press the right-arrow key to reach the Type number for the column, then type **0** (zero) to make it a Calculation column. WordPerfect moves to the Calculation Formulas list and displays the column letter.
2. Enter the formula for that column (note that you can define up to four Calculation columns).
3. Define the rest of the columns in the table, then press F7 to return to the menu.

Once you have set up a Calculation column, WordPerfect will insert an exclamation point (!) whenever you Tab to it. As with subtotals, totals, and grand totals, the result of the calculation will not appear until you select Calculate from the menu.

Mathematical Operations

```
           Yearly Sales by Region for 1987 and 1988
                   (Dollar amounts in thousands)

   Region      1988 Sales   1987 Sales   Difference   % Change

   Northeast     2481.1       1944.2       536.9!       27.6!
   Southeast     1956.5       1572.8       383.7!       24.4!
   Midwest       2764.9       3276.8      (511.9)!     -15.6!
   Mountain      1849.0       1616.3       232.7!       14.4!
   Northwest     2205.9       2360.7      (154.8)!      -6.6!
   Southwest     2915.4       2244.6       670.8!       29.9!

   Totals      14,172.8+    13,015.4+    1,157.4!
```

Figure M-9. Two Calculation columns operating on rows.

Figure M-9 shows a typical application for Calculation columns: a table that summarizes a company's sales for 1988, and compares them to sales for 1987. Numeric columns A and B list the 1988 and 1987 figures for each sales region, while Calculation columns C and D display the dollar and percentage difference between the two years.

Setting up this table requires the following steps:

1. In the blank line below the headings, press Alt-F7 to give a *Math/Columns* command, then select *Math Def* from the menu.
2. When the Math Definition menu appears, change column C's *Type* to **0** (Calculation). Column C subtracts column B from column A, so enter **A-B** for its *Calculation Formula*.
3. Change column D's *Type* to **0** and enter **C/B*100** for its *Calculation Formula*.
4. For column D, change *Negative Numbers* to - (minus).
5. For all four columns, change *# of digits to the right* to **1**.
6. Press F7 (Exit) to leave the Math Definition menu.
7. When the Math/Columns menu reappears, select *Math On*.
8. Enter the labels and data for each line, and Tab to columns C and D, to insert the ! symbols.
9. After entering **Totals**, press Tab three times. The first two Tabs insert a +, the last a !.
10. Give another Math/Columns command and select *Calculate*. WordPerfect inserts the calculated results.
11. Turn *Math Off*.

While creating a table of this kind takes a lot of steps, it's easier than making the calculations by hand.

A Macro That Performs Calculations Within a Document

Sometimes you may want to make a calculation within a document. For example, suppose you're writing a memo to one of your salespeople that includes the sentence

Your commission on the sale of the Roberts home is $

and you want to insert the commission after the dollar sign. That is, if this person earns a 6.25 percent commission and the property sold for $146,900, you want to insert the result of multiplying 146,900 by .0625.

Figure M-10 lists the keystrokes needed to create a WordPerfect 4.1 or 4.2 macro that lets you enter a calculation formula (*.0625*146900* for my example), then calculates the answer (*9,181.25*, here) and inserts it at the cursor position. As the second line of the figure shows, I have designed the macro to run when you press Alt and C (for Calculate). You may want to assign it to some other Alt-key combination or give it a name such as *CALC*.

When you press Alt-C to run this macro, WordPerfect displays the *Math Definition* screen with the cursor following an A on line 1 of *Calculation Formulas*. The macro is waiting for you to enter your formula. Type it, then press Enter. WordPerfect shows *** Please Wait *** while it calculates, then inserts the answer in your document.

This macro always produces a result that has two digits to the right of the decimal point. To change the number of digits, you can modify the macro by inserting the following lines just after the *Ctrl-PgUp* line:

Down-arrow Down-arrow Left-arrow   Move to the|"# of   digits" position
Ctrl-PgUp Enter Enter $$1Pause for keyboard input

When you run this modified macro and enter the formula, you can then specify 0 to 4 digits to the right of the decimal point.

The Alt-C macro was developed by Kenneth R. Kletzien, and appeared in the Power User column of the September 29, 1987, issue of *PC Magazine*. Column editor Neil J. Rubenking suggested the modification.

```
Ctrl-F10                          Begin macro definition
Alt-C                             Assign the macro to the Alt-C keys
Enter Enter Left-arrow            Make room for work in the document
Shift-F8 1 Space Tab F7           Set a tab stop, to be sure there is one.
                                  (A Math Calculation Column requires a
                                  tab.)
Alt-F7 2 0                        Begin a Math Definition, make the
                                  first column a Calculation Column.
Ctrl-PgUp Enter Enter Enter       Pause to let user enter the formula
                                  while the macro is running
F7 1                              End Math Definition, turn Math on
Tab Alt-F7 2                      Calculate what the user just entered
    (Now clean up the mess)
Alt-F4                            Put WordPerfect in Block mode
Shift-F2 Enter F2                 Search backward for a [HRt] code (the
                                  previous Enter keystroke)
Del y                             Delete the block
Backspace End Del Backspace       Delete the remaining things we
                                  added
Ctrl-F10                          End the macro definition
```

Figure M-10. The keystrokes to create a WordPerfect 4.1/4.2 macro that makes a calculation at the cursor position.

Editing Math Tables

If you change data in a table after performing a calculation, you must make WordPerfect recalculate any answer the change affects. That is, make your changes (but be *sure* "Math" is still on the screen) and press Alt-F7 to obtain the Math menu. When it appears, select Calculate. WordPerfect replaces the original answers with the corrected ones.

You can also insert lines or delete lines just as you would insert or delete them in a regular text table. Just be sure to recalculate where needed.

Mathematical Symbols

— See Special Characters

Menus, Selecting Options from

When you give WordPerfect a command that can do several different jobs, it displays a *menu* of the available choices. In most cases, the menu is short enough to fit on the bottom line of the screen. For example, pressing Ctrl and F4 together gives a Move command. WordPerfect 4.2 responds by displaying the following menu:

Move 1 Sentence; **2** Paragraph; **3** Page; **Retrieve 4** Column; **5** Text; **6** Rectangle: **0**

Here, WordPerfect shows the option numbers in **bold**, to indicate that you must type them to select an option. For example, typing **1** indicates that you want to move the current *Sentence*. Note that this menu also has a bold 0 (zero) at the end, to indicate the "default" choice. Typing **0** (or pressing Enter) doesn't select an option; it makes the menu disappear!

In WordPerfect 5.0, menu options also have a bold letter in their names, to indicate that you can type either the letter or the number to select that option. Thus, typing either **S** or **1** selects *Sentence* from this WordPerfect 5.0 Move menu:

Move 1 Sentence; **2 P**aragraph; **3 P**age; **4 R**etrieve: **0**

Merge Codes Command (Alt-F9 in Wordperfect 4.1 and 4.2, Shift-F9 in WordPerfect 5.0)

This command is used when you are creating a generalized letter (*primary file*) or data (*secondary merge*) file for use in a merge operation. (Merge operations are described under **Form Letters**.) When you give it, WordPerfect shows the following menu at the bottom of the screen:

^C; ^D; ^F; ^G; ^N; ^O; ^P; ^Q; ^S; ^T; ^V; :

These are WordPerfect's *merge codes*. Once the menu appears, you can insert a merge code at the current cursor position by simply typing its letter. For example, to insert ^N, type **n**.

Here is a summary of what the merge codes do:

Merge Codes Command

Code	Action
^C	Stops the merge operation temporarily, tto allow material to be inserted from the keyboard. Press the Merge R (F9) key to continue. In general, you should preced the ^C code with a prompt enclosed in ^O codes, to inform the typist what to insert. A typical example is

```
^OType the cost, then press F9 -^O^C
```

During the merge, WordPerfect displays the message at the bottom of the screen, then halts when it encounters .

^D   Inserts the current date in whatever format you selected with the Date (Shift-F5) command.

^E   *Produced in WordPerfect 4.1 and 4.2 by pressing Shift-F9.* Marks the end of a record in a secondary merge file.

^Fn^ Merges the text from field *n* (a number) in the current data record. When you select ^F from the Merge Codes menu, WordPerfect displays *Field Number?* at the bottom of the screen. Type the number, then press Enter.

^G   ^G *macro name* starts the specified macro at the end of the merge You must spell out the macro name here, even for Alt key macros. For example, to run the macro assigned to the Alt-W key combination, enter **^Galtw^G**.

^N   Skips to the next record in the secondary merge file. If there are no more records, WordPerfect ends the merge operation. The ^N code is handy for using data from several records in a document. For example, ^F1^ *and* ^N1^ inserts the F1 field from the current record, then advances to the next record (^N) and inserts its F1 data. Note that the advance operation is permanent; once WordPerfect encounters a ,^N it makes the next record current. What's in the preceding record is history.

^O   ^O*message*^O displays the specified message at the bottom of the screen. Since the message is normally a prompt to the o perator (e.g., "Type the cost, then press F9 —"), the second ^O is usually followed by a ^C (pause) code.

^P   ^P*filename* inserts the specified file. This is handy for reading "boilerplate" into a document. For example, if TERMS.DOC contains text that describes your standard terms of payment, ^Dterms.doc^P inserts it in the merged document.

^Q   Stops the merge. It may be placed in a primary or secondary merge file. For example, if you have a large secondary file (perhaps a mailing list of 500 customers) and you want to send a form letter to just a portion of it (e.g., preferred

Merge Codes Command

customers, the first 125 in the list), you could put a ^Q code after the final addressee's record.

^R *Produced by pressing F9.* Marks the end of a field in a secondary merge file.

^S *^Sfilename* switches WordPerfect to the specified secondary file. This lets you use several secondary files during a merge operation. It would be handy for merging, say, a mailing list in one file with a list of products in a second file to produce form letters.

^T Sends all text that has been merged at that point to the printer.

^U Updates (rewrites) the screen. During a merge operation, WordPerfect just shows *Merging* at the bottom of the screen. The ^U code makes it show the actual merged document.

^V Lets you insert merge codes into the document being created. For example, the sequence ^V^K^V inserts a ^K (end-of-field) code.

Combining Merge Codes

You can also combine merge codes in your documents. I have already mentioned that the ^C (pause for keyboard input) code usually follows an ^O(message) sequence, but here are some other sample combinations.

Sequence: ^O Type name of file to be inserted, then press F9 -^P^C .doc

This sequence displays the prompt at the bottom of the screen and waits for the operator to type the name of a "boilerplate" file to be inserted at that place in the document. The *.doc* at the end makes WordPerfect append that extension to whatever name the operator types.

Sequence: Type name of product, then press F9-^S^C.lst^P^D

This kind of sequence is handy when you're creating form letters for diverse recipients.

Sequence: ^O What do you want to do now? Type a command, then press F9-^G^C^G^O

This sequence lets the operator enter a command (a macro name, actually), probably at the end of a merge operation.

Inserting Merge Codes Manually

There's nothing mysterious about WordPerfect's merge codes; they are ordinary text characters. Hence, you can insert a merge code without choosing it from the Merge Codes menu, by typing a caret (^), then the appropriate letter. For example, to insert ^G, type ^, then G.

Merge E Command (Shift-F9) — WordPerfect 4.1 and 4.2

4.1
4.2

Pressing Shift and F9 in WordPerfect 4.1 or 4.2 inserts ^E at the cursor position and moves the cursor to the next line (in WordPerfect 5.0, ^E is an option in the Merge Codes menu). The code is used to mark the end of a record in a secondary merge file, so skipping to the next line is appropriate.

If you press Shift-F9 during a merge operation, WordPerfect stops merging and displays the incomplete merge document.

Merge Operations

Full details of doing merge operations are given under **Form Letters**. To stop a merge operation, press Shift and F9 simultaneously.

Merge R Command (F9)

Pressing F9 inserts R at the cursor position and moves the cursor to the next line. The ^R code is used to mark the end of a field in a secondary merge file, so skipping to the next line is appropriate.

During a merge operation, you must press F9 when you finish entering information from the keyboard in response to a ^C (pause) command

Merge/Sort Command (Ctrl-F9)

Pressing Ctrl and F9 makes WordPerfect display the following menu at the bottom of the screen:

        1 Merge; 2 Sort; 3 Sorting Sequences: 0

Full details of the merge operation are given under **Form Letters**. Similarly, the sort operation and its sorting sequences are discussed under **Sorting**.

Minus (-) Key on the Numeric Keypad

Pressing the gray minus key on the numeric keypad moves the cursor to the top line on the screen, at the current column position.

Move Command (Ctrl-F4) — WordPerfect 4.1 and 4.2

4.1
4.2

The Move command lets you *cut*, *copy*, or *delete* a sentence, paragraph, page, or the text in a selected block, column, or rectangle. You can also *append* a block; that is, add a copy of it to the end of an existing document on disk.

Cut and copy operations are similar, but cutting text removes it from the screen, while copying text simply makes a copy of it, and leaves the original intact. In both cases, you "paste" the cut or copied material in its new location by moving the cursor there and then *retrieving* it.

Like a cut, a delete operation removes text from the screen. But you normally delete something when you want to discard it, rather than use it somewhere else.

Sentences, Paragraphs, and Pages

To cut, copy, or delete a sentence, paragraph, or page, move the cursor anywhere in it and press Ctrl-F4 to give a Move command. When this menu appears:

```
Move 1 Sentence; 2 Paragraph; 3 Page; Retrieve 4 Column; 5 Text; 6 Rectangle: 0
```

type **1**, **2**, or **3**. WordPerfect highlights the text and shows

```
1 Cut; 2 Copy; 3 Delete: 0
```

at the bottom of the screen. With all three options, WordPerfect keeps a copy of the selected text internally. However, Cut and Delete remove the text from the screen, while Copy leaves it intact.

To "paste" cut or copied material somewhere else in a document (or even in a different document), move the cursor to where the material belongs and press Ctrl-F4 to give another Move command. Then type **5** to select *Text* from the Move menu.

To restore deleted text, press the F1 key to give an Undelete command. WordPerfect displays the text you most recently deleted (in highlighted form) and shows the following menu at the bottom of the screen:

```
Undelete: 1 Restore; 2 Show Previous Deletion: 0
```

Now you can type **1** to restore the highlighted text, type **2** to display the next most recent deletion (WordPerfect saves the text from up to three delete operations), or press Enter to return to editing without undeleting.

Blocks

Sometimes you may want to operate on a block of text. A block can be any amount of text you select, from a single character to the entire contents of a document. As with a sentence, page, or paragraph, you can cut, copy, or delete a block. Further, you can *append* a block, to add it to the end of an existing disk file.

To begin, put the cursor at the beginning of the block and press Alt-F4 to put WordPerfect in Block mode (a flashing **Block on** message appears at the bottom). Then move the cursor to the end of the block and press Ctrl-F4 to give a Move command. When the following menu appears at the bottom of the screen:

```
1 Cut Block; 2 Copy Block; 3 Append; 4 Cut/Copy Column; 5 Cut/Copy Rectangle: 0
```

type **1**, **2**, or **3**.

Choosing *Cut Block* or *Copy Block* makes WordPerfect save a copy of the highlighted material internally. However, cutting a block removes it from the screen, whereas copying a block leaves the original intact. To "paste" the block at its new location, move the cursor there and press Ctrl-F4 to give another Move command. Then type **5** to select *Text* from the Move menu.

The Move menu's *Append* option lets you copy the highlighted block of text to the end of a document file on disk (provided it's not a locked file). When **Append to:** appears at the bottom of the screen, enter the name of the file.

Columns and Rectangles

Columns and rectangles are special kinds of text blocks. A *column* is a vertical strip of text or numbers that was entered using tabs, indents, tab aligns, or Hard Returns (i.e., you pressed Enter at the end of each entry). A *rectangle* is the portion of a block that extends down from where the highlighting begins and right to where the highlighting ends.

To cut, copy, or delete a column or rectangle, put the cursor at its top left-hand corner and press Alt-F4 to put WordPerfect in Block mode (a flashing **Block on** message appears at the bottom). Then move the cursor to the column or rectangle's bottom right-hand corner (WordPerfect highlights everything in between) and press Ctrl-F4 to give a Move command. When the following menu appears at the bottom of the screen:

```
1 Cut Block; 2 Copy Block; 3 Append; 4 Cut/Copy Column; 5 Cut/Copy Rectangle: 0
```

type **4**, or **5**. When the following menu appears at the bottom of the screen:

```
1 Cut; 2 Copy; 3 Delete: 0
```

make your selection.

To "paste" a cut or copied column or rectangle somewhere else in a document (or even in a different document), move the cursor to where the material belongs, press Ctrl-F4 to give another Move command, and type **4** or **6** to select *Column* or *Rectangle* from the menu.

To restore a deleted column or rectangle, press the F1 key to give an Undelete command. WordPerfect displays the text you most recently deleted, highlighted, and shows the following menu at the bottom of the screen:

```
Undelete: 1 Restore; 2 Show Previous Deletion: 0
```

Now you can type **1** to restore the highlighted text, type **2** to display the next most recent deletion (WordPerfect saves the text from up to three delete operations), or press Enter to return to editing.

Move Command (Ctrl-F4) — WordPerfect 5.0

5.0   The Move command lets you *move, copy, delete,* or *append* a sentence, paragraph, page, or the text in a selected block, column, or rectangle.
Move and copy operations are similar, but moving text removes it from the screen, while copying text simply makes a copy of it, and leaves the original intact. In both cases, you "paste" the moved or copied material in its new location by moving the cursor there and then *retrieving* it.
Like a move, a delete operation removes text from the screen. But you normally delete something when you want to discard it, rather than use it somewhere else.
An append operation adds a copy of the selected text to the end of a specified document file on disk. If the file does not yet exist, WordPerfect creates it, then does the append.

Sentences, Paragraphs, and Pages

To operate on a sentence, paragraph, or page, move the cursor anywhere in it and press Ctrl-F4 to give a Move command. When this menu appears:

```
Move 1 Sentence; 2 Paragraph; 3 Page; 4 Retrieve: 0
```

type **1, 2,** or **3**. WordPerfect highlights the text and shows

```
1 Move; 2 Copy; 3 Delete; 4 Append: 0
```

If you *Move* or *Copy* text, WordPerfect assumes you want to "paste" it immediately, and displays **&Move** cursor; press Enter to

retrieve& at the bottom of the screen. You can then move to where the material belongs and press the Enter key.

However, if you want to paste later, or haven't yet created the place where the material belongs, press F1 (Cancel) to remove the prompt. Then, when you're ready to paste, press Ctrl-F4 to give another Move command and type **&4&** to choose *Retrieve*. When this menu appears:

```
Retrieve: 1 Block; 2 Tabular Column; 3 Rectangle: 0
```

type **1** for *Block*.

To restore deleted text, press the F1 key to give an Undelete command. WordPerfect displays the text you most recently deleted (in highlighted form) and shows the following menu at the bottom of the screen:

```
Undelete: 1 Restore; 2 Show Previous Deletion: 0
```

Now you can type **1** to restore the highlighted text, type **2** to display the next most recent deletion (WordPerfect saves the text from up to three delete operations), or press Enter to return to editing without undeleting.

The *Append* option lets you copy the selected text to the end of a document file (even a locked file) on disk. When **Append to:** appears at the bottom of the screen, enter the name of the file. If the file doesn't exist, WordPerfect creates it.

Blocks, Columns, and Rectangles

Sometimes you may want to operate on the text in a block, column, or rectangle. A *block* can be any amount of text you select, from a single character to the entire contents of a document. Columns and rectangles are special kinds of blocks. A *column* is a vertical strip of text or numbers that was entered using tabs, indents, tab aligns, or Hard Returns (i.e., you pressed Enter at the end of each entry). A *rectangle* is the portion of a block that extends down from where the highlighting begins and right to where the highlighting ends.

To begin, put the cursor at the beginning of the unit (the top left-hand corner of a column or rectangle) and press Alt-F4 to put Word-Perfect in Block mode; a flashing **Block on** message appears at the bottom. Then move the cursor to the end of the unit (the bottom right-hand corner of a column or rectangle) and press Ctrl-F4 to give a Move command. When the following menu appears at the bottom of the screen:

Move: 1 Block; 2 Tabular Column; 3 Rectangle: 0

choose the unit you want. WordPerfect then needs to know what you want to do with the unit. It displays

1 Move; 2 Copy; 3 Delete; 4 Append: 0

If you *Move* or *Copy* a block, column, or rectangle, WordPerfect assumes you want to "paste" it immediately, and displays **&move** cursor; press Enter to **retrieve&**. You can then either move to the insertion point and press Enter or press F1 (Cancel) to remove the prompt and paste later. When you're ready to paste, press **Ctrl-F4** to give a Move command and type **&4&** for "Retrieve". When this menu appears:

Retrieve: 1 Block; 2 Tabular Column; 3 Rectangle: 0

specify the unit you're retrieving.

To restore a deleted unit, press the F1 key to give an Undelete command. WordPerfect displays the text you most recently deleted (in highlighted form) and shows the following menu at the bottom of the screen:

Undelete: 1 Restore; 2 Show Previous Deletion: 0

Now you can type **1** to restore the highlighted text, type **2** to display the next most recent deletion (WordPerfect saves the text from up to three delete operations), or press Enter to return to editing without undeleting.

The *Append* option lets you copy the highlighted unit to the end of a document file (even a locked file) on disk. When **Append to:** appears at the bottom of the screen, enter the name of the file. If the file does not yet exist, WordPerfect creates it.

Moving Between Pages

Sometimes changes or corrections on one page will require changes on another page. Or you may suddenly think of an error or omission on some other page. WordPerfect lets you move quickly to any page in a document.

Moving is simplest if the other page is the next one up or down from where you are working. Then all you do is press PgUp to move back a page or PgDn to move ahead a page. Or, if the cursor is on the first or last line of a page, press the up-arrow key or down-arrow key to move it back a page or ahead a page, respectively.

To move to some other page, press Ctrl and Home. When **Go to** appears at the bottom of the screen, type the number of the page you want to work on, then press Enter. For example, if you are on page 4 and want to move to page 2, press Ctrl-Home, then type **2** and Enter. WordPerfect shows **Repositioning** at the bottom of the screen, then displays page 2 with the cursor at the top left-hand corner.

You can move to the beginning or end of a document without entering a page number. Just press Home twice, then either ↑ (for beginning) or ↓ (for end).

Moving Within a Document

— See **Cursor, Moving the**

MultiMate Documents

— See **Convert Program**

Multiple Copies, Printing

WordPerfect normally prints only one copy of a document. To make it print two or more copies, press Shift and F7 to give a Print command. When the Print menu appears, perform one of the following procedures:

4.1 4.2
- *For WordPerfect 4.1 or 4.2,* type **3** to select *Options* from the menu. When the *"Change Print Options Temporarily"* menu appears, type **2** to reach the *Number of Copies* field. Type a number (e.g., type **9** to get nine copies), then press Enter twice to return to the Print menu.

5.0
- *For WordPerfect 5.0,* type **n** to reach the *Number of Copies* field, then type a number (e.g., type **9** to get nine copies) and press Enter to return to the *Selection* field.

These procedures only change the number of copies for the current print operation. If you generally need a specific number of copies of everything you do (a common case in our paper-run society), you can make WordPerfect produce them for every print operation. See **Set-up** for details.

Naming Documents

— See **Filenames**

New Page Number

WordPerfect always numbers pages sequentially, starting with 1. However, if you prepare a document as several disk files, you will want to continue the numbering sequence with each file you print. Further, if you're writing a book, you may want to use Roman-style numbering (i, ii, iii, etc.) for the table of contents and preface, but switch to Arabic numbering (1, 2, 3) for the main text.

To change the page number or numbering style, move the cursor to the first page you want renumbered and do one of the following:

4.1
4.2
- **With WordPerfect 4.1 or 4.2**, press Alt-F8 to give a Page Format command. When the menu appears, type **2** to select *New Page Number*. When WordPerfect asks for the *New Page #*, enter it, then select the numbering style, Arabic or Roman.

| 5.0 | •**With WordPerfect 5.0**, press Shift-F8 to give a Format command. When the menu appears, type **2** to select *Page*, then **6** to select *New Page Number*. For New Page Number, enter the number you want in the desired numbering style, Roman or Arabic. |

New Page, Starting a

If you press Ctrl and Enter, WordPerfect will start a new page. It tells you it has done this by showing a line of equal signs across the screen (or a dashed line, in WordPerfect 4.1) and displaying *Ln 1* at the bottom right-hand corner. It also inserts a hidden [HPg] code where you pressed Ctrl-Enter. If you pressed Ctrl-Enter by mistake (say, you intended Ctrl-Home), press Alt-F3 to see the hidden codes and delete [HPg].

Newspaper-Style Columns

—See **Columns, Text**

Numeric Keypad

The keys at the right of the keyboard, shown in Figure N-1, are like the keys on a calculator. They are called a *numeric keypad* because they can be used to enter long sequences of numbers, such as item prices, grades, and population figures. The regular number keys in the typewriter section are also available, but they are rather hard to reach.

Note that four of the white keys are marked with arrows. They provide you with a way to move from one place to another on the screen. The Home, End, PgUp (Page Up), and PgDn (Page Down) keys in the keypad, and the + and - keys to the right of it, are also movement keys, but they let you move greater distances than the arrow keys do.

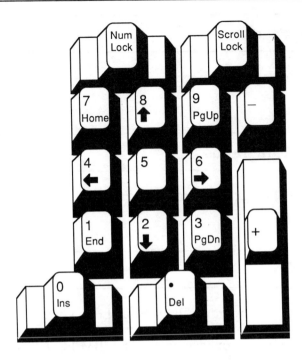

Figure N-1. Numeric keypad.

Ins (Insert) and Del (Delete) at the bottom of the keypad are used to replace existing text or remove material from it.

Note that the keys in the numeric keypad have both lowercase and uppercase markings. Pressing the Num Lock key changes these keys from one case to the other. The IBM PC AT has a special green light that indicates which case is active, but the PC and XT keyboards do not. Fortunately, WordPerfect provides an indicator; it makes *Pos* flash at the bottom right-hand corner of the screen.

Numbering Lines

— See **Print Format Command** (WordPerfect 4.1 and 4.2) or **Line Format Option** (WordPerfect 5.0)

Numbering Pages

—See **Page Numbering**

Numbering Paragraphs

—See **Paragraph Numbering**

Num Lock Key

Num Lock operates like a Shift Lock key for the numeric keypad. Pressing it changes the keys in the numeric keypad from lowercase to uppercase, or vice versa. The IBM PC AT keyboard has a green light that indicates which case is active, but the PC and XT keyboards do not. Fortunately, WordPerfect provides an indicator that tells you when Num Lock has been pressed; it makes *Pos* flash at the bottom right-hand corner of the screen.

Original Backup

— See **Backups**

Orphan Lines

— See **Widow and Orphan Lines**

Other Format Option — WordPerfect 5.0

| 5.0 | WordPerfect 5.0's Format (Shift-F8) menu provides four options, of which *Other* contains some formatting features that don't belong in any of the other options. When you type **4** from the Format menu, WordPerfect displays the Other Format menu shown in Figure O-1.

The Other Format menu lets you make the following format changes within a document:

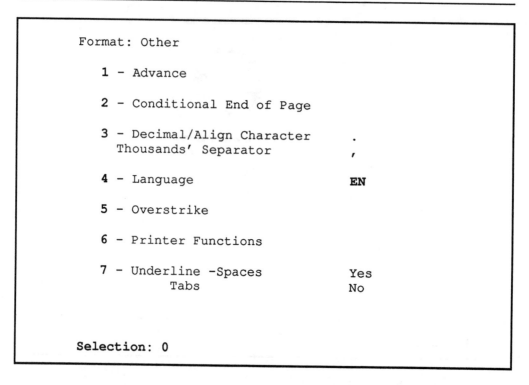

Figure O-1. WordPerfect 5.0's Other Format menu.

1. *Advance* lets you move the cursor anywhere on the screen.
2. *Conditional End of Page* lets you protect a specified number of lines (e.g., the lines in a table), to keep WordPerfect from splitting between two pages.
3. This option specifies characters that WordPerfect is to use for a Tab Align (Ctrl-F6) command. *Decimal/Align Character* (initially a period) is the character on which decimal numbers should be aligned. *Thousands' Separator* (initially a comma) is the character to be inserted between groups of "thousands" digits.
4. *Language* lets you choose the Spell, Thesaurus, and Hyphenation files in computers that have those files for more than one language. It is usually preset to *EN*, for English.
5. *Overstrike* lets you print two or more characters at the same place on a page.
6. *Printer Functions* produces a submenu of advanced printer features, including Kerning, Printer Command, Word Spacing, Letter Spacing, and Word Spacing Justification Limits.

7. *Underline* determines whether WordPerfect's Underline (F8) command is to underline spaces (preset to Yes) and tabs (preset to No) between words as well as the words themselves.

Outlines

If your document is long, you should prepare an outline before starting to work on it. You may also want to number the section titles as they'll be numbered in the document. Section numbering is especially common for term papers, research reports, and technical specifications and manuals. Further, you may want to number paragraphs as you enter them; this is often required for legal contracts.

In preparing an outline on a typewriter, the writer must supply the numbers and keep track of them—an annoying job at best. It becomes even more tedious if he or she adds or deletes a subsection, because that changes the numbering on all subsequent subsections. WordPerfect can help eliminate these problems, by inserting the numbers automatically.

| 4.1 |
| 4.2 |

WordPerfect 4.1 and 4.2 provide seven levels of numbering and three predefined styles (Paragraph, Outline, and Legal), plus an *Other* style that you can define yourself. The predefined styles produce numbers of these forms:

Paragraph	1. a. i. (1) (a) (i) 1)
Outline	I. A. 1. a. (1) (a) 1)
Legal	1., 1.1, 2, 2.1, etc.

| 5.0 |

WordPerfect 5.0 provides eight levels of numbering and four predefined styles (the three I just described, plus a *Bullets* style) and *Other*.

Each version of WordPerfect comes preset to use the *Outline* numbering style.

Preparing Outlines

When preparing an outline, you can make WordPerfect number the section titles before or after you enter them. In doing this, WordPerfect works much as you would. That is, it enters first-level (section or chapter) titles at the left-hand margin, indents second-level (subsection) titles one tab stop, indents third-level (sub-subsection) titles two tab stops, and so on. However, each time you start a new line or press Tab, WordPerfect automatically inserts the next number for that level. You needn't type the numbers or remember which one comes next, as you do when you prepare an outline on a typewriter.

Once WordPerfect is in its Outline mode, two different keys make it produce a section number:

- Pressing *Enter* makes it insert a first-level number (e.g., I, II, III) at the beginning of the next line.
- Pressing *Tab* makes it move to the next tab stop and insert the next level number there.

To make WordPerfect number an outline, enter a title (if you want one), then proceed as follows:

1. Set tabs for the section numbers and the titles that follow them.
2. **For WordPerfect 4.1 or 4.2**, press Alt-F5 to give a Mark Text command, then type **1** to select Outline. **For WordPerfect 5.0**, press Shift-F5 to give a Date/Outline command, then type **4** to select Outline. In either case, WordPerfect shows **Outline** at the bottom of the screen.
3. Press Enter to reach the line where the outline should start. Enter makes WordPerfect display *I.* at the left margin. (To put more lines between the title and the outline, continue pressing Enter.)
4. To reach the place where the text starts, press Indent (F4) to indent the text, or press the space bar, then **Tab**, to tab rather than indent. (You wouldn't want to press just Tab here, because that would make WordPerfect advance to the next numbering level.)
5. Type the section title, then press Enter. WordPerfect inserts *II.*, the next first-level number.
6. Now you have two choices:

- To produce another first-level title, enter it as described in steps 4 and 5.
- To produce a second-level title, press Tab.

As I mentioned earlier, pressing Tab makes WordPerfect advance to the next numbering level. Thus, pressing Tab once from the left margin sets up a second-level title, pressing it twice sets up a third-level title, and so on. If you accidentally overshoot the tab stop where you want a number, press Shift-Tab to tab backward.

```
     I.   Big Game Reserve

          A.   Permits
               1.   Animals
               2.   Hunting Hours
               3.   Tags
               4.   Annual Totals

          B.   Big Game Hunts and Conservation
               1.   Permit Reduction
               2.   Legal Age
               3.   Deer and Elk Exceptions

    II.   Campgrounds

   III.   Wilderness Mountain Area

    IV.   Lone Pine Reserve
```

Figure O-2. Sample outline.

To turn the Outline feature off, do another Mark Text or Date/Outline command and select *Outline* again.

Figure O-2 shows a typical outline. Here, the first-level titles (e.g., *I. Big Game Reserve*) are at the left margin, second-level titles (e.g., *A. Permits*) are at the first tab stop, and third-level titles (e.g., *1. Animals*) are at the second tab stop.

Editing Outlines

Unless your document is simple and straightforward, you will probably spend quite a bit of time preparing an outline for it. Typically, you create a preliminary outline, with perhaps only the first- and second-level titles. Then you survey this first attempt and decide what to change.

Often, you want to make the outline more detailed, by inserting new section or subsection titles. You may also want to delete titles or change their priority (say, change a second-level title to first level, or vice versa). Finally, you may want to change the order of certain sections, by moving them from one part of the outline to another.

Of course, all of these operations affect the numbering within the outline. With a typewriter, they would require you to spend hours cutting and pasting or retyping. With WordPerfect on a computer, they take only seconds—and better yet, WordPerfect renumbers everything automatically to reflect the changes!

To insert an entry into an outline, move the cursor to the end of the line that is to precede the insertion, then start as usual: by selecting *Outline* from the Mark Text or Date/Outline menu. Press Enter to start a new line and Tab to indent to the level you want. Finally, type your insertion—but *don't* press Enter after it unless you want to insert another entry. WordPerfect renumbers as you move the cursor down the screen or leave Outline mode.

You can delete an outline entry just as you delete ordinary text; you don't even have to put WordPerfect into Outline mode. When the entry disappears, WordPerfect closes the gap and renumbers to reflect the deletion.

As you know, WordPerfect numbers each outline entry based on how many tab stops you indented it. The amount of indentation determines the entry's level, and thus its number.

Fortunately, **if you indent too much or too little, and enter a title at the wrong level, you can easily correct it**. Simply move the cursor to the beginning of the number and press Backspace or Tab once for each level you want to raise or lower the entry. For example, to change a third-level title to first-level, move the cursor to its number and press Backspace twice. When you move the cursor down the screen, WordPerfect renumbers each entry to reflect the level change.

Once you prepare an outline using Outline mode, WordPerfect keeps track of the numbering. Thus, if you move or copy numbered titles using the standard techniques, WordPerfect corrects the affected numbers automatically. Generally, you move titles to change the order of the document, and copy them as a basis for creating similar entries.

Changing Numbering Styles

WordPerfect comes preset to use the *Outline* numbering style, but you can easily switch to another style. Moreover, if you are continuing an outline that began in some other document, you can specify the starting number (say, 6, if the earlier outline ended with 5). To change the style and/or numbering, move the cursor to where you want the change to begin and proceed as follows:

|4.1|
|4.2|

- **For WordPerfect 4.1**, press Alt-F5 to give a Mark Text command, then type 6 for Define and 7 for Paragraph/Outline Numbering. **For WordPerfect 4.2**, press Alt-F5 to give a Mark Text command, then type 6 for Other Options and 1 for Define Paragraph/Outline Numbering.

When the Paragraph Numbering Definition form appears, type the number of the style you want. To number the first level *1*, press Enter. To start the first level with some other number, type the number, then press Enter.

5.0

•**For WordPerfect 5.0**, press Shift-F5 to give a Date/Outline command, then type **6** to select Define. When the Paragraph Numbering Definition form appears, type the number of the style you want.

To number the first level *1*, press Enter. To start the first level with some other number, type **1** to reach *Starting Paragraph Number*, then type the starting number and press Enter. Press F7 (Exit) twice to get back to your document.

Overflow file already exists Message for WordPerfect 4.1

4.1

This message appears when you try to start WordPerfect version 4.1 after a power failure. It is followed by the menu

```
Directory is in use!  1 Exit;  2 Use Another Directory;  3 Overwrite Files: 1
```

When this happens, type **3**. WordPerfect then deletes the files that are preventing you from starting and displays its normal starting screen.

Overstrikes

WordPerfect has an *Overstrike* feature that lets you print two characters at the same position. This is handy for creating foreign language characters, such as ñ in Spanish.

Overstrike with WordPerfect 4.1 or 4.2

4.1
4.2

To construct an overstrike with WordPerfect 4.1 or 4.2, type the first character, then press Shift and F1 to give a Super/Subscript command. When the menu appears, type **3** to select *Overstrike*. The cursor will backspace to your first character (and insert a hidden [Overstk] code in your document), at which point you type the second character. Only the second character appears on the screen, but WordPerfect will print both characters.

If you accidentally mistyped one or both overstrike characters, you can easily correct your mistake. Start as before—by pressing Shift-F8 and typing **4**, then **5**—but when the Overstrike menu appears, type **2** to select Edit. WordPerfect searches backward for an overstrike. If it does not find any, it then searches forward. When the overstrike characters appear, make the necessary changes and press Enter, then press F7 (Exit) to return to your document.

Overstrike with WordPerfect 5.0

5.0

To construct an overstrike with WordPerfect 5.0, begin by pressing Shift and F8 to give a Format command. Type **4** to select *Other* from the Format menu, **5** to select *Overstrike* from the Other Format menu, and **1** to Create the overstrike. Finally, type the two overstrike characters and press Enter, then press F7 (Exit) to return to your document. Only the second character appears on the screen, but WordPerfect will print both characters.

If you accidentally mistype either or both overstrike characters, you can easily correct your mistake. Start as before—by pressing Shift-F8 and typing **4**, then **5**—but when the Overstrike menu appears, type **2** to select Edit. WordPerfect searches backward for an overstrike. If it doesn't find one, it then searches forward. When the overstrike characters appear, make the necessary changes and press Enter, then press F7 (Exit) to return to your document.

Related Features

WordPerfect also provides a variety of foreign, Greek, and graphic characters that you can insert in your documents; see **Special Characters** for details. There is also a **Strikeout Text** feature that lets you overstrike a block of text with hyphens, a common practice for legal documents.

P

Page Breaks

When you have filled a page, WordPerfect starts a new page automatically, and draws a dashed line across the screen to show where it switched pages. This is called a *soft page break*; a hidden [SPg] code marks its position in your document.

You can also force WordPerfect to start a new page by pressing Ctrl and Enter. This *hard page break* draws a line of equal signs across the screen and inserts a hidden [HPg] code in your document. (Note: WordPerfect 4.1 is an exception; it shows a dashed line across the screen for both soft and hard page breaks.)

Page Format Command (Alt-F8) — WordPerfect 4.1 and 4.2

4.1
4.2

This command differs depending on whether WordPerfect is in Block mode or regular editing mode. Pressing Alt and F8 in Block mode lets you *protect* the block; that is, keep it together on a page. Pressing Alt and F8 in editing mode makes the Page Format menu (shown in Figure P-1) appear.

Page Format Command (Alt-F8) — WordPerfect 4.1 and 4.2

```
Page Format

    1 - Page Number Position

    2 - New Page Number

    3 - Center Page Top to Bottom

    4 - Page Length

    5 - Top Margin

    6 - Headers or Footers

    7 - Page Number Column Positions

    8 - Suppress for Current page only

    9 - Conditional End of Page

    A - Widow/Orphan

Selection: 0
```

Figure P-1. Page Format menu.

Page Number Position

By selecting this option you can tell WordPerfect to print the page number at the top or bottom of each page, at the left- or right-hand margin, or centered. You can also tell it to alternate the page number position, putting it at the right margin on odd-numbered pages and at the left margin on even-numbered pages. This menu's *Page Number Column Positions* option (7) lets you set the left, right, and center positions for page numbers independent of the text's margin settings.

New Page Number

WordPerfect always numbers pages sequentially, starting with 1. However, sometime you may prepare a document as several disk files, in which case you will want to continue the numbering sequence with each file you print. When you select this option, WordPerfect asks for the new page number, then the numbering style, Arabic (1, 2, 3) or Roman (i, ii, iii).

Center Page Top to Bottom

This option arranges the text on each page so that there is the same amount of blank space at the top and bottom.

Page Length

WordPerfect is preset to print six lines per inch on regular 8-1/2 by 11-inch paper, and to put a one-inch margin at the top and bottom of each page. At six lines per inch, an 11-inch page is 66 lines long; with the one-inch margins at the top and bottom, a page can hold 54 single-spaced lines. This option lets you change to 8-1/2 by 14 legal size paper or any other length you want to specify.

Top Margin

WordPerfect is preset to provide a one-inch margin at the top. This option lets you specify a new top margin size in half-lines, or twelfths of an inch.

Headers or Footers

This option can make WordPerfect print specified text at the top (a header) or bottom (a footer) of each page. See **Headers and Footers** for details.

Page Number Column Positions

When you tell WordPerfect to print page numbers using option 1 (Page Number Position), it uses the same left and right margin position, and center position, as for the text. This option lets you specify different left, right, and center positions for page numbers. In effect, it lets you put the page numbers anywhere you want on a line.

Suppress for Current Page Only

This option lets you selectively turn off page format settings on this page, based on what you select from the menu shown in Figure P-2.

Conditional End of Page

This option lets you keep a specified number of lines, such as a table, together on a page. See the separate **Conditional End of Page** entry.

Widow/Orphan

Normally, WordPerfect doesn't care how it arranges text; it simply fills each page to capacity. Unlike a good typist, it may leave the first

Figure P-2. Suppress Page Format menu.

```
Suppress Page Format for Current Page Only

   To temporarily turn off multiple lines, include a
   "+" between menu entries. For example 5+6+2 will
   turn off Header A, Header B, and Page Numbering for
   the current page.

        1 - Turn off all page numbering, headers, and footers

        2 - Turn page numbering off

        3 - Print page number at bottom center (this page only)

        4 - Turn off all headers and footers

        5 - Turn off Header A

        6 - Turn off Header B

        7 - Turn off Footer A

        8 - Turn off Footer B

Selection(s): 0
```

line of a paragraph alone at the bottom of a page (a *widow*) or the last line at the top of a new page (an *orphan*). This option lets you break it of this sloppy habit.

Page Format Option — WordPerfect 5.0

5.0

WordPerfect's Format (Shift-F8) command provides four options, of which *Page* controls the appearance and amount of text on a page, page numbering, and the kind of form on which the document is printed. When you type **2** from the Format menu, WordPerfect displays the Page Format menu shown in Figure P-3.

The Page Format menu lets you make the following format changes within a document:

1. *Center Page (top to bottom)* arranges the text on a page so that there is the same amount of blank space at the top and bottom.
2. *Force Odd/Even Page* forces the current page to have an odd or even number. This is especially handy for ensuring that the first page of each chapter of a book or report is odd-numbered.
3. *Headers* lets you specify text that is to be printed at the top of a page. You can define two different headers. For example, you can print a section title at the top of right-hand (odd-numbered) pages and the report title at the top of left-hand (even-numbered) pages.
4. *Footers* lets you specify text that is to be printed at the bottom of a page. You can define two different footers.
5. *Top and Bottom Margins*. WordPerfect is preset to provide a one-inch margin at the top and bottom of every page, but you can make these margins wider or narrower to suit your needs.
6. *New Page Number*. WordPerfect always numbers pages sequentially, starting with 1. However, if a document is divided into several disk files, you will want to continue the numbering sequence with each file you print. This option lets you start renumbering pages with a specified Roman (i, ii, iii, etc.) or Arabic (1, 2, 3, etc.) number.
7. *Page Numbering* lets you tell WordPerfect where and on which pages to print the page number. You can choose any of eight different page positions.

8. *Paper Size and Type.* WordPerfect assumes you want to print on standard 8-1/2 by 11-inch paper, but you can choose from a variety of sizes and types.
9. *Suppress* lets you tell the printer to omit headers, footers, or page numbers (in any combination) from the current page.

Page Length

—See **Page Format Command (WordPerfect 4.1 and 4.2)**

Figure P-3. WordPerfect 5.0's Page Format menu.

```
Format: Page

    1 - Center page (top to bottom)    No

    2 - Force Odd/Even Page

    3 - Headers

    4 - Footers

    5 - Margins - Top                   1"
              Bottom                    1"

    6 - New Page Number                 1
        (example: 3 or iii)

    7 - Page Numbering                  No page numbering

    8 - Paper Size                      8.5" x 11"
              Type                      Standard

    9 - Suppress (this page only)

Selection: 0
```

Page, Lines Per

— See **Page Format Command (WordPerfect 4.1 and 4.2)**

Page, New

— See **Hard Page Command**

Page Numbering

WordPerfect always displays the current page number as a *Pg* value at the bottom right-hand corner of the screen, but it won't print page numbers unless you tell it to. There are two ways to make WordPerfect print page numbers.

Stand-Alone Page Numbers

To print just the page number itself, with no text around it, move to the first page (by pressing Home twice, then ↑) and do one of the following procedures:

4.1
4.2
- **For WordPerfect 4.1 and 4.2**, press Alt and F8 to give a Page Format command. When the menu appears, type **1** to select *Page Number Position*. That brings on a second menu that lets you tell WordPerfect where to place the page number. Make your choice, then press Enter if you are done using the Page Format menu.

5.0
- **For WordPerfect 5.0**, press Shift and F8 to give a Format command. When the menu appears, type **2** for *Page*, then **7** for *Page Numbering*. That brings on a display that lets you tell WordPerfect where to place the page number. Make your choice, then press F7 (Exit) to return to your document.

Page Numbers in Headers and Footers

You can also make WordPerfect insert the page number in a header or footer, by pressing Ctrl and B where you want it to appear. Pressing Ctrl-B puts a ^B symbol on the screen. (You can also print the current page number in regular text, by pressing Ctrl-B where you want it.)

Specifying Page Numbers

WordPerfect always numbers pages sequentially, starting with 1. However, if a document is divided into several disk files, you will want to continue the numbering sequence with each file you print. WordPerfect provides a *New Page Number* feature that lets you start renumbering pages with a specified Roman (i, ii, iii, etc.) or Arabic (1, 2, 3, etc.) number.

In WordPerfect 4.1 and 4.2, *New Page Number* is an option in the Page Format (Alt-F8) menu; in WordPerfect 5.0, it is an option in the Format (Shift-F8) command's Page Format submenu.

Page, Starting a New

— See **Hard Page Command**

Pages, Moving Between

— See **Moving Between Pages**

Paper

WordPerfect is preset to print on standard 8-1/2 by 11-inch paper. To print on some other size form (such as legal size paper or envelopes), you must give WordPerfect the form's specifications.

4.1 4.2 WordPerfect 4.1 and 4.2 specify the form size with a Page Length parameter on the Page Format menu. To change the page length, press Alt and F8 to choose Page Format, then type **4** to select *Page Length*.

The Page Length is defined by the number of single-spaced lines (at six lines per inch) on the page, while the length of the text area on a page is defined by the number of single-spaced text lines (again, at six lines per inch). The Page Length menu provides options for the two most common paper sizes, letter size (66 total lines and 54 text lines) and legal size (84 total lines and 72 text lines). It also provides an option that you can use to specify some other size.

5.0 **WordPerfect 5.0** provides a wider variety of form sizes. To select one, press Shift and F8 to give a Print command and type **2** for *Page*. When the Page Format menu appears, type **8** to reach the *Paper Size* field. Choose your paper size from the menu, then choose its type from the Paper Type menu. Finally, press F7 (Exit) to return to your document.

Paragraph Numbering

WordPerfect's Paragraph Number feature can number paragraphs, titles, and lists in a document. To make it do this, you must explicitly tell it to insert a paragraph number *every* time you want one. WordPerfect does not insert numbers automatically, as it does for outlines.

4.1 4.2 WordPerfect 4.1 and 4.2 provide seven levels of numbering and three predefined styles (Paragraph, Outline, and Legal), plus an *Other* style that you can define yourself. The predefined styles produce numbers of these forms:

Paragraph	1. a. i. (1) (a) (i) 1)
Outline	I. A. 1. a. (1) (a) 1)
Legal	1., 1.1, 2, 2.1, etc.

5.0 WordPerfect 5.0 provides eight levels of numbering and four predefined styles (the three I just described, plus a *Bullets* style), plus *Other*.

Each version of WordPerfect comes preset to use the *Outline* numbering style.

Using the Paragraph Number Feature

To start numbering paragraphs, move the cursor to where you want the first number and proceed as follows:

> **4.1**
> **4.2**

- For WordPerfect 4.1 or 4.2, press Alt-F5 for Mark Text. When the Mark Text menu appears, type **2** to select *Para #*.

> **5.0**

- For WordPerfect 5.0, press Shift-F5 for Date/Outline. When the Date/Outline menu appears, type **5** to select *Para Num*.

In either case, WordPerfect produces the prompt

```
Paragraph Level (ENTER for automatic):
```

WordPerfect is waiting for you to tell it which of two types of numbers you want, "automatic" or "fixed."

Automatic and Fixed Numbers

With automatic paragraph numbering, WordPerfect inserts the appropriate level for the tab position the cursor is currently on. That is, it inserts 1 at the first tab position, 2 at the second, and so on. By contrast, fixed paragraph numbering lets you tell WordPerfect which level of number to insert, regardless of which tab position the cursor is at. For example, you can make it insert a fourth-level number at the first tab position.

In short, there are three ways to respond to the "Paragraph Level" prompt:

- To insert an automatic number, press Enter. WordPerfect uses the level that reflects how many times you pressed Tab *before* requesting the number.
- To insert a fixed number, enter a number between 1 and 7. WordPerfect inserts the next number for that particular level.
- To return to editing without inserting a number, press F1.

When should you use fixed paragraph numbers instead of automatic ones? In general:

Use fixed numbers if you want a specific level number, regardless of which tab position the cursor is on, or if you want a numbered title centered and the number would fall between two tabs. For any other application, use automatic numbers.

Most people can probably use fixed paragraph numbers exclusively. Only those who must prepare complex technical documents such as specifications must revert to automatic numbers.

Changing Numbering Styles

WordPerfect comes preset to use the *Outline* numbering style, but you can easily switch to another style. Moreover, if you are continuing an outline that began in some other document, you can specify the starting number (say, 6, if the earlier outline ended with 5). To change the style and/or numbering, move the cursor to where you want the change to begin and do one of two things:

| 4.1 |
| 4.2 |

- **For WordPerfect 4.1**, press Alt-F5 to give a Mark Text command, then type **6** for Define and **7** for Paragraph/Outline Numbering. **For WordPerfect 4.2**, press Alt-F5 to give a Mark Text command, then type **6** for Other Options and **1** for Define Paragraph/Outline Numbering.

  When the Paragraph Numbering Definition form appears, type the number of the style you want. To number the first level *1*, press Enter. To start the first level with some other number, type the number, then press Enter.

| 5.0 |

- **For WordPerfect 5.0**, press Shift-F5 to give a Date/Outline command, then type **6** to select Define. When the Paragraph Numbering Definition form appears, type the number of the style you want.

  To number the first level *1*, press Enter. To start the first level with some other number, type **1** to reach *Starting Paragraph Number*, then type the starting number and press Enter. Press F7 (Exit) twice to get back to your document.

Parallel Columns

— See **Columns, Text**

PgUp and PgDn Keys

Pressing the PgUp (Page Up) or PgDn (Page Down) key on the numeric keypad moves the cursor to the top of the next or preceding page, respectively, of the document. Pressing PgUp from the first page, however, moves the cursor to the top of that page. Similarly, pressing PgDn from the last page moves the cursor to the bottom of that page.

If the number 9 or 3 appears when you press PgUp or PgDn, you have apparently pressed the Num Lock key accidentally. (Note that *Pos* at the bottom right-hand corner of the screen is flashing.) Press Num Lock to remove the lock.

Pitch — WordPerfect 4.1 and 4.2

> 4.1
> 4.2

The term pitch refers to the number of characters the printer produces per inch of type. WordPerfect is preset to produce ten pitch (i.e., ten characters per inch), but you can easily change it to produce some other density. (Note that the higher the pitch value the smaller the letters, because the printer must compress more characters into each inch.)

To change the pitch value within a document, move the cursor there and press Ctrl-F8 to give a *Print Format* command. When the Print Format menu appears, type 1 to select Pitch, type the new pitch value, and then press Enter *three* times to return to the document. If you want proportional spacing, type an asterisk (*) after the pitch value.

Changing the pitch makes WordPerfect insert a hidden code of the form [Font Change:*p,f*] in your document, where *p* is the pitch and *f* is the font.

Place Markers

When you retrieve a document from disk, WordPerfect always starts on the first page. Often you will want to continue working where you left off last time. That's easy if you were working at the end of the text; simply press Home twice, then press the ↓ key. However, if you were working somewhere within a document, especially a long one, it may be more difficult to locate the stopping point. (In fact, you may not even remember where you were!)

Before quitting a work session, you can mark your place by typing a character or series of characters that doesn't appear anywhere else in the document; say, a carat (^) or tilde (~). That way, the next time you start, you can do a Search operation with the place marker as the search string. Or you could do a Replace operation by entering the place marker as the search string and pressing F2 when you are asked for the replacement string. This makes WordPerfect find the marker and delete it (i.e., replace it with nothing), leaving the cursor exactly where you want to start working.

Plus (+) Key on Numeric Keypad

Pressing the + key at the bottom right-hand corner of the keyboard moves the cursor to the same column position at the bottom of the screen. Pressing Shift and + together inserts a + symbol at the cursor position.

Pos Indicator

The Pos value at the bottom right-hand corner of the screen tells you where the cursor is currently positioned on the line. If you pressed F6 or F8 to turn on bold print or underlining, the number will also be bold (although that may be difficult to see) or underlined. Further, WordPerfect 5.0 shades the Pos value while you're in Block mode.

The word *Pos* is also an indicator. WordPerfect displays it as *POS* when Caps Lock is on and makes it flash when Num Lock is on.

Power Failure

If someone accidentally dislodges the computer's power cord, the electricity goes off, or you switch off the computer without leaving WordPerfect with an Exit (F7) command, the screen will show one of two prompts when you next start WordPerfect. WordPerfect 4.1 shows **Overflow file already exists** and a menu; type **3** to select *Overwrite Files*. WordPerfect 4.2 and 5.0 show **Are other copies of WordPerfect currently running?**; type **n** for no.

Primary File in Merge Operations

The *primary file* is the generalized version of a form letter, the one in which WordPerfect is to insert the data (generally names and addresses) from a separate "secondary" file. For details on creating form letters, see **Form Letters**.

Print Command (Shift-F7) — WordPerfect 4.1 and 4.2

4.1 4.2

Pressing Shift and F7 in WordPerfect 4.2 makes the following Print menu appear:

1 Full Text; 2 Page; 3 Options; 4 Printer Control; 5 Type-thru; 6 Preview: 0

(WordPerfect 4.1's Print menu is similar, but has no Preview option.)

Full Text and Page

The first two choices make WordPerfect print the entire document you're working on (1) or just the current page (2).

Options

Choosing *Options* (3) brings on a menu that lets you specify the printer number (in case you have more than one), the number of copies, and the binding width for your next print operation.

Printer Control

Choosing *Printer Control* (4) brings on the Printer Control menu shown in Figure P-4. The menu provides ten options, four with

```
Printer Control
                            C - Cancel Print Job(s)
1 - Select Print Options        D - Display All Print Jobs
2 - Display Printers and Fonts  G - "Go" (Resume Printing)
3 - Select Printers             P - Print a Document
                                R - Rush Print Job
Selection: 0                    S - Stop Printing


Current Job

Job Number: n/a    Page Number:   n/a
Job Status: n/a    Current Copy:  n/a
Message:       The print queue is empty

Job List

Job    Document            Destination     Forms and Print Options




Additional jobs not shown: 0
```

Figure P-4. Printer Control menu for WordPerfect 4.1 and 4.2.

numbers (including 0, to leave the menu) and six with letters. Here, *Select Print Options* (1) gives you the same choices as *Options* does on the main Print menu. *Display Printers and Fonts* and *Select Printers* (2 and 3) are used to switch between printers, if you have more than one.

Of the lettered choices, you will probably use P (Print a Document) most often. That's the command that lets you print a document stored on disk. It's also the command you need to print a selected range of pages. When you press **p**, WordPerfect displays **Document name:** below **Selection**. Type the name of the document you want to print, then press Enter. (If there is no file with that name, WordPerfect displays **ERROR: File not found**.) You must then tell WordPerfect which pages to print.

4.1
4.2

WordPerfect 4.1 asks for the **Starting page** (enter its number, or press Enter to start with *1*), then the **Ending page** (enter it, or press Enter to print to the end of the document).

WordPerfect 4.2 assumes you want to print the entire document, and shows **Page(s): (All)**. If that is indeed what you want, press Enter. Otherwise, you have several choices, as follows:

- To print from the beginning of the document up to a certain page, enter a command of the form **-n**, where *n* is the ending page number. For example, to print from the beginning up to and including page 24, enter **-24**.

- To print to the end of the document, starting at a certain page number, enter a command of the form **n-**.

- To print a specific range of pages, enter a command of the form **n-m**, where *n* and *m* are the page numbers where printing is to begin and end, respectively.

- To print several nonconsecutive pages or several ranges of pages, enter their numbers separated with commas. For example, to print pages 11 through 15, 24, and 40 to the end, enter **11-15, 24, 40-**.

Of course, if you numbered a table of contents, preface, or index with Roman numbers, enter those numbers in the *Page(s)* field. For example, you could enter **i-iv** to print the first four Roman-numbered pages.

If you have divided your document into chapters or sections by restarting the page numbering from *1*, WordPerfect recognizes each section by number. To print selected pages within a specific section, type the section number, a colon (:), and the page numbers.

For example, suppose your document has three chapters, where Chapter 1 has pages numbered 1 to 20, Chapter 2 has pages numbered 1 to 13, and Chapter 3 has pages numbered 1 to 36. Some possible page ranges are:

- Entering **2:1-6** prints the first 6 pages of Chapter 2.

- Entering **2:7,3:4-** prints page 7 of Chapter 2 and from page 4 to the end of Chapter 3.

- Entering **4-2:10** prints from page 4 of Chapter 1 through page 10 of Chapter 2.

You needn't wait for a print job to finish before telling WordPerfect what to print next. WordPerfect maintains a *Job List* (shown at the bottom of the Printer Control menu) into which you can enter as many printing jobs as you want. You can also do useful work while printing is going on; simply press Enter to return to editing. The other Printer Control commands are:

- *C - Cancel Print Job(s)* lets you remove any or all printing jobs from the Job List. When WordPerfect displays "Cancel Which Job?", enter the unwanted job's number or enter an asterisk (*) to cancel all jobs.
- *D - Display All Print Jobs* shows a list of all the print jobs in the Job List; the regular Printer Control screen shows only the first three.
- *G - "Go" (Resume Printing)* is used to tell WordPerfect to proceed if you are using single-sheet paper or after you have stopped a print operation temporarily, by pressing **S**.
- *R - Rush Print Job* lets you change the priority of a print job in the Job List, putting it next in line for printing.
- *S - Stop Printing* stops the current print operation until you press **G**. This is handy if the paper has jammed, you have to answer the phone, or for any other kind of temporary interruption.

Type-thru

This option lets you use your computer like a typewriter, and "type" onto the printer. When you press **5**, WordPerfect shows

```
Type-thru printing: 1 by line; 2 by character: 0
```

The *by line* option lets you type a line of text (up to 250 characters), edit it as needed, then press Enter to send it to the printer. When you choose this option, WordPerfect displays a screen that has a typing area at the top and the following at the bottom:

Line Type-thru Printing

Function Key	Action
Move	Retrieve the previous line for editing
Print Format	Do a printer command
Enter	Print the line
Exit/Cancel	Exit without printing

Here, Move refers to the key combination Ctrl-F4, Print Format refers to Ctrl-F8, and Exit/Cancel refers to F1. Pressing **Ctrl-F8** makes WordPerfect display **Cmnd:** and waits for you to enter a numeric command that your printer understands. See the WordPerfect manual for details.

Type-thru's *by character* option sends each keystroke directly to the printer. This option only works if your printer is able to handle it; many printers can't.

For either option, printing starts wherever the print head happens to be. However, you can position it by pressing an arrow key. Up-arrow and down-arrow move the paper up or down one line, while left-arrow and right-arrow move the print head one character position to the left or right. These movement commands are handy for filling in preprinted forms.

Preview

> 4.2

This option, introduced with WordPerfect version 4.2, lets you see how each of the pages in a document or the current page will look when printed, by choosing from this menu:

```
Preview: 1 Document; 2 Page: 0
```

Type **1** to preview the first page of the document or type **2** to preview the current page. For each page, the Preview screen shows the margins, headers, footers, footnotes, endnotes, page numbers, and right justification. You can use the normal cursor-moving keys to reach other pages. You may not edit the document, however.

WordPerfect keeps the preview material in a separate, temporary disk file, as indicated by *Doc 3* on the bottom line. To switch between the preview and the actual document, press Shift-F3 for Switch. To leave the Preview screen, press F7 to Exit.

Print Command (Shift-F7) — WordPerfect 5.0

Pressing Shift and F7 makes the Print menu shown in Figure P-5 appear.

Full Text and Page

The first two choices make WordPerfect print the entire document you're working on (1) or just the current page (2).

Print Command (Shift-F7) — WordPerfect 5.0

```
Print

1 - Full Document
2 - Page
3 - Document on Disk
4 - Control Printer
5 - Type Through
6 - View Document
7 - Initialize Printer

Options

S - Select Printer          Standard Printer
B - Binding                 0"
N - Number of Copies        1
G - Graphics Quality        Medium
T - Text Quality            High


Selection: 0
```

Figure P-5. WordPerfect 5.0's Print menu.

Document on Disk

This option lets you print a document stored on disk without loading it into WordPerfect. When you type **3**, WordPerfect displays **Document name:** at the bottom of the screen. Type the name of the document, then press Enter. If WordPerfect can't find a file with that name, it displays **ERROR: File not found**.

Be aware, however, a disk document can only be printed if it was saved with WordPerfect's *Fast Save* feature turned off; WordPerfect comes with Fast Save turned on. (Fast Save saves documents in an unformatted form, which speeds up save operations.) The procedure for turning Fast Save off is described in the **Fast Save** entry.

If the file name is valid, you must specify the pages to be printed. WordPerfect assumes you want to print the entire document, and shows Page(s): (All). If that is indeed what you want, press Enter. Otherwise, you have several choices, as follows:

- To print from the beginning of the document up to a certain page, enter a command of the form **-n**, where *n* is the ending page number. For example, to print from the beginning up to and including page 24, enter **-24**.
- To print to the end of the document, starting at a certain page number, enter a command of the form **n-**.
- To print a specific range of pages, enter a command of the form **n-m**, where *n* and *m* are the page numbers where printing is to begin and end, respectively.
- To print several nonconsecutive pages or several ranges of pages, enter their numbers separated with commas. For example, to print pages 11 through 15, 24, and 40 to the end, you would enter **11-15, 24, 40-**.

Of course, if you numbered a table of contents, preface, or index with Roman numbers, enter those numbers in the *Page(s)* field. For example, you could enter **i-iv** to print the first four Roman-numbered pages.

If you have divided your document into chapters or sections by restarting the page numbering from *1*, WordPerfect recognizes each section by number. To print selected pages within a specific section, type the section number, a colon (:), and the page numbers.

For example, suppose your document has three chapters, where Chapter 1 has pages numbered 1 to 20, Chapter 2 has pages numbered 1 to 13, and Chapter 3 has pages numbered 1 to 36. Some possible page ranges are:

- Entering **2:1-6** prints the first 6 pages of Chapter 2.
- Entering **2:7,3:4-** prints page 7 of Chapter 2 and from page 4 to the end of Chapter 3.
- Entering **4-2:10** prints from page 4 of Chapter 1 through page 10 of Chapter 2.

You needn't wait for a print job to finish before telling WordPerfect what to print next. WordPerfect maintains a *Job List* (viewable using the Control Printer option) into which you can enter as many printing jobs as you want. You can also do useful work while printing is going on; simply press Enter to return to editing.

Control Printer

Choosing *Control Printer* (4) brings on the print status summary and menu shown in Figure P-6. Here is what the menu options do

1. *Cancel Job(s)* lets you remove any or all printing jobs from the Job List. When WordPerfect displays **Cancel Which Job?**, enter the unwanted job's number or enter an asterisk (*) to cancel all jobs.
2. *Rush Job* lets you change the priority of a print job in the Job List, and make WordPerfect print it next.
3. *Display Jobs* shows a list of all the print jobs in the Job List; the regular screen shows only the first three.
4. *Go (start printer)* is used to tell WordPerfect to proceed if you are using single-sheet paper or after you have stopped a print operation temporarily by choosing *Stop*.
5. *Stop* stops the current print operation until you choose*Go*. This is handy if the paper has jammed, you have to answer the phone, or for any other kind of temporary interruption

Figure P-6. WordPerfect 5.0's Control Printer menu.

```
Print: Control Printer

Current Job

Job Number:  n/a                 Page Number:   n/a
Job Status:  n/a                 Current Copy:  n/a
Paper:       n/a
Location:    n/a
Message:     No print jobs


Job List

Job    Document            Destination      Print Options




Additional Jobs Not Shown: 0


1 Cancel Job(s); 2 Rush Job; 3 Display Jobs; 4 Go
(start printer);5 Stop: 0.
```

Type Through

This option lets you use your printer just like a typewriter. When you press **5**, WordPerfect shows

```
Type Through: 1 By Line; 2 By Character: 0
```

By Line lets you type a line of text (up to 250 characters), edit it as needed, then press Enter to send it to the printer. To edit typed material, you can

- Press the arrow keys to move a line or character at a time.
- Press F1 (Cancel) or F7 (Exit) to leave the Type Through screen.
- Press Home, then ← or →, to move to the beginning or end of the current line.
- Press Ctrl-F4 (Move) to retrieve the preceding line for editing.
- Press Shift-F8 (Format) to display *Cmnd:*, and enter a command for your printer.

The *By Character* option sends each keystroke directly to the printer. This option only works if your printer is able to handle it; many printers can't.

For either option, printing starts wherever the print head happens to be. However, you can position it by pressing an arrow key. Pressing ↑ or ↓ moves the carriage up or down one line, while pressing ← or → moves the print head one character position to the left or right. These movement commands are handy for filling in preprinted forms.

View Document

This option displays a miniaturized version of the current page as it will be printed, and shows the following menu at the bottom:

```
1 100%; 2 200%; 3 Full Page; 4 Facing Pages: 3
```

Here, pressing **1** makes WordPerfect display the page in its true size, while pressing **2** displays it double-sized. Pressing **4** for *Facing Pages* shows two miniaturized pages, with an even-numbered page on the left and an odd-numbered page on the right.

To work forward or backward in the document, use the normal cursor-moving keys. (You may not edit the document, however.)

When you finish looking at the pages, press F7 (Exit) to return to your document.

Options

The Print menu also provides options that let you switch printers, include binding space (to allow for punched holes, spirals, and the like), request multiple copies, and change the print quality for text and graphics. Choosing Graphics Quality (G) or Text Quality (T) brings on a menu with these options:

```
1 Do Not Print; 2 Draft; 3 Medium; 4 High
```

Do Not Print is useful for printers that can print both graphics and text, but not in the same print operation. Here, you would turn off graphics printing (type **g**, then **1**) and print the text. Then you would reinsert the paper, turn off text printing (type **t**, then **1**), and print the graphics.

Print Format Command (Ctrl-F8) — WordPerfect 4.1 and 4.2

4.1 4.2 The Print Format command does just what its name implies: it controls how your text will look when you print it. When you press Ctrl and F8, WordPerfect displays the menu shown in Figure P-7. Let's take the options one at a time.

Pitch and Font

The term pitch refers to the number of characters the printer produces per inch of type. WordPerfect is preset to produce ten pitch (i.e., ten characters per inch), but you can easily change it to produce some other density. (Note that the higher the pitch value the smaller the letters, because the printer must compress more characters into each inch.)

To change the Pitch value, type **1** to select Pitch, type the new pitch value, and then press Enter *three* times to return to the document. To get proportional spacing (assuming your printer can produce it), type an asterisk (*) after the pitch value. For dot matrix printers, 10*

Print Format Command (Ctrl-F8) — WordPerfect 4.1 and 4.2

```
Print Format

    1 - Pitch                               10
        Font                                 1

    2 - Lines per inch                       6

    Right Justification                     On
    3 - Turn off
    4 - Turn on

    Underline Style                          5
    5 - Non-continuous Single
    6 - Non-continuous Double
    7 - Continuous Single
    8 - Continuous Double

    9 - Sheet Feeder Bin Number              1

    A - Insert Printer Command

    B - Line Numbering                      Off

Selection: 0
```

Figure P-7. Print Format menu.

produces pica type with proportional spacing; daisy wheel or thimble type printers often require 3* for the Pitch value.

Most dot matrix printers can produce two or more forms of type. In general, the form that prints quickly but is of lesser quality is referred to as "draft," while the more professional looking (but slower-printing) is called "correspondence" or "near-letter quality." Both of these forms of type are called *fonts*. Laser printers can produce a variety of fonts. To change the font, type **1** to select Pitch, press Enter to reach the Font line, enter your new value, and then press Enter *twice* to return to the document.

Changing the pitch or font makes WordPerfect insert a hidden code of the form [Font Change:*p,f*] in your document, where *p* is the pitch and *f* is the font.

Lines per Inch

WordPerfect assumes you want 6 lines per inch, but you may change it to 8. You could do this to print with a small type size—say, 16.5 characters per inch. When you change the *Lines per inch* setting, WordPerfect inserts a hidden [LPI:*n*], where *n* is the new value.

Understand, the *Lines per inch* setting simply determines how much space the printer will put between single-spaced lines. To produce double- or triple-spacing, press **Shift-F8** to give Word-Perfect a *Line Format* command and select the *Spacing* option.

Right Justification

WordPerfect is preset to make every line the same length, and produce an even right-hand margin by inserting spaces between words. If you generally print with a ragged right-hand margin, press **3** to switch to *Turn off*. When you change the right justification, WordPerfect inserts a hidden [Rt Just On] or [Rt Just Off] code in your document.

Underline Style

These four options determine how WordPerfect underlines text when you give it an *Underline* (F8) command. The terms "Single" and "Double" refer, of course, to underlining with one line or two. (Not all printers can produce double-underlining.) With continuous underlining, WordPerfect underlines the space between tabbed material; with non-continuous underlining (the preset style) it does not. When you change the underline style, WordPerfect inserts a hidden code of the form [Undrl Style:*s*] in your document, where *s* is 5, 6, 7, or 8.

Sheet Feeder Bin Number

This option lets you select which sheet feeder bin is to supply the paper, in case you have more than one bin. When you switch bins, WordPerfect inserts a hidden code of the form [Bin#:*n*] in your document, where *n* is the new bin number.

Insert Printer Command

This option is used to insert command to your printer within a document. See **Printer Commands** for further details.

Line Numbering

4.2 This option, introduced with WordPerfect 4.2, lets you number the lines in your document in a variety of ways. When you press **b** to select *Line Numbering*, WordPerfect displays the menu shown in Figure P-8. Here, the menu items reflect their preset values.

If you simply turn line numbering *On* (by typing 2), WordPerfect will number every line of text and print the numbers six-tenths of an inch from the left-hand edge of the page. It will also restart the line numbering with each new page. Further, since option 3 is set to *Y*, it will also number any blank lines that you insert by pressing Enter. WordPerfect will *not* number the blank lines between double- or triple-spaced text.

Line numbers are not visible on the screen; they only appear when you print the document. Whenever you switch Line Numbering *On* or *Off*, WordPerfect inserts a hidden [LnNum:On] or [LnNum:Off] code in your document.

Print Jobs

When you are printing disk documents (by choosing *Printer Control* from the Print menu), you may request as many different print operations as you want. WordPerfect accepts them one by one and puts them in a *Job List*. The first three items in the list appear at the bottom of the Printer Control screen. To see the complete list, press **d** to *Display All Print Jobs* (WordPerfect 4.1 or 4.2) or **3** to *Display Jobs* (WordPerfect 5.0). When you finish examining the Job List, press F7 to return to the Printer Control screen.

WordPerfect always prints documents in the order you enter them (the order shown in the Job List), but if you need a job in the list printed as soon as possible, press **r** for *Rush Print Job* (WordPerfect 4.1 or 4.2) or **2** for *Rush Job* (WordPerfect 5.0). When WordPerfect asks for the job's number, enter it (from the Job List's *Job* column).

```
Line Numbering

    1 - Turn off                                    Off
    2 - Turn on

    3 - Count blank lines?                          Y

    4 - Number every n lines, where n=              1

    5 - Position of number from left edge:          6
        (in tenths of an inch)

    6 - Restart numbering on each page?             Y


Selection: 0
```

Figure P-8. Line Numbering menu.

You can also cancel any or all of the operations in the Job List. To do this, press c for *Cancel Print Job(s)* (WordPerfect 4.1 or 4.2) or 1 for *Cancel Job(s)* (WordPerfect 5.0). When requested, enter the number of the job you want to cancel (or enter * to cancel all jobs), then type y to confirm and press Enter to leave the Printer Control menu.

Print Options — WordPerfect 4.1 and 4.2

4.1
4.2

Choosing *Options* (3) from the Print menu brings on a menu that lets you specify the printer number (in case you have more than one), the number of copies, and the binding width for your next print operation.

Binding Width

Binding width is only relevant when you are printing double-sided pages. It is the amount of extra space, in tenths of an inch, Word-

Perfect should add to the inner margin to account for holes, spirals, or other bindings.

On odd-numbered (right-hand) pages, the inner margin is the left-hand margin; on even-numbered (left-hand) pages, it is the right-hand margin. For example, if you set the binding width to 3, WordPerfect will add three-tenths of an inch to the left-hand margin of odd-numbered pages and the right-hand margin of even-numbered pages.

Print Screen (PrtSc) Key

To the immediate left of the numeric keypad is a dark key marked *PrtSc* and *. Pressing Shift and PrtSc makes WordPerfect print the material that's currently on the screen (provided, of course, that your printer is on). This gives a quick and easy way to get a printout of a block of material without waiting for WordPerfect to search for it. For example, you may want to print a table so you can view it while you're describing it on another page.

Printer Commands

WordPerfect lets you insert commands into your documents that activate special functions of your printer. The procedure for inserting printer commands depends on which version of WordPerfect you have. Specifically:

| 4.1 4.2 |

- **For WordPerfect 4.1 and 4.2,** press Ctrl and F8 to give a Print Format command. When the menu appears, type **a** to select *Insert Printer Command*. WordPerfect displays **Cmnd:** at the bottom of the screen.

| 5.0 |

- **For WordPerfect 5.0,** press Shift and F8 to give a Format command and type **4** for *Other*. When the Other Format menu appears, type **6** for *Printer Functions*, then **2** for *Printer Command*. WordPerfect displays **Command:** at the bottom of the screen.

When the printer command prompt appears, enter the appropriate command sequence (see your printer manual for details). You can enter character keys directly, but you must supply control keys as numeric codes enclosed with angle brackets (< and >).

For example, if your printer has a two-color ribbon and the command *Esc Q* switches it to the second color, enter <27>Q in response to the command prompt. (Here, 27 is the numeric code for Esc.) When you finish typing the command sequence, press Enter (WordPerfect 4.1 and 4.2) or F7 (WordPerfect 5.0) to return to your document.

WordPerfect 4.1 and 4.2 inserts a printer command in your document as a hidden code of the form [Cmnd:*command*]; WordPerfect 5.0's code is of the form [Ptr Cmnd:*command*].

Printer, Stopping the

Once a print operation has started, you can either stop it temporarily to fix a problem (say, the printer has run out of paper) or cancel it entirely.

Stopping the Printer Temporarily

To stop printing while you fix a problem or attend to other business:

1. Press Shift-F7 for *Print*, then **4** for *Printer Control*.
2. When the Printer Control menu appears, press **s** (WordPerfect 4.1 or 4.2) or **5** (WordPerfect 5.0) to stop printing.
3. When the printer stops, fix the problem, advance the paper to the top of the next page, and press **g** (4.1 or 4.2) or **4** (5.0) for *Go*.

When you give the Go command, WordPerfect reprints the page at which it stopped, then completes the job. As soon as it starts printing again, you may press Enter to get back to your document.

Canceling Print Jobs

To cancel a print operation or "job":

1. Press Shift-F7 for *Print*, then **4** for *Printer Control*.
2. When the Printer Control menu appears, press **c** (WordPerfect 4.1 or 4.2) or **1** to cancel printing. WordPerfect shows

Cancel which job? (*=All Jobs) *n*

where *n* is the number of the job being printed.
3. You now have three options:

   A. To cancel the current job, press Enter.
   B. To cancel an upcoming job, enter its number from the Job List at the bottom.
   C. To cancel all jobs, type an asterisk (*), then press Enter. Since this is a drastic action, WordPerfect lets you change your mind by displaying *Cancel All Jobs? (Y/N) N*. Press **y** to cancel the jobs or Enter to proceed with printing.

In any case, WordPerfect shows *Press ENTER if Printer Does not Respond.*

Of course, performing these operations takes time. To cancel printing quickly, you may want to set up a macro that does the job. Such a macro is described under **Canceling Print Jobs**.

Printers, Switching

— See **Switching Printers**

Printing

WordPerfect provides a variety of ways to print material from documents on either the screen or disk. For example, the *Print* (Shift-F7) command lets you print the page or document that's on the screen, or a range of pages (e.g., pages 10 through 17) from a document stored on disk. With WordPerfect 4.1, you can only print a single range of pages, but versions 4.2 and 5.0 let you specify as many ranges as you want. The Print command also has options that let you specify the number of copies you want and which printer to use, in case you have more than one.

You can also print a block of text (say, a table or a few paragraphs) in the current document, by highlighting it using WordPerfect's Block (Alt-F4) mode, then giving a Print command. And if you only want to print the text on the screen, you don't even need the Print command—simply press Shift and the gray PrtSc key.

WordPerfect's *List Files* (F5) command produces a list of the documents on a disk, from which you can select one for printing. With WordPerfect 4.2 and 5.0, you can even print several disk documents, one after another, by marking them in the list. Here, WordPerfect 4.1 and 4.2 always print an entire document, while WordPerfect 5.0 lets you print selected page ranges, as its Print command does.

For full details on these commands, see **Print Command** and **List Files Command**.

Proportional Spacing

WordPerfect lets you print documents with proportional spacing, where the printer gives each character the amount of space equal to its width. For example, it gives M's more space than i's. Of course, this assumes that your printer can produce proportional spacing; not all can.

| 4.1 |
| 4.2 |

With **WordPerfect 4.1 and 4.2**, you must explicitly ask for proportional spacing. To begin, press Ctrl and F8 to obtain the Print Format menu. To switch to proportional spacing, type **1** to select *Pitch*, then enter **10*** for Pitch and **3** for Font. Finally, press Enter once more to return to your document.

| 5.0 |

With **WordPerfect 5.0**, you get proportional spacing by selecting a printer that produces it. When you select a printer, WordPerfect displays a "Printer Helps and Hints" screen that tells you whether it can do proportional spacing.

Protecting Blocks of Text

— See **Block Command**

Protecting Lines of Text

—See **Conditional End of Page**

PrtSc (Print Screen) Key

—See **Print Screen (PrtSc) Key**

Quit Printing

Once a print operation has started, you can either stop it temporarily to fix a problem (say, the printer has run out of paper) or cancel it entirely.

Stopping the Printer Temporarily

To stop printing while you fix a problem or attend to other business:

1. Press Shift-F7 for Print, then **4** for *Printer Control*.
2. When the Printer Control menu appears, press **s** (WordPerfect 4.1 or 4.2) or **5** (WordPerfect 5.0) to stop printing.
3. When the printer stops, fix the problem, advance the paper to the top of the next page, and press **g** (4.1 or 4.2) or **4** (5.0) for *Go*.

When you give the Go command, WordPerfect reprints the page at which it stopped, then completes the job. As soon as it starts printing again, you may press Enter to get back to your document.

Canceling Print Jobs

To cancel a print operation or "job":

Quit Printing

4.1
4.2

1. Press Shift-F7 for Print, then **4** for *Printer Control*.
2. When the Printer Control menu appears, press **c** (WordPerfect 4.1 or 4.2) or **1** to cancel printing. WordPerfect shows

   ```
   Cancel which job? (*=All Jobs) n
   ```

   where *n* is the number of the job being printed.
3. You now have three options:

   A. To cancel the current job, press Enter.
   B. To cancel an upcoming job, enter its number from the Job List at the bottom.
   C. To cancel all jobs, type an asterisk (*), then press Enter. Since this is a drastic action, WordPerfect lets you change your mind by displaying *Cancel All Jobs? (Y/N) N*. Press **y** to cancel the jobs or Enter to proceed with printing.

In any case, WordPerfect shows *Press ENTER if Printer Does not Respond*.

Of course, performing these operations takes time. To cancel printing quickly, you may want to set up a macro that does the job. Such a macro is described under **Canceling Print Jobs**.

Rectangles, Drawing

— See **Lines, Drawing**

Rectangular Blocks of Text — WordPerfect 4.1 and 4.2

4.1
4.2

WordPerfect lets you cut, copy, or delete a rectangular block of text. For example, you can copy two adjacent columns in a four-column table, for use somewhere else. The procedure is:

1. Move the cursor to the beginning of the block and press Alt-F4 to put WordPerfect into Block mode.
2. Using the arrow keys, move the cursor to the end of the block. WordPerfect highlights everything in between.
3. Press Ctrl-F4 to obtain the following *Move* menu:

```
1 Cut Block; 2 Copy Block; 3 Append; 4 Cut/Copy Column; 5 Cut/Copy Rectangle: 0
```

4. Press **5** to select *Cut/Copy Rectangle*.
5. When WordPerfect displays

                1 Cut; 2 Copy; 3 Delete: 0

> select the option you want. (WordPerfect 4.1's menu has no *Delete* option.)
6. If you cut or copied the rectangle, move to the place where you want to insert it, and press Ctrl-F4 for *Move*.
7. When the following menu appears:

Move 1 Sentence; 2 Paragraph; 3 Page; **Retrieve** 4 Column; 5 Text; 6 Rectangle: 0

> type 6 to select *Rectangle*.

Rectangular Blocks of Text — WordPerfect 5.0

5.0 WordPerfect lets you cut, copy, delete, or append (add to another file) a rectangular block of text. For example, you can copy two adjacent columns in a four-column table, for use somewhere else. The procedure is:

1. Move the cursor to the beginning of the block and press Alt-F4 to put WordPerfect into Block mode.
2. Using the arrow keys, move the cursor to the end of the block. WordPerfect highlights everything in between.
3. Press Ctrl-F4 to obtain the following *Move* menu:

        Move: 1 Block; 2 Tabular Column; 3 Rectangle: 0

4. Type 5 to select *Rectangle*.
5. When WordPerfect displays

        1 Move; 2 Copy; 3 Delete; 4 Append: 0

> select the option you want.
6. If you moved or copied the rectangle, move to the place where you want to insert it, and press Ctrl-F4 for *Move*.
7. When the following menu appears:

        Move: 1 Sentence; 2 Paragraph; 3 Page; 4 Retrieve: 0

> type 4 for *Retrieve*.
8. Finally, when this menu appears:

Retrieve: 1 Block; **2** Tabular Column; **3** Rectangle: **0**

type **3** for *Rectangle*.

Redlining Text — WordPerfect 4.1 and 4.2

4.1
4.2

When people make additions to a document (say, add a new clause to a contract or rewrite a portion of it), they often indicate the new material by drawing a vertical line to the left of it. This is called a *redline*, after the common practice of indicating changes with a red pencil. WordPerfect can redline new or existing text.

Redlining New Text

To add material to a document, and print a vertical line beside it, move to where the new text is to start and do the following:

1. Press Alt-F5 to give WordPerfect a *Mark Text* command.
2. When the following menu appears:

1 Outline; **2** Para #; **3** Redline; **4** Short Form; **5** Index; **6** Other Options: **0**

press **3** to select *Redline*. WordPerfect shows a + to the right of the Pos (position) value at the bottom right-hand corner of the screen.
3. Enter the text you want redlined. When you finish, press Alt-5 again and press **3** for *Redline*.

Redlining Existing Text

To print a vertical line beside existing text, move to the beginning of it and do the following:

1. Press Alt-F4 to put WordPerfect in *Block* mode.
2. Move the cursor to the last character you want redlined.
3. Press Alt-F5 to give WordPerfect a *Mark Text* command.
4. When the following menu appears:

1 ToC; **2** List; **3** Redline; **4** Strikeout; **5** Index; **6** ToA: **0**

press **3** to select *Redline*.

Removing Redline Markings

To remove all redline markings from a document—and delete all strikeout text (see that entry)—press Alt-F5 to get the Mark Text menu, and then

> 4.1
> 4.2

- •For WordPerfect 4.1, type **4** for *Remove*.
- •For WordPerfect 4.2, type **6** for *Other Options*. When the Other Mark Text Options menu appears, type **6**.

When the prompt appears, type **y**.

Redlining Text — WordPerfect 5.0

When people make additions to a document (say, add a new clause to a contract or rewrite a portion of it), they often indicate the new material by drawing a line beside it. This is called a *redline*, after the common practice of indicating changes with a red pencil. WordPerfect can redline mark new or existing text.

Redlining New Text

To add material to a document and print a redline mark beside it, move to where the new text is to start and do the following:

1. Press Ctrl-F8 to give WordPerfect a *Font* command.
2. When this Font menu appears:

   ```
   1 Size; 2 Appearance; 3 Normal; 4 Base Font; 5 Print Color: 0
   ```

   press **2** to select *Appearance*.
3. When WordPerfect displays the Appearance menu, press **8** to select *Redln*.
4. Enter the text you want redlined. When you finish, press the → key to move past WordPerfect's hidden Redline Off code.

Redlining Existing Text

To print redline marks beside existing text, move to the beginning of it and do the following:

1. Press Alt-F4 to put WordPerfect in *Block* mode.
2. Move the cursor to the last character you want redlined.
3. Press Ctrl-F8 to give WordPerfect a *Font* command.
4. When the following menu appears:

    Attribute: 1 Size; 2 Appearance: 0

    press **2** to select *Appearance*.
5. When WordPerfect displays the Appearance menu, type **8** to select *Redln*.

Selecting the Redline Character

WordPerfect is preset to redline text based on a "redline string" in the active printer's Printer Definition file. However, you can specify how redlined text is to be marked by doing the following:

1. Press Shift-F8 to display the Format menu.
2. Type **3** to select *Document*.
3. When the Document Format menu appears, type **3** for *Redline Method*.
4. When WordPerfect shows

Redline Method: 1 Printer Dependent; 2 Red; 3 Left; 4 Alternating: 1

choose the option you want.

The *Red* option prints redlined text in red on color printers. *Left* marks redlined text with a vertical line in the left-hand margin. *Alternating* marks redlined text with a vertical line in the left margin for even-numbered pages and in the right margin for odd-numbered pages.

Choosing *Left* or *Alternating* makes WordPerfect display **Redline character:** and the current redline character, which is usually a vertical line. To continue using that character, press Enter; to use some other character, type it and then press Enter.

Removing Redline Markings

To remove all redline markings from a document—and delete all strikeout text (see that entry)—press Alt-F5 to get the Mark Text menu, and type **6** for Generate. When the Generate menu appears, type **1**; when the prompt appears, type **y**.

Reformatting Documents

Sometimes you must reformat an entire document. For example, you may have double-spaced a report so you could edit it easily, but want to print the final version single-spaced. Reformatting a document is easiest if you entered it using WordPerfect's automatic format settings. Then you simply move the cursor to the beginning of the document (by pressing Home twice, then ↑) and do one or more Line Format commands to specify your new settings.

It's also easy to reformat a document that uses the same format settings throughout. Move the cursor to the beginning and give a Reveal Codes (Alt-F3) command. The Reveal Codes display shows a Tab Set, Margin Set, or Line Spacing code if you set the tabs, margins, or spacing. To change one of these values, delete its code by moving the cursor just ahead of it and pressing Del, or just beyond it and pressing Backspace. Then get back to editing and specify the settings you want. WordPerfect makes the change throughout the document automatically.

Reformatting a document that includes format changes is a little trickier. In that case, you must locate each format code you want to change, then delete the code and enter the settings you want. Suppose, for example, that you have a double-spaced report that includes single-spaced tables, and you want everything single-spaced.

Single-Spacing a Double-Spaced Document

| 4.1 4.2 |
| 5.0 |

To single-space a double-spaced document, move the cursor to the beginning of the document and use Reveal Codes to delete the Line Spacing code. ([Spacing Set:2] in WordPerfect 4.1 and 4.2; [Ln Spacing:2] in WordPerfect 5.0.) This makes WordPerfect revert to its default, single-spacing, which means it will single-space everything up to the next Line Spacing code.

At this point, of course, you could move through the document looking for where double-spacing begins again and delete the code. But it's easier to let WordPerfect find each code and delete it for you!

With the cursor at the beginning of the document, you can delete every Line Spacing code by doing the following:

1. Press Alt-F2 to start a Replace operation and type **n** when WordPerfect asks **w/Confirm? (Y/N) N**.
2. When the **-?Srch:** prompt appears, do one of the following:

   | 4.1 |
   | 4.2 |

   - **For WordPerfect 4.1 or 4.2**, press Shift-F8 to give a Line Format command. When the Line Format menu appears, type **4** for Spacing ([Spacing Set] appears in the response field), then press F2.

   | 5.0 |

   - **For WordPerfect 5.0**, press Shift-F8 to give a Format command and type **1** for *Line*. When the Line Format menu appears, type **5** for *Line*, and **3** for *Line Spacing* ([Ln Spacing] appears in the response field), then press F2.

3. When the **Replace with:** prompt appears, press F2 to start replacing. (Pressing F2 here tells WordPerfect to replace each Line Spacing code with nothing; that is, delete it.)

WordPerfect searches through your entire document, and deletes spacing codes as it goes. When it finishes, the document appears in single-spaced form.

Deleting Other Codes

You can also use Replace operations to locate and delete other codes in a document. For example, you can eliminate bold print, centering, or underlining by pressing F6, Shift-F6, or F8 in response to the **->Srch:** prompt. Furthermore, you can eliminate selected occurrences of these formats by typing **y** in response to **w/Confirm? (Y/N) N**.

Reformatting the Screen

— See **Auto Rewrite**

Removing Tabs

— See **Tabs**

Renaming Files

— See **List Files Command**

Repeating Commands or Characters

— See **Esc (Escape) Key**

Replace Command (Alt-F2)

WordPerfect has a Replace command that searches for a specified *string* (a sequence of characters) and replaces it with another string. You can use Replace to:

- Correct a common misspelling throughout a document.
- Update a document to account for changes in names, titles, dates, or locations.
- Change prices, rates, or terms in an invoice or contract.
- Change a part number or order number in a technical manual.
- Replace an overused or inappropriate phrase throughout a report.

The procedure to replace a string is:

1. Move the cursor to where you want the search to start and press Alt-F2. WordPerfect displays *w/Confirm? (Y/N)* N at the bottom of the screen.
2. You have three options:

- To make WordPerfect replace all occurrences of the search string automatically, type **n** or press Enter (this is called a *global* search and replace operation).
- To make WordPerfect stop each time it finds the string and ask if you want to replace it, type **y**.
- To cancel the Replace operation, press F1.

If you type **n** or **y**, WordPerfect shows *->Srch:* on the bottom line.

The - symbol indicates that WordPerfect will search forward through the document. With WordPerfect 5.0, you can make it search backward by pressing the ↑ key.

| 5.0 |

3. Type the string you want to search for, then press F2. The form of the search string determines what WordPerfect will search for. Specifically:

- If you type the search string in lowercase form, WordPerfect will search for every occurrence of it.
- If you type it in capitalized form, WordPerfect will only search for capitalized occurrences.

For example, suppose you want to search for the phrase "oil well." To find every instance of it (i.e., *oil well,Oil Well*, and *OIL WELL*), type **oil well** as the string. To find only capitalized instances, (i.e., *Oil Well* and *OIL WELL*), type **Oil well** as the string.

Either way, *don't* press Enter after you type the search string. Pressing Enter would make WordPerfect search only for occurrences that are followed by an Enter—those at the ends of paragraphs. (If you accidentally press Enter, WordPerfect shows it as the code [HRt], for Hard Return; press Backspace to delete the code.)

4. When WordPerfect shows *Replace with:* on the bottom line, Enter the replacement string, then press F2.

Note that you can just press F2 here if you want to replace the string with nothing (i.e., delete it). You might do this, for example, to update someone's title from "Assistant Vice President" to "Vice President" throughout a report or interview. Here, you should search for "Assistant " and replace it with nothing.

WordPerfect begins searching when you press F2. If *w/Confirm?* is *Y*, it stops at each instance of the search string and shows the prompt *Confirm? (Y/N) N*. Type **y** to replace the string, **n** to proceed to the next occurrence, or F1 to cancel the replace operation. If WordPerfect cannot find another occurrence of the search string, it leaves the cursor where you last started searching and displays * *Not Found* *.

Changing the Search String

4.2

Once you have done a Replace, WordPerfect assumes that you want to search for the same string the next time. This is convenient if you want to replace the same string in another document. But if you actually want to search for a different string, you can either type it directly or, if the new string is similar (and you have WordPerfect version 4.2 or later), edit the current string.

To move within a search string you're editing, you can press ← or → to reach the preceding or next character, End to reach the end of the string, or Home, then ← to reach the beginning of it. As in regular text, WordPerfect inserts typed characters unless you press Ins (for *Typeover*); then it replaces string characters with those you type.

WordPerfect doesn't remember the replacement string, however. You must enter it again when you start a new Replace operation.

Selecting Search Strings

If the string you are looking for is long or distinctive, such as "International Products Division" or "NASA," you probably won't have any trouble with unexpected matches. However, if it is not distinctive, WordPerfect may stop at places you never intended. For example, if you tell WordPerfect to search through a report on cigarette smoking for each mention of "tar," it will stop at "target," "start," "retarding," and "Tareyton."

One solution to this problem is to put a space in front of the string. For example, you could tell WordPerfect to search for " tar." If you put a space *after* "tar." WordPerfect will not find occurrences followed by a period, a comma, or other punctuation. Even a space in front can cause problems with occurrences such as "(tar)."

Wildcard Searches

Sometimes you may want to search for any of several similarly-spelled words. You can do this by typing Ctrl-VX—that is, hold Ctrl down and press V, then X—in the "->Srch:" string for each character that may differ from one occurrence to another. (With WordPerfect 4.1, type Ctrl-X rather than Ctrl-VX.) To WordPerfect, Ctrl-VX (shown as ^X) is a *wildcard* character; it acts as shorthand for "any single character." You may compare it with the Joker in popular card games, a free number in Bingo, or a blank tile in Scrabble.

For example, suppose you sometimes mistype *term* as *tern*, because N is next to M on the keyboard. WordPerfect's spelling checker will not locate this mistake because tern is a valid word in its dictionary. Here, you could give a Replace command and enter **ter^X** as the search string and **term** as the replacement string. Of course, this also makes WordPerfect stop on words such as *character*, *enter*, and *terminate*. To avoid potential problems, you should always answer *Yes* to "w/Confirm?."

You cannot enter ^X as the first character in a search string, but you can put it anywhere else. You can even put several ^X's in a search string. For example, you could use **19-^X^X-3657** to find all mentions of part numbers that start with 19 and end with 3657.

Replace Example

Figure R-1 shows a document that illustrates the use of the replace options. We want to update this notice for the 1988 annual meeting to be held at the same place on Friday, June 3, 1988. To do this, we will perform the following operations:

1. Replace automatically each occurrence of *1987-88* with*1988-89*.
2. Replace automatically each occurrence of *June 5* with *June 3*.
3. Find all occurrences of *1987* and replace them with *1988*. We must be careful here to avoid changing historical dates accidentally.

To replace *1987-88* automatically with *1988-89*, do the following:

1. Put the cursor at the beginning of the first line of the text, then press Alt-F2.
2. In response to *w/Confirm? (Y/N) N*, press Enter to accept *N*.
3. For *->Srch:*, type **1987-88**, then press F2. (Note that WordPerfect encloses the hyphen in brackets, as [-]. Don't worry about this, it's normal.)
4. For *Replace with*, type **1988-89** and press F2 again.

Replace Command (Alt-F2)

```
                    NOTICE OF STOCKHOLDERS' MEETING

     The 1987 Annual Stockholders' Meeting for International
     Consolidated Industries will be held at company headquarters,
     19870 Pine Street, Des Moines, Iowa on Friday, June 5, 1987. The
     following matters will be considered:

        1)   Election of the Board of Directors for the 1987-88 fiscal
             year.
        2)   Designation of Smith, Brown, and Little as the company's
             independent auditors for the 1987-88 fiscal year.
        3)   Amendments to the Employees' Qualified Stock Ownership
             Plan (ESOP) in accordance with new regulations.
        4)   Other amendments and matters as they may be brought to the
             attention of the Secretary of the Corporation.

     Anyone wishing to have matters considered at that meeting must
     notify the Secretary by registered mail on or before May 15,
     1987. In accordance with regulations adopted at the annual
     meeting of June 11, 1982, such notifications must be presented on
     forms provided by the Secretary and must contain notarized
     signatures representing no fewer than 1% of the common stock of
     the Corporation of record May 15th, 1987. In accordance with
     guidelines adopted at a special Board of Directors meeting on
     February 1, 1987, the board has the final authority on whether to
     accept notifications that are presented after May 17th, 1987 or
     that contain an insufficient number of signatures.
```

Figure R-1. Original search document.

WordPerfect immediately makes the replacements, and leaves the cursor at the last occurrence. Press the - (minus) key on the numeric keypad to reach the top of the screen.

To replace *June 5* with *June 3*, start by pressing Alt-F2 and **n** to select automatic (global) replacement. For *->Srch:*, enter **June 5**, then press F2. Enter the **June 3** replacement string similarly. Now the meeting notice looks like Figure R-2.

To replace *1987* with *1988* selectively, proceed as follows:

1. Press - to reach the top of the screen.
2. Press Alt-F2 to start a new Replace operation.
3. In response to *w/Confirm? (Y/N) N*, type **y** for yes.
4. For *->Srch:*, type **1987**, then press F2.
5. For *Replace with*, type **1988**, then F2 again.

WordPerfect will immediately find a match in the second word. You must press **y** to make the replacement.

The next match is unexpected: WordPerfect finds *1987* at the beginning of the company's address. Here you must press **n** to make

```
                    NOTICE OF STOCKHOLDERS' MEETING

     The 1987 Annual Stockholders' Meeting for International
Consolidated Industries will be held at company headquarters,
19870 Pine Street, Des Moines, Iowa on Friday, June 3, 1987. The
following matters will be considered:

     1)   Election of the Board of Directors for the 1988-89 fiscal
          year.
     2)   Designation of Smith, Brown, and Little as the company's
          independent auditors for the 1988-89 fiscal year.
     3)   Amendments to the Employees' Qualified Stock Ownership
          Plan (ESOP) in accordance with new regulations.
     4)   Other amendments and matters as they may be brought to the
          attention of the Secretary of the Corporation.

     Anyone wishing to have matters considered at that meeting must
notify the Secretary by registered mail on or before May 15,
1987. In accordance with regulations adopted at the annual
meeting of June 11, 1982, such notifications must be presented on
forms provided by the Secretary and must contain notarized
signatures representing no fewer than 1% of the common stock of
the Corporation of record May 15th, 1987. In accordance with
guidelines adopted at a special Board of Directors meeting on
February 1, 1987, the board has the final authority on whether to
accept notifications that are presented after May 17th, 1987 or
that contain an insufficient number of signatures.
```

Figure R-2. Revised document after automatic replacements.

WordPerfect continue forward without replacing. You must do this again later when WordPerfect finds *1987* as part of "a special Board of Directors meeting on February 1, 1987,". That is a historical date, and you must not change it.

When WordPerfect finishes, the document looks like Figure R-3.

How Search Strings Affect Replace Operations

As I mentioned earlier, the form of the search string tells WordPerfect what to search for. (A lowercase string makes it search for every occurrence, while an uppercase string makes it search only for capitalized occurrences.) The search string can affect what WordPerfect *replaces* as well as what it *finds*.

When replacing, WordPerfect uses the following guidelines:

- If the search string consists of lowercase characters, WordPerfect finds every occurrence of it and replaces that occurrence with your replacement string *exactly*.

```
                    NOTICE OF STOCKHOLDERS' MEETING

     The 1988 Annual Stockholders' Meeting for International
     Consolidated Industries will be held at company headquarters,
     19870 Pine Street, Des Moines, Iowa on Friday, June 3, 1988. The
     following matters will be considered:

          1)   Election of the Board of Directors for the 1988-89 fiscal
               year.
          2)   Designation of Smith, Brown, and Little as the company's
               independent auditors for the 1988-89 fiscal year.
          3)   Amendments to the Employees' Qualified Stock Ownership
               Plan (ESOP) in accordance with new regulations.
          4)   Other amendments and matters as they may be brought to the
               attention of the Secretary of the Corporation.

     Anyone wishing to have matters considered at that meeting must
     notify the Secretary by registered mail on or before May 15,
     1988. In accordance with regulations adopted at the annual
     meeting of June 11, 1982, such notifications must be presented on
     forms provided by the Secretary and must contain notarized
     signatures representing no fewer than 1% of the common stock of
     the Corporation of record May 15th, 1988. In accordance with
     guidelines adopted at a special Board of Directors meeting on
     February 1, 1987, the board has the final authority on whether to
     accept notifications that are presented after May 17th, 1988 or
     that contain an insufficient number of signatures.
```

Figure R-3. Final form of document.

- If the search string contains an uppercase character, WordPerfect finds occurrences in which the same character is capitalized and replaces it with the *matching* form of your replacement string.

This can cause problems in some Replace operations. For example, suppose you have prepared a letter using the singular form (e.g., "I would like . . ." and "Still, I want . . .") and your spouse or business partner asks you to change every "I" to "we."

To do this, you would normally type I for the search string and **we** for the replacement string, and fully expect WordPerfect to make the corrections. However, because your search string contains an uppercase letter, WordPerfect replaces every "I" with "We," and changes phrases such as "Still, I want" to "Still, We want" (with "we" capitalized, mistakenly).

Things get worse if you try to change a capitalized word to lowercase, because WordPerfect won't make the replacements. Worse yet, it won't even tell you that it hasn't made the replacements! For example, suppose you entered "Winter" instead of "winter" throughout a document. If you do a Replace operation with *Winter* as the search string and *winter* as the replacement string, WordPerfect will go merrily along, but leave "Winter" intact in each case.

To eliminate these problems, you should replace each uppercase string by using Search (described under **Search Commands**), rather than Replace. That is, make WordPerfect find the string you want to replace, then delete the entire string (or just the capitalized letter in it) and type the replacement. Of course, this involves doing a Search operation for each occurrence. As an alternative, you can set up a *macro* to do the job. See **Macros, Introduction to** and other entries dealing with macros.

Extended Searches

WordPerfect normally searches only regular text, but with version 4.2 and later, you can make it include headers, footers, footnotes, and endnotes as well. To do this, press Home before entering your Replace command.

Replacing Hidden Codes

You can also replace or delete hidden codes, by entering them in Replace's ->*Srch:* and *Replace with:* strings. For example, you could put an extra line of spacing after an emboldened title by searching for [b] and replacing it with [b][HRt]. Similarly, you could remove emboldening by searching for [b] (or [B], bold's starting code) and replacing it with nothing. For details, see *Searching for Hidden Codes* under **Codes, Hidden**.

Abbreviations

Replace also allows you to use abbreviations when typing a document. This is like the common practice in note-taking of jotting down UN for "United Nations" or DoD for "United States Department of Defense."

For example, if you are writing a report on European sales, you may simply type UK for "United Kingdom," WG (West Germany) for "Federal Republic of Germany," and EEC for "European Economic Community." Then, when you finish, do replace operations to expand the abbreviations. Be sure that your abbreviations are distinct (note, for instance, that you will find US in USSR) and don't conflict with each other (such as using UF for "United Fund" and "University of Florida").

Replace has the advantage of making WordPerfect—not *you*—expand the abbreviations.

Restoring Deleted Text

— See **Undeleting**

Retrieve Command (Shift-F10)

Pressing Shift and F10 tells WordPerfect to load in a new document from disk. When the **Document to be Retrieved:** prompt appears on the bottom line, type the filename of the document you want (precede it with a disk drive name or hard disk subdirectory name, if necessary), then press Enter. WordPerfect copies the document onto the screen, starting at the cursor position.

If WordPerfect can't find the file, however, it shows **ERROR: File not found** and brings back the prompt and the name you entered. If you simply mistyped the filename, correct it (use the left or right arrow key to move through the name), then press Enter.

Finding Out What's on a Disk

If you don't remember the name of the document you want to retrieve, press F5 (List Files) to get a list of the available files. When the list appears, highlight the file you want and choose *Retrieve* from the menu.

Retrieving One Document into Another

WordPerfect does *not* clear the screen before it retrieves a document. Thus, if you Retrieve onto a screen that already contains text, WordPerfect will *insert the retrieved document into your text* at the cursor position.

Of course, you may really want to insert a disk document if it contains, say, "boilerplate" text you want to reproduce in a contract or form letter. However, if you absent-mindedly Retrieve a document without first clearing the screen, you must either Exit without saving to disk (press F7 and type **n** at the prompt) or delete the retrieved material manually.

Other Retrieve Operations

If you tell WordPerfect 4.2 to retrieve a document that was created using version 4.1, or tell WordPerfect 5.0 to retrieve a 4.2 document, it converts the older document into its own format. You can then save the document in its new format by giving a Save (F10) or Exit (F7) command. To save a converted document in its original format, however, you must give a Text In/Out (Ctrl-F5) command and choose *Save in WordPerfect 4.1 format* or *Save WP 4.2* from the menu. Text In/Out also has options that let you save or retrieve a DOS text file (see that entry).

Returning From DOS

The Shell (Ctrl-F1) command lets you leave WordPerfect temporarily to perform disk operations using DOS. It also tells you how to return to WordPerfect by displaying the prompt

```
Enter 'EXIT' to return to WordPerfect
```

Don't make the mistake of assuming that *EXIT* here refers to WordPerfect's Exit *key* (F7). It doesn't. Instead, you must take this prompt literally; that is, to leave DOS, you must type the word **exit**, then press Enter.

Return Key

— See **Enter Key**

Reveal Codes Command (Alt-F3)

WordPerfect tells your printer how to format text by sending it special codes. The printer interprets each code as a command and does whatever that command indicates. For example, when you press Ctrl and Enter to switch pages, WordPerfect inserts a "new page" code at that place in your document. When you print the document, the printer receives that code and advances the paper to the next page before it starts printing.

WordPerfect does not show these formatting codes on the screen; it hides them. However, you can display the codes by pressing Alt-F3, to give a Reveal Codes command. Reveal Codes encloses each hidden code in brackets ([and]); for a complete list of the codes, see **Codes, Hidden**. Further, Reveal Codes shows the current cursor position as [^] in WordPerfect 4.1, as a blinking underscore (_) in WordPerfect 4.2, and as a shaded rectangle in WordPerfect 5.0.

Deleting

To delete a code or character from within the Reveal Codes screen, move the cursor to the left of it and press Del, or to the right of it and press Backspace.

Editing on the Reveal Codes Screen

The Reveal Codes screen for WordPerfect 4.1 and 4.2 only lets you delete codes and move forward or backward through the text. Pressing any character key or function key sends WordPerfect back to the editing screen. However, WordPerfect 5.0's Reveal Codes screen lets you insert characters, perform commands (e.g., change the tabs), or do virtually any other operation.

Leaving Reveal Codes

To leave the Reveal Codes screen in WordPerfect 4.1 or 4.2, you can press either F1 or Enter; to leave it in WordPerfect 5.0, you must press Alt-F3.

Rewriting the Screen

— See **Auto Rewrite**

Right-Aligning Text

— See **Flush Right Command**

Right Indent

— See **Indent Commands**

Right-Justifying

— See **Justification**

Roman Numerals for Numbering Pages

When you tell WordPerfect to number the pages in a document (see **Page Numbering**), it assumes you want them numbered in standard Arabic (1, 2, 3) fashion. However, the table of contents, preface, and other frontal matter of a book or report are usually numbered in Roman style, with i, ii, iii, and so on. The procedure for switching to Roman numbering depends on which version of WordPerfect you have.

Roman Numbering With WordPerfect 4.1 or 4.2

| 4.1 |
| 4.2 |

To switch to Roman numbering with WordPerfect 4.1 or 4.2, press Alt-F8 to give a Page Format command. When the menu appears, type **2** to select *New Page Number*. When WordPerfect asks for the *New Page #*, enter it (enter **1** if it's the first page), then type **2** to select the Roman numbering style.

When you finish creating Roman-numbered pages, do another New Page Number procedure, but enter **1** for the new page number and type **1** to select *Arabic*.

Roman Numbering with WordPerfect 5.0

5.0 To switch to Roman numbering with WordPerfect 5.0, press Shift-F8 to give a Format command. When the menu appears, type **2** to select *Page*, then **6** to reach the *New Page Number* field. Enter the Roman number you want to start with (usually *i*), then press F7 (Exit) to return to your document.

When you finish creating Roman-numbered pages, repeat the same procedure, but enter **1** (or some other Arabic number) for New Page Number.

Running a Macro at Startup

— See **Macros, Running at Startup**

S

Save Command (F10)

Pressing F10 for Save lets you store a copy of the current document on disk, then resume working on it. (The similar Exit command lets you save the document and retrieve a different one, or leave WordPerfect. See **Exit Command** for details.)

Saving New Documents

If the document being saved is one that you haven't yet stored on disk, WordPerfect asks for the **Document to be Saved:** at the bottom of the screen. Type the document's name (and an extension, if you want one), then press Enter.

After saving a document, WordPerfect 4.2 and 5.0 display the names of the disk drive, disk directory, and file at the bottom left-hand corner of the screen. (This is handy for those Friday afternoon sessions when you forget what you're working on.) For example, if you save REPORT.DOC to the WP (WordPerfect) directory on Drive C, the screen shows **C:\WP\REPORT.DOC**.

Saving Existing Documents

If the document you're saving is one you loaded in from disk, WordPerfect displays its name in a prompt of the form **Document to be Saved:** *d:\docname.ext,* where *d* is the name of the floppy disk drive or, on a hard disk, the name of the drive and subdirectory (e.g., C:\WP). To save the document under that name, press Enter; to save it under a different name or save it to a different disk or directory, type the name you want, then press Enter.

If you press Enter at the first prompt, WordPerfect asks whether you want the current version to replace the version stored on disk. It asks **Replace** *d:\docname.ext?* **(Y/N) N**. To make the *Document to be Saved* prompt reappear (if, say, you meant to save to a different directory), type **n** or press Enter; to make this version replace the existing one, type **y**.

Saving in Other Formats

If you tell WordPerfect 4.2 to retrieve a WordPerfect 4.1 document, or tell WordPerfect 5.0 to retrieve a WordPerfect 4.2 document, it converts the older document into its own format. You can then save the document in its new format by giving a Save or Exit command. To save a converted document in its original format, however, you must give a Text In/Out (Ctrl-F5) command and choose *Save in WordPerfect 4.1 format* or *Save WP 4.2* from the menu.

Text In/Out can also save or retrieve a locked file or a DOS text file, or save in a "generic" word processor format. See **Text In/Out Command** for details.

Screen Command (Ctrl-F3) — WordPerfect 4.1 and 4.2

4.1
4.2

The Screen command lets you change the way WordPerfect displays material. Pressing Ctrl and F3 makes the following menu appear at the bottom:

```
0 Rewrite; 1 Window; 2 Line Draw; 3 Ctrl/Alt keys; 4 Colors; 5 Auto Rewrite: 0
```

Rewrite and Auto Rewrite

When you add or delete material, WordPerfect rearranges text on the screen automatically. If you find this distracting, set *Auto Rewrite* to **n**, for No. WordPerfect will then only reformat when you move down the screen or give a *Rewrite* command.

Window

This option lets you divide the screen into two separate text areas, or *windows*, where each can display a different document or different parts of the same document. Once you have set up the second window, you can work in either of them.

Why would you want to use two windows? You can, for example:

1. Examine previous correspondence, a contract, or other document while writing a letter. You may even want to copy sections from that document.
2. Look back at an earlier report to be sure you are using the same format, terminology, or spelling.
3. Examine an outline while you write, and check off sections as you finish them.
4. Take figures, tables, or terminology from old versions of a document or from standard forms. Thus, you could use part of last year's report or the last project's contract in a new report or contract. You could also combine weekly reports into a monthly report or excerpt a brief synopsis from a complete project report.

WordPerfect's main work area is itself a window (#1, as indicated by *Doc 1* on the status line). WordPerfect will label the second window *Doc 2*.

When you choose *Window* from the Screen menu, WordPerfect displays the prompt

```
# Lines in this Window: 24
```

where the 24 indicates that the current window occupies 24 lines on the screen; in other words, the entire screen.

Now you can either enter the number of lines you want in the active window (2 or more) or press the ↑ or ↓ key until the reverse-video Tab Ruler bar appears. Note that the # *Lines* value changes as you move the Tab Ruler. Continue pressing the arrow key until the bottom window is the size you want, then press Enter.

At this point, the second window is visible, but the original window is still active. To switch to the second window (i.e., make it active), press Shift-F3 for Switch. The cursor moves to the top of the second window. Now you can create a new document or retrieve an existing one. To switch back to the first window, press Shift-F3 again.

Note that the windows are independent. Once you Retrieve a document into a window, it is a separate entity. You can work on it without affecting the document in the other window.

WordPerfect treats the active window just like the full screen. You can edit, move the cursor, retrieve or save a document, issue commands, and so on.

The only special part of moving text to another window is that you must remember to switch windows. That is, you go through the usual process of using the Move command to select the text and either Cut or Copy it. You must then press Shift-F3 to switch windows. Now you can finish the task by moving the cursor to where you want the text and doing another Move to paste it.

To close a window, press Shift-F3 to switch to the other window, then press Ctrl-F3 to obtain the Screen menu and select *Window*. When the # **Lines in this Window** message appears, enter **24**. The Tab Ruler and window text disappear.

Closing a window does not affect its contents, it simply makes WordPerfect take the window off the screen. You can still reach a closed window with Switch. Thus, if you give an Exit command from either window, WordPerfect will display the *Save* and *Exit* prompts for each document, Doc 1 and Doc 2.

Line Draw

This option lets you draw lines and boxes within a document. See **Lines, Drawing** for details.

Ctrl/Alt Keys

This option lets you assign key combinations where pressing Ctrl or Alt and a letter key makes WordPerfect insert a geometric shape, foreign character, or other character that can't be produced from the keyboard. See **Special Characters** for details.

Colors

This option lets you change the foreground and background colors on a color screen.

Screen Command (Ctrl-F3) — WordPerfect 5.0

The Screen command lets you change the way WordPerfect displays material. Pressing Ctrl and F3 makes the following menu appear at the bottom:

```
0 Rewrite; 1 Window; 2 Line Draw: 0
```

Rewrite

When you add or delete material, WordPerfect rearranges text on the screen automatically. If you find this distracting, obtain the Setup menu (by pressing Shift-F1) and type **3** for *Display*. Then type **3** again to reach the *Automatically Format and Rewrite* field and type **n** to turn automatic formatting off. WordPerfect will then only reformat when you move down the screen or give a *Rewrite* command.

Window

This option lets you divide the screen into two text areas, or *windows*, where each can display a different document or different parts of the same document. Once you have set up the second window, you can work in either of them.

Why would you want to use two windows? You can, for example:

1. Examine previous correspondence, a contract, or other document while writing a letter. You may even want to copy sections from that document.
2. Look back at an earlier report to be sure you are using the same format, terminology, or spelling.
3. Examine an outline while you write, and check off sections as you finish them.
4. Take figures, tables, or terminology from old versions of a document or from standard forms. Thus, you could use part of last year's report or the last project's contract in a new report or contract. You could also combine weekly reports into a monthly report or excerpt a brief synopsis from a complete project report.

WordPerfect's main work area is itself a window (#1, as indicated by *Doc 1* on the status line). WordPerfect will label the second window *Doc 2*.

When you choose *Window* from the Screen menu, WordPerfect displays the prompt

```
Number of lines in this window: 24
```

where the 24 indicates that the current window occupies 24 lines on the screen; in other words, the entire screen.

Now you can either enter the number of lines you want in the active window (2 or more) or press the ↑ or ↓ key until a reverse-video bar (the Tab Ruler) appears. Note that the *Number of Lines* value changes as you move the Tab Ruler. Continue pressing the arrow key until the bottom window is the size you want, then press Enter.

At this point, the second window is visible, but the original window is still active. To switch to the second window (i.e., make it active), press Shift-F3 for Switch. The cursor moves to the top of the second window. Now you can create a new document or retrieve an existing one. When you want to switch back to the first window, press Shift-F3 again.

Note that the windows are independent. Once you Retrieve a document into a window, it is a separate entity. You can work on it without affecting the document in the other window.

WordPerfect treats the active window just like the full screen. You can edit, move the cursor, retrieve or save a document, issue commands, and so on.

The only special part of moving text to another window is that you must remember to switch windows. That is, you go through the usual process of using the Move command to select the text and either Move or Copy it. You must then press Shift-F3 to switch windows. Now you can finish the task by moving the cursor to where you want the text and doing another Move to paste it.

To close a window, press Shift-F3 to switch to the other window, then press Ctrl-F3 to obtain the Screen menu and select *Window*. When the **Number of lines in this window** message appears, enter 24. The Tab Ruler and window text disappear.

Closing a window does not affect its contents; it simply makes WordPerfect take the window off the screen. You can still reach a closed window with Switch. Thus, if you give an Exit command from either window, WordPerfect will display the *Save* and *Exit* prompts for each document, Doc 1 and Doc 2.

Line Draw

This option lets you draw lines and boxes within a document. See **Lines, Drawing** for details.

Screen is Blank

— See **Blank Screen**

Scroll Lock Key

Scroll Lock, the dark key at the top right-hand corner of the keyboard, does nothing within WordPerfect. But if you enter a DOS *Dir* (Directory) command to get a list of the available files, pressing Ctrl and Scroll Lock makes the scrolling stop.

Search Commands (F2 and Shift-F2)

WordPerfect has Search commands that search forward or backward through a document looking for a sequence or *string* of characters. (It also has a Replace command that both searches for a string and replaces it; see **Replace Command**.) You can use the search features to locate a customer's name in a mailing list or check for occurrences of obsolete or revised names, titles, dates, or terms.

Search Procedure

The procedure to search for a string is:

1. Move the cursor to where you want the search to begin and press F2 to search forward or Shift-F2 to search backward. WordPerfect displays **->Srch:** or **<- Srch:** at the bottom of the screen.

2. Type the search string, then press F2 to start searching. The form of the search string determines what WordPerfect will search for. Specifically:

   • If you type the search string in lowercase form, WordPerfect will search for every occurrence of it.

   • If you type it in capitalized form, WordPerfect will only search for capitalized occurrences.

   For example, suppose you want to search for the phrase "oil well." To find every instance of it (i.e., *oil well*, *Oil Well*, and *OIL WELL*), type **oil well** as the string. To find only capitalized instances, (i.e., *Oil Well* and *OIL WELL*), type **Oil well** as the string.
   Either way, *don't* press Enter after you type the search string. Pressing Enter would make WordPerfect search only for occurrences that are followed by an Enter—those at the ends of paragraphs. (If you accidentally press Enter, WordPerfect shows it as the code [HRt], for Hard Return; press Backspace to delete the code.)

3. If WordPerfect finds an instance of the string, it puts the cursor just past the last character. Your options at this point are:

   A. To search for the next occurrence of the string, press F2 *twice*.
   B. To return to your starting location, press Ctrl-Home (Go To) *twice*.

If WordPerfect cannot find the search string, it leaves the cursor at its original position and displays *** Not found *** on the bottom line.

Changing the Search String

Once you have done a Search, WordPerfect assumes you want to search for the same string the next time. This is convenient if you want to resume a search after making changes or corrections. But if you actually want to search for a different string, you can either type it directly or, if the new string is similar (and you have WordPerfect version 4.2 or later), edit the current string.

To move within a search string you're editing, you can press ← or → to reach the preceding or next character, End to reach the end of the string, or Home, then ← to reach the beginning of it. As in regular text, WordPerfect inserts typed characters unless you press

Ins (for *Typeover*); then it replaces string characters with those you type.

Extended Searches

WordPerfect normally searches only regular text, but with version 4.2 and later, you can make it include headers, footers, footnotes, and endnotes in the search. Simply press Home before entering your Search command.

Selecting Search Strings

If the string you are looking for is long or distinctive, such as "International Products Division" or "NASA,"tar you probably won't have any trouble with unexpected matches. However, if it is not distinctive, WordPerfect may stop at places you never intended. For example, if you tell WordPerfect to search through a report on cigarette smoking for each mention of "tar," it will stop at "target," "start," "retarding," and "Tareyton."

One solution to this problem is to put a space in front of the string. For example, you could tell WordPerfect to search for " tar." If you put a space *after* "tar," WordPerfect will not find occurrences followed by a period, a comma, or other punctuation. Even a space in front can cause problems with occurrences such as "(tar)."

Wildcard Searches

Sometimes you may want to search for any of several similarly-spelled words. You can do this by typing Ctrl-VX—that is, hold Ctrl down and press V, then X—in the search string for each character that may differ from one occurrence to another. (With WordPerfect 4.1, type Ctrl-X rather than Ctrl-VX.) To WordPerfect, Ctrl-VX (shown as ^X) is a *wildcard* character that acts as shorthand for "any single character." You may compare it with the Joker in popular card games, a free number in Bingo, or a blank tile in Scrabble.

For example, to find every mention of dates in the 1970s, you could perform a Search command using **197^X** as the search string. This makes WordPerfect stop on 1970, 1971, 1972, and so on.

You cannot enter ^X as the first character in a search string, but you can put it anywhere else. You can even put several ^X's in a search string. For example, you could use **19-^X^X-3657** to find all mentions of part numbers that start with "19" and end with "3657."

Search Commands in Macros

— See **Macros, Chaining**

Searching a Disk for a Word

— See **Word Search**

Secondary Merge File

A secondary merge file is a disk file that WordPerfect combines or *merges* with another file (called the *primary file*) to produce form letters or other personalized documents. In a merge operation, the primary file holds the generalized form of the document, while the secondary merge file holds the data (names, addresses, part numbers, etc.) to be inserted into that document. See **Form Letters** for full details on merge operations.

Selecting Blocks of Text

— See **Block Command**

Selecting Printers

— See **Switching Printers**

Setting Tabs

— See **Tabs**

Set-Up — WordPerfect 4.1 and 4.2

WordPerfect comes preset to operate in a certain way. For example, it assumes you want tabs at every fifth column position, the left margin at column 10, the right margin at column 74, and so on. You can change these settings from within a document, but those changes only apply to that document. To change the settings for *every* document you create, you must change WordPerfect's Set-up menu.

To obtain the Set-up menu, start WordPerfect by entering **wp/s** (instead of the usual **wp**). Figure S-1 shows the Set-up menu for WordPerfect 4.2. WordPerfect 4.1's Set-up menu is similar, except it separates *Set Beep and Screen Options* into two options, *Set Screen Size* (3) and *Set Beep Options* (5).

End Set-Up

Typing **0** (zero) records the changes you made to the Set-up menu and puts you into WordPerfect. You can also press F1 (Cancel) to discard Set-up menu changes and return to DOS

```
Set-up Menu

    0 - End Set-up and enter WP

    1 - Set Directories or Drives for Dictionary and
    Thesaurus Files
    2 - Set Initial Settings
    3 - Set Screen and Beep Options
    4 - Set Backup Options

    Selection:

Press Cancel to ignore changes and return to DOS.
```

Figure S-1. WordPerfect 4.2's Set-up menu.

354 Setting Tabs

Set Directories or Drives

Normally, the dictionary and thesaurus files are kept on their regular floppy disks or in the WordPerfect hard disk subdirectory, but you can make WordPerfect look for them anywhere in the system by choosing this option.

The main dictionary is a file named LEX.WP. If you add words to it, WordPerfect stores them in a supplementary dictionary file called {WP}LEX.SUP. The thesaurus is contained in TH.WP.

When you type 1 to choose this option, WordPerfect displays the prompt

```
Where do you plan to keep the dictionary (LEX.WP)?
Enter full pathname: LEX.WP
```

If LEX.WP is in its standard subdirectory or drive, simply press Enter. Otherwise, if LEX.WP is in a different subdirectory or drive, type the pathname, then press Enter. For example, if LEX.WP is in the subdirectory \WP\DICT (i.e., a DICT subdirectory one level below WordPerfect's WP subdirectory), enter **\wp\dict\lex.wp**.

Pressing Enter brings on a similar prompt for the supplementary dictionary. Pressing Enter again brings on a prompt for the thesaurus. Finally, pressing Enter once more makes WordPerfect return to the Set-up menu.

Set Initial Settings

Typing 2 brings on a table menu with key names in the left-hand column and the parameters these keys affect in the right-hand column. To change a parameter, press the key whose name appears to the left of it. When the key's menu appears, select the parameter you want to change. (For details about this option and a summary of the preset values, see **Initial Settings for WordPerfect 4.1 and 4.2**.)

Set Screen and Beep Options

The *Screen* options here let you specify the size of the screen's text area in rows and columns, and whether *hard returns* (the code that WordPerfect generates when you press Enter) and the document name are to be displayed on the screen. Initial settings are 25 rows and 80 columns (the full screen), with hard returns appearing as blanks (i.e., they are invisible) and a filename on the status line.

WordPerfect is preset to beep the speaker when it needs a hyphenation decision (see **Hyphenation**), but there is a *Beep* option that lets you turn this beeping off. You can also make WordPerfect beep when a search operation fails or when an error message appears on the screen.

Set Backup Options

Using these options, you can make WordPerfect create a backup copy of your document automatically, at either regular intervals (called *Timed Backup*) or when you do a Save (F10) operation (called *Original Backup*). See **Backups** for a discussion of these features.

Set-Up — WordPerfect 5.0

WordPerfect comes preset to operate in a certain way. For example, it assumes you want tabs at every fifth column position, one-inch margins at the top, bottom, left, and right, and so on.

You can change these settings for the current document using Format (Shift-F8) and other commands. To change them for *every* document you create, you must change WordPerfect's Setup menu. To obtain the Setup menu (shown in Figure S-2), press Shift and F1 to give a Setup command.

Backup

Using this option, you can make WordPerfect create a backup copy of your document automatically, at either regular intervals (called *Timed Backup*) or when you do a Save (F10) operation (called *Original Backup*). See **Backups** for details.

Cursor Speed

When you hold the → or ← key down, the cursor moves across the screen at a rate of 30 characters per second. To make it move faster or slower, enter a higher or lower value here.

```
Setup

    1 - Backup

    2 - Cursor Speed                       30 cps

    3 - Display

    4 - Fast Save (unformatted)            Yes

    5 - Initial Settings

    6 - Keyboard Layout

    7 - Location of Auxiliary Files

    8 - Units of Measure



Selection: 0
```

Figure S-2. WordPerfect 5.0's Setup menu.

Display

This option controls what information appears on the screen and how it's displayed. Choosing it makes WordPerfect produce the Display Setup menu shown in Figure S-3.

Most users will probably only consider changing these three options:

- *Automatically Format and Rewrite* (1) is preset to Yes, which makes WordPerfect rearrange text on the screen as you make additions or deletions. If you find this distracting, type n for No to make Word-Perfect reformat only when you move through a document.

- *Display Document Comments* (3) is preset to Yes, which makes Word-Perfect show document comments along with regular text. (See **Document Comments** for details.) Typing **n** for No makes Word-Perfect hide the comments. Either way, document comments are never printed.

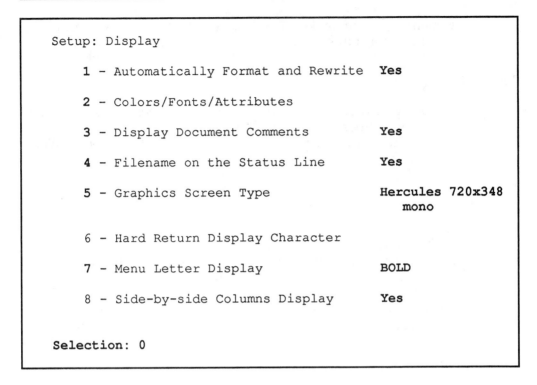

Figure S-3. WordPerfect 5.0's Display Setup menu.

- *Side-by-side Columns Display* (8) is preset to Yes, which makes WordPerfect display text columns (see **Columns, Text**) as they appear on the printed page. Typing **n** for No makes WordPerfect display each column on a separate page.

When you finish changing the Display Setup menu, press F7 (Exit) to save your changes and return to the main Setup menu, or press F1 (Cancel) to discard the changes.

Fast Save

WordPerfect is preset to store documents on disk in "unformatted" form, which speeds up Save (F10) and Exit (F7) operations. A potential drawback, however, is that a Fast-Saved document cannot be printed from disk directly. Instead, you must either print it from the screen or add the formatting, *then* print it from disk; see **Fast Save** for details. However, if you're willing to sacrifice speed for convenience, you can make WordPerfect store documents in printable, formatted form by entering **n** for No in the Fast Save field.

Initial Settings

Choosing this option brings on a menu that lets you specify a variety of settings under which WordPerfect should operate. For details and a summary of the preset values, see **Initial Settings for WordPerfect 5.0**.

Keyboard Layout

As you know, many keys and key combinations do specific jobs within WordPerfect. For example, WordPerfect does a Save operation when you press F10, and starts a new page when you press Ctrl and Enter. The Keyboard Layout option lets you create disk files that make any key or combination do whatever *you* want. This is particularly handy for creating a macro *library*, a file that installs a set of macros when you activate it. See **Keyboard Layout** for details.

Location of Auxiliary Files

This option tells WordPerfect where to look for auxiliary disk files, such as the Speller's main and supplementary dictionaries, printer files, and the thesaurus. See **Auxiliary Files**.

Units of Measure

WordPerfect normally displays numeric values such as margins and tabs in inches, and it displays the status line's *Ln* and *Pos* values in lines and column positions, respectively. With this option, you can make WordPerfect display measurements in any form you want. For example, you can make it display margin and tab settings in centimeters. See **Units of Measure** for details.

Shell Command (Ctrl-F1)

Pressing Ctrl and F1 makes WordPerfect display

`1` Go to DOS: `0`

Typing **1** here takes you out of WordPerfect temporarily so you can run another program, format disks, copy files, or do anything else you can do with the DOS prompt on the screen. When you finish using DOS, type the word **exit** and press Enter. This puts you back in WordPerfect, at the place where you pressed Ctrl-F1.

Single-Sheet Paper

— See **Paper**

Single-Spacing

— See **Spacing**

Soft Hyphens

— See **Hyphenation**

Soft Page Breaks

When you attempt to enter material onto a page that is filled to capacity, WordPerfect draws a dashed line across the screen and puts the excess text below it. The dashed line indicates a *soft page break*, one that WordPerfect generated automatically. The term "soft" here distinguishes this kind of page break from a *hard page break*, which you create by pressing Ctrl and Enter together. Word-Perfect 4.2 and 5.0 indicate a hard page break by drawing a line of equal signs across the screen.

Sorting

Many people need to work with lists or tables whose entries are arranged in some specific order. A telephone list is an obvious example; it must be arranged alphabetically. A mailing list is another; companies generally want it sorted by ZIP code, to take advantage of bulk postage rates. Further, an accountant may want accounts receivable listed chronologically, with the most delinquent accounts first. Regardless of what kind of list or table you have, WordPerfect can usually sort it to meet your needs.

WordPerfect can *sort* lines, paragraphs, or groups of text in a document in either ascending or descending order. Moreover, it can perform the sort on up to nine "key words." This means, for example, that you can make it sort a telephone list by both last name (the main key word) and first name (the secondary key word), to break "ties."

Further, you can make WordPerfect sort material that is on the screen or in a file on disk. Similarly, you can tell it to display the result on the screen or store it on disk.

Finally, WordPerfect can *select* entries from a list based on criteria you specify. For example, you can request a list of customers who live in Florida, or those whose accounts are delinquent, or both (all delinquent Floridians).

General Procedure for Sorting

Before starting a sort operation, you must tell WordPerfect the following (in this general order):

- Where to obtain the sort material; from the screen or a disk file.
- Where to send the sorted result; to the screen or a disk file.
- Whether to sort by lines, paragraphs, or groups of text.
- The type of each key word; whether it is a word or number.
- The location of each key word; its position on the line and (for paragraphs and groups) its line number.
- Whether to sort in ascending or descending order.

```
          Tyner, Mavis          965-2694
        : Lane, Lois            557-1332
          Edgewood, Bill        847-3896
          Grayson, Edgar        744-6743
          Grayson, Dr. Leonard  931-5410
          Brown, Byron          356-7732
          Carlson, Joan         753-6844
          Michelle, Pam         602-5419
          Raymond, Morris       705-5537
```

Figure S-4. Telephone list for sorting.

A Simple One-Key Sort Operation

Suppose you have entered the telephone list shown in **Figure S-4** and saved it on disk. (**Important:** Unless you're an expert at sorting, *always save to disk before you sort*. That way you can start over if you foul up the sort operation.) Sort the list as follows:

1. Press Ctrl-F9 to give a Merge/Sort command.
2. When this menu appears at the bottom of the screen:

    `1 Merge; 2 Sort; 3 Sorting Sequences: 0`

    type **2** for *Sort*.
3. When WordPerfect shows

    Input file to sort: (Screen)

    press Enter.
4. Press Enter again when this prompt appears:

    Output file for sort: (Screen)

    WordPerfect shows the Tab Ruler, followed by its *Sort* menu (Figure S-5).

The Sort menu looks fairly complex, so instead of trying to do anything with it (we will, later), let's just proceed and see what hap-

―――――――――――――― Sort by Line ――――――――――――――

Key	Typ	Field	Word	Key	Typ	Field	Word	Key	Type	Field	Word
1	a	1	1	2				3			
4				5				6			
7				8				9			

Select

Action	Sort	Type of Sort
Sort	Ascending	Line Sort

1 Perform Action; 2 View; 3 Keys; 4 Select; 5 Action; 6 Order;
7 Type: **0**

Figure S-5. Sort menu.

pens. After all, it *does* show "Sort by Line" at the top—and that's what we want to do. So, with the Sort menu on the screen, type **1** to select *Perform Action* (i.e., sort by line).

The Sort menu disappears and WordPerfect instantly sorts the list. Now the list looks like Figure S-6. Note that WordPerfect sorted the list correctly except for one thing: it put Dr. Leonard Grayson ahead of Edgar Grayson. Apparently, it thought "Dr." was a first name!

To put the list in proper order, you must sort by first names as well as last names. This involves telling WordPerfect where to *find*

```
Brown, Byron           356-7732
Carlson, Joan          753-6844
Edgewood, Bill         847-3896
Grayson, Dr. Leonard   931-5410
Grayson, Edgar         744-6743
Lane, Lois             557-1332
Michelle, Pam          602-5419
Raymond, Morris        705-5537
Tyner, Mavis           965-2694
```

Figure S-6. Telephone list after first sort operation.

the first name on any given line. To do this, you must know something about how WordPerfect handles entries in a sort list—and that entails understanding the special terminology the WordPerfect manual uses for sort operations. The manual refers to "records," "fields," and "words."

Records, Fields, and Words

A *record* is an individual entry (a line or paragraph) in the document WordPerfect is to sort. For example, each name and number in a telephone list is a record.

A *field* is a portion of a record. For example, our sample telephone list has two fields: name and number. WordPerfect numbers fields from left to right, and requires you to separate them with indents or tabs.

A *word* is a unit that makes up a field. As expected, words are divided by spaces. WordPerfect can count words within a field from left to right (if you give it a positive number such as 1, 2, or 3) or from right to left (if you give it a negative number such as -1 or -2).

You would count words right to left if a field can contain various numbers of words. For example, our telephone list's name field contains two words (last and first name) in all but one entry: "Grayson, Dr. Leonard" has a three-word name field in which the first name is the third word. Due to this single exception, to sort the list by first names as well as last names, we must use a negative number to tell WordPerfect where to find the first name. Throughout the list, the first name is always the rightmost word, so we must use *-1* to identify its location. (You would also use negative numbering to sort a list in which a field contains some names that have middle initials and others that don't.)

Sorting on Two Key Words

Now let's sort the telephone list again, but this time sort on the first name as well as the last. Begin as before, and stop when the Sort menu appears. Let's spend a few minutes discussing the Sort menu (refer back to Figure S-5).

The menu's header, *Sort by Line*, indicates that WordPerfect assumes you want to sort lines rather than paragraphs. (The Select option lets you sort paragraphs.) The Sort menu provides for nine *Keys* (because WordPerfect can sort up to nine levels), and each has space for a *Typ*, *Field*, and *Word* parameter. As before, WordPerfect assumes that you want to sort on only one key word, so it fills in the first entry. Let's discuss the parameters.

Typ, short for Type, indicates whether the key word is alphanumeric (a) or numeric (n). Here's how they differ:

- *Alphanumeric* key words can be either words or numbers. However, alphanumeric numbers must have the same length in every record. ZIP codes, telephone numbers, employee numbers, and social security numbers all meet this criteria—they are always the same length.
- *Numeric* key words can only be numbers. These may be numbers of different lengths (e.g., ages, salaries, or bowling scores) and may include dollar signs, commas, and decimal points.

Field identifies the field that contains the key word. Again, fields are numbered left-to-right (*1* is the first field, *2* is the second, and so on) and are separated with tabs or indents.

Word identifies the key word in the field. WordPerfect can number words from left to right (with positive numbers) or from right to left (with negative numbers).

Hence, WordPerfect's automatic choices for Key 1 indicate that it wants to base the sort operation on an alphanumeric word (*Typ* is "a"), the first word of the first field (*Word* and *Field* are both "1"). These are the correct choices for the telephone list, because our primary sort key should refer to the last names—and that is indeed what "a 1 1" does.

Now, to make WordPerfect include first names in the sort criteria, type **3** to select *Keys*. WordPerfect puts the cursor on the "a" parameter of Key 1. Press the right-arrow key three times to reach the Key 2 parameters. WordPerfect shows "a" for *Typ*. This is what we want (because first names, like last names, are alphanumeric), so press right-arrow again. Now "1" appears for both *Field* and *Word*.

Field should indeed be "1," because first names are in the leftmost field. However, *Word* should be "-1," because first names appear at the end of the field. To replace the *Word* value, press right-arrow to reach it, then Backspace to delete it. Now, type **-1** and press F7 to leave the Key part of the menu. Finally, type **1** for Perform Action. When WordPerfect finishes sorting, the telephone list should look like Figure S-7.

```
Brown, Byron          356-7732
Carlson, Joan         753-6844
Edgewood, Bill        847-3896
Grayson, Edgar        744-6743
Grayson, Dr. Leonard  931-5410
Lane, Lois            557-1332
Michelle, Pam         602-5419
Raymond, Morris       705-5537
Tyner, Mavis          965-2694
```

Figure S-7. Final form of telephone list.

Sorting Paragraphs

WordPerfect can also sort paragraphs. This is handy for arranging catalogs, bibliographies, lists of tasks, and other kinds of descriptive lists. For sorting purposes, paragraphs may be no longer than a page and must have at least one blank line or a page break between them.

To sort paragraphs, start as you would to sort lines. That is, press Ctrl-F9 for Merge/Sort, type **2** for *Sort*, and specify the "Input file" and "Output file." When the Sort menu appears, however, type **7** for *Type*, then **3** for *Paragraph*. WordPerfect displays a new Sort menu that has "Sort by Paragraph" at the top. The Key fields also have an additional parameter, *Line*, and look like this:

```
Key Typ Line Field Word
 1   a   1    1    1
```

As you may have guessed, the *Line* parameter indicates which line of the paragraph contains the key word. WordPerfect lets you specify line numbers in either top-to-bottom order (where *1* is the top line) or bottom-to-top order (where *-1* is the bottom line).

So, to sort paragraphs, fill in the Key(s), then type **1** for Perform Action.

Sorting Groups of Text

You may also want to sort groups of line-oriented information, such as names and addresses or product specifications. To do this, you must prepare the material as a so-called *secondary merge file*.

Within a secondary merge file, each entry (e.g., an individual's name and address) is called a *record*. Records are separated by

"Merge E" codes, which you produce by pressing Shift-F9 or (in WordPerfect 5.0) choosing it from the Merge Codes list. WordPerfect shows ^E on the screen and moves the cursor to the next line.

Each record is comprised of *fields*. Fields are separated by "Merge R" codes, which you produce by pressing F9. WordPerfect shows ^R and moves the cursor to the next line. Fields are numbered from top to bottom; thus, *1* is the field that starts on the first line.

Note that I just said "the field that *starts* on the first line." Fields in secondary merge files can contain as many lines as you want. For example, to create an address list of business associates, you might want to make the "company name" field three lines long. By reserving three lines, you can construct records that require only a company name (one line), a company name and division name (two lines), or a company, division, and department name (three lines). To start a new line within a field, press Enter.

You can put any number of fields in a record, but any given field must always contain the same type of information or nothing at all. For example, suppose you are creating a secondary merge file that contains the names and addresses of both your friends and business associates. If field 2 is set aside for a company name, you would enter the name and ^R for business associates, but enter only ^R for friends.

To sort secondary merge files, start as you would to sort lines or paragraphs. That is, press Ctrl-F9 for Merge/Sort, type **2** for *Sort*, and specify the "Input file" and "Output file." When the Sort menu appears, type **7** for *Type*, then **1** for *Merge*. WordPerfect displays a new Sort menu that has "Sort Secondary Merge File" at the top. The Key fields have the same four parameters they do for paragraphs: Typ, Line, Field, and Word.

So, to sort a secondary merge file, enter the Key(s), press F7, then type **1** for Perform Action.

Merge/Sort Example

Figure S-8 shows a mailing list (albeit a rather small one) you could sort as a secondary merge file. Create it like an ordinary document, but remember to enter a ^R after each field and a ^E after each record. To enter ^R, press F9; to enter ^E, press Shift-F9 in WordPerfect 4.1 or 4.2, or Shift-F9 and **e** in WordPerfect 5.0.

Suppose we want the list sorted by ZIP codes and last names. To do this, save the document on disk (name it *mailing.lst*) and start a sort operation as usual. When the Sort menu appears, type **7** for

```
Mr. Harold S. Woods^R
Woods Flying School^R
13 Paris Circle^R
Ocala,^R
FL 32787^R
^E
Mr. Phillip T. Grange^R
Newton Plastics Corporation^R
1865 Industrial Way^R
Newton,^R
FL 32786^R
^E
Mr. Terry Briggs^R
Modern Designs, Inc.^R
17565 Canard St.^R
Newton,^R
FL 32786^R
^E
Dr. Howard L. Alberts^R
^R
1305 Sunnyland Rd.^R
Newton,^R
FL 32786^R
^E
Mrs. Viola Wilson^R
Wilson & Associates, Inc.^R
4399 Beach St.^R
Ocala,^R
FL 32787^R
^E
```

Figure S-8. Secondary merge file before sorting.

Type, then **1** for Merge. Now you must set up the Keys to select the ZIP code as the Key 1 and the last name as Key 2.

The ZIP code is a number, the second word in the fifth field (which is also the fifth line). Type **3** to choose Keys and change Key 1 to

Key	Typ	Line	Field	Word
1	n	1	5	2

The last name is an alphanumeric word, the last word of the first field and line. (Note that I said *last* word because some records have four words in the first field, while others have three. Hence, you must enter **-1** for the Word value.) Move the cursor to the Key 2 field and enter

Key	Typ	Line	Field	Word
2	a	1	1	-1

```
Dr. Howard L. Alberts^R
^R
1305 Sunnyland Rd.^R
Newton,^R
FL 32786^R
^E
Mr. Terry Briggs^R
Modern Designs, Inc.^R
17565 Canard St.^R
Newton,^R
FL 32786^R
^E
Mr. Phillip T. Grange^R
Newton Plastics Corporation^R
1865 Industrial Way^R
Newton,^R
FL 32786^R
^E
Mrs. Viola Wilson^R
Wilson & Associates, Inc.^R
4399 Beach St.^R
Ocala,^R
FL 32787^R
^E
Mr. Harold S. Woods^R
Woods Flying School^R
13 Paris Circle^R
Ocala,^R
FL 32787^R
^E
```

Figure S-9. Secondary merge file after sorting.

Finally, press F7 to leave the Keys form, then type **1** to start sorting. The sorted list should look like Figure S-9.

Selecting

WordPerfect can also select records from a list, and generate a second, "result" list, based on criteria you specify. For example, if the main list contains employee information for a company, you could tell WordPerfect to produce a list of Marketing personnel, or people who earn more than $30,000.

You can also combine criteria. You could, for example, request a list of Marketing and Engineering personnel who earn more than $30,000. WordPerfect normally produces the result list in sorted form, but you can request it unsorted.

To make WordPerfect select records from a list, you must give it the ground rules. If WordPerfect was a human being, you could simply tell it something like "List all of my customers who live in

Utah." and it would do that. Being a computer program, WordPerfect doesn't understand plain English. But it *does* understand commands entered in the form of a so-called *select statement.*

A select statement tells WordPerfect which Key (or Keys) to use for selecting and what criteria to apply to it. For example, if Key 3 refers to state abbreviations in a customer list, the select statement

key3=UT

tells WordPerfect to select the records for all the customers who live in Utah.

The equal sign (=) is just one symbol you can use in select statements. WordPerfect provides eight symbols in all; they are:

+ (OR)   combines two key definitions, and tells WordPerfect to select records that satisfy *either* condition.
* (AND) also combines two key definitions, but it tells WordPerfect to select records that satisfy *both* conditions.
=   Equal to
<>   Not equal to
>   Greater than
<   Less than
>=   Greater than or equal to
<=   Less than or equal to

Figure S-10 shows a list of names and credit limits from which we could make WordPerfect select records. Some typical select statements are:

(Name)	(Init.)	(ST)	(Credit Limit)
Simpson	L	TX	75,000.
Chang	P	PA	150,000.
Albers	B	CA	300,000.
Massey	C	MD	95,000.
Wilder	G	CA	425,000.
Chamberlain	I	MD	600,000.
Raymond	S	CA	80,000.
Anderson	H	FL	160,000.
Gladstone	W	CA	150,000.
Acerson	J	UT	250,000.

Figure S-10. Credit limit list.

Statement	Selects records of ...
key3=UT + key3=TX	clients from Utah or Texas
key3=CA * key4>80,000	California clients whose credit limit is more than $80,000
key3=MD * key4=95,000	Maryland clients whose credit limit is $95,000
key3<>MD	all clients except those from Maryland
key4=75,000	clients whose credit limit is $75,000 or more
key4>75,000 * key4<100,000	clients whose credit limit is between $75,000 and $100,000 (exclusive)

Note this about the format of select statements: You must enter a space between + or * symbols and *key* names, but enter other symbols and words (or numbers) with no space between them.

You can also use parentheses in a select statement, to keep WordPerfect from getting confused. For example,

key475,000 * (key3=TX + key3=PA)

selects all clients in Texas and Pennsylvania whose credit limit is more than $75,000. If you omit the parentheses, WordPerfect would select Texas clients whose credit limit is more than $75,000 and *all* Pennsylvania clients.

Finally, WordPerfect lets you use a shortcut to select all the records that contain a certain key word, regardless of which field it's in or where it's located within a field. To do this, simply type **g** after *key*. For example,

keyg=American

would select "Acme American, Inc.," "American Buggywhip Corp.," and every other record that contains the word "American."

Now that you know something about select statements, we can discuss how to use them to select and sort a list.

Select and Sort Procedure

To perform a select and sort operation on a list, retrieve it from disk (or create it and save it), then do the following:

1. Start a sort operation as usual, by pressing Ctrl-F9 and choosing Sort from the menu.
2. When the Sort menu appears, use the Keys option to set up your keys. Unless you're using the "keyg" form of the select statement, be sure to enter Key parameters for the field(s) you want to select as well as those you want to sort. Press F7 when you finish.
3. Type 4 to choose *Select* from the menu. WordPerfect replaces the menu with a list of the available select statement symbols.
4. Enter your select statement, then press F7 to get back to the menu.
5. Type 1 for *Perform Action*. WordPerfect sorts and selects, then displays the result.

Selecting Without Sorting

Sometimes you may want to select records without sorting them. For example, with a long list that's already sorted, you can save some time by just selecting from it. You may also want to skip the sorting if you plan to select from two different lists, then combine them (Retrieve one into the other) and sort the result.

To select without sorting, enter your select statement, then choose *Action* from the Sort menu. When the screen shows

```
1 Select and Sort; 2 Select Only: 0
```

type 2.

Using Sorted Material in a Document

Whenever WordPerfect performs a sort operation, it sorts the *entire document*. This can produce unexpected results if you include regular text as well as the actual list. For example, if you sort a list that has a title, WordPerfect will put your title at the appropriate place in the sorted result list. To avoid this kind of problem, you could prepare the material to be sorted as a separate document.

An easier solution is to define the material as a block, then sort the block. To do this, obtain Block mode, highlight the material to be sorted, then continue defining the sort menu. Finally, when you tell WordPerfect to sort, it will sort only the highlighted material; the remainder of the document will be unaffected.

Spacing

WordPerfect comes preset for single-spacing, but you can easily make it double-space, triple-space, or produce any other kind of spacing.

To change the spacing in a WordPerfect 4.1 or 4.2 document, press Shift-F8 to give a Line Format command. When the Line Format menu appears, type **4** to select *Spacing*. WordPerfect shows

```
[Spacing Set] n
```

where *n* is the current spacing value (1, 2, or whatever). To change the spacing, type a new value, then press Enter.

To change the spacing in a WordPerfect 5.0 document, press Shift-F8 to give a Format command and type **1** to select *Line*. When the Line Format menu appears, type **6** to reach the *Line Spacing* field. Enter a new spacing value, then press F7 (Exit) to return to your document.

When you change the spacing, WordPerfect inserts a hidden [Spacing Set:*n*] (WordPerfect 4.1 or 4.2) or [Ln Spacing:*n*] code in your document and applies the new spacing to everything that follows, up to the next spacing code (if any).

The **Reformatting Documents** entry describes a procedure for single-spacing a double-spaced document.

Special Characters

Sometimes you may want to produce characters that aren't available on the keyboard. WordPerfect provides a wide variety of special characters that you can insert into text. They include:

- Geometric shapes, such as "smiling faces," the symbols on playing cards, triangles, arrows, and musical notes.
- Various combinations of lines, from which you can construct rectangles and other forms.
- Mathematical symbols.
- The Greek alphabet.

- Characters that are used in Spanish, French, and other foreign languages.

Each version of WordPerfect provides a feature that lets you insert these characters into your document directly, by specifying them with key commands. WordPerfect 4.1 and 4.2 also let you assign the characters to a key combination consisting of Alt or Ctrl and a letter key. After that, you can press those keys to insert the character.

Inserting Special Characters Directly

To insert a special character in your document with WordPerfect 4.1 or 4.2, begin by pressing Ctrl and V at the same time. When WordPerfect shows **n =** at the bottom of the screen, type a number between 1 and 254, then press Enter. (These characters are listed in the IBM BASIC manual's *ASCII Character Codes* appendix.) For example, pressing Ctrl-V, 1, and Enter inserts a "happy face" symbol in your text. You can also give the Ctrl-V *number* sequence in the search string of a Search or Replace command, to locate a special character.

To insert a special character in your document with WordPerfect 5.0, use the Compose feature. See that entry for details.

Assigning a Special Character to a Key Combination

To assign a special character to an Alt-key or Ctrl-key combination, do the following:

1. Press Ctrl and F3 to give WordPerfect a Screen command.
2. When the Screen menu appears, type **3** to select *Ctrl/Alt keys*. This brings on a screen that lists the available Alt-key and Ctrl-key combinations (i.e., Alt-A through Alt-Z and Ctrl-A through Ctrl-Z), with a 0 (zero) after each one. The 0 indicates that a combination is unassigned.
3. Press the keys you want to assign to a special character. For example, to make WordPerfect insert a character when you press Alt and A, press Alt-A. WordPerfect replaces that combination's *Value* with a solid rectangle. Now it's time to select the character for that key combination.

The bottom of the screen shows the characters in a numbered grid of five rows and fifty columns. Each row is preceded by a starting value (0, 100, 150, 200, or 250) and each column is marked with a digit that represents the distance from the starting (row) value. For example, the column digits 0 through 9 at the beginning of row 100 represent the values 100 through 109, respectively.

4. To assign a special character to the key combination you have specified, add its row and column values, and enter that number from the keyboard. WordPerfect shows the number and its corresponding character in the list.

   For example, suppose you want to assign the Greek *Pi* symbol to your active key combination. Pi is on the 200 row, at column position 7 in the third group of digits. The third group of digits represents the *20's*, so Pi is actually at column 27. Adding 27 to 200 (the row value) produces 227—and that's the number you must enter.

5. Assign other key combinations you want similarly. When you finish, press Enter to return to your document or press the F1 (Cancel) key to discard the key assignments.

If you no longer need a special character, you can free up or *unassign* its key combination. To do this, perform the assign procedure, but when the key combination screen appears, select the character's combination and set its *Value* to **0** (zero).

Special Character Keys and Macros

You can also assign an Alt-key combination to a macro (see **Macros, Introduction to**). If you have done this, *don't* assign the same combination to a special character. If you do, WordPerfect will insert the character (rather than run the macro) when you press those keys.

Spell Command (Ctrl-F2)

WordPerfect includes a Speller that can check a document, or a portion of one, for spelling errors. It does this by looking for each word in its dictionary. If a word is not there, the Speller highlights it and displays a list of close words from the dictionary; you can then choose from the list. If the word you're after is not in the list, you can tell the Speller to

•Skip it (e.g., it's a proper name or part of a book title),

Spell Command (Ctrl-F2)

- Add it to a supplementary dictionary (e.g., it's a technical term not found in most dictionaries),
- Let you correct it manually, or
- Produce a list of words that match the general pattern of, or sound similar to, the misspelled word.

Starting the Speller

WordPerfect can spell-check a word, a page, or an entire document. To begin, put the Speller disk in drive B (replacing the data disk), then press Ctrl and F2 to give a Spell command. This produces the following menu at the bottom of the screen:

```
Check: 1 Word; 2 Page; 3 Document; 4 Change Dictionary; 5 Look Up; 6 Count
```

Now, type **1**, **2**, or **3**. The Speller displays a ***Please Wait*** message while it checks each word against its dictionary.

If the Speller can't find a word in the dictionary, it highlights the word, displays a list of possible replacements (if any), and shows this menu at the bottom:

```
Not Found! Select Word or Menu Option (0 = Continue): 0
1 Skip Once; 2 Skip; 3 Add Word; 4 Edit; 5 Look Up; 6 Phonetic
```

The list of replacements produced by WordPerfect 4.1's Speller includes words that are different by a single letter and those where two letters may have been transposed. The Spellers for WordPerfect 4.2 and 5.0 also list *homonyms*; words that sound like the highlighted word.

If the word you want appears in the list, simply type the letter that precedes it. Otherwise, if the word is not listed, choose from the options on the bottom line. Here's what these options do:

1. *Skip Once* tells the Speller to resume spell-checking, but stop at the next occurrence of the word (if there is one).
2. *Skip* tells the Speller to skip this word and any subsequent occurrences of it. This lets you ignore a word you don't use often enough to add to the dictionary.
3. *Add Word* makes the Speller create a supplementary dictionary (if it doesn't already exist) and add this word to it. In future spell-checking operations, the Speller will automatically search the extra dictionary as well as the main one.
4. *Edit* lets you correct a word manually. When the Speller moves the cursor to the word, make your changes, then press Enter.

5. *Look Up* makes WordPerfect search its dictionary for a word that you enter. You can also make it search for words that match a generalized form, or *pattern*. More about this option later.
6. *Phonetic* makes the Speller display words that sound like this one. (In reality, this option is only useful for WordPerfect 4.1, because the Spellers for both 4.2 and 5.0 include phonetics in their replacement lists. In fact, WordPerfect 5.0's menu doesn't even have a *Phonetic* option!)

When the Speller finishes, it shows a word count and **Press any key to continue** at the bottom of the screen. At that point, you can remove the Speller disk from drive B and replace it with the data disk on which you want to save the corrected document. Then press Enter.

Duplicated Words

The Speller also checks for duplicated words, as in "I drove the the car." If it encounters a duplication, it displays

```
Double Word!  1 2 Skip;  3 Delete 2nd;  4 Edit;  5 Disable double word checking
```

Here, you would normally type **3** to delete the second word. But you can also type **1** or **2** to skip this occurrence (but not subsequent ones), **4** to edit (say, to insert a hyphen between the words), or **5** to ignore double words altogether.

Spelling Correction Example

As an example of using the Speller, consider the letter in Figure S-11. With the aid of *Webster's New World Misspeller's Dictionary*, a few typing mistakes, and a little ingenuity, I have introduced several spelling errors. If you try this example on your own, don't be restricted by my mistakes; surely you can make bigger, better, or different ones.

Once you have entered the letter, insert the Speller disk in drive B, then press Ctrl and F2 for Spell. When the Check menu appears, type **3** for *Document*.

The Speller then searches the document for words that are not in its dictionary. Besides misspellings, these may include proper names, abbreviations, and technical terms. In this case, it finds ten unmatched words (starting with "rikwest" in the first paragraph),

```
                            2211 Washington Street
                            San Diego, CA 92121
                            May 16, 1988

Mr. Carl Johnson
1236 Summit Drive
San Diego, CA 92121

Dear Mr. Johnson:

In response to your recent rikwest, we need the following
information to cunsider a credit applivdation:

    1) Name and adddress of your bank, along with your account
       number.
    2) Three credit references.
    3) A signed corprate resullution indicating trepponsabillity
       for payment.

You may either use our enclosed form or sumbit a standard one of
your own.  Please indicate any ratings you may have from credit
burows.

                            Sincerely yours,


                            Marie F. Gerard
                            Assistant Credit Manager

Enclosure
```

Figure S-11.   Credit application letter with misspellings.

and displays the Not Found menu at the bottom of the screen each time.

Dealing With Unmatched Words

Since WordPerfect Corporation has improved the Speller with each new version, how we deal with the ten unmatched words depends somewhat on which version of WordPerfect is being used. With version 4.2's Speller, we do the following:

- The words *rikwest, cunsider, adddress, corprate, resullution, sumbit,* and *burows* were so close to those in the dictionary that the Speller was able to produce a list that included the correct form. Hence, we typed the identifying letter to make the replacement. For *rikwest,* for example, the Speller showed

378 Spell Command (Ctrl-F2)

A.	raciest	B.	racist	C.	reaccused
D.	recast	E.	recessed	F.	recused
G.	request	H.	requested	I	requisite
J.	richest	K.	rockiest	L.	roughcast

Here, we pressed **g** for *request*.

- We typed **3** to add *Gerard* to a supplementary dictionary. (Surprisingly, the Speller already had *San Diego, CA;Carl; Johnson; Marie;* and *F.* in its main dictionary!)
- We typed **4** to manually change *applivdation* to *application* and *trepponsabillity* to *responsabillity*. In the second case, however, the Speller marked *responsabillity* as still misspelled. But then, the list it produced gave us the correct form, so we were home free.

Spell-Checking a Block of Text

You can also spell-check a sentence, paragraph, or any other selected portion of a document. To do this, put the cursor where you want to start, then press Alt and F4 to put WordPerfect into Block mode. Finally, move the cursor just past the last word you want to check (WordPerfect highlights everything in between) and press Ctrl and F2 to start the Speller.

Looking Up Words

Selecting option 5 (*Look Up*) from either the Check menu or the Not Found menu makes the prompt **Word or Word Pattern:** appear. Here, you may enter either a word or a word *pattern*.

Entering a word in response to **Word or Word Pattern:** makes the Speller produce a list of *homonyms*; words that sound like the one you entered. This is handy for finding the correct form of a word you aren't reasonably sure how to spell. For example, entering **reconsiliation** makes the Speller produce the correct *reconciliation*, and entering **iridesent** or **eradesent** makes it produce *iridescent*.

You can also enter a word pattern for **Word or Word Pattern:**. The pattern can include "wildcard" symbols to represent letters you want the Speller to supply. Specifically, you can enter a question mark (?) to represent a single letter or an asterisk (*) to represent an unspecified number of consecutive letters.

The question mark is useful for determining which vowel belongs in a word. For example, if you're not sure whether "durable" is spelled *durable*, *dureble*, or *durible*, enter **dur?ble**; the Speller lists only *durable*. Similarly, entering **hom?ly** produces both *homely* and *homily*; choose the word you want.

The asterisk is especially handy for determining whether a word contains one or two occurrences of a letter. For example, if you're not sure how to spell "accommodate" (two c's and two m's, one c and two m's, etc.), enter **ac*m*date**; the Speller produces *accommodate*. Similarly, entering **rec*om*end** produces the correct form *recommend*. Note that * can represent any number of letters, even no letters, whereas ? can only represent a single letter. Thus, if you enter **rec?om?end** (as in the preceding example), the Speller will not find the form you want.

The asterisk is also useful for finding the correct combination of two or more letters. For example, entering **finag*** informs you that the correct form is *finagle* (rather than *finagel*) and entering **us*ble** produces *usable* (rather than *useable*).

The Look Up option is also handy for less important tasks, such as solving crossword puzzles. Some examples are:

- Entering the pattern **r?nt** makes the Speller display four-letter words that start with "r" and end with "nt"—*rant*, *rent*, and *runt*, in this case.
- Entering **ran??** makes it display three- to five-letter words that start with "ran." This produces *ran*, *randy*, *range*, *ranks*, and so on.
- The similar form **ran*** makes it display all words that start with "ran," regardless of their length.
- Entering **r*n** makes it display words that start with "r" and end with "n." This includes words as short as *ran* and as long as *radiosterilization*.

Alternate Main Dictionaries — WordPerfect 5.0

When you spell-check a document, the Speller checks words against a dictionary file on disk. WordPerfect comes with a dictionary written for a particular language. The English-language file is called LEX.WP (in WordPerfect 4.1 and 4.2) or WP{WP}EN.LEX (in WordPerfect 5.0). However, WordPerfect Corporation offers dictionaries in a variety of languages for WordPerfect 5.0. These dictionary files have names of the form WP{WP}nn.LEX. For example, WP{WP}DE.LEX and WP{WP}ES.LEX are German and Spanish dictionaries, respectively.

The Speller is preset to use the supplied dictionary. To make it use a different one, press Shift-F8 to give a Format command and type

4 to select *Other*. When the Other Format menu appears, type **4** to reach the *Language* field.

This field contains the last two letters of the current dictionary's filename. This is usually **EN**, which selects WP{WP}EN.LEX. Enter the last two letters of the file you want to use, then press F7 to leave the Other Format menu.

You can also perform this procedure to make the Speller use a *custom* dictionary that you have created.

Custom Dictionaries

Sometimes you may create a document that contains words the Speller would ordinarily treat as misspellings. For example, you may write a science fiction novel that has unusual character and place names—perhaps Aert, Grax, and Hubix. Because you only need those names for that particular project, you probably won't want to add them to the Speller's dictionary.

Fortunately, WordPerfect lets you create custom dictionaries that you can tell it to use for special-purpose documents. To see how custom dictionaries fit in, let's take a brief look at how WordPerfect conducts a Spell operation.

When you do a Spell operation, the Speller checks each word against a "main" dictionary called LEX.WP (WordPerfect 4.1 or 4.2) or WP{WP}EN.LEX (WordPerfect 5.0). If it can't find the word there, it searches through a "supplementary" dictionary called {WP}LEX.SUP (4.1 or 4.2) or WP{WP}EN.SUP (5.0). (This dictionary doesn't come with WordPerfect. The Speller creates it the first time you choose *Add Word* from the Not Found menu.) But these are simply the Speller's default dictionaries. You can easily create a main dictionary, supplementary dictionary, or both, and make the Speller use those dictionaries for spell-checking.

Creating Custom Dictionaries

To create a custom main dictionary, you must use WordPerfect's *Spell* program. See **Spell Utility Program** for details.

To create a custom supplementary dictionary, you can either use the Spell utility or type in the words you want (separated by spaces) from within WordPerfect and save them in a disk file.

Which technique you use to create a supplementary dictionary depends mainly on its length. It's easier to create a dictionary using WordPerfect, but the Speller will take longer to search through it. By contrast, Spell arranges dictionary entries in alphabetical order, which speeds up searches. As a rule of thumb, create short or very temporary dictionaries with WordPerfect and use Spell to create all others.

Since dictionaries created from within WordPerfect are standard WordPerfect files, you can edit them like any regular document. (The {WP}LEX.SUP and WP{WP}EN.SUP dictionaries are also in WordPerfect format, incidentally. You can add or delete words by simply loading them into WordPerfect.) However, you cannot use Spell to edit a WordPerfect-created dictionary, or vice versa.

Using Custom Dictionaries

The procedure for making the Speller use custom dictionaries depends on which version of WordPerfect you have.

4.1 4.2 **With WordPerfect 4.1 or 4.2,** start the Speller and choose *Change Dictionary* from the Check menu. When **Enter new main dictionary name: LEX.WP** appears, press Enter to accept LEX.WP or enter the name of a custom main dictionary. Similarly, when **Enter new supplementary dictionary name: {WP}LEX.SUP** appears, press Enter to accept {WP}LEX.SUP or enter the name of a custom supplementary dictionary. The Speller will then use the specified dictionaries until you do another *Change Dictionary* or leave WordPerfect, in which case it reverts back to LEX.WP and {WP}LEX.SUP.

5.0 **With WordPerfect 5.0,** specifying custom main and supplementary dictionaries takes separate operations. To specify a main dictionary, follow the procedure described earlier under *Alternate Main Dictionaries — WordPerfect 5.0.* Be sure to give your dictionary file a name of the form WP{WP}*nn*.LEX.

To specify a supplementary dictionary, start the Speller and choose *New Sup. Dictionary* from the Check menu. When **New supplemental dictionary name:** appears, enter the name of your file.

The Speller will then use the specified dictionaries until you do another new-dictionary operation or leave WordPerfect, in which case it reverts back to WP{WP}EN.LEX and WP{WP}EN.SUP.

Spell Utility Program

WordPerfect's Speller disk contains a special program called *Spell* that lets you operate on dictionaries used by the Speller. With Spell, you can:

- Create a new dictionary.
- Add words to or delete words from an existing dictionary, including the main dictionary. You may enter the words from the keyboard or specify a disk file that contains them.
- Display the common word list, the part of a dictionary the Speller searches first.
- Find out whether a word is located in a dictionary's main or common word list.
- Look up a word or a phonetic, "sound-alike" spelling of it.

Starting Spell

To start the Spell utility with floppy disks:

1. Obtain the A> prompt.
2. Insert the data disk that contains your dictionaries, supplementary word lists, or files of words to be added or deleted into Drive B.
3. Insert the Speller disk into Drive A.
4. Type **spell b:** and then press Enter.

To start Spell from a hard disk, change to its directory, then type **spell** and press Enter.

Either way, Spell displays the menu shown in Figure S-12. Let's look at each option.

Exit

Typing **0** (zero) records the changes you made and then returns you to the DOS prompt. This is the *only* way to leave the Spell menu! Pressing F1 (Cancel) does nothing, nor does pressing Enter—because there is no default Selection, as there is for most menus.

Change/Create Dictionary

As the top right-hand corner of the Spell menu shows, when you start Spell, it always assumes you want to operate on LEX.WP (or WP{WP}EN.LEX in WordPerfect 5.0), the disk file that contains WordPerfect's main dictionary. To operate on some other dictionary or create a new one, type **1** and enter its name.

```
Spell — WordPerfect Speller Utility LEX.WP

    0 — Exit
    1 — Change/Create dictionary
    2 — Add words to dictionary
    3 — Delete words from dictionary
    4 — Optimize dictionary
    5 — Display common word list
    6 — Check location of word
    7 — Look up
    8 — Phonetic look up

Selection:
```

Figure S-12. Spell utility menu.

Realize, however, that *Spell cannot operate on {WP}LEX.SUP or WP{WP}EN.SUP*, the supplementary dictionary that WordPerfect creates automatically, because it is a standard WordPerfect document, not a dictionary. If you attempt to change this or any other WordPerfect document, Spell displays **ERROR: Invalid dictionary file**, and ignores your command. On the other hand, since the supplementary dictionary is a regular document, you can retrieve, edit, and save it from within WordPerfect.

If you enter the name of a dictionary that does not exist, Spell shows a message of the form

```
Dictionary filename not found.
Create a new dictionary named filename (Y/N)? n
```

To create this dictionary, type **y**; to enter a different name (if, say, you misspelled it), type **n** or press Enter.

Once you enter a valid dictionary name, the Spell menu reappears with this name at the top. Any operations you perform from here on will apply to that dictionary.

Add Words to Dictionary

You can add words to a dictionary by entering them from the keyboard or copying them from a WordPerfect document file (including {WP}LEX.SUP or WP{WP}EN.LEX). Typing **2** to choose *Add words to dictionary* makes Spell display the following menu:

Spell — Add Words LEX.WP

0 - Cancel - do not add words
1 - Add to common word list (from keyboard)
2 - Add to common word list (from a file)
3 - Add to main word list (from keyboard)
4 - Add to main word list (from a file)
5 - Exit

The only difference between adding words to the common or main word list is that when you add them to the common list, Spell also adds them to the main list automatically. Unless you're building an unusually large dictionary, you should probably add them to the common word list, using option 1 or 2.

When you choose either keyboard option, 1 or 3, Spell displays **Enter word(s):**. Type the words to be added, with a space between them, and press Enter when you finish. Pressing Enter here makes Spell add the words to the dictionary, then alphabetize the entries. Type **5** to *Exit* to the Spell menu.

If you try to add a word that's already in the dictionary, Spell simply ignores it.

Delete Words from Dictionary

You can delete words from a dictionary by entering them from the keyboard or listing them in a WordPerfect document file. Typing **3** to choose *Delete words from dictionary* makes Spell display a menu that's similar to the Add Words menu in the previous section, except the options read "Delete" rather than "Add."

Of course, Spell can only delete words that are actually in the dictionary. If you tell it to delete a nonexistent word, it simply ignores your command.

Optimize Dictionary

Frankly, I'm not sure what this option does, nor are the people in WordPerfect's Customer Support staff. At any rate, optimize any dictionaries you change, to play it safe.

Display Common Word List

Typing 5 makes Spell list the words in the dictionary's common word list, 51 words at a time. (The main dictionary's common word list contains about 1,500 words.) To see the next screenful, press Enter. To return to the Spell menu, press F1 (Cancel).

Check Location of Word

This option lets you find out whether a specified word is contained in a dictionary's main or common word list. If it's in neither place, Spell shows *Not found*. Press F1 (Cancel) to return to the Spell menu.

Look Up

This option lets you look up a word in the dictionary. It does the same thing as when you *Look Up* a word from within the Speller, except it only searches the dictionary that's listed at the top of the screen. As with the Speller, you can enter a *word pattern*, a generalized form of the word that includes * and ? wildcard characters (see *Looking Up Words* under **Spell Command**).

Phonetic Look Up

If you're not sure how to spell a word, you can look it up by entering its phonetic or "sound-alike" form. For example, to check whether recommend is in the dictionary, you could enter **rekomend**. Spell will produce *recombined, recommend, recumbent*, and (surprisingly) *reexamined*.

Splitting the Screen

WordPerfect lets you divide the screen into two separate text areas, or *windows*. Each can display a different document. Once you have set up the second window, you can work in either of them. The procedure for splitting the screen into two windows is described under **Screen Command**.

Spreadsheet Files, Using

Without a doubt, the most popular business program is the electronic spreadsheet. If your reports involve tables of numbers requiring arithmetic manipulation, an electronic spreadsheet can save you a lot of hand calculations.

To explain what an electronic spreadsheet does, let us consider a practical application. Suppose you own a clothing store and want to find out how your business is doing. You could take a large piece of paper and rule it off into rows and columns. Each row would correspond to a different department: men's suits, children's wear, sportswear, women's fashions, and so on.

The first 12 columns would be monthly sales totals, followed by yearly totals, comparisons with previous months or previous years, commissions, sales taxes, and so forth. You could add down the monthly columns (giving monthly totals) and add across the rows (giving annual totals for a given department). You could also figure annual receipts, net profits (receipts minus costs), and other results.

How would you do this by hand? You would enter the numbers from your account books and use a calculator to add each row and column, one after the other. Surely, this would be a long, tedious, error-prone task. The electronic spreadsheet can do all the calculations simultaneously. It lets you label rows and columns and tell the computer how they are related.

For example, you could label the monthly columns with the names of the months. You could then specify that the *Yearly Total* column is the sum of the monthly columns. Similarly, you could say that the *Monthly Cost* row is the sum of all departmental costs for a particular month. After you tell the computer what the rows and columns mean, you then enter your data.

The computer quickly and automatically performs all the calculations at once. It's like having many calculators, each doing its specific task and passing its results on if other calculators need them. You can also change any number on the spreadsheet, and the program will instantly recalculate everything the number affects.

You can copy the results of a spreadsheet such as Lotus' *1-2-3* or Microsoft's *Multiplan* into a WordPerfect document. For example, you might be preparing a loan proposal to a bank for a possible expansion of your clothing store. To begin, you develop a spreadsheet that lists income, costs, and profits for the last five years and uses them to make five-year projections under reasonable assumptions about inflation rates, profit margins, operating costs, and so forth.

You save this spreadsheet as a DIF file on your data disk, then use the CONVERT program's *Spreadsheet DIF to WordPerfect Secondary Merge* option (9) to convert it to a WordPerfect document. When you reach the point where the spreadsheet is to appear, copy it into the loan proposal document with a Retrieve command. After that, you can reformat, expand, or otherwise change the spreadsheet just as you would change standard WordPerfect text.

An electronic spreadsheet is a great timesaver for an accountant, banker, insurance agent, purchasing manager, sales manager, broker, or anyone else who works with figures. Furthermore, it ensures greater accuracy and allows the user to calculate more results and try out variables such as inflation, interest rates, market penetration, or foreign exchange rates.

Lotus 1-2-3 Procedure

Lotus 1-2-3 produces spreadsheets in its own unique format called *WKS* (for "worksheet," which is what Lotus Development Corp. calls a spreadsheet). WordPerfect cannot convert the WKS format directly, but the 1-2-3 program contains a procedure to convert a WKS file to a DIF file—and DIF is a format WordPerfect *can* handle. Hence, we must make two separate conversions: WKS to DIF (using 1-2-3), then DIF to WordPerfect (using WordPerfect). The procedure is as follows:

1. Start 1-2-3 as usual.
2. Create the worksheet or load it in from disk with a /File Retrieve command.
3. Put your WordPerfect data disk in drive B.
4. Select /File Xtract, then Formulas.
5. When 1-2-3 asks for the Xtract filename, enter **b:** and the name you want to give the file. (For example, **b:salespro** would be suitable for a table of sales projections.)
6. When 1-2-3 asks for the Xtract range, enter the beginning column and row, two periods, the ending column and row, and then press Return. For example, to extract rows 6 through 24 of columns A through G, enter **A6..G24**.
7. When the top right-hand corner of the screen shows *READY*, select /Quit and Yes to leave 1-2-3.
8. When the Lotus Access System command menu appears, select Translate, then WKS to DIF.
9. For the source disk drive, specify B.

10. When the computer asks you to *Select file for processing*, use the down-arrow key to highlight the filename you entered in step 5, then press Return.
11. For the destination disk drive, specify B.
12. Select Yes to proceed with the translation.
13. When the screen shows *Press any key to clear display and continue*, press Return.
14. When the File Translation System menu reappears, select Quit and Yes.
15. When the Lotus Access System command menu appears, select Exit and Yes to leave Lotus.

Your data disk now contains two versions of the worksheet, one in Lotus 1-2-3 worksheet format (e.g., SALESPRO.WKS) and another in DIF format (e.g., SALESPRO.DIF). To convert the DIF file to a WordPerfect document, do the following:

1. Put your WordPerfect Learning disk in drive A, replacing the Lotus disk, and enter **a:convert**.
2. When the "Name of Input File?" prompt appears, enter the filename and **.dif** (e.g., enter **salespro.dif**).
3. When the "Name of Output File?" prompt appears, enter the same filename, but give it a different extension. Since the result will be a secondary merge file, *.sf* is a reasonable choice (e.g., enter **salespro.sf**).
4. When the Convert menu appears, type **9** to select *Spreadsheet DIF to WordPerfect Secondary Merge*.

Once you have converted a spreadsheet to a WordPerfect file, you can copy it into any other document using the regular Retrieve command.

Using Wide Spreadsheets

A problem with spreadsheets is that they are often wider than your paper. (For example, Lotus 1-2-3 provides 2,048 rows and 254 columns!) To use a wide spreadsheet, set up margins for it, *Retrieve* it, then distribute it over several pages with column move and copy operations; see **Column Operations**.

Starting a New Page

— See **Hard Page Command**

Starting WordPerfect

Most people generally start WordPerfect by entering **wp** or (to start with a specific document) **wp** *filename*. However, you may start it with any of several commands; Table S-1 lists the most useful ones.

The letters following WP in this table are *switches*. With the exception of /S, you can use any combination of switches in a single startup command. For example, starting WordPerfect with the following command sets the backup interval to 15 minutes, runs a macro called *START*, then loads a document called *REPORT.DOC*:

wp/b-15/m-start report.doc

Table S-1. Commands that start WordPerfect.

Command	Action
WP	Start without loading a document.
WP/B-*minutes*	During this work session, save documents at *minutes* intervals; see *Automatic Backups* under **Backups**.
WP *filename*	Start by loading a specified document.
WP/M-*macroname*	Start by running a specified macro (e.g., START or ALTF).
WP/NF	Startup command required by some compatibles and windowing programs (other than TopView).
WP/R	Loads a set of menus and error messages into memory, which can make WordPerfect run faster.
WP/S	*With WordPerfect 4.1 or 4.2 only:* Obtain the Set-up menu, to change some of WordPerfect's initial settings permanently. See **Set-Up WordPerfect** 4.1 and 4.2 for details.

Starting WordPerfect

A Hard Disk Startup File for WordPerfect

When you turn on a computer that has a hard disk, it always starts in the primary or *root* directory. To switch it to the WordPerfect subdirectory, you must first type **cd \wp** (or **cd \wp50** in WordPerfect 5.0). Then, to start WordPerfect, you must type **wp** and press Enter. This requires only a few simple commands, but remembering commands is bothersome. To make your job easier, let's create a short program or *file* that changes directories and starts WordPerfect when you type **wp** and Enter.

To create the startup file, proceed as follows:

1. Type **cd ** and press Enter to put the computer in the root directory (in case it isn't there already).
2. Type **copy con: wp.bat** and Enter.
3. Type **cd \wp** and Enter.
4. Type **wp %1** and press the *F6* function key, then Enter.

Status Line

The line at the bottom of the screen is called the status line. It shows the name of the document you're working on, the document number (*Doc 1* or *2*), and the cursor's current page, line, and column position. The document number reflects the fact that WordPerfect can work with two different documents at the same time, in separate *windows* (see **Windows, Document**).

The *Pos* label is itself an indicator. When you press Caps Lock (the computer's version of a typewriter's Shift Lock key), it appears as *POS*. When you press Num Lock (to type numbers using the numeric keypad), it appears as a flashing *Pos*.

The number following *Pos* can also function as an indicator. WordPerfect displays it in bold when you press F6 (Bold) and underlines it when you press F8 (Underline).

WordPerfect also displays messages and prompts on the status line, where the document name normally appears.

Stop Merging

To stop a merge operation, press Shift and F9. For full details on merge operations, see **Form Letters**.

Stop Printing

Once a print operation has started, you may either stop it temporarily to fix a problem (say, the printer has run out of paper) or cancel it entirely.

Stopping the Printer Temporarily

To stop printing while you fix a problem or attend to other business:

1. Press Shift-F7 for *Print*, then 4 for *Printer Control*.
2. When the Printer Control menu appears, press **s** (WordPerfect 4.1 or 4.2) or **5** (WordPerfect 5.0) to stop printing.
3. When the printer stops, fix the problem, advance the paper to the top of the next page, and press **g** (4.1 or 4.2) or **4** (5.0) for *Go*.

When you give the Go command, WordPerfect reprints the page at which it stopped, then completes the job. As soon as it starts printing again, you may press Enter to get back to your document.

Canceling Print Jobs

To cancel a print operation or "job":

1. Press Shift-F7 for *Print*, then 4 for *Printer Control*.
2. When the Printer Control menu appears, press **c** (WordPerfect 4.1 or 4.2) or **1** to cancel printing. WordPerfect shows

   ```
   Cancel which job? (*=All Jobs) n
   ```

   where *n* is the number of the job being printed.
3. You now have three options:

   A. To cancel the current job, press Enter.
   B. To cancel an upcoming job, enter its number from the Job List at the bottom.
   C. To cancel all jobs, type an asterisk (*), then press Enter. Since this is a drastic action, WordPerfect lets you change your mind by displaying *Cancel All Jobs? (Y/N) N*. Press **y** to cancel the jobs or Enter to proceed with printing.

In any case, WordPerfect shows *Press ENTER if Printer Does not Respond*.

Of course, performing these operations takes time. To cancel printing quickly, you may want to set up a macro that does the job. Such a macro is described under **Canceling Print Jobs**.

Stop Replacing

To stop a Replace operation, press F1 to give WordPerfect a *Cancel* command.

Stopping Operations

— See **Cancel Command**

Strikeout Text — WordPerfect 4.1 and 4.2

When lawyers or legislators change a legal document, they often mark text to be deleted by striking through it with hyphens. WordPerfect provides a *strikeout* feature that lets you do this.

To apply the strikeout to text, select it in Block mode, then press Alt and F5 to give WordPerfect a *Mark Text* command. When the following menu appears:

```
Mark for: 1 ToC; 2 List; 3 Redline; 4 Strikeout; 5 Index; 6 ToA: 0
```

type 4 for Strikeout. WordPerfect leaves Block mode and returns you to editing.

For example, suppose your will includes the sentence

The estate is to be equally distributed among John, Mary, Elizabeth, and Jason Cane.

Later, in an act of heartless vengeance, you decide to disinherit Elizabeth. To do this, move the cursor to the "E" and press Alt-F4 for Block mode. Then highlight "Elizabeth, ", press Alt-F5 for Mark Text, and type **1** for Strikeout. When you print the will, the sentence will appear as

The estate is to be equally distributed among John, Mary, ~~Elizabeth,~~ and Jason Cane.

WordPerfect will strikeout characters with a hyphen (-) unless you tell it to use something else. To change the strikeout character, refer to the "Printer Program" section of the Installation manual.

Deleting Strikeout Text

To delete all strikeout text—and remove all redline markings (see **Redlining Text**)—from a document, press Alt-F5 to get the Mark Text menu, and then

> **4.1**
> **4.2**

- **For WordPerfect 4.1**, type **4** for Remove.
- **For WordPerfect 4.2**, type **6** for Other Options. When the Other Mark Text Options menu appears, type **6**.

When the prompt appears, type **y**.

Strikeout Text — WordPerfect 5.0

> **5.0**

When lawyers or legislators change a legal document, they often mark text to be deleted by striking through it with hyphens. WordPerfect 5.0 can *strikeout* (print hyphens through) new or existing text.

Strikeout New Text

To add material to a document and print strikeout marks through it, move to where the new text is to start and do the following:

1. Press Ctrl-F8 to give WordPerfect a *Font* command.
2. When this Font appears:

```
1 Size; 2 Appearance; 3 Normal; 4 Base Font; 5 Print Color: 0
```

Press **2** to select *Appearance*.
3. When WordPerfect displays the Appearance menu, press **9** to select *Stkout*.
4. Enter the text you want to strike out. When you finish, press the → key to move past WordPerfect's hidden Strikeout Off code.

Strikeout Existing Text

To print strikeout marks through existing text, move to the beginning of it and do the following:

1. Press Alt-F4 to put WordPerfect in *Block* mode.
2. Move the cursor to the last character you want to strike out.
3. Press Ctrl-F8 to give WordPerfect a *Font* command.
4. When the following menu appears:

       Attribute: 1 Size; 2 Appearance: 0

   press **2** to select *Appearance*.
5. When WordPerfect displays the Appearance menu, type **9** to select *Stkout*.

For example, suppose your will includes the sentence

The estate is to be equally distributed among John, Mary, Elizabeth, and Jason Cane.

Later, in an act of heartless vengeance, you decide to disinherit Elizabeth. To do this, move the cursor to the "E" and press Alt-F4 for Block mode. Then highlight "Elizabeth, ", press Ctrl-F8 for Font, and type **2** for Appearance, then **9** for Stkout. When you print the will, the sentence will appear as

The estate is to be equally distributed among John, Mary, ~~Elizabeth,~~ and Jason Cane.

Deleting Strikeout Text

To delete all strikeout text—and all redline markings (see **Redlining Text**)—from a document, press Alt-F5 to get the Mark Text menu, and type **6** for *Generate*. When the Generate menu appears, type **1**; when the prompt appears, type **y**.

Style Command (Alt-F8) — WordPerfect 5.0

5.0 WordPerfect provides a variety of commands for changing the tabs, line spacing, margins, justification, and other format settings. However, in practice you will probably use a few formats (e.g., single-spaced business letters or double-spaced reports) most of the time.

Rather than making you set the same values repeatedly, WordPerfect lets you save them as a standard format called a *style*. Moreover, WordPerfect lets you record the styles you need in a list called a *style sheet*. All you must do then is obtain a style sheet from within a document and select the style you want to use. You can even change a document's format (e.g., go from draft style to final form or from one journal or company's standard to another's) simply by changing styles.

Components of a Style

A style sheet consists of a list of format combinations called *styles*, where each style has a name, type, description, and code definition.

The style *name* consists of up to 11 characters that suggest the style's function. For example, you might use **busletter** for the format of a business letter, **indentlist** for an indented list, or **rightjust** to turn on right justification.

A style can be either of two *types*, paired or open. A *paired* style has two sets of formatting codes, one set that turns the style on and another set that turns it off. An *open* style has only one set of formatting codes, to turn the style on. Hence, a paired style is used to change the format of a block of text temporarily, while an open style is used to change the format for the rest of the document.

The *description* is an optional parameter that lets you describe what the style means in more detail than its name.

The *code definition* consists of the codes that WordPerfect inserts when you use the style in a document.

Creating Styles

To create a style, do the following:

1. Press Alt and F8 to give a Style command. WordPerfect displays a style sheet that has the headings *Name*, *Type*, and *Description* at the top and this menu at the bottom:

```
1 On; 2 Off; 3 Create; 4 Edit; 5 Delete; 6 Save; 7 Retrieve; 8 Update: 4
```

2. Type **3** for *Create* to obtain the Edit Styles menu (Figure S-13).

3. Type **1** to reach the *Name* field and enter a name (up to 11 characters) for the style you're creating.

4. Type **2** to select *Type*.

5. When WordPerfect displays

```
1 Paired; 2 Open: 0
```

select the type of style you want. (Selecting *Open* makes the menu's Enter option disappear.)

6. To include a description in the style, type **3** and enter it. The description text may extend to the end of the line, which means it can be up to 54 characters long.

7. Type **4** to begin entering the *Codes* you want for this style. WordPerfect shows the Reveal Codes screen.

8. What you do next depends on whether you're creating a Paired or Open style.

For a Paired style, WordPerfect displays the cursor at the top of the screen and the prompt **Place Style On Codes above, and Style Off Codes below** in a box below it. Do the following:

```
Styles: Edit

    1 - Name

    2 - Type                          Paired

    3 - Description

    4 - Codes

    5 - Enter                         HRt


Selection: 0
```

Figure S-13. Edit Styles menu.

A. Give WordPerfect commands to produce the codes you want inserted when the style is turned on, then press the ↓ key to move below the box.
B. Generate the codes you want inserted when the style is turned off.
C. Press F7 (Exit) to leave the Codes screen and return to the Edit Styles menu.
D. Type **5** to obtain the Enter menu.
E. Specify what you want the Enter key to do within the style. Type **1** to make it produce a hard return (its usual function), **2** to make it turn the style off, or **3** to make it turn the style off, then turn it back on.

For an Open style, give WordPerfect commands to produce the codes you want inserted when the style is turned on, then press F7 (Exit) to leave the Codes screen.

9. Press F7 (Exit) to return to the style sheet.
10. If you're finished working with the style sheet, press F7 to return to your document.

Using Styles

Once you have created a style, you can use it in the document. *To apply a style to new text*, do the following:

1. Move the cursor to where you want to insert the style.
2. Press Alt-F8 to obtain the style sheet.
3. Press the ↓ key until the style you want is highlighted.
4. Type **1** to turn the style *On*.
5. Type the text you want styled.
6. If you are using a Paired style, press Alt-F8 and type **2** to turn the style *Off* or (if you defined Enter as *Off* or *Off/On*), press Enter.

To apply a Paired style to existing text, do the following:

1. Move the cursor to the first character you want to style.
2. Press Alt-F4 to put WordPerfect in Block mode.
3. Move the cursor to the last character you want to style (WordPerfect highlights everything in between).
4. Press Alt-F8 to obtain the style sheet.
5. Press the ↓ key until the style you want is highlighted.

6. Type **1** to turn the style *On*. WordPerfect inserts a hidden [Style On] code ahead of the text and a [Style Off] code after it.

Editing Styles

Sometimes you may want to modify a style definition, to rename it, change its description, or insert or delete codes. To do this, press Alt-F8 to obtain the style sheet, highlight the style you want to edit, and type **4** to select *Edit* from the menu. When the Edit Style menu appears, make your changes. When you finish, press F7 (Exit) to return to the style sheet. From then on, the style will have the changes you made to it.

Deleting Styles

To delete a style, press Alt-F8 to obtain the style sheet, highlight the appropriate style, type **5** to choose *Delete* from the menu, and type **y** to confirm the deletion.

Saving Style Sheets on Disk

When you save a document on disk, WordPerfect also saves any styles you have created for it. In effect, the style sheet is "attached" to that document. Thus, whenever you retrieve the document and press Alt-F8 (Style), WordPerfect displays the corresponding style sheet.

If you use certain styles often, you will want to be able to activate them whenever they're needed. Fortunately, you can use a style sheet in any document by saving it as a separate file on disk.

To save a style sheet on disk, type **6** to choose *Save* from the Style menu, and enter a filename when WordPerfect requests it. Similarly, to use a style sheet that has been saved on disk, type **7** to choose *Retrieve* from the Style menu and enter the style sheet's filename.

As with a regular document, when you retrieve a style sheet, WordPerfect only *copies* it into your document; the original remains intact on disk. However, if you edit the sheet and then save it on disk under the original filename, WordPerfect replaces the old version with the new one.

If you try to retrieve a style sheet that has one or more styles with the same names as a document's attached sheet, WordPerfect displays **Styles Conflict, Overwrite? (Y/N) N**. Press **n** to retrieve only the styles that don't conflict, or **y** to retrieve every style on the disk-based style sheet.

Style Library

As you know, when you create a new document, WordPerfect provides built-in or "default" settings for the tabs, margins, and other format features, as defined in its Setup menu. Similarly, if you press Alt-F8 to give a Style command in a document that has no defined styles, WordPerfect retrieves a default style sheet called the *style library*.

Initially, the style library is empty; it has no predefined styles. However, if you use certain styles in many of your documents, you can put them in a style library. Once you do that, WordPerfect will retrieve those styles whenever you give a Style command from a new document.

To obtain the style library, WordPerfect uses the "pathname" (floppy disk drive name or hard disk directory, plus filename) specified by the *Style Library Filename* parameter in the Setup menu's Location of Files submenu. Hence, before creating a style library, you must enter the library's pathname for *Style Library File*, as follows:

1. Press Shift-F1 to obtain the Setup menu
2. Type **7** for *Location of Files*.
3. Type **6** to reach the *Auxiliary Style Library Filename* field.
4. Enter the pathname for the style library you will create. For example, to name the library STYLE.LIB and store it in the current directory, enter **style.lib** for the pathname. To store it in some other directory, precede the filename with the directory name (e.g., **c:\auxfiles\style.lib** means that STYLE.LIB will be stored in a directory called AUXFILES on drive C:).
5. Press F7 (Exit) to return to your document.

Now that you have told WordPerfect where to find the style library, you must create the library and save it to disk. To do this:

1. Create the style sheet you want to use as the style library.
2. Type **6** to select Save from the Style menu.
3. When WordPerfect asks for the filename, enter the same pathname you used for *Style Library Filename*.
4. Press F7 to return to your document.

Subscripts

— See **Super/Subscript Command (WordPerfect 4.1 and 4.2)** or **Font Command (WordPerfect 5.0)**

Summing Columns

— See **Math/Columns Command**

Superscripts

— See **Super/Subscript Command (WordPerfect 4.1 and 4.2)** or **Font Command (WordPerfect 5.0)**

Super/Subscript Command (Shift-F1) — WordPerfect 4.1 and 4.2

WordPerfect lets you produce subscripts that are printed below the line and superscripts that are printed above it.

Subscripts

If your report includes chemical formulas such as H_2O or mathematical notations such as A_i, you will need subscripts that appear below the line. The procedure differs depending on whether you want to subscript new or existing material.

To apply a subscript to new text, begin by pressing Shift and F1 to obtain the following Super/Subscript menu:

```
1 Superscript; 2 Subscript; 3 Overstrike; 4 Adv Up; 5 Adv Dn; 6 Adv Ln: 0
```

What you do next depends on how much material you want to subscript, as follows:

- *To subscript the next character you type*, enter **2** to select "Subscript" (an *s* appears at the bottom left-hand corner), then type the character. For example, to produce H_2O, type **H**, press Shift-F1 and **2** (for Subscript), then type 2 and O.

- *To subscript the next string of characters you type*, enter **5** to select "Adv Dn" (an upside-down triangle appears at the bottom left-hand corner) and type the characters. When you finish typing the subscripted material, press Shift-F1 to get the Super/Subscript menu and enter 4 for "Adv Up." For example, to produce U_{235}, enter **U**, press Shift-F1 and **5**, type **235**, then press Shift-F1 and **4**.

To subscript existing material, put WordPerfect in Block mode, highlight the material, then press Shift-F1 and **2**.

Superscripts

If your report includes footnotes, references, or mathematical formulas such as $E = mc^2$ or $c^3 = a^6 + b^9$, you will need superscripts that appear above the line. As with subscripts, the procedure differs depending on whether you want to superscript new or existing material.

To apply a superscript to new text, press Shift-F1 to obtain the Super/Subscript menu, then do one of the following:

- *To superscript the next character you type,* enter **1** to select "Superscript" (an S appears at the bottom left-hand corner), then type the character. For example, to produce $E = mc^2$, enter **E = mc**, press Shift-F1 and **1**, then type **2**.

- *To superscript the next string of characters you type,* enter **4** to select "Adv Up" (a triangle appears at the bottom left-hand corner) and type the characters. When you finish typing the superscripted material, press Shift-F1 to get the Super/Subscript menu and enter **5** for "Adv Dn." Note that this procedure is the reverse of what you do for a subscript.

To superscript existing material, put WordPerfect in Block mode, highlight the material, then press Shift-F1 and **1**.

Removing Subscripts and Superscripts

WordPerfect precedes each subscript or superscript character with a hidden [SubScrpt] or [SuprScrpt] code. Similarly, it precedes advance down or advance up material with a hidden [Adv ▼] or [Adv ▲] code. To remove these features, press Alt and F3 to give a *Reveal Codes* command, then find the code and delete it.

Switch Documents Command (Shift-F3)

WordPerfect can work with two different documents (or different portions of the same document) at a time, by putting each in a text area called a *window*. The starting screen is itself a document window, as indicated by *Doc 1* on the status line at the bottom. To switch to a different document, but leave the current one intact, begin by pressing Shift and F3, to give a Switch Documents command. WordPerfect clears the screen and shows *Doc 2* on the status line. Now you can Retrieve the second document into this window and press Shift-F3 whenever you want to switch documents.

You can also split the current screen to view two different documents at the same time; see **Splitting the Screen**. Here too, pressing Shift-F3 moves the cursor from one document to the other.

Switching Printers — WordPerfect 4.1 and 4.2

4.1
4.2

As part of WordPerfect's installation procedure, you give it a list of up to six printers you will be using. These needn't be six *different* printers, however. If you have only one printer, for example, you can give it several numbers; say, one for continuous form paper, another for single-sheet paper, and so on. You can change the printer number for a single print job or for every job until you exit WordPerfect.

Switching Printers for a Single Job

To switch printers for a single print job, press Shift-F7 to give WordPerfect a Print command and type **3** to select *Options*. When the Change Print Options Temporarily menu appears, type **1** to select *Printer Number*. Then type the number of the printer you want and press Enter. When the Print menu reappears, choose the option you want to proceed with the print operation.

Switching Printers for This Work Session

To switch to a different printer until you exit WordPerfect, press Shift-F7 to give a Print command and type **4** to select *Printer Con-*

trol. When the Printer Control menu appears, type **1** to *Select Print Options*. When the Select Print Options menu appears, type **1** to select *Printer Number*. Then type the number of the printer you want and press Enter. When the Print menu reappears, choose the option you want to proceed with the print operation.

Switching Printers — WordPerfect 5.0

5.0 WordPerfect 5.0's Print (Shift-F7) command has a *Select Printers* feature that maintains a list of printers that are available with your computer. To select a printer for use during print operations, do the following:

1. Press Shift and F7 to give a Print command.
2. When the Print menu appears, type **s** for *Select Printer*.
3. Using the ↑ and ↓ keys, move the highlighting to the name of the printer you want to use.
4. Press Enter to select the highlighted printer. WordPerfect marks it with an asterisk (*).
5. Press F7 (Exit) *twice* to return to your document.

WordPerfect will use the printer you selected until you do another Select Printer operation.

Tab Align Command (Ctrl-F6)

WordPerfect lets you align text or numbers around a tab stop by pressing Ctrl and F6 (instead of Tab) to reach that tab position. (With WordPerfect 4.2 or 5.0, you can also align material by defining a tab as *Decimal*, and press Tab to reach it. For details on decimal tabs, see **Tabs**.)

When you press Ctrl-F6 to reach a tab stop, WordPerfect moves the cursor and shows **Align Char = .** at the bottom of the screen. After that, WordPerfect automatically aligns any number you enter at that tab position. That is, it shifts everything left until you type a decimal point, then puts anything else you enter to the right.

For example, suppose your organization is raising money for a charity and you want to list how much each member has collected, as follows:

```
Member                  Collections
Brown, John             $1,504.36
Carlson, Ray                65.77
Decker, Patricia,          668.43
Garnett, Vance             769.03
Evans, Sue                 779.56
Gerard, Roy              1,056.90
Morton, Mary               800.00
Stevens, George            863.96
```

You must set a tab directly below the "t" in "Collections." Then you simply press Ctrl-F6 (Tab Align) after entering each name, and type the amount. WordPerfect will align it automatically around the tab position.

For example, as you enter **$1,504** on the first line, WordPerfect will put each character at the tab position and shift all preceding characters left. Then, when you type the decimal point, WordPerfect will stop shifting and put the next two digits (**36**) to the right of the decimal point.

Changing the Alignment Character

WordPerfect assumes you want to align material around a decimal point, but you can easily change it to align around any character. For example, you may want to use a slash (/) to align a column of fractions. To change the alignment character, use one of the following procedures:

| 4.1 4.2 |

- **With WordPerfect 4.1 or 4.2**, press Shift and F8 to give a Line Format command. When the Line Format menu appears, type **6** to select *Align Char*. When the **Align Char = .** prompt appears, type the character you want.

| 5.0 |

- **With WordPerfect 5.0**, press Shift and F8 to give a Format command, then type **4** for *Other*. When the Other Format menu appears, type **3** to reach the *Decimal/Align Character* field. Type the decimal character you want, then type the thousands' separator character (or press Enter to retain the comma). Finally, press F7 (Exit) to return to your document.

Tab Key

The dark key with both left and right arrows (left of Q) is Tab. It is used to move right, just as on a typewriter. You can also move left, by pressing Shift and Tab together. How WordPerfect aligns text at a tab stop depends on what kind of tab is set there. For information on tab settings, see **Tabs**.

Table of Authorities

A table of authorities is a specialized table of contents that lists the pages where cases and statutes are referred to in a legal brief. Since this feature is only useful for members of the legal profession, I simply mention it here. For full details, refer to your WordPerfect manual.

Table of Contents — WordPerfect 4.1 and 4.2

4.1
4.2

WordPerfect can generate a table of contents if you tell it what to include. You can specify any of five different numbering styles, including no page numbers, a page number following each entry, or page numbers at the right-hand margin.

Building a Table of Contents

To build a table of contents, you must tell WordPerfect what to include. To do this:

1. Move the cursor to the beginning of the first section title you want to include (or to its number, if it has one) and press Alt-F4 to put WordPerfect in Block mode.
2. Press End to select the rest of the line.
3. Press Alt-F5 to give a Mark Text command. WordPerfect displays

```
Mark for: 1 ToC; 2 List; 3 Redline; 4 Strikeout; 5 Index; 6 ToA: 0
```

4. Type **1** to select ToC (Table of Contents).
5. When WordPerfect shows **ToC Level:**, type a number between 1 and 5 to specify the level of this particular title. The number tells WordPerfect how much to indent the title in the table of contents. Typing **1** puts the title at the left margin, typing **2** indents it one tab stop, and so on.

Repeat these steps for each title you want to include in the table of contents. When you finish, move the cursor to where the table of contents belongs (generally, it follows the title page) and start a new page with Ctrl-Enter. Then enter a heading (if you want one) and set tabs for the table. Now you must tell WordPerfect which format or *numbering style* to use.

Defining the Numbering Style

WordPerfect can generate a table of contents in any of five numbering styles. They are:

1. No page numbers (only numbers and titles).
2. Page numbers follow entries.
3. Page numbers follow entries, but are enclosed in parentheses. For example, if the "Major Products" entry is on page 43, this option would produce

    Major Products (43)

4. Flush right page numbers; that is, numbers aligned along the right-hand margin.
5. Flush right page numbers with leaders; WordPerfect inserts periods between the end of the title and the page number.

To select the style, begin by pressing Alt-F5 and typing **6** for Other Options. When the Other Mark Text Options menu appears, type **2** for Define Table of Contents. WordPerfect displays its *Table of Contents Definition* menu (Figure T-1).

The prompt at the top is asking how many levels of indentation you want in your table of contents. To put every entry at the left-hand margin, type **1**; otherwise, type a number between **2** and **5**, depending on how many levels you marked.

WordPerfect then asks **Display last level in wrapped format? (Y/N) N**. To put each last-level (highest-numbered) entry on a separate line, type **n**; to list them consecutively, in paragraph form, type **y**.

WordPerfect next needs to know the Page Number Position for each level. It normally assumes you want *Flush Right Page Numbers with Leaders* (format 5) throughout. However, if you specified "wrapped format" for the last level, it suggests *(Page Numbers) Follow Entries* (format 3) for that level. For example, here is how the beginning of a two-level table looks if Level 1 uses format 5 and Level 2 uses format 3:

1. TOOLS AND HOW TO USE THEM 1
    Selecting a Hammer (3); How to Drive Nails (4); First Aid for Thumbs

```
Table of Contents Definition

Number of levels in table of contents (1-5): 0


                    Page Number Position
        Level 1
        Level 2
        Level 3
        Level 4
        Level 5


    Page Number Position
    1 - No Page Numbers
    2 - Page Numbers Follow Entries
    3 - (Page Numbers) Follow Entries
    4 - Flush Right Page Numbers
    5 - Flush Right Page Numbers with Leaders
```

Figure T-1. Table of Contents Definition menu for WordPerfect 4.1 and 4.2.

To accept WordPerfect's suggested format for a particular level, press Enter; to specify a different format, type its number, then press Enter. When your document reappears, you can generate the table of contents.

Generating a Table of Contents

To make WordPerfect generate the table of contents, obtain the Mark Text menu (Alt-F5) and select *Other Options*, then *Generate Tables and Index*. When the screen shows

```
Existing tables, lists, and indexes will be replaced.
Continue? (Y/N): Y
```

type y. Finally, WordPerfect begins creating the table of contents, and displays **Generation in progress** at the bottom of the screen. When it finishes, your table of contents appears.

WordPerfect indents table of contents entries according to their level numbers. However, each will have the same print format as in the document. That is, bold text will be bold in the table, underlined text will be underlined, and so on. You may want to edit the table of contents to remove these formats.

Updating a Table of Contents

Usually you generate the table of contents when you finish a document, so it remains unchanged thereafter. However, if you are subject to higher authority (who isn't?), someone may suggest—or demand—changes that alter the final form. If these changes only affect a few words, you can simply make the revisions and reprint the document. But if they affect page numbering or require adding or deleting references, you must update the document.

To *add* entries to a table of contents perform the procedure I just described for building one.

To *remove* an entry from a table of contents, you must delete either its text or the invisible code that identifies it as an entry. WordPerfect marks each table of contents entry by placing a hidden code of the form *[Mark:ToC,n]* ahead of it and *[EndMark:ToC,n]* after it; in each case, the *n* indicates the table of contents level.

Therefore, to remove an entry from a table of contents, use Reveal Codes (Alt-F3) to locate the beginning Mark code and press Del or Backspace to delete it (WordPerfect deletes the matching EndMark code automatically).

If you have altered a table of contents, you must produce an updated version of it. To do this, select *Generate Tables and Index* from the Other Mark Text Options menu. When WordPerfect asks **Existing tables, lists, and indexes will be replaced. Continue?**, type **y**, as usual. This makes WordPerfect delete the existing table and generate a new one.

Table of Contents — WordPerfect 5.0

5.0 WordPerfect can generate a table of contents if you tell it what to include. You can choose from five different numbering styles, including no page numbers, a page number following each entry, or page numbers at the right-hand margin.

Building a Table of Contents

To build a table of contents, you must tell WordPerfect what to include. To do this:

1. Move the cursor to the beginning of the first section title you want to include (or to its number, if it has one) and press Alt-F4 to put WordPerfect in Block mode.
2. Press End to select the rest of the line.
3. Press Alt-F5 to give a Mark Text command. WordPerfect displays

    ```
    Mark for: 1 ToC; 2 List; 3 Index; 4 ToA: 0
    ```

4. Type 1 to select ToC (Table of Contents).
5. When WordPerfect shows **ToC Level:**, enter a number between 1 and 5 to specify the level of this particular title. The number tells WordPerfect how much to indent the title in the table of contents. Typing **1** puts the title at the left margin, typing **2** indents it one tab stop, and so on.

Repeat these steps for each title you want to include in the table of contents. When you finish, move the cursor to where the table of contents belongs (generally, it follows the title page) and start a new page with Ctrl-Enter. Then enter a heading (if you want one) and set tabs for the table. Now you must tell WordPerfect which format or *numbering style* to use.

Defining the Numbering Style

WordPerfect can generate a table of contents in any of five numbering styles. They are:

1. No page numbers (only numbers and titles).
2. Page numbers follow entries.
3. Page numbers follow entries, but are enclosed in parentheses. For example, if the "Major Products" entry is on page 43, this option would produce

Major Products (43)

4. Flush right page numbers; that is, numbers aligned along the right-hand margin.
5. Flush right page numbers with leaders; WordPerfect inserts periods between the end of the title and the page number.

To select the style, begin by pressing Alt-F5 and typing **5** for *Define*. When the Define Mark Text menu appears, type **1** for *Define Table of Contents*. WordPerfect displays its Table of Contents Definition menu (Figure T-2).

As the figure shows, WordPerfect assumes you want only one level in your table of contents, with the last level unwrapped (more on this shortly) and each page number aligned against the right-hand margin, with a dot leader separating it from the title. If you want something else, you must change one or more of the options.

The *Number of Levels* option (1) determines how many title levels will appear in the table. Type **1** to reach this field, then type a number between **2** and **5**, depending on how many levels you marked.

The *Display Last Level in Wrapped Format* option (2) tells WordPerfect whether to put each last-level (highest-numbered) entry on a separate line (No) or list them consecutively, in paragraph form (**Yes**).

Page Number Position (3) determines the numbering style for each level. WordPerfect assumes you want flush right page numbers with dot leaders throughout, unless you told it to "wrap" the last level. In that case, WordPerfect suggests **(Page #) follows entry** for the last level. For example, here is how the beginning of a two-level table looks if you accept WordPerfect's formatting suggestions:

1. TOOLS AND HOW TO USE THEM 1
   Selecting a Hammer (3); How to Drive Nails (4); First Aid for Thumbs (6)

To select a different numbering style for a level, begin by typing **3** to reach the Level 1 field. WordPerfect shows the following menu at the bottom:

1 None; **2** Pg # Follows; **3** (Pg #) Follows; **4** Flush Rt; **5** Flush Rt with Leader: 0

To specify the style for a level, type its menu number; to reach the next level's format field, press Enter.

When you finish working with the Table of Contents Definition menu, press F7 (Exit) to return to your document. Now you can generate the table of contents.

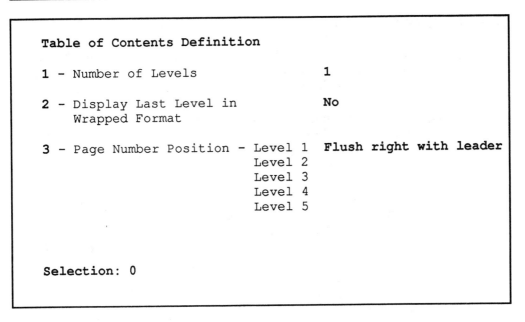

Figure T-2. Table of Contents Definition menu for WordPerfect 5.0.

Generating a Table of Contents

To make WordPerfect generate the table of contents, obtain the Mark Text menu (Alt-F5) and type 6 for *Generate*, then 5 for *Generate Tables, Indexes, Automatic References, etc*. When the screen shows

```
Existing tables, lists, and indexes will be replaced.
Continue? (Y/N) Y
```

type y. Finally, WordPerfect begins creating the table of contents, and displays **Generation in progress** at the bottom of the screen. When it finishes, your table of contents appears.

WordPerfect will indent table of contents entries according to their level numbers. However, each will have the same print format as in the document. That is, bold text will be bold in the table, underlined text will be underlined, and so on. You may want to edit the table of contents to remove these formats.

Updating a Table of Contents

Usually you generate the table of contents when you finish a document, so it remains unchanged thereafter. However, if you are subject to higher authority (who isn't?), someone may suggest—or demand—changes that alter the final form. If these changes only affect a few words, you can simply make the revisions and reprint the document. But if they affect page numbering or require adding or deleting references, you must update the document.

To *add* entries to a table of contents, perform the procedure I just described for building one.

To *remove* an entry from a table of contents, you must either delete its text or delete the invisible code that identifies it as an entry. WordPerfect marks each table of contents entry by placing a hidden code of the form *[Mark:ToC,n]* ahead of it and *[EndMark:ToC,n]* after it; in each case, the *n* indicates the table of contents level.

Therefore, to remove an entry from a table of contents, use Reveal Codes (Alt-F3) to locate the beginning Mark code and press Del or Backspace to delete it (WordPerfect deletes the corresponding EndMark code automatically).

If you have altered a table of contents, you must produce an updated version of it. To do this, select *Generate* from the Mark Text menu, then *Generate Tables, Indexes, Automatic References, etc.* from the Generate menu. When WordPerfect asks **Existing tables, lists, and indexes will be replaced. Continue?**, type **y**, as usual. This makes WordPerfect delete the existing table and generate a new one.

Tab Ruler

When you give a Reveal Codes (Alt-F3) command, do a *Window* operation from the Screen (Ctrl-F3) menu, or do a *Sort* operation from the Merge/Sort (Ctrl-F9) menu, WordPerfect displays a lighted bar called the *Tab Ruler*. The Tab Ruler marks the current tab stops with triangles, the left-hand margin with a [symbol, and the right-hand margin with a] symbol. When a tab stop and margin setting are in the same place, WordPerfect displays a { or } symbol there.

Tabs

Each version of WordPerfect provides preset tab stops. Specifically:

4.1
4.2
- WordPerfect 4.1 has a tab stop every five spaces (0, 5, 10, 15, etc.) up to column 155.
- WordPerfect 4.2 has a tab stop every five spaces up to column 160, and every 10 spaces from column 160 to 250.

5.0
- WordPerfect 5.0 has a tab stop every 0.5" up to 8.5" (the right edge of a standard piece of paper).

If these settings aren't right for your work, you can easily change them.

Changing Tab Settings

To change WordPerfect's tab settings, move the cursor to where you want to put the new settings into effect and do one of these operations:

4.1
4.2
- **For WordPerfect 4.1 or 4.2,** press Shift-F8 to give a *Line Format* command. When the Line Format menu appears, type **1** to select *Tabs*. This makes WordPerfect replace the bottom five lines with the Tabs menu shown in Figure T-3. (**Note:** The Tabs menu for WordPerfect 4.1 shows a T, rather than an L, at each tab stop.)

5.0
- **For WordPerfect 5.0,** press Shift-F8 to give a Format command, then type **1** for *Line*. When the Line Format menu appears, type **8** to select *Tab Set*. WordPerfect 5.0's Tabs menu is similar to 4.2's, except positions are marked in inches (1", 2", etc.).

Here, the top line shows an *L* for each tab stop, while the second and third lines show the column numbers (e.g., the *4* to the right of *30* indicates column 34). The fourth line lists the available options. You can:

- Clear all tabs from the cursor position to the end by pressing Ctrl-End. (WordPerfect 4.2 and later put the cursor at the column position where you selected *Tabs*.)
- Set a new tab by either typing its column number and pressing Enter or moving the cursor to the appropriate column and pressing Tab.

```
            L....L....L....L....L....L....L....L....L....L....L....L....L....
            0123456789012345678901234567890123456789012345678901234567890121234
                    20        30        40        50        60        70
            Delete EOL (clear tabs); Enter number (set tab), Del (clear tab);
            Left; Center; Right; Decimal; .= Dot leader; Press EXIT when done
```

Figure T-3. Tabs menu for WordPerfect 4.2.

- Delete a tab by moving the cursor to it and pressing Del or Backspace. (Pressing Backspace here deletes *at* the cursor position, not ahead of it, as with regular text.)

The fifth line of the Tabs menu lists the types of tabs that WordPerfect can produce.

Types of Tabs

If you set a tab by entering its column number or pressing Tab, WordPerfect makes it the standard *L* (left-justify) type, where the left-hand edge of text is aligned flush with the tab stop. However, WordPerfect versions 4.2 and later can work with seven different types of tabs, where each has a different effect on text. Table T-1 lists the tab types and the key(s) you must press to set them.

When you enter text at a Decimal (D) tab stop, WordPerfect aligns it around a prescribed alignment character, initially a period. As you type characters, WordPerfect shifts them left. It stops shifting when you type a period, and puts anything you type next to the right.

WordPerfect assumes you want to align material around a period, but you can easily change it to align around any character. For example, you may want to align a column of fractions around a slash (/). To change the alignment character, use one of the following procedures:

| 4.1 |
| 4.2 |

- **With WordPerfect 4.1 or 4.2**, press Shift and F8 to give a Line Format command. When the Line Format menu appears, type **6** to select *Align Char*. When the **Align Char** = . prompt appears, type the character you want.

| 5.0 |

- **With WordPerfect 5.0**, press Shift and F8 to give a Format command, then type **4** for *Other*. When the Other Format menu appears,

Table T-1. Types of tabs.

Entry at tab position	Effect on text:
L	Left-justify text
R	Right-justify text
D	Decimal-align text
C	Center text
L, then . (period	Left-justify text, precede it with a dot leader
R, then . (period	Right-justify text, precede it with a dot leader
D, then . (period	Decimal-align text, precede it with a dot leader

type **3** to reach the *Decimal/Align Character* field. Type the decimal character you want, then type a new *Thousands' Separator* character or press Enter to retain the comma. Finally, press F7 (Exit) to return to your document.

Figure T-4 shows an example of each of the four types of tabs. I have inserted a vertical line above each example to mark the tab stop it is keyed on. Tabbed text with dot leaders (produced by typing a letter and a period at the same position) looks similar, except it is preceded with a line of dots separated by spaces, as used in a table of contents.

Setting Multiple Tabs

If you want to create a table using evenly-spaced tabs in WordPerfect 4.2 or later, you needn't set the tabs individually; you can set them all at once! To set a group of evenly-spaced, left-justified (L) tabs, enter the position of the first tab stop, followed by a comma and the spacing value. For example, to set a tab at column 15 and every ten spaces thereafter (15, 25, 35, etc.) in WordPerfect 4.2, enter **15,10**. Similarly, to set a tab at 1.5" and every half-inch thereafter (1.5", 2.0", 2.5", etc.) in WordPerfect 5.0, enter **1.5,0.5**.

When you specify a group of tabs, WordPerfect adds them to the ones that are already there. To make your new tabs replace the existing ones, begin by pressing Home *twice*, then ←, to reach the beginning of the Tabs form. Then press Ctrl and End to delete the existing tabs. Now that the form is clear, you can enter your tab command(s).

```
....L........................R.........D...........C..............
01234567890123456789012345678901234567890123456789012345678901234
         20        30        40        50        60        70
    Left-justified text

         Right-justified text

                                      $136.25

                                                  Centered text
```

Figure T-4. Examples of tabbed text.

You can also set multiple *R*, *D*, *C*, or dot leader tabs, by simply typing its letter at the first tab stop, then entering the multiple tab stop command. For example, to set decimal tabs every ten spaces, starting at column 15, type **D** at column 15, then enter **15,10**.

Text Files

You can load a text file into WordPerfect by selecting either *Text In* from the List Files (F5) menu or *Retrieve* from the Text In/Out (Ctrl-F5) menu. Text In/Out also lets you save a WordPerfect document as a text file. See **List Files Command** or **Text In/Out Command** for details.

Text In/Out Command (Ctrl-F5) — WordPerfect 4.1

4.1 WordPerfect 4.1's Text In/Out command can do the following jobs:

- Save the document on the screen as an ASCII "DOS" text file.
- Retrieve a DOS text file into WordPerfect.
- Save the document on the screen in a "locked" form, for security purposes.
- Retrieve a locked document into WordPerfect.

Text In/Out Command (Ctrl-F5) — WordPerfect 4.1

When you press Ctrl and F5 to give a Text In/Out command, WordPerfect displays the menu shown in Figure T-5.

Saving and Retrieving DOS Text Files

Most computers transfer information internally as pure text. The WordPerfect manual refers to this format as "DOS text." Elsewhere in the computer field, it is usually called *ASCII*, short for "American Standard Code for Information Interchange."

DOS text is, in essence, the generic computer format. Nearly every program can both read text information and produce text results. Thus, you would use DOS text to communicate with programs that cannot produce any of the formats that WordPerfect's CONVERT program can use. For example, you would work with it to use documents produced by a non-CONVERTible word processor.

Menu option 1 is used to save the document on the screen as a DOS text file whose name you specify. In making the conversion, WordPerfect translates codes for the Date, Paragraph Numbering, and Outline Numbering into text; strips off codes for Bold, Underline, Subscript, and other print formats; replaces codes for Tab, Tab Align, Flush Right, Indent, and Center with spaces; and discards footnotes and endnotes.

Option 2 retrieves a specified DOS text file into WordPerfect and arranges it within the active margin settings. Unfortunately, however, this only works well for files that contain line-oriented material such as lists. If a file contains paragraphs whose lines extend past the right-hand margin, WordPerfect moves the excess material to the next line and puts a hidden [SRt] (Soft Return) code at the end of the shortened line. It also puts an [HRt] (Hard Return) code at the original end-of-line position.

Document Conversion and Locking

1 - Save current document as a DOS text file
2 - Retrieve a DOS text file
3 - Lock and save current document
4 - Unlock and retrieve a locked document

Figure T-5. WordPerfect 4.1's Text In/Out menu.

In regular text, WordPerfect inserts an [SRt] code when it moves excess material to a new line; it inserts an [HRt] code when *you* press Enter at the end of a paragraph. Thus, in effect, option 2 splits a text file paragraph into several paragraphs. To eliminate this problem, you can make your margins wider than normal. For example, if the text is 80 columns wide, you can set the margins to 0 and 85.

Saving and Retrieving Locked Documents

Options 3 and 4 of the Text In/Out menu let you save and retrieve documents in a "locked" format, for security purposes. A locked document is one to which you assign a password. After that, no one (not even you!) can retrieve the document unless they first enter the correct password.

To save the current document in locked format, choose option 3. When WordPerfect shows **Enter Password:**, enter a password of up to 75 characters. (Note that the password does not appear on the screen.) When it shows **Re-enter Password:**, enter the same password again. Finally, save the document as usual.

To retrieve and unlock a locked document, clear the screen, then press Ctrl-F5 and choose option 4. When WordPerfect shows **Document to be Retrieved:**, enter its name. When **Enter Password:** appears, enter the password you used to lock the document. When you're ready to send the document back to disk, you can either save it in locked format using option 3, or save an unlocked version of it under a different name using the regular Save or Exit command (here, press Enter when **Enter Password:** appears).

Another security feature is that locked documents can only be printed from the screen (by pressing Shift-PrtSc); neither the Print command nor the List Files *Print* option work with them.

Note that once a document has been locked, you cannot retrieve it unless you know the password. Therefore, be selective in deciding which documents to lock. Don't lock *anything* unless it's absolutely necessary. Finally, choose your password carefully, make it easy to remember (use, say, your Social Security number or birth date), and use the same password for every document you lock.

Text In/Out Command (Ctrl-F5) — WordPerfect 4.2

4.2

WordPerfect 4.2's Text In/Out command can do the following jobs:

- Save the document on the screen as an ASCII "DOS" text file, or retrieve a DOS text file into WordPerfect.
- Save the document on the screen in a "locked" form, for security purposes, or retrieve a locked document into WordPerfect.
- Save the document on the screen in a generic word processing format.
- Save the document on the screen in WordPerfect 4.1 format.
- Create and edit nonprinting document summaries and comments.

When you press Ctrl and F5 to give a Text In/Out command, WordPerfect displays the menu shown in Figure T-6.

Saving and Retrieving DOS Text Files

Most computers transfer information internally as pure text. The WordPerfect manual refers to this format as "DOS text." Elsewhere in the computer field, it is usually called *ASCII*, short for "American Standard Code for Information Interchange."

DOS text is, in essence, the generic computer format. Nearly every program can both read text information and produce text results. Thus, you would use DOS text to communicate with programs that cannot produce any of the formats that WordPerfect's CONVERT program can use. For example, you would work with it to use documents produced by a non-CONVERTible word processor.

Menu option 1 is used to *Save* the document on the screen as a DOS text file whose name you specify. In making the conversion, WordPerfect translates codes for the Date, Paragraph Numbering, and Outline Numbering into text; strips off codes for Bold, Underline, Subscript, and other print formats; replaces codes for Tab, Tab Align, Flush Right, Indent, and Center with spaces; and discards footnotes and endnotes.

Options 2 and 3 both *Retrieve* a specified DOS text file into WordPerfect, but as the parenthesized comments indicate, they use different rules to arrange the text. Choosing option 2 makes WordPerfect copy the specified text file onto the screen and arrange it within the active margin settings.

However, option 2 only works well for files that contain line-oriented material such as lists. If a file contains paragraphs whose lines extend past WordPerfect's active right-hand margin, option 2 moves the excess material to the next line and puts a hidden [SRt] (Soft Return) code at the end of the shortened line. It also puts an [HRt] (Hard Return) code at the original end-of-line position.

```
Document Conversion, Summary and Comments

DOS Text File Format
   1 - Save
   2 - Retrieve (CR/LF becomes [HRt])
   3 - Retrieve (CR/LF in H-Zone becomes [SRt])

Locked Document Format
   4 - Save
   5 - Retrieve

Other Word Processor Formats
   6 - Save in a generic word processor format
   7 - Save in WordPerfect 4.1 format

Document Summary and Comments
   A - Create/Edit Summary
   B - Create Comment
   C - Edit Comment
   D - Display Summary and Comments
```

Figure T-6. WordPerfect 4.2's Text In/Out menu.

In regular text, WordPerfect inserts an [SRt] code when it moves excess material to a new line; it inserts an [HRt] code when *you* press Enter at the end of a paragraph. Thus, in effect, option 2 splits a text file paragraph into several paragraphs. As Figure T-7 shows, option 2's paragraph-reformatting technique may produce WordPerfect text that's nowhere near what you want.

Fortunately, there's another way to retrieve a text file into Word-Perfect: by choosing option 3. Unlike option 2 (and the List Files command's equivalent option, Text In), the option 3 *Retrieve* simply rearranges a text file paragraph to fit within WordPerfect's margins. It remains one paragraph, not several. Choosing option 3 is usually the better way to retrieve a text file.

Saving and Retrieving Locked Documents

Options 4 and 5 of the Text In/Out menu let you save and retrieve documents in a "locked" format, for security purposes. A locked

```
The following is a paragraph within a text file:

    Text files are files on disk that contain only characters;
that is, letters or symbols. They contain no special control
codes (not even tabs), and therefore cannot represent bold,
underlined, subscripted, or superscripted material.

This is how the same paragraph is arranged when you load it into
WordPerfect using the Text In/Out option 2:

    Text files are files on disk that contain only characters;
that is, letters
or symbols. They contain no special control codes (not even
tabs), and therefore
cannot represent bold, underlined, subscripted, or superscripted
material.
```

Figure T-7. The effect of the Text In/Out command's *Retrieve* option 2 on a paragraph within a text file.

document is one to which you assign a password. After that, no one (not even you!) can retrieve the document unless they first enter the correct password.

To save the current document in locked format, choose option 4. When WordPerfect shows **Enter Password:**, enter a password of up to 75 characters. (Note that the password does not appear on the screen.) When it shows **Re-enter Password:**, enter the same password again. Finally, save the document as usual.

To retrieve and unlock a locked document, clear the screen, then press Ctrl-F5 and choose option 5. When WordPerfect shows **Document to be Retrieved:**, enter its name. When **Enter Password:** appears, enter the password you used to lock the document. When you're ready to send the document back to disk, you can either save it in locked format using option 4, or save an unlocked version of it under a different name using the regular Save or Exit command (here, press Enter when **Enter Password:** appears).

Another security feature is that locked documents can only be printed from the screen (by pressing Shift-PrtSc); neither the Print command nor the List Files *Print* option work with them.

Note that once a document has been locked, you cannot retrieve it unless you know the password. Therefore, be selective in deciding which documents to lock. Don't lock *anything* unless it's absolutely necessary. Finally, choose your password carefully, make it easy to remember (use, say, your Social Security number or birth date), and use the same password for every document you lock.

Document Summary and Comments

WordPerfect lets you attach a nonprinting document summary to your documents and insert nonprinting comments throughout a document. These features are described under **Document Summary** and **Document Comments**.

Text In/Out Command (Ctrl-F5) — WordPerfect 5.0

5.0

WordPerfect 5.0's Text In/Out command can do the following jobs:

- Save the document on the screen as an ASCII "DOS" text file, or retrieve a DOS text file into WordPerfect.
- Save the document on the screen in a "locked" form, for security purposes, or retrieve a locked document into WordPerfect.
- Save the document on the screen in a generic word processing format.
- Save the document on the screen in WordPerfect 4.2 format.
- Create and edit nonprinting document comments.

When you press Ctrl and F5 to give a Text In/Out command, WordPerfect displays the following menu at the bottom of the screen:

```
1 DOS Text; 2 Password; 3 Save Generic; 4 Save WP 4.2; 5 Comment: 0
```

Saving and Retrieving DOS Text Files

Most computers transfer information internally as pure text. The WordPerfect manual refers to this format as "DOS text." Elsewhere in the computer field, it is usually called *ASCII*, short for "American Standard Code for Information Interchange."

DOS text is, in essence, the generic computer format. Nearly every program can both read text information and produce text results. Thus, you would use DOS text to communicate with programs that cannot produce any of the formats that WordPerfect's CONVERT program can use. For example, you would work with it to use documents produced by a non-CONVERTible word processor.

When you type **1** to choose *DOS Text* from the Text In/Out menu, WordPerfect displays the following submenu:

`1 Save; 2 Retrieve (CR/LF to HRt]); 3 Retrieve (CR/LF to [SRt] in HZone): 0`

Menu option 1 is used to *Save* the document on the screen as a DOS text file whose name you specify. In making the conversion, WordPerfect translates codes for the Date, Paragraph Numbering, and Outline Numbering into text; strips off codes for Bold, Underline, Subscript, and other print formats; replaces codes for Tab, Tab Align, Flush Right, Indent, and Center with spaces; and discards footnotes and endnotes.

Options 2 and 3 both *Retrieve* a specified DOS text file into WordPerfect, but as the parenthesized comments indicate, they use different rules to arrange the text. Choosing option 2 makes WordPerfect copy the specified text file onto the screen and arrange it within the active margin settings.

However, option 2 only works well for files that contain line-oriented material such as lists. If a file contains paragraphs whose lines extend past WordPerfect's active right-hand margin, option 2 moves the excess material to the next line and puts a hidden [SRt] (Soft Return) code at the end of the shortened line. It also puts an [HRt] (Hard Return) code at the original end-of-line position.

In regular text, WordPerfect inserts an [SRt] code when it moves excess material to a new line; it inserts an [HRt] code when *you* press Enter at the end of a paragraph. Thus, in effect, option 2 splits a text file paragraph into several paragraphs. (See Figure T-7 in the **Text In/Out Command** entry for WordPerfect 4.2.)

Fortunately, there's another way to retrieve a text file into WordPerfect: by choosing option 3. Unlike option 2 (and the List Files command's equivalent, Text In), the option 3 *Retrieve* simply rearranges a text file paragraph to fit within WordPerfect's margins. It remains one paragraph, not several. Choosing option 3 is usually the better way to retrieve a text file.

Saving and Retrieving Locked Documents

Option 2 of the Text In/Out menu lets you save and retrieve documents in a "locked" format, for security purposes. A locked document is one to which you assign a password. After that, no one (not even you!) can retrieve the document unless they first enter the correct password.

To save the current document in locked format, type **2** to choose *Password* from the Text In/Out menu. When WordPerfect displays this menu:

Password: 1 Add; **2** Remove: 0

type **1** for *Add*. When WordPerfect shows **Enter Password:**, enter a password of up to 25 characters. (Note that the password does not appear on the screen.) When it shows **Re-enter Password:**, enter the same password again. Finally, save the document as usual, with a Save (F10) or Exit (F7) command.

Another security feature is that locked documents can only be printed from the screen (by pressing Shift-PrtSc); neither the Print command nor the List Files *Print* option work with them.

Note that once a document has been locked, you cannot retrieve it unless you know the password. Therefore, be selective in deciding which documents to lock. Don't lock *anything* unless it's absolutely necessary. Finally, choose your password carefully, make it easy to remember (use, say, your Social Security number or birth date), and use the same password for every document you lock.

You can also unlock a document, by removing the password. To begin, retrieve the document into WordPerfect by giving a Retrieve (Shift-F10) command or giving a List Files (F5) command and choosing *Retrieve* from the menu. When WordPerfect shows **Enter Password:**, enter the password you used to lock the document. When you're ready to send the document back to disk, press Ctrl-F5 to give a Text In/Out command and type **2** for *Password*, then **2** to *Remove* the password. WordPerfect unlocks the document, and you can save or retrieve it without giving a password.

Document Comments

Option 5 of the Text In/Out menu lets you insert nonprinting comments throughout a document. This feature is described under **Document Comments**.

Thesaurus Command (Alt-F1)

WordPerfect's Thesaurus can display synonyms and (with Word-Perfect 4.2 or later) antonyms for a word on the screen, and replace that word with one from its list. It can also look up synonyms and antonyms for a word you type.

To begin, put the Thesaurus disk in drive B (replacing the data disk), then move the cursor to the word you want to look up—or to where that word belongs, if you haven't yet typed it. Finally, press Alt and F1 to give WordPerfect a Thesaurus command.

Finding Synonyms for Existing Words

When you start the Thesaurus, it searches for the specified word, then does one of two things. If the Thesaurus does not contain that particular word, it displays the message **Word not found** and the prompt **Word:** at the bottom of the screen. You can then enter another word (if, say, it's misspelled on the screen) or press the F1 (Cancel) key twice to get back to your document.

If your word is one the Thesaurus recognizes, it lists the synonyms—nouns, verbs, and adjectives—and antonyms, and shows this menu at the bottom of the screen:

```
1 Replace Word; 2 View Doc; 3 Look Up Word; 4 Clear Column: 0
```

Your choices are:

1. *Replace Word* makes the Thesaurus replace the word with one from the list. When you type **1**, the screen shows **Press letter for word**. Type the identifying letter of the synonym you want; the Thesaurus makes the replacement.
2. *View Doc* lets you leave the Thesaurus temporarily so you can display other parts of your text. Move through your document as you do during editing: with the arrow keys, PgUp, PgDn, and so on. To return to the Thesaurus (and to the original place in your text), press the F7 (Exit) key.
3. *Look Up Word*. If a synonym in the list is close to what you want, and it is preceded by a bullet, use this option to obtain synonyms for the listed word. The bullets mark words for which the Thesaurus has synonyms.

    Pressing **3** makes **Word:** and your word appear at the bottom of the screen. To obtain synonyms for a bulleted word, type its identifying letter and press Enter. The Thesaurus displays them in the next available column, and moves the lettering to that column. The lettered column is the active one. To activate a different column, press the → or ←key to select the next column or the preceding one.

4. *Clear Column* erases the active column and moves the lettering to the preceding column. It's handy if you looked up a word with option 3 and decided you didn't want any of the synonyms it produced. Clearing the column opens up more screen space for a preceding set of synonyms.

Finding Synonyms for New Words

You can also make the Thesaurus list synonyms for a word you haven't yet typed. To do this, put the cursor on the space where the new word belongs, then start the Thesaurus. When **Word:** appears at the bottom of the screen, enter the word you want to look up. The operation then proceeds just as it would with an existing word.

Time, Inserting the

— See **Date Command** (for WordPerfect 4.1 or 4.2) or **Date/Outline Command** (for WordPerfect 5.0)

Timed Backup

— See **Backups**

Top Margin

WordPerfect is preset to provide a one-inch margin at the top of each page. If you are printing on letterhead paper, you may want to increase this margin.

Top Margin for the Current Document

To change the current document's top margin, do one of the following:

Top Margin

**4.1
4.2**
- **For WordPerfect 4.1 or 4.2**, press Alt and F8 to obtain the Page Format menu, and type **5** to select *Top Margin*. WordPerfect measures the top margin in "half-lines." Since it prints six lines per inch of paper, it displays the prompt

    ```
    Set half-lines (12/inch) from 12 to
    ```

    and waits for you to enter a new value. To provide a two-inch margin at the top, for example, enter **24**.

5.0
- **For WordPerfect 5.0**, press Shift and F8 to give a Format command and type **2** for *Page*. When the Page Format menu appears, type **6** to reach the *Margins - Top* field. Enter the margin value you want (e.g., enter **2** for two inches), then press F7 (Exit) to return to your document.

Top Margin for New Documents

You can also change the top margin value permanently, so WordPerfect uses it for each document you create. To do this:

**4.1
4.2**
- **For WordPerfect 4.1 or 4.2**, start WordPerfect by entering **wp/s** (instead of the usual **wp**). When the Set-up Menu appears, type **2** for *Set Initial Settings*. When the Initial Settings menu appears, press Alt-F8, give a Page Format command, and change the Top Margin using the procedure I just described.

5.0
- **For WordPerfect 5.0**, press Shift and F1 to obtain the Setup menu and type **5** to select *Initial Settings*. When the Initial Settings menu appears, type **5** for *Initial Codes*, then use the WordPerfect 5.0 procedure I just described.

Totals

— See **Math/Columns Command**

Triple-Spacing

— See **Spacing**

Typeover Mode (Ins)

WordPerfect normally inserts characters as you type them, by pushing existing material to the right. However, by pressing the Ins key (bottom left-hand corner of the numeric keypad), you can put WordPerfect in a *Typeover* mode in which it replaces old characters with ones you type. WordPerfect reminds you that Typeover is active by showing **Typeover** at the bottom left-hand corner of the screen. The Typeover mode remains in effect until you press Ins again.

Typeover is handy for making corrections that are about the same length as the originals, but quite different. For example, suppose you type "He can precede" instead of "He may proceed." To correct this error, move the cursor to the "c" in "can," press Ins to put WordPerfect in Typeover mode, type **may proceed**, then press Ins again to put WordPerfect back in the Insert mode. Sometimes typing over characters is quicker and more natural than inserting and deleting them.

Special Keys for Typeover Mode

In Typeover mode, the Backspace and Tab keys work differently than they do in the normal Insert mode. Pressing Backspace in Typeover mode moves the cursor to the preceding character and replaces that character with a space. Pressing Tab in Typeover mode moves the cursor to the next tab stop, but does not affect the text it passes over (nor does it insert a [Tab] code in the text).

WordPerfect 5.0 also has key sequences that let you force WordPerfect into Typeover or Insert mode, regardless of which mode it was in originally. Specifically, pressing Home, then Ins forces WordPerfect into Typeover mode, while pressing Home *twice*, then Ins, forces it into Insert mode. These commands come in handy in macros, where you can't anticipate which mode WordPerfect is in when the user runs the macro.

Typing Directly to the Printer

WordPerfect provides a *Type-thru* (spelled *Type Through* in WordPerfect 5.0) option that makes your computer operate like a typewriter, by printing lines of text or characters as you enter them. For details, see **Print Command**.

Undeleting

This book's **Deleting** entry describes the ways you can delete material with WordPerfect. You can delete a character by pressing Del or Backspace, a word by pressing Ctrl-Backspace, and the rest of a line or page by pressing Ctrl-End or Ctrl-PgDn. You can also delete a sentence, clause, or paragraph you selected with a Move command, or delete a block you selected in Block mode.

When you delete text using any of these methods, WordPerfect does not immediately discard it but instead temporarily saves it in the computer's memory. In fact, WordPerfect retains text from the last *three* deletions.

To recycle deleted text, move the cursor to where you want it to appear and press the F1 (Cancel) key. Here, Cancel serves as an *Undelete* key, and makes WordPerfect show the text, highlighted, at the cursor position and display the following menu at the bottom of the screen:

```
Undelete 1 Restore; 2 Show Previous Deletion: 0
```

Now you have three choices: to undelete or restore the shaded text, type **1**; to show the text from the preceding deletion, type **2**; to return to editing (if you pressed F1 by mistake), press Enter.

As an illustration of restoring deleted text, let's suppose you absent-mindedly transposed Raymond Morris' name in the telephone list—entering *Raymond, Morris* instead of *Morris, Raymond*—so you must switch these words. To begin, move the cursor to the "R" in "Raymond," then press Ctrl and Backspace. "Raymond, " disappears. Then move the cursor to the space after Morris and type a comma and a space. The cursor is now where *Raymond* belongs, so press F1, then 1, to retrieve "Raymond, " from memory and insert it. (Note that the word is still in memory, so you can insert it somewhere else if you want to.) Finally, press Backspace twice to delete the extra space and the comma.

Underlining

Writers use underlining for emphasis, or to indicate a new term, a book title, or a magazine name. You can also use it to create mathematical symbols such as > or +.

Underlining Existing Text

To underline material, put the cursor at the start of it, press Alt and F4 to put WordPerfect in Block mode, extend the highlighting to cover the text to be underlined, then press the F8 to give WordPerfect an Underline command. Remember, you can select a word with Ctrl and →, a line with End, a sentence by typing the ending punctuation mark, or a paragraph by pressing Enter. For example, if your sales letter says

We must reduce the inventories of bedspreads this month.

you may want to underline *must* for emphasis. To do this, move the cursor to *m*, then press Alt-F4 (for Block mode), → four times (to extend the highlighting), and F8 (to underline the block). Pressing F8 here takes WordPerfect out of Block mode.

Underlining New Text

You can also make WordPerfect underline material as you type it. When you get to where the underlining should begin, press F8. After that, WordPerfect will underline everything—even spaces—until you press F8 again. For example, suppose you want to enter

Our company's name is <u>Frank O. Gold, Inc.</u>, not Franco Goldink, as in your recent article.

To produce it, you would type normally up to the *F* in *Frank*, then press F8. Type **Frank O. Gold, Inc.** (WordPerfect underlines it), press F8 again, and finish the sentence.

Note, incidentally, that while underlining is active, WordPerfect underlines the *Pos* value at the bottom right-hand corner of the screen.

Removing Underlining

When you underline something, WordPerfect precedes it with a hidden [U] code and follows it with a [u] code (or [UNDRLN] and [undrln], in WordPerfect 5.0). To remove the underlining, put the cursor on the first underlined character, then press Alt and F3 to give a Reveal Codes command. When the Reveal Codes screen appears, move the cursor just ahead of the [U] and press Del to delete it. (WordPerfect deletes the matching [u] code automatically.) Then press Alt-F3 to return to your document.

Double-Underlining

Besides underlining material, WordPerfect can also put a double underline beneath it. For details, see **Double-Underlining**.

Underline Styles

WordPerfect is preset to underline words and the spaces between them, but not the space created when you move the cursor with a Tab, Tab Align (Ctrl-F6), Flush Right (Alt-F6), or Indent (F4 or Shift-F4) operation. However, this is simply the underline style that WordPerfect assumes you want. You can easily switch to a different style.

4.1
4.2

WordPerfect 4.1 and 4.2 provide four different underline styles, called *Non-continuous Single* (the preset style), *Non-continuous Double*, *Continuous Single*, and *Continuous Double*. The Continuous styles underline Tabs, Tab Aligns, and so on; the Non-continuous styles do not. To change the underline style, press Ctrl and F8 to give a Print Format command. When the Print Format menu appears, type **5**, **6**, **7**, or **8** to select the new style. Note that besides specifying whether underlining should be continuous or non-continuous, your menu selection determines whether pressing the F8 (Underline) key should produce single- or double-underlining.

5.0 WordPerfect 5.0 is more flexible; it lets you specify whether regular spaces, as well as Tabs, etc., are to be underlined. To change the underline style, press Shift and F8 to give a Format command, and type **4** for *Other*. When the Other Format menu appears, type **7** for *Underline,* then type **y** or **n** to control underlining for Spaces and Tabs. When you finish, press F7 (Exit) to return to your document. WordPerfect will then use your underlining rules for both single and double underlining.

When you switch underline styles, WordPerfect 4.1 and 4.2 insert a hidden code of the form [Undrl Style:*n*] in your document, where *n* is the style number (5, 6, 7, or 8). WordPerfect 5.0 marks an underline style change with a code of the form [Undrl:Spaces,Tabs], where the word *Spaces* appears if spaces get underlined and *Tabs* appears if Tabs, Tab Aligns, etc. get underlined. The code [Undrl:] indicates that neither spaces nor tabs get underlined (i.e. WordPerfect only underlines text).

Units of Measure — WordPerfect 5.0

5.0 WordPerfect normally displays margins, tab settings, box dimensions, and other measurements in inches, and it displays the status line's *Ln* and *Pos* values in lines and columns, respectively. However, you easily can make it use one of several other units of measure. To do this, press Shift and F1 to give a Setup command, and type **8** to obtain the *Units of Measure* menu shown in Figure U-1.

As you can see, the menu provides options that let you specify the units for numeric values (e.g., margin and tab settings) and the status line's *Ln* and *Pos* values. Type **1** or **2** to select the option you want to change, then type the character that represents the new unit. That is, type **"** or **i** for inches, **c** for centimeters, **p** for points, or **u** for the WordPerfect 4.2-style units—lines for vertical values and columns for horizontal values. (A *point* is a common measuring unit in the typesetting field. It represents 1/72 inches.) When you finish, press F7 (Exit) to record your changes and return to editing.

```
Setup: Units of Measure

1 - Display and Entry of Numbers      "
    for Margins, Tabs, etc.

2 - Status Line Display               u

Legend:

" = inches
i = inches
c = centimeters
p = points
u = WordPerfect 4.2 Units (Lines/Columns)


Selection: 0
```

Figure U-1. WordPerfect 5.0's Units of Measure menu.

Unlocking Documents

— See **Text In/Out Command**

Uppercase Letters

— See **Capitalizing**

Using Other Programs With WordPerfect

— See **Convert Program**

V

Variables — WordPerfect 5.0

5.0

As you may know, WordPerfect lets you record a sequence of keystrokes in a *macro*. When you create a macro, you must either give it a name or assign it to an Alt-*letter* key combination (Alt-A, Alt-B, etc.). After that, you can make WordPerfect replay your keystrokes by invoking the macro by name or key combination.

With WordPerfect 5.0, you can also use the ten Alt-*number* key combinations (that is, Alt-0 through Alt-9) to hold *variables*. A variable can be an integer (a number with no decimal point, such as 3 or 122), a simple calculation, or a block of text. Once you create a variable, you can insert its integer, calculation result, or block by pressing the Alt-*number* keys.

To assign an integer to an Alt-*number* combination, press Ctrl and PgUp, which the WordPerfect manual calls "Macro Commands." When the **Variable:** prompt appears on the bottom line, type the number you want (0 to 9). When the **Value:** prompt appears, enter the integer you want. For example, to make WordPerfect insert 567 whenever you press Alt-4, enter **4** for **Variable:**, then **567** for **Value:**.

If you assign a calculation to an Alt-*number* combination, Word-Perfect will insert the result of the calculation. The calculation must be fairly simple, however. It can only consist of two numbers, and both must be integers. If we call the numbers *v1* and *v2*, the available calculations are:

- **v1+v2** adds v1 and v2 and assigns the sum to the variable.
- **v1-v2** subtracts v2 from v1 and assigns the difference to the variable.
- **v1*v2** multiplies v1 by v2 and assigns the product to the variable.
- **v1/v2** divides v1 by v2 and assigns the integer quotient to the variable.
- **v1%v2** divides v1 by v2 and assigns the *remainder* to the variable.

For example, if you type **1** for **Variable:** and enter **25*36** for **Value:**, WordPerfect will insert 900 whenever you press Alt-1.

To assign a block of text to a variable, highlight it in Block mode, press Ctrl-PgUp, and type a number in response to the **Variable:** prompt. WordPerfect includes any Tab, Indent, Hard Page (Ctrl-Enter), and Required Hyphen codes in the block, but discards other formatting codes. Thus, the block you insert will not have any bold text, underlines, subscripts, and so on.

You can think of variables as temporary macros; they only exist until you leave WordPerfect.

Vertical Line Precedes Text

— See **Redlining Text**

View Document Option — WordPerfect 5.0

5.0

WordPerfect 5.0 has a *View Document* feature that shows how pages in your document will look when you print them. Besides text, the View Document screen shows headers, footers, footnotes, endnotes, margins, graphics, and any other elements on a page.

To begin, move to the first page you want to preview, press Shift and F7 to give a Print command, then type **6** to *View Document*. WordPerfect displays a miniaturized version of the current page as it will be printed, and shows the following menu at the bottom:

```
1 100%; 2 200%; 3 Full Page; 4 Facing Pages: 3
```

Here, typing **1** makes WordPerfect display the page in its true size, while typing **2** displays it double-sized. Typing **4** produces two miniaturized *Facing Pages*, with an even-numbered page on the left and an odd-numbered page on the right.

You can move forward or backward through the document using the regular cursor-moving keys. (You may not edit the document, however.) When you finish looking at your handiwork, press F7 (Exit) to return to your document.

Widow and Orphan Lines

When you enter material into a document, WordPerfect simply fills each page to capacity. Unlike a good typist, it may leave the first line of a paragraph alone at the bottom of a page (a *widow*) or leave the last line at the top of a new page (an *orphan*). Fortunately, you can break it of this habit.

To make WordPerfect keep the first and last two lines of a paragraph together on a page, put the cursor at the beginning of your document (press Home *twice*, then ↑ will do the job) and perform one of the following procedures.

4.1
4.2
- **For WordPerfect 4.1 or 4.2**, press Alt and F8 to give a Page Format command. When the Page Format menu appears, type **a** for *Widow/Orphan*. When WordPerfect shows **Widow/Orphan Protect (Y/N): N**, type **y** (for yes). Press Enter to return to editing.

5.0
- **For WordPerfect 5.0**, press Shift and F8 to give a Format command, and type **1** for *Line*. When the Line Format menu appears, type **9** to reach the *Widow/Orphan Protection* field. Type **y** (for yes), then press F7 (Exit) to return to your document.

WordPerfect only applies widow/orphan protection to paragraphs that have four or more lines. (That's reasonable. If a paragraph has three lines, WordPerfect would have to put two on one page and one on the other, regardless of what kind of protection you specified.)

Winding Columns

— See **Columns, Text**

Windows, Document

WordPerfect lets you work with two different documents (or two different parts of the same document) at a time, by putting each in a text area called a *window*. Once you have set up the second window, you can work in either of them.

Why would you want to use two windows? You can, for example:

1. Examine previous correspondence, a contract, or other document while writing a letter. You may even want to copy sections from that document.
2. Look back at an earlier report to be sure you are using the same format, terminology, or spelling.
3. Examine an outline while you write, and check off sections as you finish them.
4. Take figures, tables, or terminology from old versions of a document, partial or extended versions, or standard forms. Thus, you could use part of last year's report or the last project's contract in a new report or contract. You could also combine weekly reports into a monthly report or excerpt a brief synopsis from a complete project report.

WordPerfect's main work area is itself a window (#1, as indicated by *Doc 1* on the status line). WordPerfect will label the second window *Doc 2*.

WordPerfect gives you two ways to display windows. You can make it show each window as a separate screen or you can make it split the screen horizontally, and show both windows at the same time.

Full-Screen Windows

To make WordPerfect show the second window as a separate screen, press Shift and F3 to give a Switch command. This brings on a blank screen with the cursor at the top left-hand corner and *Doc 2* at the beginning of the status line. Now you can create a new document or retrieve an existing one. When you want to switch back to the first window, press Shift-F3 again.

Note that the windows are independent. Once you Retrieve a document into a window, it is a separate entity. You can work on it without affecting the document in the other window.

Splitting the Screen

To divide the editing screen into two windows, press Ctrl-F3 for Screen. When the Screen menu appears, type 1 for *Window*. This produces the prompt

```
# Lines in this Window: 24
```

where the 24 indicates that the current window occupies 24 lines; in other words, the entire screen.

Now you can either enter the number of lines you want in the active window (2 or more) or press the up-arrow or down-arrow key until a reverse-video bar (the Tab Ruler) appears. Note that the # *Lines* value changes as you move the Tab Ruler. Continue pressing the arrow key until the bottom window is the size you want, then press Enter.

Activating Windows

At this point, the second window is visible, but the original window is still active. To switch to the second window (i.e., make it active), press Shift-F3 for Switch. The cursor moves to the top of the second window. Pressing Shift-F3 again reactivates the first window.

Operating on Windows

WordPerfect treats the active window just like the full screen. You can edit, move the cursor, retrieve or save a document, issue commands, and so on.

The only special part of moving text to another window is that you must remember to switch windows. That is, you go through the usual process of using the Move command to select the text and either Move or Copy it. You must then press Shift-F3 to switch windows. Now you can finish the task by moving the cursor to where you want the text and doing another Move to paste it.

Closing a Window

When you finish using a window, you can close it. To close a full-screen window—one that you switched to by pressing Shift-F3—press F7 to give an Exit command. Then respond to WordPerfect's **Save Document?** prompt (and, if you answered yes, to the **Document to be Saved** and **Replace** prompts) and type **n** or press Enter when **Exit Doc 2?** appears.

To close a window on a split screen, press Shift-F3 to switch to the other window, then press Ctrl-F3 to obtain the Screen menu and select *Window*. When the **# Lines in this Window** message appears, enter **24**. The Tab Ruler and window text disappear.

Closing a split-screen window does not affect its contents; it simply makes WordPerfect move those contents to the alternate, full-screen window. You can still reach that window with Switch. Thus, if you give an Exit command from either window, WordPerfect will display the *Save* and *Replace* prompts for that window, then ask if you want to *Exit* to the other window.

Word Count

To get a count of the number of words in a document, press Ctrl and F2 to give WordPerfect a Spell command. When the Spell menu appears, type **6** to select *Count*. WordPerfect shows *** Please Wait *** while it counts, then displays the word count at the bottom of the screen. Press Enter twice to return to your document.

Counting Words in a Block

Choosing the Spell command's *Count* option makes WordPerfect count the words in the entire document. To make it count words in some portion of a document, such as a paragraph or a poem, highlight the text in Block mode and press Ctrl-F2 to give a Spell command. This makes WordPerfect spell-check the block. If you only care about the word count, and not whether there are misspellings, type 1 (for Skip) whenever the *Not Found!* message appears. WordPerfect will show the word count when it finishes spell-checking.

Word Left and Right Commands (Ctrl-← and Ctrl-→)

Pressing Ctrl-← moves the cursor to the beginning of the preceding word or (if the cursor is not at the beginning of a word) current word. Pressing Ctrl-→ moves the cursor to the beginning of the next word, regardless of the initial cursor position.

Word Search

Sometimes you want to determine whether a specific word or phrase appears in your current document. To find out, follow the procedures described under **Search Commands**. You may also want to find out which documents on a disk contain a specific word or phrase (say, a company name); this is described under **List Files Command**.

WordPerfect Commands

— See **Appendix A, B, or C**

WordPerfect, Leaving

You should always use the Exit command to leave WordPerfect, rather than just turn the computer off. That is, press F7 to give an Exit command, save the current document (unless you have already done so or want to discard it), then type **y** in response to the **Exit WP?** prompt. When the DOS prompt (B> or C>) appears, simply switch the power off if you are done.

WordPerfect, Starting

— See **Starting WordPerfect**

WordPerfect, Using Other Programs With

— See **Convert Program**

WordStar Files

— See **Convert Program**

Appendix A
WordPerfect 4.1 Features

Advance Down	Shift-F1, 5
Advance to Line	Shift-F1, 6
Advance Up	Shift-F1, 4
Align Character	Shift-F8, 6
Alt Key Mapping	Ctrl-F3, 3
Append Block	Alt-F4, Ctrl-F4, 3
Auto Rewrite	Ctrl-F3, 5
Bin Number, Sheet Feeder	Ctrl-F8, 9
Binding Width	Shift-F7, 3, 3
Block	
Append	Alt-F4, Ctrl-F4, 3
Center	Alt-F4, Shift-F6
Copy	Alt-F4, Ctrl-F4, 2
Cut	Alt-F4, Ctrl-F4, 1
Delete	Alt-F4, Del, Y
Mode	Alt-F4
Protect	Alt-F4, Alt-F8
Bold	F6
^C (Text from Keyboard)	Alt-F9, C
Cancel	F1
Cancel Merge Operation	Shift-F9
Cancel Print Job(s)	Shift-F7, 4, C
Capitalize text	Alt-F4, Shift-F3, 1
Center Line	Shift-F6
Center Page Top to Bottom	Alt-F8, 3
Change Directory	F5, Enter, 7
Change Print Options	Shift-F7, 3

Colors, Screen	Ctrl-F3, 4
Columns, Text	
Definition	Alt-F7, 4
On/Off	Alt-F7, 3
Comment, Document	
Create	Ctrl-F5, B
Edit	Ctrl-F5, C
Conditional End of Page	Alt-F8, 9
Copy	Ctrl-F4
Block	Alt-F4, Ctrl-F4, 2
Column	Alt-F4, Ctrl-F4, 4
File	F5, Enter, 8
Page	Ctrl-F4, 3, 2
Paragraph	Ctrl-F4, 2, 2
Rectangle	Alt-F4, Ctrl-F4, 5
Sentence	Ctrl-F4, 1, 2
Ctrl Key Mapping	Ctrl-F3, 3
Cut (Move)	
Block	Alt-F4, Ctrl-F4, 1
Column	Alt-F4, Ctrl-F4, 4
Page	Ctrl-F4, 3, 1
Paragraph	Ctrl-F4, 2, 1
Rectangle	Alt-F4, Ctrl-F4, 5
Sentence	Ctrl-F4, 1, 1
^D (Date)	Alt-F9, D
Date	
Format	Shift-F5, 2
Function	Shift-F5, 3
Text	Shift-F5, 1
Define	
Index	Alt-F5, 6, 8
List	Alt-F5, 6, 1-5
Macro	Ctrl-F10
Paragraph/Outline Numbering	Alt-F5, 6, 7
Table of Contents	Alt-F5, 6, 6
Delete	
Block	Alt-F4, Del
Character	Del (current) or Backspace (preceding)
End of Line	Ctrl-End
End of Page	Ctrl-PgDn
File	F5, Enter, 2
Page	Ctrl-F4, 3, 1

Paragraph	Ctrl-F4, 2, 1
Sentence	Ctrl-F4, 1, 1
Word	Ctrl-Backspace
Display All Print Jobs	Shift-F7, 4, D
Display Printers and Fonts	Shift-F7, 4, 2
DOS, go to	Ctrl-F1, 1
DOS Text File	
Retrieve	Ctrl-F5, 2
Save	Ctrl-F5, 1
Double Underline	Ctrl-F8, 6 or 8, then F8
Draw Line	Ctrl-F3, 2
^E (End of Record)	Shift-F9
End of Page, Conditional	Alt-F8, 9
Endnote	
Create	Ctrl-F7, 5
Edit	Ctrl-F7, 6
E-Tabs	Shift-F8, 2
Exit and Save Document	F7, Enter, Enter, Y, Y
^F (Field)	Alt-F9, F
Flush Right	Alt-F6
Font	Ctrl-F8, 1
Fonts, Display	Shift-F7, 4, 2
Footers	Alt-F8, 6
Footnote	
Create	Ctrl-F7, 1
Edit	Ctrl-F7, 2
New Number	Ctrl-F7, 3
Options	Ctrl-F7, 4
^G (Start Macro)	Alt-F9, G
Generate Table of Contents, Lists, and Index	Alt-F5, 7, Y
Go (Resume Printing)	Shift-F7, 4, G
Go To	Ctrl-Home
Go to DOS	Ctrl-F1, 1
Headers	Alt-F8, 6
Help	F3
Hyphenation	Shift-F8, 5
Indent	
Left	F4

Left/Right	Shift-F4
Index	
Define	Alt-F5, 6, 8
Mark for	Alt-F4, Alt-F5, 5
Justification, Right	
Off	Ctrl-F8, 3
On	Ctrl-F8, 4
Left Indent	F4
Left/Right Indent	Shift-F4
Line	
Draw	Ctrl-F3, 2
Format	Shift-F8
Spacing	Shift-F8, 4
Lines per Inch	Ctrl-F8, 2
List	
Define	Alt-F5, 6, 1-5
Mark for	Alt-F4, Alt-F5, 2
List Files	F5, Enter
Locked Document	
Retrieve	Ctrl-F5, 4
Save	Ctrl-F5, 3
Look at (View) File	F5, Enter, 6
Lowercase, convert text to	Alt-F4, Shift-F3, 2
Macro	
Define	Ctrl-F10
Start	Alt-F10
Margin Release	Shift-Tab
Margins	
Left/Right	Shift-F8, 3
Top	Alt-F8, 5
Mark Block	
for Index	Alt-F4, Alt-F5, 5
for List	Alt-F4, Alt-F5, 2
for Redline	Alt-F4, Alt-F5, 3
for Strikeout	Alt-F4, Alt-F5, 4
for Table of Contents	Alt-F4, Alt-F5, 1
Mark Text	
Index	Alt-F5, 5
Outline	Alt-F5, 1
Paragraph Number	Alt-F5, 2
Redline	Alt-F5, 3

Short Form	Alt-F5, 4
Math	
On	Alt-F7, 1
Definition	Alt-F7, 2
Merge	Ctrl-F9, 1
Cancel	Shift-F9
Codes	Alt-F9
E (^E)	Shift-F9
R (^R)	F9
Move	Ctrl-F4
Block	Alt-F4, Ctrl-F4, 1
Column	Alt-F4, Ctrl-F4, 4
Page	Ctrl-F4, 3, 1
Paragraph	Ctrl-F4, 2, 1
Rectangle	Alt-F4, Ctrl-F4, 5
Sentence	Ctrl-F4, 1, 1
^N (Next Record)	Alt-F9, N
Name Search	F5, Enter, (name)
New Page	Ctrl-Enter
New Page Number	Alt-F8, 2
Number of Copies	Shift-F7, 3, 2
^O (Display Message)	Alt-F9, O
Outline	Alt-F5, 1
Overstrike	Shift-F1, 3
^P (Primary File)	Alt-F9, P
Page	
Center Top to Bottom	Alt-F8,3
Format	Alt-F8
Format, Suppress	Alt-F8, 8
Length	Alt-F8, 4
New	Ctrl-Enter
New Number	Alt-F8,2
Number Column Positions	Alt-F8, 7
Number Position	Alt-F8, 1
Print	Shift-F7, 2
Paragraph	
Number, insert	Alt-F5, 2
Numbering Definition	Alt-F5, 6, 7
Pitch	Ctrl-F8, 1
Print	Shift-F7
Block	Alt-F4, Shift-F7

Appendix A: WordPerfect 4.1 Features

Disk Document	Shift-F7, 4, P or F5, Enter, 4
Format	Ctrl-F8
Full Text (Document)	Shift-F7, 1
Job(s), Cancel	Shift-F7, 4, A
Jobs, Display All	Shift-F7, 4, D
List Files	F5, Enter, 4
Options, Change	Shift-F7, 3
Options, Select	Shift-F7, 4, 1
Page	Shift-F7, 2
Screen	Shift-PrtSc
Printer	
Command	Ctrl-F8, A
Control	Shift-F7, 4
Number	Shift-F7, 3, 1
Printers, Display	Shift-F7, 4, 2
Printers, Select	Shift-F7, 4, 3
Printing, Resume (Go)	Shift-F7, 4, G
Printing, Stop	Shift-F7, 4, S
Proportional Spacing	Ctrl-F8, 1
^Q (Stop Merge)	Alt-F9, Q
^R (End of Field)	Alt-F9, R
Redline	Alt-F5, 3
Remove Redline/Strikeout	Alt-F5, 4, Y
Rename File	F5, Enter, 3
Repeat Next Command	Esc
Replace	Alt-F2
Resume Printing (Go)	Shift-F7, 4, G
Retrieve	
Cut or Copied Column	Ctrl-F4, 4
Cut or Copied Rectangle	Ctrl-F4, 6
Cut or Copied Text or Block	Ctrl-F4, 5
Document	Shift-F10 or F5, Enter, 1
Text File	F5, Enter, 5 or Ctrl-F5, 2 or 3
Return to Previous Place	Ctrl-Home, Ctrl-Home
Rewrite Screen	Ctrl-F3, 0
Reveal Codes	Alt-F3
Right Justification	
Off	Ctrl-F8, 3
On	Ctrl-F8, 4
Rush Print Job	Shift-F7, 4, R
^S (Secondary File)	Alt-F9, S

Save
  Document   F10
  Document and Exit   F7, Enter, Enter, Y, Y
  DOS Text File   Ctrl-F5, 1
  Locked Document   Ctrl-F5, 3
Screen   Ctrl-F3
Screen Colors   Ctrl-F3, 4
Screen, Split   Ctrl-F3, 1
Search
  Backward   Shift-F2
  Forward   F2
Select Print Options   Shift-F7, 4, 1
Select Printers   Shift-F7, 4, 3
Sheet Feeder Bin Number   Ctrl-F8, 9
Shell   Ctrl-F1
Sort   Ctrl-F9, 2
Sorting Sequences   Ctrl-F9, 3
Spacing, Line   Shift-F8, 4
Spell   Ctrl-F2
Split Screen   Ctrl-F3, 1
Start Macro   Alt-F10
Stop Printing   Shift-F7, 4, S
Strikeout, mark text for   Alt-F4, Alt-F5, 4
Strikeout text, remove   Alt-F5, 4, Y
Subscript   Shift-F1, 2
Superscript   Shift-F1, 1
Suppress Page Format   Alt-F8, 8
Switch Windows   Shift-F3

^T (Send to Printer)   Alt-F9, T
Tab Align   Ctrl-F6
Tab Set   Shift-F8, 1
Table of Contents
  Define   Alt-F5, 6, 6
  Mark for   Alt-F4, Alt-F5, 1
Text In (List Files)   F5, Enter, 5
Text In/Out   Ctrl-F5
Thesaurus   Alt-F1
Top Margin   Alt-F8, 5
Typeover On/Off   Ins
Type-thru   Shift-F7, 5

^U (Rewrite Screen)   Alt-F9, U
Undelete   F1

Feature	Keys
Underline	F8
Underline, Double	Ctrl-F8, 6 or 8, then F8
Underline Style	Ctrl-F8, 5 - 8
Uppercase, convert text to	Alt-F4, Shift-F3, 1
^V (Insert Merge Code)	Alt-F9, V
Widow/Orphan Protect	Alt-F8, A
Window	Ctrl-F3, 1
Word Count	Ctrl-F2, 6
Word Search	F5, Enter, 9

Initial Settings

Following is a summary of WordPerfect 4.1's initial settings. To change a setting, start WordPerfect by entering **wp/s**, instead of the usual **wp**. When the Set-up Menu appears, type **2** to select *Set Initial Settings*. When the Change Initial Settings menu appears, obtain the feature you want to change by pressing the keys listed in the right-hand column.

Feature	**Initially set to**	**To obtain, press**
Align Character	. (period)	Shift-F8, 6
Auto Rewrite	On (reformat screen automatically)	Ctrl-F3
Binding Width	0 (Enter 1/10-inch values)	Shift-F7, 3
Date Format	Month Day, Year (e.g., May 29, 1988)	Shift-F5
Endnote numbering mode	0 (Numbers)	Ctrl-F7, 6
E-Tabs	Every 10 spaces, starting at column 160	Shift-F8, 2
Font	1	Ctrl-F8, 1, Enter
Foonote numbering mode	0 (Numbers)	Ctrl-F7, 5
Footnotes at bottom of page	Yes	Ctrl-F7, 8

Hyphenation	Off	Shift-F8, 5
Insert/Typeover	Insert mode	Ins
Line separating text and footnotes	1 (2-inch line)	Ctrl-F7, 8
Line Spacing	Single	Shift-F8, 4
Lines in notes to keep together	3	Ctrl-F7, 3
Lines per inch	6	Ctrl-F8, 2
Margin, Top	12 half-lines (one inch)	Alt-F8, 5
Margins, Side	Left = 10, Right = 74 (one-inch margins)	Shift-F8, 3
Note numbering mode	Numbers	Ctrl-F7, 4
Number of Copies	1	Shift-F7, 2
Outline Numbering Style	Outline	Alt-F5, 1
Page Length	66 lines total, 54 text lines (8 1/2 by 11-inch paper)	Alt-F8, 4
Page Number Column Positions	Left = 10, Center = 42, Right = 74	Alt-F8, 7
Page Number Position	No page numbers	Alt-F8, 1
Paragraph/Outline Numbering Style	Outline	Alt-F5, 1
Pitch	10 characters per inch	Ctrl-F8, 1
Printer Number	1	Shift-F7, 1
Repeat value for Esc	8	Esc
Right Justification	On (Even right-hand margin)	Ctrl-F8, 3 or 4
Sheet Feeder Bin Number	1	Ctrl-F8, 9
Spacing, line	Single	Shift-F8, 4
Spacing between notes	1	Ctrl-F7, 2
Spacing within notes	1	Ctrl-F7, 1
Tabs	Every 5 spaces	Shift-F8, 1
Top Margin	12 half-lines (one inch)	Alt-F8, 5
Underline Style	Non-continuous single	Ctrl-F8, 5-8
Widow/Orphan Protect	No	Alt-F8, A

Appendix B
WordPerfect 4.2 Features

Advance Down	Shift-F1, 5
Advance to Line	Shift-F1, 6
Advance Up	Shift-F1, 4
Align Character	Shift-F8, 6
Alt Key Mapping	Ctrl-F3, 3
Append Block	Alt-F4, Ctrl-F4, 3
Auto Rewrite	Ctrl-F3, 5
Bin Number, Sheet Feeder	Ctrl-F8, 9
Binding Width	Shift-F7, 3, 3
Block	
Append	Alt-F4, Ctrl-F4, 3
Copy	Alt-F4, Ctrl-F4, 2
Cut	Alt-F4, Ctrl-F4, 1
Delete	Alt-F4, Del, Y
Mode	Alt-F4
Protect	Alt-F4, Alt-F8
Bold	F6
^C (Text from Keyboard)	Alt-F9, C
Cancel	F1
Cancel Merge Operation	Shift-F9
Cancel Print Job(s)	Shift-F7, 4, C
Capitalize text	Alt-F4, Shift-F3, 1
Center	Shift-F6
Center Page Top to Bottom	Alt-F8, 3
Change Directory	F5, Enter, 7
Change Print Options	Shift-F7, 3
Colors	Ctrl-F3, 4

Columns, Text	
Definition	Alt-F7, 4
Display side-by-side	Alt-F7, 5
On/Off	Alt-F7, 3
Comment, Document	
Create	Ctrl-F5, B
Edit	Ctrl-F5, C
Conditional End of Page	Alt-F8, 9
Copy	Ctrl-F4
Block	Alt-F4, Ctrl-F4, 2
Column	Alt-F4, Ctrl-F4, 4
File	F5, Enter, 8
Page	Ctrl-F4, 3, 2
Paragraph	Ctrl-F4, 2, 2
Rectangle	Alt-F4, Ctrl-F4, 5
Sentence	Ctrl-F4, 1, 2
Ctrl Key Mapping	Ctrl-F3, 3
Cut (Move)	
Block	Alt-F4, Ctrl-F4, 1
Column	Alt-F4, Ctrl-F4, 4
Page	Ctrl-F4, 3, 1
Paragraph	Ctrl-F4, 2, 1
Rectangle	Alt-F4, Ctrl-F4, 5
Sentence	Ctrl-F4, 1, 1
^D (Date)	Alt-F9, D
Date	
Format	Shift-F5, 2
Function	Shift-F5, 3
Text	Shift-F5, 1
Define	
Index	Alt-F5, 6, 5
List	Alt-F5, 6, 3
Macro	Ctrl-F10
Paragraph/Outline Numbering	Alt-F5, 6, 1
Table of Authorities	Alt-F5, 6, 4
Table of Contents	Alt-F5, 6, 2
Delete	
Block	Alt-F4, Del
Character	Del (current) or Backspace (preceding)
End of Line	Ctrl-End
End of Page	Ctrl-PgDn
File	F5, Enter, 2

Appendix B: WordPerfect 4.2 Features   461

Page	Ctrl-F4, 3, 3
Paragraph	Ctrl-F4, 2, 3
Sentence	Ctrl-F4, 1, 3
Word	Ctrl-Backspace
Display All Print Jobs	Shift-F7, 4, D
Display Printers and Fonts	Shift-F7, 4, 2
Document Comments	Ctrl-F5, B or C
Document Summary	Ctrl-F5, A
DOS, go to	Ctrl-F1, 1
DOS Text File	
Retrieve (CR/LF to [HRt])	Ctrl-F5, 1, 2
Retrieve (CR/LF to [SRt])	Ctrl-F5, 1, 3
Save	Ctrl-F5, 1, 1
Double Underline	Ctrl-F8, 6 or 8, then F8
Draw Line	Ctrl-F3, 2
^E (End of Record)	Shift-F9
Edit Table of Authorities Full Form	Alt-F5, 6, 7
End of Page, Conditional	Alt-F8, 9
Endnote	
Create	Ctrl-F7, 5
Edit	Ctrl-F7, 6
Exit and Save Document	F7, Enter, Enter, Y, Y
^F (Field)	Alt-F9, F
Flush Right	Alt-F6
Font	Ctrl-F8, 1
Fonts, Display	Shift-F7, 4, 2
Footers	Alt-F8, 6
Footnote	
Create	Ctrl-F7, 1
Edit	Ctrl-F7, 2
New Number	Ctrl-F7, 3
Options	Ctrl-F7, 4
^G (Start Macro)	Alt-F9, G
Generate Tables, Index, and Lists	Alt-F5, 6, 8
Generic Word Processor Format	Ctrl-F5, 6
Go (Resume Printing)	Shift-F7, 4, G
Go To	Ctrl-Home
Go to DOS	Ctrl-F1, 1

Headers	Alt-F8, 6
Help	F3
Hyphenation	Shift-F8, 5
Indent	
Left	F4
Left/Right	Shift-F4
Index	
Define	Alt-F5, 5
Mark for	Alt-F4, Alt-F5, 5
Justification, Right	
Off	Ctrl-F8, 3
On	Ctrl-F8, 4
Left Indent	F4
Left/Right Indent	Shift-F4
Line	
Draw	Ctrl-F3, 2
Format	Shift-F8
Numbering	Ctrl-F8, B
Spacing	Shift-F8, 4
Lines per Inch	Ctrl-F8, 2
List	
Define	Alt-F5, 6, 3
Mark for	Alt-F4, Alt-F5, 2
List Files	F5, Enter
Locked Document	
Retrieve	Ctrl-F5, 5
Save	Ctrl-F5, 4
Look at (View) File	F5, Enter, 6
Lowercase, convert text to	Alt-F4, Shift-F3, 2
Macro	
Define	Ctrl-F10
Start	Alt-F10
Margin Release	Shift-Tab
Margins	
Left/Right	Shift-F8, 3
Top	Alt-F8, 5
Mark Block	
for Index	Alt-F4, Alt-F5, 5
for List	Alt-F4, Alt-F5, 2
for Redline	Alt-F4, Alt-F5, 3

Appendix B: WordPerfect 4.2 Features 463

for Strikeout	Alt-F4, Alt-F5, 4
for Table of Authorities	Alt-F4, Alt-F5, 6
for Table of Contents	Alt-F4, Alt-F5, 1
Mark Text	
Index	Alt-F5, 5
Outline	Alt-F5, 1
Paragraph Number	Alt-F5, 2
Redline	Alt-F5, 3
Table of Auth. Short Form	Alt-F5, 4
Math	
On	Alt-F7, 1
Definition	Alt-F7, 2
Merge	Ctrl-F9, 1
Cancel	Shift-F9
Codes	Alt-F9
E (^E)	Shift-F9
R (^R)	F9
Move	Ctrl-F4
Block	Alt-F4, Ctrl-F4, 1
Column	Alt-F4, Ctrl-F4, 4
Page	Ctrl-F4, 3, 1
Paragraph	Ctrl-F4, 2, 1
Rectangle	Alt-F4, Ctrl-F4, 5
Sentence	Ctrl-F4, 1, 1
^N (Next Record)	Alt-F9, N
New Page	Ctrl-Enter
New Page Number	Alt-F8, 2
Number of Copies	Shift-F7, 3, 2
^O (Display Message)	Alt-F9, O
Outline	Alt-F5, 1
Overstrike	Shift-F1, 3
^P (Primary File)	Alt-F9, P
Page	
Center Top to Bottom	Alt-F8, 3
New Number	Alt-F8, 2
Format	Alt-F8
Format, Suppress	Alt-F8, 8
Length	Alt-F8, 4
New	Ctrl-Enter
New Number	Alt-F8, 2
Number Column Positions	Alt-F8, 7

Number Position	Alt-F8, 1
Print	Shift-F7, 2
Paragraph	
Number, insert	Alt-F5, 2
Numbering Definition	Alt-F5, 6, 1
Pitch	Ctrl-F8, 1
Preview	Shift-F7, 6
Print	Shift-F7
Block	Alt-F4, Shift-F7
Disk Document	Shift-F7, 4, P or F5, Enter, 4
Format	Ctrl-F8
Full Text (Document)	Shift-F7, 1
Job(s), Cancel	Shift-F7, 4, A
Jobs, Display All	Shift-F7, 4, D
List Files	F5, Enter, 4
Options, Change	Shift-F7, 3
Options, Select	Shift-F7, 4, 1
Page	Shift-F7, 2
Screen	Shift-PrtSc
Printer	
Command	Ctrl-F8, A
Control	Shift-F7, 4
Number	Shift-F7, 3, 1
Printers, Display	Shift-F7, 4, 2
Printers, Select	Shift-F7, 4, 3
Printing, Resume (Go)	Shift-F7, 4, G
Printing, Stop	Shift-F7, 4, S
Proportional Spacing	Ctrl-F8, 1
^Q (Stop Merge)	Alt-F9, Q
^R (End of Field)	Alt-F9, R
Redline	Alt-F5, 3
Remove Redline/Strikeout	Alt-F5, 6, 6, Y
Rename File	F5, Enter, 3
Repeat Next Command	Esc
Replace	Alt-F2
Replace Macro	Ctrl-F10
Replace, Extended	Home, Alt-F2
Resume Printing (Go)	Shift-F7, 4, G
Retrieve	
Cut or Copied Column	Ctrl-F4, 4
Cut or Copied Rectangle	Ctrl-F4, 6
Cut or Copied Text	Ctrl-F4, 5

Document	Shift-F10 or F5, Enter, 1
Text File	F5, Enter, 5 or Ctrl-F5, 2 or 3
Return to Previous Place	Ctrl-Home, Ctrl-Home
Rewrite Screen	Ctrl-F3, 0
Reveal Codes	Alt-F3
Right Justification	
Off	Ctrl-F8, 3
On	Ctrl-F8, 4
Rush Print Job	Shift-F7, 4, R
^S (Secondary File)	Alt-F9, S
Save	
Document	F10
Document and Exit	F7, Enter, Enter, Y, Y
DOS Text File	Ctrl-F5, 1
in Generic Word Proc. Format	Ctrl-F5, 6
in WordPerfect 4.1 Format	Ctrl-F5, 7
Locked Document	Ctrl-F5, 4
Screen	Ctrl-F3
Screen Colors	Ctrl-F3, 4
Screen, Split	Ctrl-F3, 1
Search	
Backward	Shift-F2
Backward, Extended	Home, Shift-F2
Forward	F2
Forward, Extended	Home, F2
Select Print Options	Shift-F7, 4, 1
Select Printers	Shift-F7, 4, 3
Sheet Feeder Bin Number	Ctrl-F8, 9
Shell	Ctrl-F1
Sort	Ctrl-F9, 2
Sorting Sequences	Ctrl-F9, 3
Spacing, Line	Shift-F8, 4
Spell	Ctrl-F2
Split Screen	Ctrl-F3, 1
Start Macro	Alt-F10
Stop Printing	Shift-F7, 4, S
Strikeout	Alt-F5, 4
Subscript	Shift-F1, 2
Superscript	Shift-F1, 1
Suppress Page Format	Alt-F8, 8
Switch Windows	Shift-F3
^T (Send to Printer)	Alt-F9, T

466 Appendix B: WordPerfect 4.2 Features

Tab Align	Ctrl-F6
Tab Set	Shift-F8, 1
Table of Authorities	
Define	Alt-F5, 6, 4
Edit Full Form	Alt-F5, 6, 7
Full Form	Alt-F4, Alt-F5, 6
Short Form	Alt-F5, 4
Table of Contents	
Define	Alt-F5, 6, 2
Mark for	Alt-F4, Alt-F5, 1
Text In (List Files)	F5, Enter, 5
Text In/Out	Ctrl-F5
Thesaurus	Alt-F1
Top Margin	Alt-F8, 5
Typeover On/Off	Ins
Type-thru	Shift-F7, 5
^U (Rewrite Screen)	Alt-F9, U
Undelete	F1
Underline	F8
Underline, Double	Ctrl-F8, 6 or 8, then F8
Underline Style	Ctrl-F8, 5 - 8
Uppercase, convert text to	Alt-F4, Shift-F3, 1
^V (Insert Merge Code)	Alt-F9, V
Widow/Orphan Protect	Alt-F8, A
Window	Ctrl-F3, 1
Word Count	Ctrl-F2, 6
Word Search	F5, Enter, 9
WordPerfect 4.1 Format	Ctrl-F5, 7

Initial Settings

Following is a summary of WordPerfect 4.2's initial settings. To change a setting, start WordPerfect by entering **wp/s**, instead of the usual **wp**. When the Set-up Menu appears, type **2** to select *Set Initial Settings*. When the Change Initial Settings menu appears, obtain the feature you want to change by pressing the keys listed in the right-hand column.

Feature	Initially set to	To obtain, press
Align Character	. (period)	Shift-F8, 6
Auto Rewrite	On (reformat screen automatically)	Ctrl-F3
Binding Width	0 (Enter 1/10-inch values)	Shift-F7, 3
Date Format	Month Day, Year (e.g., May 29, 1988)	Shift-F5
Endnote numbering mode	0 (Numbers)	Ctrl-F7, 6
Enter Document Summary on Save/Exit	No	Ctrl-F5
Font	1	Ctrl-F8, 1, Enter
Foonote numbering mode	0 (Numbers)	Ctrl-F7, 5
Footnotes at bottom of page	Yes	Ctrl-F7, 8
Hyphenation	Off	Shift-F8, 5
Insert/Typeover	Insert mode	Ins
Line Numbering	Off	Ctrl-F8, B
Line separating text and footnotes	1 (2-inch line)	Ctrl-F7, 7
Line Spacing	Single	Shift-F8, 4
Lines in notes to keep together	3	Ctrl-F7, 3
Lines per inch	6	Ctrl-F8, 2
Margin, Top	12 half-lines (one inch)	Alt-F8, 5
Margins, Side	Left = 10, Right = 74 (one-inch margins)	Shift-F8, 3
Note numbering mode	Numbers	Ctrl-F7, 4
Number of Copies	1	Shift-F7, 2
Outline Numbering Style	Outline	Alt-F5, 1
Page Length	66 lines total, 54 text lines (8 1/2 by 11-inch paper)	Alt-F8, 4
Page Number Column Positions	Left = 10, Center = 42, Right = 74	Alt-F8, 7
Page Number Position	No page numbers	Alt-F8, 1
Paragraph/Outline Numbering Style	Outline	Alt-F5, 1

Pitch	10 characters per inch	Ctrl-F8, 1
Printer Number	1	Shift-F7, 1
Repeat value for Esc	8	Esc
Right Justification	On (Even right-hand margin)	Ctrl-F8, 3 or 4
Sheet Feeder Bin Number	1	Ctrl-F8, 9
Spacing, line	Single	Shift-F8, 4
Spacing between notes	1	Ctrl-F7, 2
Spacing within notes	1	Ctrl-F7, 1
Table of Authorities	Dot leaders, no underlining, blank line between authorities	Alt-F5, 2
Tabs	Every 5 spaces	Shift-F8, 1
Top Margin	12 half-lines (one inch)	Alt-F8, 5
Underline Style	Non-continuous single	Ctrl-F8, 5-8
Widow/Orphan Protect	No	Alt-F8, A

Appendix C
WordPerfect 5.0 Features

Advance	
Down	Shift-F8, 4, 1, 2
Left	Shift-F8, 4, 1, 4
Right	Shift-F8, 4, 1, 5
to Column	Shift-F8, 4, 1, 6
to Line	Shift-F8, 4, 1, 3
Up	Shift-F8, 4, 1, 1
Align Character	Shift-F6, 4, 3
Appearance Attributes	Ctrl-F8, 2
Append	
Block	Alt-F4, Ctrl-F4, 1, 4
Page	Ctrl-F4, 3, 4
Paragraph	Ctrl-F4, 2, 4
Rectangle	Alt-F4, Ctrl-F4, 3, 4
Sentence	Ctrl-F4, 1, 4
Tabular Column	Alt-F4, Ctrl-F4, 2, 4
Auto Rewrite	Ctrl-F3, 0
Automatic Reference	
Generate	Alt-F5, 6
Mark for	Alt-F5, 1
Base Font	Ctrl-F8, 4
Binding Width	Shift-F7, B
Block	
Append	Alt-F4, Ctrl-F4, 1, 4
Copy	Alt-F4, Ctrl-F4, 1, 2
Delete	Alt-F4, Del, Y
Mode	Alt-F4
Move	Alt-F4, Ctrl-F4, 1, 1

Protect	Alt-F4, Shift-F8
Bold	F6 or Ctrl-F8, 2, 1
^C (Text from Keyboard)	Shift-F9, C
Cancel	F1
Cancel Merge Operation	F1
Cancel Print Job(s)	Shift-F7, 4, 1
Capitalize text	Alt-F4, Shift-F3, 1
Center block	Alt-F4, Shift-F6
Center line	Shift-F6
Center Page Top to Bottom	Shift-F8, 2, 1
Change List Files Directory	F5, Enter, 7
Color, Print	Ctrl-F8, 5
Columns, Text	
Definition	Alt-F7, 4
Display side-by-side	Alt-F7, 5
On/Off	Alt-F7, 3
Comment	
Convert Text to	Alt-F4, Ctrl-F5, Y
Convert to Text	Ctrl-F5, 5, 3
Create	Ctrl-F5, 5, 1
Edit	Ctrl-F5, 5, 2
Compare Screen to Disk Document	Alt-F5, 6, 2
Compose	Ctrl-2
Concordance	Alt-F5, 5, 3
Condense Master Document	Alt-F5, 6, 4
Conditional End of Page	Shift-F8, 4, 2
Control Printer	Shift-F7, 4
Copy	
Block	Alt-F4, Ctrl-F4, 1, 2
Column	Alt-F4, Ctrl-F4, 2, 3
File	F5, Enter, 8
Page	Ctrl-F4, 3, 2
Paragraph	Ctrl-F4, 2, 2
Rectangle	Alt-F4, Ctrl-F4, 3, 2
Sentence	Ctrl-F4, 1, 2
Create Directory	F5, =
Create Style	Alt-F8, 3
^D (Date)	Shift-F9, D
Date	
Code	Shift-F5, 2
Format	Shift-F5, 3

Text	Shift-F5, 1
Decimal/Align Character	Shift-F8, 4, 3
Define (Mark Text)	Alt-F5, 5
Define Macro	Ctrl-F10
Define Style	Alt-F5, 6
Define Variable	Ctrl-PgUp
Delete	
Block	Alt-F4, Del
Character, current	Del
Character, preceding	Backspace
File	F5, Enter, 2
Page	Ctrl-F4, 3, 3
Paragraph	Ctrl-F4, 2, 3
Sentence	Ctrl-F4, 1, 3
to End of Line	Ctrl-End
to End of Page	Ctrl-PgDn
Word	Ctrl-Backspace
Word Left	Home, Backspace
Word Right	Home, Delete
Display	
All Print Jobs	Shift-F7, 4, 3
Pitch	Shift-F8, 3, 1
Document Comments	Ctrl-F5, 5
Document Compare	Alt-F5, 6, 2
Document Summary, Create	Shift-F8, 3, 4
DOS, go to	Ctrl-F1, 1
DOS Text File	
Retrieve (CR/LF to [HRt])	Ctrl-F5, 1, 2
Retrieve (CR/LF to [SRt])	Ctrl-F5, 1, 3
Save	Ctrl-F5, 1, 1
Double Underline	Ctrl-F8, 2, 3
Draw Line	Ctrl-F3, 2
^E (End of Record)	Shift-F9, E
Edit Macro	Ctrl-F10
Edit Table of Authorities Full Form	Alt-F5, 5, 5
End of Page, Conditional	Shift-F8, 4, 2
Endnote	
Create	Ctrl-F7, 2, 1
Edit	Ctrl-F7, 2, 2
New Number	Ctrl-F7, 2, 3
Options	Ctrl-F7, 2, 4
Placement	Ctrl-F7, 3

Exit and Save Document	F7, Enter, Y, Y
Expand Master Document	Alt-F5, 6, 3
^F (Field)	Shift-F9, F
Figure Box, Graphics	Alt-F9, 1
Fine Print	Ctrl-F8, 1, 3
Flush Right	Alt-F6
Font, Base	Ctrl-F8, 4
Footers	Shift-F8, 2, 4
Footnote	
Create	Ctrl-F7, 1, 1
Edit	Ctrl-F7, 1, 2
New Number	Ctrl-F7, 1, 3
Options	Ctrl-F7, 1, 4
Format	Shift-F8
Forms	Shift-F7, S, 3, 4
^G (Start Macro)	Shift-F9, G
Generate (Mark Text)	Alt-F5, 6
Generate Tables, Index, and Automatic References	Alt-F5, 6, 5
Generic Word Processor Format	Ctrl-F5, 3
Go (Start Printer)	Shift-F7, 4, 4
Go To	Ctrl-Home
Go to DOS	Ctrl-F1, 1
Graphics	
Figure Box	Alt-F9, 1
Line, Horizontal	Alt-F9, 5, 1
Line, Vertical	Alt-F9, 5, 2
Quality	Shift-F7, G
Table Box	Alt-F9, 2
Text Box	Alt-F9, 3
User-defined Box	Alt-F9, 4
Hard	
Page	Ctrl-Enter
Return	Enter
Space	Home, Spacebar
Headers	Shift-F8, 2, 3
Help	F3
Horizontal Line, Graphics	Alt-F9, 5, 1
Hyphenation	Shift-F8, 1, 1
Hyphenation Zone	Shift-F8, 1, 2

Indent Left	F4
Indent Left and Right	Shift-F4
Index	
Define	Alt-F5, 3
Mark for	Alt-F4, Alt-F5, 3
Initial Settings (Format)	Shift-F8, 3, 2
Initialize Printer	Shift-F7, 7
Insert, Forced	Home, Home, Ins
Insert Variable	Alt-number
Italics	Ctrl-F8, 2, 4
Justification, Right	Shift-F8, 1, 3
Kerning	Shift-F8, 4, 6, 1
Language	Shift-F8, 4, 4
Large Print	Ctrl-F8, 1, 5
Left Indent	F4
Left/Right Indent	Shift-F4
Left/Right Margins	Shift-F8, 1, 7
Line	
Draw	Ctrl-F3, 2
Format	Shift-F8, 1
Graphics	Alt-F9, 5
Height	Shift-F8, 1, 4
Numbering	Shift-F8, 1, 5
Spacing	Shift-F8, 1, 6
List	
Define	Alt-F5, 5, 2
Mark for	Alt-F4, Alt-F5, 2
List Files	F5
Look at File	F5, Enter, 6
Lowercase, convert text to	Alt-F4, Shift-F3, 2
Macro	
Define, edit, or replace	Ctrl-F10
Start	Alt-F10
Margin Release	Shift-Tab
Margins	
Left/Right	Shift-F8, 1, 7
Top/Bottom	Shift-F8, 2, 5
Mark Block	
for Index	Alt-F4, Alt-F5, 3
for List	Alt-F4, Alt-F5, 2

for Table of Authorities	Alt-F4, Alt-F5, 4
for Table of Contents	Alt-F4, Alt-F5, 1
Mark Text	
for Automatic Reference	Alt-F5, 1
for Index	Alt-F5, 3
for Subdocument	Alt-F5, 2
for Table of Auth. Short Form	Alt-F5, 4
Master Document	
Condense	Alt-F5, 6, 4
Expand	Alt-F5, 6, 3
Subdocument	Alt-F5, 2
Math	
On	Alt-F7, 1
Definition	Alt-F7, 2
Merge	Ctrl-F9, 1
Cancel	F1
Codes	Shift-F8
R (^R)	F9
Move	
Block	Alt-F4, Ctrl-F4, 1, 1
Column	Alt-F4, Ctrl-F4, 2, 1
Page	Ctrl-F4, 3, 1
Paragraph	Ctrl-F4, 2, 1
Rectangle	Alt-F4, Ctrl-F4, 3, 1
Sentence	Ctrl-F4, 1, 1
^N (Next Record)	Shift-F9, N
Name Search	F5, Enter, N
New Page	Ctrl-Enter
New Page Number	Shift-F8, 2, 6
Normal Text (Turn off attributes)	Ctrl-F8, 3
Number of Copies	Shift-F7, N
^O (Display Message)	Shift-F9, O
Other Directory	F5, Enter, 7
Outline	Shift-F5, 4
Outline Print (Attribute)	Ctrl-F8, 2, 5
Overstrike	Shift-F8, 4, 5
^P (Primary File)	Shift-F9, P
Page	
Format	Shift-F8, 2
Format, Suppress	Shift-F8, 2, 9

Hard (New)	Ctrl-Enter
Number, New	Shift-F8, 2, 6
Numbering	Shift-F8, 2, 7
Print	Shift-F7, 2
Paper Size/Type	Shift-F8, 2, 8
Paragraph	
Number, insert	Shift-F5, 5
Numbering Definition	Shift-F5, 6
Password	Ctrl-F5, 2
Print	
Block	Alt-F4, Shift-F7
Color	Ctrl-F8, 5
Document on Disk	Shift-F7, 3
Full (Entire) Document	Shift-F7, 1
List Files	F5, Enter, 4
Job(s), Cancel	Shift-F7, 4, 1
Jobs, Display	Shift-F7, 4, 3
Page	Shift-F7, 2
Screen	Shift-PrtSc
Printer	
Command	Shift-F8, 4, 6, 2
Select	Shift-F7, S
Settings	Shift-F7, S, 3
Printing, Resume (Go)	Shift-F7, 4, 4
Printing, Stop	Shift-F7, 4, 5
^Q (Stop Merge)	Shift-F9, Q
^R (End of Field)	Shift-F9, R
Redline	Ctrl-F8, 2, 8
Redline Method	Shift-F8, 3, 3
Remove Redline/Strikeout	Alt-F5, 6, 1
Rename File	F5, Enter, 3
Repeat Next Command	Esc
Replace	Alt-F2
Replace, Extended	Home, Alt-F2
Replace Macro	Ctrl-F10
Resume Printing (Go)	Shift-F7, 4, 4
Retrieve	
Document	Shift-F10
Moved or Copied Block	Enter or Ctrl-F4, 4, 1
Moved or Copied Column	Enter or Ctrl-F4, 4, 2
Moved or Copied Rectangle	Enter or Ctrl-F4, 4, 3
Text File	F5, Enter, 5 or Ctrl-F5, 2 or 3

Return to Previous Place	Ctrl-Home, Ctrl-Home
Rewrite Screen	Ctrl-F3, 0
Reveal Codes (on or off)	Alt-F3
Right Justification	Shift-F8, 1, 3
Rush Print Job	Shift-F7, 4, 2
^S (Secondary File)	Shift-F9, S
Save	
Document	F10
Document and Exit	F7, Enter, Enter, Y, Y
DOS Text File	Ctrl-F5, 1
in Generic WP Format	Ctrl-F5, 3
in WordPerfect 4.2 Format	Ctrl-F5, 4
Screen	Ctrl-F3
Screen Colors	Ctrl-F3, 4
Screen, Split	Ctrl-F3, 1
Search	
Backward	Shift-F2
Backward, Extended	Home, Shift-F2
Forward	F2
Forward, Extended	Home, F2
Select Printer	Shift-F7, S
Setup	Shift-F1
Shadow Print	Ctrl-F8, 2, 6
Shell	Ctrl-F1
Size Attributes	Ctrl-F8, 1
Small Caps	Ctrl-F8, 2, 7
Small Print	Ctrl-F8, 1, 4
Sort	Ctrl-F9, 2
Sort Order	Ctrl-F9, 3
Spacing, Line	Shift-F8, 1, 6
Spell	Ctrl-F2
Split Screen	Ctrl-F3, 1
Start Macro	Alt-F10
Stop Printing	Shift-F7, 4, 5
Strikeout	Ctrl-F8, 2, 9
Style	Alt-F8
Subscript	Ctrl-F8, 1, 2
Superscript	Ctrl-F8, 1, 1
Suppress Page Format	Shift-F8, 2, 9
Switch Windows	Shift-F3
^T (Send to Printer)	Shift-F9, T
Tab Align	Ctrl-F6

Feature	Keystrokes
Tab Set	Shift-F8, 1, 8
Table Box, Graphics	Alt-F9, 2
Table of Authorities	
Define	Alt-F5, 5, 4
Edit Full Form	Alt-F5, 5, 5
Full Form	Alt-F4, Alt-F5, 4
Short Form	Alt-F5, 4
Table of Contents	
Define	Alt-F5, 5, 1
Mark for	Alt-F4, Alt-F5, 1
Text Box, Graphics	Alt-F9, 3
Text In (List Files)	F5, Enter, 5
Text In/Out	Ctrl-F5
Text File, DOS	
Retrieve	Ctrl-F5, 1, then 2 or 3
Save	Ctrl-F5, 1, 1
Thesaurus	Alt-F1
Thousands' Separator	Shift-F8, 4, 3
Top/Bottom Margins	Shift-F8, 2, 5
Type Through	Shift-F7, 5
Typeover On/Off	Ins
Typeover, Forced	Home, Ins
^U (Rewrite Screen)	Shift-F9, U
Undelete	F1
Underline	F8 or Ctrl-F8, 2, 2
Uppercase, convert text to	Alt-F4, Shift-F3, 1
User-defined Box, Graphics	Alt-F9, 4
^V (Insert Merge Code)	Shift-F9, V
Variable	
Define	Ctrl-PgUp
Insert	Alt-number
Vertical Line, Graphics	Alt-F9, 5, 2
Very Large Print	Ctrl-F8, 1, 6
View Document	Shift-F7, 6
Widow/Orphan Protection	Shift-F8, 1, 9
Window	Ctrl-F3, 1
Word/Letter Spacing	Shift-F8, 4, 6, 3
Word Count	Ctrl-F2, 6
Word Search	F5, Enter, 9
Word Spacing Justification Limits	Shift-F8, 4, 6, 4

WordPerfect 4.2 Format   Ctrl-F5, 4

Initial Settings

Following is a summary of WordPerfect 5.0's initial settings. To change a setting, press Shift and F1 to give a Setup command. When the Setup Menu appears, press the keys listed in the right-hand column to obtain the feature you want to change.

Feature	Initially set to	Setup Menu keys
Automatically Format and Rewrite	Yes	3, 1
Auxiliary Files, Location of	Main WordPerfect directory	7
Backup		
Original Document	No	1, 2
Timed Document	No	1, 1
Beep Options		
Beep on Error	No	5, 1, 1
Beep on Hyphenation	Yes	5, 1, 2
Beep on Search Failure	No	5, 1, 3
Center Page top-to-bottom	No	5, 4, Shift-F8, 2, 1
Cursor Speed	30 chars/second	2
Date Format	Month Day, Year (e.g., May 29, 1988)	5, 2
Decimal/Align Character	. (period)	5, 4, Shift-F8, 4, 3
Display Document Comments	Yes	3, 3
Display Pitch	Automatic, 10 chars/inch	5, 4, Shift-F8, 3, 1
Document Comments, Display	Yes	3, 3
Document Summary		
Create on Save/Exit	No	5, 3, 1

Subject Search String	RE:	5, 3, 2
Esc key, Repeat Value for	8	5, 5
Fast Save (unformatted)	Yes	4
Filename on Status Line	Yes	3, 4
Hard Return Display Char.	Space	3, 6
Hyphenation	No (off)	5, 4, Shift-F8, 1, 1
Hyphenation Zone	L=0.7", R=0.25"	5, 4, Shift-F8, 1, 2
Initial Font	Courier 10 Pitch	5, 4, Shift-F8, 3, 3
Justification	Yes (even right margin)	5, 4, Shift-F8, 1, 3
Kerning	No (off)	5, 4, Shift-F8, 4, 6, 1
Keyboard Layout	Standard	6
Language	EN (English)	5, 4, Shift-F8, 4, 4
Left and Right Margins	L=1", R=1"	5, 4, Shift-F8, 1, 7
Line Height	Auto	5, 4, Shift-F8, 1, 4
Line Numbering	No	5, 4, Shift-F8, 1, 5
Line Spacing	1 (single-space)	5, 4, Shift-F8, 1, 6
Location of Auxiliary Files	Main WordPerfect directory	7
Margins, Left and Right	L=1", R=1"	5, 4, Shift-F8, 1, 7
Margins, Top and Bottom	T=1", B=1"	5, 4, Shift-F8, 2, 5
Menu Letter Display	Bold	3, 7

New Page Number	1	5, 4, Shift-F8, 2, 6
Original Document Backup	No	1, 2
Page Number, New	1	5, 4, Shift-F8, 2, 6
Page Numbering	No page numbers	5, 4, Shift-F8, 2, 7
Paper		5, 4, Shift-F8, 4, 8
Size	8.5" x 11"	
Type	Standard	
Print Color	Black	5, 4, Ctrl-F8, 5
Redline Method	Printer Dependent	5, 4, Shift-F8, 3, 3
Repeat Value for Esc key	8	5, 5
Side-by-side Columns Display	Yes	3, 8
Spacing, Line	1 (single-space)	5, 4, Shift-F8, 1, 6
Table of Authorities		
Dot Leaders	Yes	5, 6, 1
Underlining Allowed	No	5, 6, 2
Blank Line between Authorities	Yes	5, 6, 3
Tab Set	Every 0.5"	5, 4, Shift-F8, 1, 8
Thousands Separator	, (comma)	5, 4, Shift-F8, 4, 3
Timed Document Backup	No	1, 1
Top and Bottom Margins	T=1", B=1"	5, 4, Shift-F8, 2, 5
Underline Spaces, Tabs	S=Yes, T=No	5, 4, Shift-F8, 4, 7
Units of Measure		
Numbers for Margins, Tabs, etc.	" (inches)	8, 1
Status Line Display	u (lines/columns)	8, 2

Widow/Orphan Protection	No	5, 4, Shift-F8, 1, 9
Width Adjustment		5, 4, Shift-F8, 4, 6, 3
Word Spacing	Optimal	
Letter Spacing	Optimal	
Word Spacing Justification		5, 4, Shift-F8, 4, 6, 4
Compressed to	60%	
Expanded to	400%	

Index

*as a grand total in Math operation, 259
*as a wildcard character, 83, 189, 378
= (total in Math operation), 259
- (minus key on numeric keypad), 269
+ (plus key on numeric keypad), 301
+ (subtotal in Math operation), 258
? (wildcard character for spell-checking), 378
~ (tilde) in macro programming commands, 205

1-2-3 (Lotus) spreadsheets—See **Convert program** and **Spreadsheet files, using**

Abbreviations
  Expanding with macros, 175, 243
  Replacing, 1, 337
Activating document windows, 445
Add Word (spell-checking option), 375
Adding rows or columns, 1, 257
Advance options, 2–5
  WordPerfect 4.1 and 4.2, 2
  WordPerfect 5.0, 4
Aided hyphenation, 149
Aligning on a character, 5, 405–406
Alt (Alternate) key, 6
Alt-*number* keys for variables, 439
ALTRNAT.WPK (WordPerfect 5.0 keyboard definition file), 172
Antonyms, 6
Appending text to a file, 7–8
  Blocks, columns, and rectangles, 7
  Sentences, paragraphs, and pages, 8
Arabic (1, 2, 3) page numbers, 277, 296
Are other copies of WordPerfect currently running? prompt, 8
Are you sure (Y/N)? (DOS prompt), 87
Arrow keys, 8–9
ASCII text files—See **DOS text files**
Asterisk (*)
  Grand total in Math operations, 259
  Wildcard character, 83, 189, 378
Authorities, table of, 407
Auto Rewrite, 9
Automatic backups, 16, 389
Automatic paragraph numbers, 298
Automatic reference—WordPerfect 5.0, 10–12
  Creating an automatic reference, 10
  Generating references, 11
  Multiple references, 12
Auxiliary files—WordPerfect 5.0, 12–14, 358
  Specifying the language, 14

^B (page number), 296
Backspace key, 15
Backup Directory parameter, 13
Backup options, 355
Backups
  Automatic, 16, 389
  Manual, 15
  Timed Backup versus Original Backup, 17
Base Font (WordPerfect 5.0 Font command option), 107
Beep sound, 17–18, 206, 355
Bin Number, Sheet Feeder, 313
Binding width, 18–19, 315
BK! (extension for backup file), 16
Blank screen, 19

484   Index

Blank space, inserting, 19
Block command (Alt-F4), 19–22
  Block operations, 20–21
  Rehighlighting a block, 22
Block on message, 19
Blocks
  Appending to a file, 7
  Centering, 28
  Counting words in, 446
  Moving and copying, 270–271, 273–274
  Right-aligning, 103
  Sorting, 367–370
  Spell-checking, 382
Bold command (F6), 22
  Removing emboldening, 22
Bold letters in WordPerfect 5.0 menus, 265
Borders for graphics boxes, 137–138
Bottom margin, 248, 252
Boxes, drawing—See **Lines, drawing**
Boxes, graphics—WordPerfect 5.0, 132
Breaking pages—See **Hard Page command**

Calculation columns, formulas in, 260–262
Calculations, a macro that performs, 263
Calculations in variables, 443–444
Cancel command (F1), 25
Canceling print jobs, 26–27
  A macro to cancel printing, 26–27
Can't create new printer files on WP disk message, 27
Capitalizing, 27–28
Caps Lock key, 28
CD (DOS Change Directory command), 85
Center command (Shift-F6), 28–29
  Centering a block of text, 28–29
  Centering a column heading, 29
  Centering a line, 28
  Uncentering, 29
Center Page top to bottom, 31, 295, 298
Centimeters, measurements in, 4, 440
Chaining macros, 236–238
Change Directory (List Files option), 193
Character, aligning on a, 6, 405–406
Characters per inch—See **Pitch**
CHKDSK (DOS Check Disk command), 85
Clear Column (Thesaurus option), 428
Closing document windows, 446
Code definition in Style command, 396
Codes, hidden—WordPerfect 4.1 and 4.2, 30–37
  Searching for hidden codes, 33–37
Codes, hidden—WordPerfect 5.0, 37–47
  Searching for hidden codes, 42–47

Colors
  Print (WordPerfect 5.0 Font command option), 108
  Screen (WordPerfect 4.1 and 4.2 option), 347
Column headings, centering, 29
Column operations, 47–50
  Adjusting the format, 48
  Column insert example, 48–49
  Deleting columns, 49–50
  Inserting columns, 48
  Moving and copying columns, 47
Columns
  Adding numbers in, 261
  Appending to a file, 7
  Moving and copying, 273–274
Columns, text, 50–54
  Column styles, 50–51
  Defining the columns, 51–52
  Editing columns, 53
  Entering Newspaper-Style Columns, 52
  Entering Parallel Columns, 53
  Displaying individual columns, 53–54
  Turning columns on, 52
Comments
  Document—See **Document Comments**
  Macro, 211
Common word list in Speller's dictionary, 385
Compose feature—WordPerfect 5.0, 54
Concordance file, 54–55
Condensing master documents, WordPerfect 5.0, 255
Conditional End of Page, 55–56, 282, 292
Continuous paper—See **Paper**
Continuous underline style, 313
Control (Ctrl) key, 59
Control Printer (WordPerfect 5.0 print option), 308–309
Convert program, 56–58
Converting between comments and text, 76
Converting WordPerfect 4.2 macros to WordPerfect 5.0, 238–239
Copy
  DOS command, 86
  List Files option, 193–194
  Operations—See **Move command**
Counting words, 446–447
Cross-references in documents—See **Automatic reference**
Ctrl (Control) key, 59
Ctrl/Alt keys option—WordPerfect 4.1 and 4.2, 59

Cursor
  Drawing with the, 185
  Moving the, 60, 212
  Speed, 355
Custom dictionaries, 380–381
Cut and Copy operations—See **Move Command**

Database files, using, 61–63
  Producing form letters from database files, 62–63
Dashed line across the screen, 61
Date command (Shift-F5)—WordPerfect 4.1 and 4.2, 63–66
  Insert Text and Insert Function options, 63
  Format option, 65
Date/Outline command (Shift-F5)—WordPerfect 5.0, 66–68
  Date Text and Date Code options, 66–67
  Date Format option, 67
  Outline, Para Num, and Define options, 68
dBASE II and III files—See **Convert program** and **Database files, using**
DCA (Document Content Architecture) files—See **Convert program**
Decimal/Align Character, 282
Decimal tabs, 68, 416
Del (Delete) key, 68
Delete [code]? (Y/N) N prompt, 69
Delete (List Files option), 191
Deleted text, undeleting, 69–70
Deleting
  Columns, 49–50
  Disk files, 87, 191
  Footnotes and endnotes, 110, 112
  Hard disk subdirectories, 73, 89
  Hidden codes, 71
  Strikeout text, 76, 393, 394
  Styles, 402
  Text, 70
  Words in Spell dictionary, 384
Dictionaries for spell-checking
  Alternate, 379–380
  Custom, 380–381
  Common word list in, 385
  Main, 382
  Supplementary, 383
DIF (Data Interchange Format) spreadsheets—See **Convert program**
DIR (DOS Directory command), 86–87
Disk directories
  Change (DOS command), 85
  Creating, 72, 8890

Deleting (removing), 73, 89
  In WordPerfect 4.1 and 4.2 Set-up menu, 354–355
  Making WordPerfect use, 72–74, 193
Disk document, saving an edited, 95–96
Disk file(s)
  Appending text to, 7–8
  Copying, 86, 193–194
  Deleting, 87, 191
  Extensions, 102–103
  Naming—See **Filenames**
  Operating on—See **DOS operations** and **List Files command**
  Printing, 191
  Renaming, 89, 191
  Retrieving, 191
  Searching through, 194–195
Disk full message, 73
DISKCOPY (DOS command), 87
Disks, formatting, 88
Display options, WordPerfect 5.0, 356
Displaying
  Document Summary, 79, 81
  Graphics lines, 188
  Individual text columns, 53
Doc indicator on status line, 73, 306, 390
Document comments, 74–76
  Comment codes, 75
  Converting between comments and text, 76
  Creating comments, 74
  Editing comments, 75
  Hiding comments, 75
Document Compare—WordPerfect 5.0, 76
  Removing redline markings and strikeout text, 76
Document Format option—WordPerfect 5.0, 77
Document names—See **Filenames**
Document, starting WordPerfect with a, 393
Document Summary—WordPerfect 4.2, 78–79
  Creating and editing a Document Summary, 78
  Hiding a Document Summary, 79
  Viewing a Document Summary, 79
Document Summary—WordPerfect 5.0, 80–82
  Creating and editing a Document Summary, 80–81
  Displaying a Document Summary, 81
  Letting WordPerfect fill In the Subject/Account field, 81–82
Document was Fast Saved message, 101

486 Index

Document windows—See **Windows, document**
Documents
  Locking and unlocking—See **Text In/Out command**
  Operating on—See **Disk file(s)**
  Reformatting, 331–332
DOS (Disk Operating System) operations, 82–90
  CD (Change Directory) command, 85
  CHKDSK (Check Disk) command, 85
  Common DOS operations, 84
  COPY command, 86
  DIR (Directory) command, 86–87
  DISKCOPY command, 87
  ERASE command, 87
  Filenames, 83
  FORMAT command, 88
  List Files equivalents of DOS commands, 90
  MD (Make Directory) command, 88
  Operating on groups of files, 83
  RD (Remove Directory) command, 89
  RENAME command, 89
  Starting DOS, 82
DOS, returning from, 90, 339
DOS text files, 91, 419, 422, 424
Dot leaders, 91, 106, 418
Double-sided pages, printing—See **Binding width**
Double-spacing—See **Spacing**
Double-underlining, 92–93, 435
Drawing boxes and lines, 184–188
Duplicated words during spell-checking, 376

^E (Merge E code), 268
Edit (spell-checking option), 375
Editing
  Columns, 53
  Disk documents, 95–96
  Document comments, 75
  Document Summary, 78–79, 80–81
  Footnotes and endnotes, 110, 112
  Graphic images, 135
  Graphics boxes, 136
  Headers and footers, 144, 146
  Macros, 203, 239–240
  Math tables, 264
  Outlines, 285–286
  Reveal Codes screen, 340
  Styles, 398
  Text columns, 53

Two documents—See **Switch Documents command**
Editor, Macro—See **Macro programming commands**
Emboldened text—See **Bold command**
EN language specifier (English), 13, 282
End key, 97
Endnotes, 97, 111
ENHANCED.WPK (WordPerfect 5.0 keyboard definition file), 172
Enter 'EXIT' to return to WordPerfect prompt, 179
Enter key, 97–98
  Ctrl and Enter starts a new page, 98
  Pressing Enter in a menu, 97
Envelopes, printing, 123
Equal signs, line of (hard page break), 98
ERASE (DOS command), 87
Erasing material—See **Deleting**
Error messages
  Are other copies of WordPerfect currently running?, 8
  Can't create new printer files on WP disk, 27
  Disk full, 73
  Document was Fast Saved, 101
  File not found, 99
  Insufficient disk space, 85
  Invalid dictionary file, 383
  Overflow file already exists, 287
Esc (Escape) key, 99–101
Exit command (F7), 100
Expanding master documents, 254–255
Extended search and replace operations, 144, 146
Extensions, disk file, 102–103

F1–F10 keys, 130
Fast Save—WordPerfect 5.0, 101–102, 357
Feeders, paper, 313
Fields in sort operation, 363
Figure Box definition form, 133–134
File not found message, 99
File, appending text to a, 7–8
File operations—See **DOS operations** and **List Files command**
Filenames, 102–103
  Reserved extensions, 103
Filespec (drive, directory, and filename), 104
Fixed paragraph numbers, 302
Flush Right command (Alt-F6), 103–105
  Flush Right with dot leaders for WordPerfect 4.2, 104
  Right-aligning a block of text, 103

Index

Font command (Ctrl-F8)—WordPerfect 5.0, 105–108
  Appearance, 106
  Base Font, 107
  Normal, 106
  Print Color, 108
  Size/Position, 106
Fonts, printer—WordPerfect 4.1 and 4.2, 108
Footers—See **Headers and footers**
Footnote command (Ctrl-F7)—WordPerfect 4.1 and 4.2, 109–110
  Creating notes, 109
  Deleting notes, 110
  Editing notes, 110
Footnote command (Ctrl-F7)—WordPerfect 5.0, 111–114
  Creating notes, 111
  Editing notes, 112
  Deleting notes, 112
  Generating endnotes, 113
  Note options, 114
  Renumbering notes, 112–113
Force Odd/Even Page—WordPerfect 5.0, 114–116, 293
Force Typeover or Insert mode, 434
Foreign characters—See **Special characters**
Formatting disks, 88
Form letters, 116–128
  Canceling a merge operation, 123
  Contents of a Secondary Merge File, 118
  Creating a Primary File, 118
  Creating form letters from mailing lists, 117
  Customizing form letters from the keyboard, 123
  Form letter prepared as a macro, 125–128
  Merging form letters, 119
  Merging to the printer, 121
  Printing envelopes, 123
  Printing form letters, 121
  Using macros with merge operations, 124
  Using multiple Primary Files, 125
Form letters, producing from database files, 61–63
FORMAT (DOS command), 88
Format command (Shift-F8)—WordPerfect 5.0, 128
Forms, 128–130
  Contents of a form-processing macro, 128
Formulas in Calculation columns, 260–262
Fractions, aligning a column of, 406
Function keys (F1–F10), 130

Generating
  Automatic references, 11
  Endnotes, 113
  Indexes, 155, 158
  Lists, 195, 197
  Table of contents, 409–410, 413
Global search and replace operations, 330
Go To command (Ctrl-Home), 131–132
  Backtracking with the Go To command, 131
Go To DOS—See **Shell command**
Grand total in Math operation, 259
Graphic images, editing, 135
Graphics command (Alt-F9)—WordPerfect 5.0, 132–139
  Box options, 137–139
  Box types, 133
  Creating a graphics box, 132
  Defining boxes, 133
  Editing boxes, 136
  Editing options for graphic images, 135
  Renumbering boxes, 137
  Viewing boxes, 136
Graphics lines, 184–188
Greek alphabet, 372
Gutter—See **Binding width**

H (units of horizontal measure), 4
Half-spacing—See **Advance**
Hand-fed paper—See **Paper**
Hanging paragraphs, 155
Hard disk
  Root directory, 71
  Startup file for WordPerfect, 142, 394
  Subdirectories, 72
  Warning about DOS Format command, 88
Hard Page command (Ctrl-Enter), 98, 142, 293
Hard space (Home, Spacebar), 142
Headers and footers—WordPerfect 4.1 and 4.2, 143–144
  Creating a header or footer, 143
  Editing and canceling headers and footers, 144
  Searching through headers and footers, 144
Headers and footers—WordPerfect 5.0, 144–146
  Creating a header or footer, 145
  Editing and canceling headers and footers, 146
  Searching through headers and footers, 146
Headings in indexes, 155
Help command (F3), 146

488   Index

Hidden codes
  Deleting, 71
  Replacing, 337
  WordPerfect 4.1 and 4.2, 30–37
  WordPerfect 5.0, 37–47
Highlighting—See **Block command**
Home key, 147–148
Homonyms, 375
Hyphenation, 148–150
  Aided (Manual) and Auto hyphenation, 149
  Soft hyphens, 150
  Turning Hyphenation on and off, 148
Hyphenation Module(s) parameter, 13
Hyphenation Zone, 150–151
Hyphens, printing to strike out text, 393, 394

IF structures for macro programming, 227–230
Inches, measurements in, 4, 436
Indent commands (F4 and Shift-F4), 153–155
  Indenting from the left margin, 153
  Indenting from both margins, 154
  Hanging paragraphs, 155
  Removing indentation, 155
Indexes, 155–159
  Building an index, 156
  Defining the numbering style, 157
  Generating an index, 158
  Headings and subheadings, 155
  Removing entries from an index, 158
Initial settings
  WordPerfect 4.1 and 4.2, 159–160
  WordPerfect 5.0, 160–167
Ins (Insert) key, 167, 430
Insert mode, 430
Inserting
  Blank space, 19
  Columns, 48
  Merge codes manually, 268
  Printer commands, 320–321
  Special characters, 372
  Variables in macro definitions, 213
  WordPerfect 5.0 subdocuments, 254
Insufficient disk space (DOS error message), 85
Integers in variables, 439
Invalid dictionary file (Spell error message), 383
Invisible codes—See **Codes, hidden**

Justification, 169–170, 313

Keeping text together, 171
KEY CMD macro programming message, 231
Key words in sort operations, 360
Keyboard/Macro Files parameter, 13
Keyboard definition files, WordPerfect 5.0, 172–175
Keyboard layout—WordPerfect 5.0, 171–177, 362
  Creating keyboard files, 175–176
  Creating key definitions, 176
  Operating on key definitions, 176–177
  Predefined keyboard definition files, 172–175
  Using keyboard files, 175
Keypad, numeric, 282–283

Language field, 14, 282
Leading (line height), 183
Leaving
  DOS, 179
  List Files, 195
  Reveal Codes, 340
  Spell utility program, 381–382
  WordPerfect, 179–180
  WordPerfect 4.1 and 4.2 Set-up menu, 353
Left Indent—See **Indent commands**
Left margin, 249, 251
Legal size paper, 180
Letterhead paper, 180–181
LEX.WP (main dictionary for WordPerfect 4.1 and 4.2), 379
Library
  Macro, 204
  Style, 394
Line, dashed (soft page break), 61
Line Format
  Command (Shift-F8)—WordPerfect 4.1 and 4.2, 181–182
  Option—WordPerfect 5.0, 183–184
Line numbering—See **Print Format command** (WordPerfect 4.2) or **Line Format option** (WordPerfect 5.0)
Line of equal signs (hard page break), 98
Line spacing—See **Spacing**
Lines, centering, 28
Lines, drawing, 184–188
  Drawing with the cursor, 185
  Drawing graphics lines with WordPerfect 5.0, 185–188
  Viewing graphics lines, 188
Lines per inch—WordPerfect 4.1 and 4.2, 188–189, 317

Lines per page—See **Page Format command—WordPerfect 4.1 and 4.2**
List Files command (F5), 189–195
　Copy, 193
　Delete, 191
　Leaving List Files, 195
　Look, 193
　Name Search, 194
　Operating on multiple files, 190
　Other Directory, 193
　Print, 191
　Rename, 191
　Retrieve, 191
　Specifying the files to be listed, 189
　Text In, 192
　The List Files screen, 190
　Word Search, 194
List Files equivalents of DOS commands, 90
List, selecting records from a, 368–371
Lists, 195–198
　Building a list, 195
　Defining the numbering style, 196
　Generating a list, 197
　Removing entries from a list, 197
Loading documents from disk—See **Retrieve command** or **List Files command**
Location of Auxiliary Files (WordPerfect 5.0 parameter), 362
Locking documents—See **Text In/Out command**
Look (List Files option), 193
Look Up (spell-checking option), 376
Look Up Word (Thesaurus option), 427
Lotus 1–2–3 spreadsheets, 391, see also **Convert program**
Lowercase, converting text to, 199

MACRO CMD macro programming message, 235
Macro command (Alt-F10), 201
Macro Define command (Ctrl-F10)— WordPerfect 4.1 and 4.2, 201–202
　Defining new macros, 201
　Replacing macros, 202
Macro Define command (Ctrl-F10)—WordPerfect 5.0, 202–204
　Defining new macros, 203
　Replacing and editing macros, 203
Macro Editor, WordPerfect 5.0—See **Macro programming commands**
Macro files, operating on, 204
Macro, form-processing, 128

Macro libraries—WordPerfect 5.0, 204
Macro programming commands—WordPerfect 5.0, 204–235
　Exception commands, 223–224
　Execution-control commands, 219–223
　IF structures, 227–230
　Inserting cursor-moving and text-editing commands, 212
　Inserting programming commands, 211
　Inserting variables, 213
　Macro-chaining commands, 230
　Single-step commands, 230–235
　STATE command, 225
　Types of programming commands, 205
　User interface commands, 213–219
Macro, repeating a, 235–236
Macro resource (.MRS) files, 13
MACROCNV (WordPerfect 5.0 macro conversion program), 238
Macros, chaining, 236–238
　Example: Format-changing macro, 236
　Repeating chains, 237
Macros, converting from WordPerfect 4.2 to WordPerfect 5.0, 238–239
Macros, editing, 239–240
Macros, introduction to, 240–243
　Macros can generate commonly-used phrases, 243
　Naming permanent macros, 242
　Naming temporary macros, 242
　Permanent and temporary macros, 242
　Using macros, 243
Macros, running at startup, 243, 393
Macros that perform commands
　WordPerfect 4.1 and 4.2, 244–245
　WordPerfect 5.0, 245–247
MACROS.WPK (WordPerfect 5.0 keyboard definition file), 172
Mail merge—See **Merge/Sort command**
Mailing lists, creating form letters from, 117
Main Dictionary(s) parameter, 13
Manual backups, 15
Margin Release (Shift-Tab)—See **Indent commands**
Margins—WordPerfect 4.1 and 4.2, 248–250
　Codes for margin changes, 250
　Left and right margins, 249
　Top and bottom margins, 248
Margins—WordPerfect 5.0, 250–251
　Codes for margin changes, 251
　Left and right margins, 251
　Top and bottom margins, 250
Mark Text command (Alt-F5)

WordPerfect 4.1 and 4.2, 251–252
WordPerfect 5.0, 252–253
Markers, place, 305
Master Documents—WordPerfect 5.0, 254–256
   Condensing master documents, 256
   Expanding master documents, 255
   Inserting subdocuments into master documents, 254
Math indicator, 257
Math/Columns command (Alt-F7), 256
Mathematical operations, 256–264
   Adding columns, 257
   Editing math tables, 264
   Macro for performing calculations, 263
   Operating on rows, 259
   Producing totals and grand totals, 259
Mathematical symbols—See **Special characters**
MD (DOS Make Directory command), 88
Measure, Units of, WordPerfect 5.0, 436–437
Menus, selecting options from, 265
Merge Codes command, 265–268
   Combining merge codes, 267
   Inserting merge codes manually, 268
Merge E command (Shift-F9)—WordPerfect 4.1 and 4.2, 268
Merge operations—See **Form letters**
Merge R command (F9), 268
Merge/Sort command (Ctrl-F9), 269
Messages, error—See **Error messages**
Minus (-) key on numeric keypad, 269
Move command (Ctrl-F4)—WordPerfect 4.1 and 4.2, 269–272
   Blocks, 270
   Columns and rectangles, 271
   Sentences, paragraphs, and pages, 270
Move command (Ctrl-F4)—WordPerfect 5.0, 272–274
   Blocks, columns and rectangles, 273
   Sentences, paragraphs, and pages, 272
Moving between pages, 274–275
Moving within a document—See **Cursor, moving the**
.MRS (extension for macro resource files), 13
MultiMate documents—See **Convert program**
Multiple
   Copies, printing, 275–276
   Tabs, setting, 417–418

Name Search (List Files option), 194
Naming

Documents—See **Filenames**
Macros, 242
Navy DIF spreadsheets, 57–58
New Directory = (List Files prompt), 193
New page number, 277, 291, 295
New page, starting a, 278
Newspaper-style columns—See **Columns, text**
Non-continuous underline style, 313
Numeric keypad, 278–279
Numbering lines—See **Print Format command** (WordPerfect 4.1 or 4.2) or **Line Format option** (WordPerfect 5.0)
Numbering pages—See **Page numbering**
Numbering paragraphs—See **Paragraph numbering**
Numbering styles
   Index, 157
   List, 196
   Outline, 286–287
   Paragraph, 299
   Table of contents, 408–409, 411–412
Num Lock key, 280, 390

Open style, 395
Original Backup option—See **Backups**
Orphan lines—See **Widow and orphan lines**
Other Format option—WordPerfect 5.0, 281–282
Outlines, 283–286
   Preparing outlines, 283–285
   Editing outlines, 285–286
   Changing numbering styles, 286–287
Overflow file already exists message, 287
Overstrikes, 287–288
Overstrikes with WordPerfect 4.1 or 4.2, 288
Overstrikes with WordPerfect 5.0, 288
   Related features, 288

Page breaks, 289
Page, centering top-to-bottom, 29, 291, 293
Page Format command (Alt-F8)—WordPerfect 4.1 and 4.2, 289–293
   Page Number Position, 290
   New Page Number, 291
   Center Page Top to Bottom, 291
   Page Length, 291
   Top Margin, 291
   Headers or Footers, 291
   Page Number Column Positions, 291
   Suppress for Current Page Only, 292
   Conditional End of Page, 292
   Widow/Orphan, 292–293

Index 491

Page Format option—WordPerfect 5.0, 293
Page Length (WordPerfect 4.1 and 4.2 parameter), 291
Page, new—See **Hard Page command**
Page number, force odd or even—WordPerfect 5.0, 114–116
Page Number
  Column Positions (WordPerfect 4.1 and 4.2 option), 291
  Position (WordPerfect 4.1 and 4.2 option), 290
Page numbering, 293, 295–296
  Stand-alone page numbers, 295
  Page numbers in headers and footers, 296
  Specifying page numbers, 296
Page numbers in Print commands, 304, 308
Page, starting a new—See **Hard Page command**
Pages
  Appending to a file, 8
  Moving and copying, 270, 272
  Moving between, 278–279
Paired style, 395
Paper, 296–297
Paper, legal size, 180
Paper, letterhead, 180–181
Paper Size and Type (WordPerfect 5.0 parameter), 297
Paragraph numbering, 297
  Using the Paragraph Number feature, 298
  Automatic and fixed numbers, 298–299
  Changing numbering styles, 299
Paragraphs
  Appending to a file, 8
  Hanging, 155
  Moving and copying, 270, 272
  Sorting, 368
Parallel columns—See **Columns, text**
Passwords in locked documents—See **Text In/Out command**
Permanent macros, 242
PgUp and PgDn keys, 300
Phonetic (spell-checking option), 376
Pitch—WordPerfect 4.1 and 4.2, 300, 311–312
Place markers, 300–301
Plus (+) key on numeric keypad, 301
Points (type measure, 1/72 inches), 4, 336
Pos (horizontal position indicator), 305, 390
Power failure, 301–302
Previewing pages (WordPerfect 4.2 option), 306
Primary file in merge operations, 118–119, 302

Print Color (WordPerfect 5.0 Font command option), 108
Print command (Shift-F7)—WordPerfect 4.1 and 4.2, 302–306
  Full Text and Page, 302
  Options, 302
  Printer Control, 302–305
  Type-thru, 305–316
  Preview, 306
Print command (Shift-F7)—WordPerfect 5.0, 306–311
  Full Text and Page, 306
  Document on Disk, 308–309
  Control Printer, 313
  Type Through, 310
  View Document, 310–311
  Options, 311
Print Format command (Ctrl-F8)—WordPerfect 4.1 and 4.2, 311–314
  Pitch and Font, 311–312
  Lines per Inch, 313
  Right Justification, 313
  Underline Style, 313
  Sheet Feeder Bin Number, 313
  Insert Printer Command, 314
  Line Numbering, 314
Print jobs, 314
Print options—WordPerfect 4.1 and 4.2, 315
  Binding Width, 315–316
Print Screen (PrtSc) key, 316
Printer
  Commands, 314, 316–318
  Control (Print command option), 302–305
  Definition (.PRS) files, 14
  Files parameter, 14
  Fonts—WordPerfect 4.1 and 4.2, 108
  Functions, 282
  Helps and Hints screen, WordPerfect 5.0, 319
  Stopping the, 317
  Typing directly to the, 305–306, 310
Printers, switching, 402–403
Printing
  Double-sided pages—See **Binding width**
  Envelopes, 123
  Graphics and text individually, 311
  Hyphens to strike out text, 393, 394
  Multiple copies, 275–276
Proportional spacing, 312, 319
Protecting
  Blocks of text—See **Block command**
  Lines—See **Conditional end of page**

.PRS (extension for printer definition files), 14
PrtSc (Print Screen) key, 316

Question mark (?) wildcard character, 378
Quit printing, 321–322
  Stopping the printer temporarily, 321
  Canceling print jobs, 321–322

^R (Merge R code), 268
RD (Remove Directory) command, 89
Records in sort operations, 363
Rectangles
  Appending to a file, 7
  Drawing—See **Lines, drawing**
Rectangular blocks of text
  WordPerfect 4.1 and 4.2, 323–324
  WordPerfect 5.0, 324–325
Redlining text—WordPerfect 4.1 and 4.2, 325–326
  Redlining new text, 325
  Redlining existing text, 325–326
  Removing redline markings, 326
Redlining text—WordPerfect 5.0, 326–328
  Redlining new text, 326
  Redlining existing text, 327
  Selecting the redline character, 327
  Removing redline markings, 328
Reformatting documents, 328
  Single-spacing a double-spaced document, 328–329
  Deleting other codes, 329
Reformatting the screen—See **Auto Rewrite**
Rehighlighting a block, 22
Removing
  Bold, 22
  Centering, 29
  Indentation, 155
  Index entries, 158
  List entries, 197
  Redline markings, 325, 326
  Strikeout text, 392, 400
  Subscripts and superscripts, 400
  Tabs—See **Tabs**
  Underlining, 434
RENAME (DOS command), 89
Renaming files—See **List Files command**
Renumbering
  Footnotes and endnotes, 112–113
  Graphics boxes, 137
Repeat Value = 8 (WordPerfect 5.0 Esc message), 99
Repeating commands or characters—See **Esc (Escape) key**
Replace command (Alt-F2), 330–332
  Changing the search string, 332
  Selecting search strings, 332
  Wild-card searches, 332–333
  Replace example, 333–335
  How search strings affect Replace operations, 335–337
  Extended searches, 337
  Replacing hidden codes, 337
  Abbreviations, 337–338
Replace Word (Thesaurus option), 427
Replacing
  Hidden codes, 337
  Macros, 202, 203
Repositioning message, 275
Reserved extensions for disk files, 102–103
Restoring deleted text—See **Undeleting**
Retrieve command (Shift-F10), 338–339
  Finding out what's on a disk, 338
  Retrieving one document into another, 338–339
  Other retrieve operations, 339
Retrieve (List Files option), 191
Retrieving one document into another, 191, 341
Returning from DOS, 339
Return key—See **Enter key**
Reveal Codes command (Alt-F3), 340
  Deleting, 340
  Editing on the Reveal Codes screen, 340
  Leaving Reveal Codes, 343
Rewriting the screen—See **Auto Rewrite**
Right
  Aligning text—See **Flush Right command**
  Indent—See **Indent commands**
  Justification, 169–170, 313
  Margin, 248, 251
Roman numerals (i, ii, iii) for pages, 341–342
Root directory on a hard disk, 71
Rotating graphic images, 135–136
Rows, operating on, 259–260
Running macros at startup, 243, 389

Save command (F10), 343–344
  Saving new documents, 343
  Saving existing documents, 344
  Saving in other formats, 344
Saving
  DOS text files, 419–420, 421–422, 424–425
  Edited disk documents, 95–98
  Locked documents, 422–423, 425–426
  Style sheets, 398–399

Index 493

WordPerfect 4.2 documents in 4.1 format, 421
WordPerfect 5.0 documents in 4.2 format, 421
Scaling graphic images, 135
Screen colors, 347
Screen command (Ctrl-F3)—WordPerfect 4.1 and 4.2, 344–347
  Rewrite and Auto Rewrite, 345
  Window, 345–346
  Line Draw, 346
  Ctrl/Alt Keys, 346
  Colors, 347
Screen command (Ctrl-F3)—WordPerfect 5.0, 347–349
  Rewrite, 347
  Window, 347–348
  Line Draw, 349
Screen
  Blank, 19
  Options, 354–355
  Splitting the, 385
Scroll Lock key, 349
Search commands (F2 and Shift-F2), 349–351
  Search procedure, 349–350
  Changing the search string, 350–351
  Extended searches, 351
  Selecting search strings, 351
  Wild-card searches, 351
Search commands in macros—See **Macros, chaining**
Searching
  For hidden codes, 33–37, 42–47
  For words on a disk—See **Word Search**
  Through headers and footers, 144, 146
Secondary Merge File, 118, 352
Select statements for sort operations, 370
Selecting
  Blocks of text—See **Block command**
  Printers—See **Switching Printers**
  Records from a list, 368–370
  Without sorting, 371
Sentences
  Appending to a file, 8
  Moving and copying, 270, 272
Setting tabs—See **Tabs**
Set-up—WordPerfect 4.1 and 4.2, 353–355
  End Set-Up, 353
  Set Directories or Drives, 354
  Set Initial Settings, 354
  Set Screen and Beep Options, 354–355
  Set Backup Options, 355
Set-up—WordPerfect 5.0, 355–358

Backup, 355
Cursor Speed, 355
Display, 356–357
Fast Save, 357–358
Initial Settings, 358
Keyboard Layout, 358
Location of Auxiliary Files, 358
Units of Measure, 358
Set-up menu, initial settings in the, 159, 163–167, 354, 358
Sheet Feeder Bin Number, 313
Shell command (Ctrl-F1), 358–359
Single-sheet paper—See **Paper**
Single-spacing—See **Spacing**
Single-step macro programming commands, 230
Skip and Skip Once (spell-checking options), 375
Soft hyphens, 150
Soft page breaks, 289, 359
Sorting, 360–371
  General procedure for sorting, 360–361
  A simple one-key sort operation, 361–363
  Records, fields, and words, 363
  Sorting on two key words, 363–365
  Sorting paragraphs, 365
  Sorting groups of text, 365–366
  Merge/Sort example, 366–368
  Selecting, 368–370
  Select and Sort procedure, 370–371
  Selecting without sorting, 371
  Using sorted material in a document, 371
Spacing, 372
Special characters, 372–373
  Inserting special characters directly, 373
  Assigning a special character to a key combination, 373–374
  Special character keys and macros, 374
Speed, cursor, 355
Spell command (Ctrl-F2), 374–381
  Starting the Speller, 375–376
  Duplicated words, 376
  Spelling correction example, 376–377
  Dealing with unmatched words, 377–378
  Spell-checking a block of text, 378
  Looking up words, 378–379
  Alternate main dictionaries—WordPerfect 5.0, 379–380
  Custom dictionaries, 380
  Creating custom dictionaries, 380–381
  Using custom dictionaries, 381
Spell utility program, 381–385
  Starting Spell, 382

Exit, 382
Change/Create Dictionary, 382-383
Add Words to Dictionary, 383-384
Delete Words from Dictionary, 384
Optimize Dictionary, 384
Display Common Word List, 385
Check Location of Word, 385
Look Up, 385
Phonetic Look Up, 385
Splitting the screen, 385
Spreadsheet files, using, 386-387
Lotus 1-2-3 procedure, 387-388
Using wide spreadsheets, 388
Starting
DOS, 84
New page—See **Hard Page command**
Spell utility program, 381-382
Speller, 375-376
With a macro, 243
WordPerfect, 389
STATE (macro programming command), 209, 225
Status line, 390
Stop
Merging, 390
Printing, 321, 391
Replacing, 392
Stopping operations—See **Cancel command**
Strikeout text—WordPerfect 4.1 and 4.2, 392-393
Deleting strikeout text, 393
Strikeout text—WordPerfect 5.0, 393-394
Strikeout new text, 393-394
Strikeout existing text, 394
Deleting strikeout text, 394
Style command (Alt-F8)—WordPerfect 5.0, 395-399
Components of a style, 395
Creating styles, 395-397
Using styles, 397-398
Editing styles, 398
Deleting styles, 398
Saving style sheets on disk, 398
Style library, 399
Style Library Filename parameter, 13
Styles Conflict prompt, 399
Styles, underline, 287, 317, 435-436
Subdirectories, hard disk, 72
Subdocuments, WordPerfect 5.0, 254
Subheadings in indexes, 155
Subscripts—See **Super/Subscript command—WordPerfect 4.1 and 4.2 or Font command—WordPerfect 5.0**

See also **Advance options**
Subtotal in Math operation, 256
Summing columns—See **Math/Columns command**
Super/Subscript command (Shift-F1)—WordPerfect 4.1 and 4.2, 400-401, see also **Advance options**
Subscripts, 400-401
Superscripts, 401
Removing subscripts and superscripts, 401
Supplementary Dictionary(s) parameter, 14
Suppress formats for current page, 292, 294
Switch Documents command (Shift-F3), 19, 402
Switching printers
WordPerfect 4.1 and 4.2, 402-405
WordPerfect 5.0, 403

Tab Align command (Ctrl-F6), 405-406
Changing the alignment character, 406
Tab key, 406
Table of authorities, 407
Table of contents—WordPerfect 4.1 and 4.2, 407-410
Building a table of contents, 407-408
Defining the numbering style, 408-409
Generating a table of contents, 409-410
Updating a table of contents, 410
Table of contents—WordPerfect 5.0, 410-414
Building a table of contents, 411
Defining the numbering style, 411-412
Generating a table of contents, 413
Updating a table of contents, 414
Tab Ruler, 414
Tabs, 415-418
Changing tab settings, 415-416
Types of tabs, 416-417
Setting multiple tabs, 417-418
Temporary macros, 242
Text-editing commands, inserting in macro definitions, 212-213
Text files, 418
Text In (List Files option), 192
Text In/Out command (Ctrl-F5)—WordPerfect 4.1, 418-420
Saving and retrieving DOS text files, 419-420
Saving and retrieving locked documents, 420
Text In/Out command (Ctrl-F5)—WordPerfect 4.2, 420-424
Saving and retrieving DOS text files, 421-422

Saving and retrieving locked documents, 422–423
Document summary and comments, 423
Text In/Out command (Ctrl-F5)—WordPerfect 5.0, 424–426
  Saving and retrieving DOS text files, 424–425
  Saving and retrieving locked documents, 425–426
  Document comments, 426
TH.WP (WordPerfect 4.1 and 4.2 thesaurus file), 354
Thesaurus command (Alt-F1), 426–428
  Finding synonyms for existing words, 427–428
  Finding synonyms for new words, 428
Thesaurus parameter, 14
Thousands Separator (WordPerfect 5.0 parameter), 282
Tilde (~) in macro programming commands, 205
Time, inserting the—See **Date command** (WordPerfect 4.1 or 4.2) or **Date/Outline command** (WordPerfect 5.0)
Timed Backup—See **Backups**
Top margin, 248, 250, 291, 293, 428–429
  For the current document, 429
  For new documents, 429
Totals—See **Math/Columns command**
Triple-Spacing—See **Spacing**
Two-sided pages, printing—See **Binding width**
Type-thru (type to printer) feature, 305–306, 310
Typeover mode (Ins), 430
  Special keys for Typeover mode, 430
Typing directly to the printer, 305–310, 431

Uncentering text, 29
Undeleting, 433–434
Underline styles, 283, 313, 434–436
Underlining, 434–436
  Underlining existing text, 434
  Underlining new text, 434–435
  Removing underlining, 435
  Double-underlining, 435
  Underline styles, 435–436
Units of measure—WordPerfect 5.0, 358, 436–437
Unlocking documents—See **Text In/Out command**
Updating a table of contents, 414
Uppercase letters—See **Capitalizing**

Using other programs with WordPerfect—See **Convert program**

V (units of vertical measure), 4
Variables—WordPerfect 5.0, 439–440
Variables, inserting in macro definitions, 213
Vertical line precedes text—See **Redlining text**
View Doc (Thesaurus option), 427
View Document option—WordPerfect 5.0, 310–311, 440–441
Viewing
  Document Summary, 79, 81
  Graphics lines, 188

Wide spreadsheets, using, 388
Widow and orphan lines, 292–293, 443–444
Wildcard characters
  List Files command, 189
  Replace command, 330–332
  Spell command, 374–375
Winding columns—See **Columns, text**
Windows, document, 444–446
  Full-screen windows, 445
  Splitting the screen, 445
  Activating windows, 445
  Operating on windows, 445–446
  Closing a window, 446
Word count, 446
  Counting words in a block, 446
Word Left and Right commands, 447
Word Search (List Files option), 194, 447
WordPerfect
  Commands—See Appendix A, B, and C
  Hard disk startup file for, 142, 390
  Leaving, 447
  Starting, 389
  Using other programs with—See **Convert program**
WordPerfect 4.1 format, saving WordPerfect 4.2 documents in, 421–422
WordPerfect 4.2 format, saving WordPerfect 5.0 documents in, 424–425
Words
  Duplicated during spell-checking, 376
  In sort operations, 363
WordStar files—See **Convert program**
.WPK (extension for keyboard definition files, 172
{WP}BACK.1 and .2 (Automatic Backup files), 16
{WP}LEX.SUP (WordPerfect 4.1 and 4.2 supplementary dictionary), 380

WP{WP}EN.HYL (WordPerfect 5.0 hyphenation file), 13
WP{WP}EN.LEX (WordPerfect 5.0 main dictionary), 13, 380
WP{WP}EN.SUP (WordPerfect 5.0 supplementary dictionary), 14, 380
WP{WP}EN.THS (WordPerfect 5.0 thesaurus file), 14